ECCLESIAZUSAE

To the memory of Sylvia Warmingham

THE COMEDIES OF ARISTOPHANES: VOL. 10

ECCLESIAZUSAE

edited with translation and commentary by

ALAN H. SOMMERSTEIN

ARIS & PHILLIPS LTD – WARMINSTER – ENGLAND

British Library Cataloguing-in-Publication Data
A catalogue record of this book is available from the British Library

ISBNS
0 85668 707 3 cloth
0 85668 708 1 limp

Printed and published in England by Aris & Phillips Ltd, Teddington House, Warminster, Wiltshire BA12 8PQ

Contents

Preface

This is the penultimate volume of the series *The Comedies of Aristophanes*. The final volume, *Wealth*, will include *addenda et corrigenda* to earlier volumes (some of which have been incorporated in reprints of those volumes) and a consolidated index to the series.

Once again it is a pleasure to acknowledge the assistance and advice I have received from many scholars while working on this volume, and before that while studying *Ecclesiazusae* over many years. Among them pride of place must go to Professor S. Douglas Olson, who in addition to much other important work on this play has done more than anyone towards clarifying the extent to which we can identify with each other the many anonymous characters who appear in different scenes, and whose arguments always command respect even on occasions when they cannot command my agreement. I am particularly grateful to Professor Olson for permitting me to cite an unpublished paper of his.

This is also an appropriate occasion to record my gratitude to the many students, undergraduate and postgraduate, who over the last twenty-four years have studied Aristophanes with me at Nottingham. The questions they have raised, the insights some of them have shown, have been of immense help to me in more ways than I can now trace. I wish especially to remember one of them, who raised a fundamental question about this play that I could not and still cannot answer, and who tragically is no longer here to read this. Her name will be found facing the title page; I hope she would have enjoyed this volume, and I hope it will stimulate and challenge her successors.

ALAN H. SOMMERSTEIN
Nottingham, September 1998

References and Abbreviations

(A) Collections of Fragments

All citations of fragments of Greek authors (other than comic dramatists) made in this volume either are from one of the collections in the following list or else are accompanied by the abbreviated title of the edition cited or by the name(s) or initial(s) of the editor(s); fuller particulars will be found in list (C) below if there might otherwise be difficulty in identifying the edition. If no editor or edition is designated and the author is not listed here, it may be assumed that the author is an Attic comic dramatist and the citation is from *PCG* (see (C) below).

Aeschylus	S.L. Radt, *TrGF* iii (Göttingen, 1985)
Alcaeus	D.A. Campbell, *Greek Lyric I* (Cambridge MA, 1982)
Archilochus	M.L. West, *Iambi et Elegi Graeci*[2] i (Oxford, 1989)
Astydamas	B. Snell, *TrGF* i (Göttingen, 1971)
Callimachus	R.H. Pfeiffer, *Callimachus* (Oxford, 1949-53)
Euripides	A. Nauck, *Tragicorum Graecorum Fragmenta*[2] (Leipzig, 1889)
Hypereides	F.G. Kenyon, *Hyperidis Orationes et Fragmenta* (Oxford, n.d. [1906])
Lysias	T. Thalheim, *Lysiae Orationes* (Leipzig, 1901)
Hesiod	R. Merkelbach and M.L. West, *Fragmenta Hesiodea* (Oxford, 1967)
Little Iliad	M. Davies, *Epicorum Graecorum Fragmenta* (Göttingen, 1988)
Pindar	H. Maehler, *Pindari Carmina cum Fragmentis: Pars II* (Leipzig, 1989)
Sappho	D.A. Campbell, *Greek Lyric I* (Cambridge MA, 1982)
Semonides, Solon	M.L. West, *Iambi et Elegi Graeci*[2] ii (Oxford, 1992)
Sophocles	S.L. Radt, *TrGF* iv (Göttingen, 1977)

(B) Abbreviations: Ancient Authors and Works

Ach.	*Acharnians.*
Aesch.	Aeschylus.
Ag.	*Agamemnon* (Aeschylus).
Airs	*Airs, Waters and Places* (Hippocratic treatise).
Aj.	*Ajax* (Sophocles).
Alc.	*Alcestis* (Euripides).
Alex.	*Alexander* (Plutarch).
Anab.	*Anabasis* (Xenophon).
Andoc.	Andocides.
Andr.	*Andromache* (Euripides).
Ant.	*Antony* (Plutarch).
AP	*Ars Poetica* (Horace) or *Anthologia Palatina.*
ap.	*apud* (= cited by).
Apol.	*Apology of Socrates* (Plato)

Apoll.	(Pseudo-)Apollodorus (mythographer).
Ar.	Aristophanes.
Arist.	Aristotle.
Arist.	*Aristeides* (Plutarch).
Ath.	Athenaeus.
Ath.Pol.	*Athenaiōn Polīteiā* (Aristotle).
Ba.	*Bacchae* (Euripides).
Bacch.	Bacchylides.
Bekk. *An.*	*Anecdota Graeca* ed. I. Bekker (Berlin, 1814-21)
Callim.	Callimachus.
Carm.	*Carmina (Odes)* (Horace).
Char.	*Characters* (Theophrastus).
Charm.	*Charmides* (Plato).
Cho.	*Choephoroi* (Aeschylus).
Cim.	*Cimon* (Plutarch).
com.	comic dramatist.
com. adesp.	*comica adespota* (anonymous fragments of comedy; cited from *PCG* viii)
Crat.	*Cratylus* (Plato).
Cycl.	*Cyclops* (Euripides).
Cyr.	*Cyropaedia* (Xenophon).
Dein.	Deinarchus.
Dem.	Demosthenes.
D.H.	Dionysius of Halicarnassus.
Diosc.	Dioscorides.
D.S.	Diodorus Siculus.
Dysk.	*Dyskolos* (Menander).
Eccl.	*Ecclesiazusae.*
Ecl.	*Eclogae* (Phrynichus the grammarian).
El.	*Electra* (Sophocles or Euripides).
Ep.	*Epitome* (of Apollodorus' *Bibliotheca*).
Epid.	*Epidemics* (Hippocratic treatise)
Epitr.	*Epitrepontes* (Menander).
Eth.Nic.	*Nicomachean Ethics* (Aristotle).
Eum.	*Eumenides* (Aeschylus)
Eur.	Euripides.
Euthyd.	*Euthydemus* (Plato).
fr.	fragment.
fr. dub.	fragment doubtfully ascribed.
Gen.	*Genesis* (Old Testament).
Gorg.	*Gorgias* (Plato).
Gyn.	*Gynaikeia (Diseases of Women)* (Hippocratic treatise).
HA	*Historia Animalium* (Aristotle).
Hdt.	Herodotus.
Hec.	*Hecuba* (Euripides).
Hel.	*Helen* (Euripides).

Hell.	*Hellenica* (Xenophon).
Hell.Oxy.	*Hellenica Oxyrhynchia*
Hes.	Hesiod.
HF	*Hercules Furens (The Madness of Heracles)* (Euripides)
h.Hom.(Dem.)	*Homeric Hymn (to Demeter).*
Hipp.	*Hippolytus* (Euripides).
Hipp.Maj.	*Hippias Major* (Plato)
Hippocr.	Hippocratic treatise(s).
Hor.	Horace.
HP	*Historia Plantarum* (Theophrastus).
IA	*Iphigeneia at Aulis* (Euripides)
Isoc.	Isocrates.
IT	*Iphigeneia in Tauris* (Euripides).
Lac.	*Lacedaemoniorum Respublica (The Spartan State)* (Xenophon).
Leocr.	*Against Leocrates* (Lycurgus).
Lex.Bachm.	Συναγωγὴ λέξεων χρησίμων ... in L. Bachmann, *Anecdota Graeca e codd. mss. Bibliothecae Regiae Parisinae* i (Leipzig, 1828)
Lyc.	Lycurgus.
Lyc.	*Lycurgus* (Plutarch).
Lys.	Lysias.
Lys.	*Lysistrata* (Aristophanes) or *Lysander* (Plutarch).
Med.	*Medea* (Euripides).
Mem.	*Memorabilia* (Xenophon).
Men.	Menander.
Men.	*Meno* (Plato).
Menex.	*Menexenus* (Plato).
Mis.	*Misoumenos* (Menander).
Mor.	*Moralia* (Plutarch).
Nem.	*Nemeans* (Pindar).
NH	*Naturalis Historia* (Pliny the Elder).
Nic.	*Nicias* (Plutarch).
OC	*Oedipus at Colonus* (Sophocles).
Od.	*Odyssey.*
Oec.	*Oeconomicus* (Xenophon).
Olymp.	*Olympians* (Pindar).
OT	*Oedipus Tyrannus* (Sophocles).
Paus.	Pausanias.
Pelop.	*Pelopidas* (Plutarch).
Per.	*Pericles* (Plutarch).
Phd.	*Phaedo* (Plato).
Phdr.	*Phaedrus* (Plato).
Phil.	*Philoctetes* (Sophocles).
Phoen.	*Phoenician Maidens* (Euripides).

Phryn. Phrynichus[1].
Pind. Pindar.
Pl. Plato.
Plin. Pliny the Elder.
Plut. Plutarch.
Poet. *Poetics* (Aristotle).
Pol. *Politics* (Aristotle).
Probl. *Problems* (Aristotle).
Prom. *Prometheus Bound* (ascribed to Aeschylus).
Prooem. *Prooemia* (Demosthenes).
Prot. *Protagoras* (Plato).
PS *Praeparatio Sophistica* (Phrynichus the grammarian).
Rep. *Republic* (Plato).
Rhes. *Rhesus* (ascribed to Euripides).
Rhet. *Rhetoric* (Aristotle)
Rhet. ad Alex. *Rhetorica ad Alexandrum* (ascribed to Aristotle).
Sam. *Samia* (Menander).
Sat. *Satyricon* (Petronius).
Sik. *Sikyonios* (Menander).
schol. scholium or scholia (ancient and medieval commentaries)
Sol. *Solon* (Plutarch).
Soph. Sophocles.
Supp. *Suppliants* (Aeschylus or Euripides)
Symp. *Symposium* (Plato or Xenophon).
Theaet. *Theaetetus* (Plato).
Them. *Themistocles* (Plutarch).
Theocr. Theocritus.
Thes. *Theseus* (Plutarch).
Thesm. *Thesmophoriazusae.*
Thg. *Theogony* (Hesiod).
Thphr. Theophrastus.
Thuc. Thucydides.
Tim. *Timaeus* (Plato)
Top. *Topics* (Aristotle).
Trach. *Trachiniae* (Sophocles).
trag. adesp. *tragica adespota* (anonymous fragments of tragedy; cited from *TrGF* ii)
Tro. *Troades* (Euripides)
Xen. Xenophon.

[*author*] (used to designate works traditionally but wrongly ascribed to the author)

1 Unless otherwise stated, citations from "Phrynichus" are from the Atticistic grammarian of the second century AD.

(C) Abbreviations: Modern Authors and Publications

ABSA — *Annual of the British School at Athens*
AC — *L'Antiquité Classique*
AD — Ἀρχαιολογικόν Δελτίον
Agora iii — R.E. Wycherley, *The Athenian Agora* iii: *Literary and Epigraphical Testimonia* (Princeton, 1957).
Agora xiv — H.A. Thompson and R.E.Wycherley, *The Agora of Athens: The History, Shape and Uses of an Ancient City Center* (Princeton, 1972)
Agora xv — B.D. Meritt and J.S. Traill, *The Athenian Agora* xv: *The Athenian Councillors* (Princeton, 1974)
AJA — *American Journal of Archaeology*
AJP — *American Journal of Philology*
Barrett — D. Barrett, "The Assemblywomen", in D. Barrett and A.H. Sommerstein, *Aristophanes: The Knights, Peace, The Birds, The Assemblywomen, Wealth* (Harmondsworth, 1978) 215-264
BCH — *Bulletin de Correspondance Hellénique*
BICS — *Bulletin of the Institute of Classical Studies, University of London*
Bonner & Smith — R.J. Bonner and G. Smith, *The Administration of Justice from Homer to Aristotle* (Chicago, 1930-8)
Burkert — W. Burkert, *Greek Religion: Archaic and Classical* tr. J. Raffan (Oxford, 1985)
CAG — *Commentaria in Aristotelem Graeca*
CAH — *Cambridge Ancient History*
Campbell — D.A. Campbell, *Greek Lyric* (Cambridge MA, 1982-93)
CGFP — C. Austin, *Comicorum Graecorum Fragmenta in Papyris Reperta* (Berlin, 1973)
CIL — *Corpus Inscriptionum Latinarum*
C&M — *Classica et Mediaevalia*
CP — *Classical Philology*
CQ — *Classical Quarterly*
CR — *Classical Review*
Csapo & Slater — E.G. Csapo and W.J. Slater, *The Context of Ancient Drama* (Ann Arbor, 1994)
CSCA — *California Studies in Classical Antiquity*
Dalby — A. Dalby, *Siren Feasts: A History of Food and Gastronomy in Greece* (London, 1996)
Dale — A.M. Dale, *The Lyric Metres of Greek Drama*, 2nd ed. (Cambridge, 1968)
David — E. David, *Aristophanes and Athenian Society of the Early Fourth Century B.C.* (Leiden, 1984)
Davidson — J.N. Davidson, *Courtesans and Fishcakes: The Consuming Passions of Classical Athens* (London, 1997)

Davies	J.K. Davies, *Athenian Propertied Families 600-300 BC* (Oxford, 1971)
Denniston	J.D. Denniston, *The Greek Particles*, 2nd ed. (Oxford, 1954)
Dickey	E. Dickey, *Greek Forms of Address from Herodotus to Lucian* (Oxford, 1996)
D-K	H. Diels, *Die Fragmente der Vorsokratiker* (rev. W. Kranz) (Berlin, 1951-2)
Dover *AC*	K.J. Dover, *Aristophanic Comedy* (Berkeley, 1972)
Dover *GPM*	K.J. Dover, *Greek Popular Morality in the Time of Plato and Aristotle* (Oxford, 1974)
Edwards	M.W. Edwards, *The Iliad: A Commentary* v: *Books 17-20* (Cambridge, 1991)
EH	*Entretiens sur l'antiquité classique* (Fondation Hardt, Geneva)[2]
FGrH	F. Jacoby et al., *Die Fragmente der griechischen Historiker* (Berlin/Leiden, 1923-).
Funke	P. Funke, *Homonoia und Arché* (Wiesbaden, 1980)
G&R	*Greece and Rome*
GRBS	*Greek, Roman and Byzantine Studies*
Harrison	A.R.W. Harrison, *The Law of Athens* (Oxford, 1968-71)
Henderson	J.J. Henderson, *The Maculate Muse* (New Haven, 1975)
Henderson^2	J.J. Henderson, *The Maculate Muse*, 2nd ed. (New York, 1991)[3]
HSCP	*Harvard Studies in Classical Philology*
IG	*Inscriptiones Graecae*
" i^3	*Voluminis I editio tertia: Inscriptiones Atticae Euclidis anno anteriores* ed. D.M. Lewis and L. Jeffery (Berlin, 1981-94)
" ii^2	*Voluminis II et III editio minor: Inscriptiones Atticae Euclidis anno posteriores* ed. J. Kirchner (Berlin, 1913-40)
" xii[5]	*Voluminis XII fasciculus 5: Inscriptiones Cycladum praeter Tenum* ed. F. Hiller von Gaertringen (Berlin, 1903)
" xii[8]	*Voluminis XII fasciculus 8: Inscriptiones insularum maris Thracici* ed. C. Friedrich (Berlin, 1909)
JHS	*Journal of Hellenic Studies*
Kaibel	G. Kaibel, *Comicorum Graecorum Fragmenta* i.1: *Doriensium comoedia, mimi, phlyaces* (Berlin, 1899)
LCM	*Liverpool Classical Monthly*
LGPN	M.J. Osborne and S.G. Byrne, *A Lexicon of Greek Personal Names: 2. Attica* (Oxford, 1994)[4]
LIMC	*Lexicon Iconographicum Mythologiae Classicae* (Zürich, 1981-97)

---

2 *EH* 38 (1993) = J.M. Bremer and E.W. Handley ed. *Aristophane*.

3 This edition is identical with the first except for the addition of a preface and addenda; it is cited only for material not contained in the first edition.

4 A reference such as "*LGPN* 2" means that the person so denoted is the 2nd person of that name listed in this volume of the *Lexicon*.

LSCG F. Sokolowski, *Lois sacrées des cités grecques* (Paris, 1969)
LSJ H.G. Liddell and R. Scott, *A Greek-English Lexicon*, 9th ed. (rev. H. Stuart Jones) (Oxford, 1940)
LSS F. Sokolowski, *Lois sacrées des cités grecques: Supplément* (Paris, 1962)
MacDowell D.M. MacDowell, *Aristophanes and Athens* (Oxford, 1995)
MCr *Museum Criticum*
MDAI(A) *Mitteilungen des Deutschen Archäologischen Instituts (Athenische Abteilung)*
Müller C. Müller, *Fragmenta Historicorum Graecorum* (Paris, 1841-70)
Nesselrath H.G. Nesselrath, *Die attische Mittlere Komödie* (Berlin, 1990)
Oakley & Sinos J.H. Oakley and R.H. Sinos, *The Wedding in Ancient Athens* (Madison, 1993)
PA J. Kirchner, *Prosopographia Attica* (Berlin, 1901-3)
Parke H.W. Parke, *Festivals of the Athenians* (London, 1977)
Parker L.P.E. Parker, *The Songs of Aristophanes* (Oxford, 1997)
PCG R. Kassel and C. Austin, *Poetae Comici Graeci* (Berlin, 1983-)
PCPS *Proceedings of the Cambridge Philological Society*
Pickard-Cambridge[3] A.W. Pickard-Cambridge, *The Dramatic Festivals of Athens*, 3rd ed. revised by J. Gould and D.M. Lewis (Oxford, 1988)
PMG D.L. Page, *Poetae Melici Graeci* (Oxford, 1962)
POxy *The Oxyrhynchus Papyri* (London, 1898-); citations are by serial number of papyrus
QSt *Quaderni di Storia*
QUCC *Quaderni Urbinati di Cultura Classica*
Rau P. Rau, *Paratragodia: Untersuchung einer komischen Form des Aristophanes* (Munich, 1967)
RE *Paulys Realencyclopädie der klassischen Altertumswissenschaft*
REG *Revue des Études Grecques*
RFIC *Rivista di Filologia e di Istruzione Classica*
RhM *Rheinisches Museum für Philologie*
Rogers B.B. Rogers, *The Ecclesiazusae of Aristophanes* (London, 1902)
Rothwell K.S. Rothwell, *Politics and Persuasion in Aristophanes' Ecclesiazusae* (Leiden, 1990)
Russo C.F. Russo, *Aristophanes: An Author for the Stage* tr. K. Wren (London, 1994)
Schwyzer E. Schwyzer, *Griechische Grammatik* (Munich, 1939-53)
SAWB *Sitzungsberichte der Deutschen Akademie der Wissenschaften zu Berlin*
SEG *Supplementum Epigraphicum Graecum*
Segal E. Segal ed. *Oxford Readings in Aristophanes* (Oxford, 1996)

Shafarevich	I.R. Shafarevich, *The Socialist Phenomenon* tr. W. Tjalsma (New York, 1980)
Slater	N.W. Slater, "Waiting in the wings: Aristophanes' *Ecclesiazusae*", *Arion* n.s. 5 (1997) 97-129.
Stone	L.M. Stone, *Costume in Aristophanic Comedy* (New York, 1981)
Strauss	B.S. Strauss, *Athens after the Peloponnesian War* (London, 1986)
Taaffe	L.K. Taaffe, *Aristophanes and Women* (London, 1993)
Taillardat	J. Taillardat, *Les images d'Aristophane*, 2nd ed. (Paris, 1965)
Thiercy	P. Thiercy, *Aristophane: Théâtre complet* (Paris, 1997)
Threatte	L. Threatte, *The Grammar of Attic Inscriptions* (Berlin, 1980-96)
Tod	M.N. Tod, *A Selection of Greek Historical Inscriptions* (Oxford, 1946-8)
Traill	J.S. Traill, *The Political Organization of Attica = Hesperia* Suppl. 14 (1975)
TrGF	*Tragicorum Graecorum Fragmenta* (Göttingen, 1971-)
Ussher	R.G. Ussher, *Aristophanes: Ecclesiazusae* (Oxford, 1973)
Vetta	M. Vetta (and D. Del Corno), *Aristofane: Le Donne all'Assemblea* (Milan, 1989)
West	M.L. West, *Iambi et Elegi Graeci*, 2nd ed. (Oxford, 1989-92)
White	J.W. White, *The Verse of Greek Comedy* (London, 1912)
Wilamowitz *KS*	U. von Wilamowitz-Moellendorff, *Kleine Schriften* (Berlin, 1962-72)
WJA	*Würzburger Jahrbücher für die Altertumswissenschaft*
Zimmermann	B. Zimmermann, *Untersuchungen zur Form und dramatischen Technik der aristophanischen Komödien* (Königstein/Frankfurt, 1984-7)
ZPE	*Zeitschrift für Papyrologie und Epigraphik*

(D) Metrical Symbols

–	a heavy (long) syllable
∪	a light (short) syllable
×	a position that may be occupied by a syllable of either kind ("anceps")
oo	the "aeolic base": two syllables, at least one of which is heavy

Introduction

1. Date and Background

Ecclesiazusae (The Assemblywomen) is one of two surviving plays of Aristophanes that were produced in the early years of the fourth century BC, during the so-called Corinthian War (395-387/6). For its precise date of production no explicit evidence survives[1], and suggestions have ranged from 393[2] to 389[3], with 392 and 391 the most popular choices. The evidence for dating the play is almost wholly internal, consisting of references (and, to some extent, failures to refer) to contemporary events and personalities in public life – of which, therefore, some account must first be given, which will also serve to indicate part of the social and political background to the play.

After the surrender of Athens in 404 and the rule of the Thirty, the democratic régime at Athens had been restored in 403/2, and an amnesty decreed for most past offences which, while sometimes circumvented (as it perhaps was in the notorious case of Socrates), proved remarkably effective in stabilizing the political system, which indeed was never again challenged until Athens fell under Macedonian domination in 322. Sparta meanwhile dominated the affairs of Greece and the Aegean; but fear of her power, and resentment at her sometimes arrogant exercise of it, had already begun to alienate from her the most important of her Greek allies in the great war recently ended, Thebes and Corinth, and their disaffection increased as time went on. Meanwhile, too, the friendship between Sparta and Persia, which had been crucial in the defeat of Athens, gave place to hostility: the death of Darius II in the spring of 404[4] led to civil war between his elder son and successor Artaxerxes II and his younger son Cyrus, who had financed the Spartan war effort in its final phase and was the close friend of Sparta's great military and naval leader Lysander. Cyrus was killed at Cunaxa in 401, at the head of an army which included 700-800 hoplites sent officially by the Spartan state[5]; and shortly afterwards, on an appeal from the Greek cities of Asia Minor for protection against the satrap Tissaphernes

---

1 A statement in the scholia to line 193, whose author knew the date of production but which unfortunately does not provide us with reliable evidence about it, will be considered below (p. 5).

2 So e.g. Rogers, Ussher, and (tentatively) S. Halliwell, *Aristophanes: Birds, Lysistrata, Assembly-Women, Wealth* (Oxford, 1997) lxxxi, 145.

3 So G. Goetz, *De temporibus Ecclesiazuson Aristophanis commentatio* (Leipzig, 1874) 365ff; W. Judeich, *Kleinasiatische Studien* (Marburg, 1892) 89 n.1.

4 Which came just too late to give any hope to Athens (D.S. 13.108.1).

5 Xen. *Anab.* 1.4.3, D.S. 14.19.5; the Spartans also sent him 25-35 warships (Xen. *Anab.* 1.2.21, 1.4.2; D.S. *loc.cit.*; cf. Xen. *Hell.* 3.1.1).

who had replaced Cyrus as governor of the region, Sparta sent an army to Asia, which presently gained considerable successes first under Dercylidas and later, from 396, under Agesilaus, one of Sparta's two kings.

Persia now had every reason to seek to embroil Sparta in a Greek war, and with anti-Spartan feeling widespread in Greece the circumstances were favourable for her. In 395 Sparta attempted to prevent the formation of a Persian-financed coalition against her by launching a two-pronged invasion of Boeotia[6]. Thebes appealed to Athens for assistance, and Athens made a defensive alliance[7] and sent her army to the Thebans' aid. This enabled the Thebans to march westwards to Haliartus, where Lysander, who was attacking the town, was defeated and killed; after which the Athenians and Thebans joined forces there, and though another Spartan-led army had meanwhile arrived under the second king, Pausanias, it did not feel strong enough to offer battle and was forced to make a humiliating withdrawal from Boeotia. Soon afterwards the Theban-Athenian alliance was expanded into a much broader league involving also Corinth, Argos and several minor states[8], with the powerful support of the Persian fleet commanded since 397 by the Athenian admiral Conon; and the Spartans, as Persia had hoped, presently ordered Agesilaus home.

Before his arrival in 394 the Spartans had been driven from most of northern and central Greece, and had suffered a major naval defeat off Cnidus at the south-west tip of Asia Minor; and Spartan victories on land, at Nemea near Corinth and (under Agesilaus) at Coronea in Boeotia, had no strategic effect. The land war became static, with the allies controlling Corinth and fortifying the Isthmus, and Sparta unable to dislodge them; and meanwhile in 393 Conon crossed the Aegean, raided the Peloponnese, brought his fleet to Peiraeus, and brought with it Persian money to help complete the rebuilding, already begun[9], of the Peiraeus fortifications and the Long Walls connecting the port with Athens. With three of her four major enemies of a dozen years earlier turned into allies, with the Aegean once again controlled by a fleet under an Athenian's command and based at the Peiraeus, protected from Spartan assault by the Isthmus barrier and with her own fortifications being restored,

---

6 The war arose out of Theban intervention in a quarrel between her neighbours Phocis and Locris; but according to Xenophon (*Hell.* 3.5.5) – whose account is otherwise very pro-Spartan and anti-Theban -- the Spartans "gladly seized an excuse for attacking Thebes".

7 *IG* ii^2 14 = Tod 101; cf. Xen. *Hell.* 3.5.16, Lys. 16.13, Andoc. 3.25. The Haliartus campaign is described by Xen. *Hell.* 3.5.17-24 and Plut. *Lys.* 28-29.

8 D.S. 14.82.1-2; cf. Andoc. 3.22.

9 Cf. *IG* ii^2 1656 = Tod 107 (before the end of the Athenian year 395/4). A series of inscriptions recording expenditure on the project (*IG* ii^2 1658-64) ends in 392/1, and that winter the work was still in progress (Andoc. 3.12, 37); soon afterwards it seems to have been suspended indefinitely, for in 378 the Peiraeus had still not been provided with defensible gates (Xen. *Hell.* 5.4.20, 34).

Athens seemed more secure than ever before, and to many Athenians there can have seemed no reason why they should not attempt to regain their old empire.

But on the naval side, Athens' recovered power was an illusion, for it depended entirely on Persian support; and Sparta now made a determined effort to detach Persia from her enemies' side. Probably in the spring or summer of 392[10] Sparta sent a mission to the satrap Tiribazus at Sardis to seek peace with Persia; the Athenians and their allies sent embassies of their own to counter this move (Conon leading the Athenian delegation), and there resulted what was virtually a conference to consider a general peace. Sparta's terms for this were that she would cease to dispute Persian supremacy over the Greek cities on the Asian mainland, and that all other Greek cities and islands should be autonomous – which would have deprived Athens of her recent acquisitions of Lemnos, Imbros and Scyros in the north-eastern Aegean, deprived Thebes of her control of Boeotia, and aborted the impending union of Corinth with Argos[11], and was thus totally unacceptable to Sparta's main Greek enemies. Tiribazus was willing to play Sparta's game, and put Conon under arrest[12]; but when he reported back to the King, he was dismissed from office. Nevertheless, although his successor Struthas was pro-Athenian, and hostilities between Persia and Sparta on Asian soil were resumed for a time, Persian financial and naval support for Athens was at an end.

Meanwhile in the autumn of 392[13] the allied position at Corinth was seriously threatened when the Spartans captured and demolished the long walls linking Corinth with its western port of Lechaeum, and proceeded to seize and garrison two fortresses beyond the Isthmus[14]. The news of this defeat created such a sense of crisis in Athens that an appeal was made for voluntary contributions from rich citizens and non-citizens "to secure the safety of the City"[15]; but Sparta was still anxious for peace on suitable terms, and she now proposed, and hosted, a second peace conference[16], at which she put forward a fresh offer: Athens was now to be

---

10 See T.T.B. Ryder, *Koine Eirene* (Oxford, 1965) 165-9; Funke 86 n.48; Strauss 147 n.57.

11 For which cf. Xen. *Hell.* 4.4.6, 4.5.1, 4.8.15, 4.8.34; Andoc. 3.26-27; D.S. 14.92.1 (dating it, probably wrongly, to 390/89). See C.J. Tuplin, *CQ* 32 (1982) 75-83. Corinth and Argos sent separate delegations to Sardis (Xen. *Hell.* 4.8.13), so at that time the union had not yet been formally completed.

12 Conon soon escaped from custody (or, less likely, was released on Tiribazus' recall), but he died soon afterwards in Cyprus (Lys. 19.38-41).

13 For the date see Strauss 147 n.62.

14 Xen. *Hell.* 4.4.7-13; cf. Andoc. 3.18.

15 Cf. Isaeus 5.37-38: many who promised contributions did not pay them, perhaps because the prospect of peace which appeared soon afterwards made it seem unnecessary.

16 We know about this conference from Philochorus (*FGrH* 328 F 149) and from the published version of Andocides' speech to the Assembly recommending acceptance of

allowed to retain Lemnos, Imbros and Scyros, and Thebes to keep its hegemony over the Boeotian states with the exception of Orchomenus. Argos (now incorporating Corinth) rejected these terms, but Thebes was apparently ready to accept them[17], and the Athenian delegation was also favourably impressed. The Athenian Assembly, however, was not; it rejected the draft treaty, and the ambassadors who had recommended acceptance were prosecuted[18] and fled into exile to avoid trial.

Athens was thus committed to continuing the war and, in the absence of Persian ships and funds, to creating and financing an effective navy. This proved a hard task: it was probably not till 390[19] that the first Athenian naval expedition, comprising no more than 40 ships, was sent out under Thrasybulus, and even three years later Athenian naval resources were so limited that the Spartan admiral Antalcidas had only to assemble 80-90 ships at the Hellespont in order to put an unbreakable stranglehold on the straits and therefore on Athens' corn supply[20].

This action, which ended the war, was the result of Persia's decision, at long last, to take sides with Sparta. Athens – possibly on the assumption that Persia and Sparta were bound to remain enemies – had since 390 been giving active support to Euagoras of Cyprus, who had been made an Athenian citizen many years before, and awarded further honours in 393 for his role in the victory of Cnidus[21], but was now in rebellion against the King[22]; by 389/8 she was also in alliance with another anti-Persian rebel, Acoris of Egypt[23]. Artaxerxes' response was to reappoint Tiribazus to his old satrapy and, soon afterwards, agree that he would make war together with Sparta against whoever did not accept the peace terms that he himself would lay down. These terms, announced by Tiribazus at Sardis late in 387, were essentially the Sardis terms of 392, except that Athens was allowed on the one hand to keep the three north-eastern islands but on the other had to abandon Euagoras[24]; they were accepted by all the Greek states, though Thebes, Corinth and Argos submitted only after a show of force. Spartan domination of the Greek world, in alliance with Persia and with Dionysius I of Syracuse, was more complete than ever.

---

the Spartan terms (Andocides 3). Philochorus dates the prosecution and exile of the four Athenian ambassadors to the Athenian year 392/1.

17 Cf. Andoc. 3.13, 20, 24-25, 28, 32.

18 By Callistratus, nephew of Agyrrhius (see on 102).

19 For the date see Funke 96 n.91.

20 Xen. *Hell.* 4.8.25, 5.1.28.

21 *IG* i³ 113 (c. 410 BC); *SEG* xxix 86 (see D.M. Lewis and R.S. Stroud, *Hesperia* 48 [1979] 180-193); Isoc. 9.54-57, 68; [Dem.] 12.10; Paus. 1.3.2.

22 Xen. *Hell.* 4.8.24, 5.1.10.

23 *Wealth* 178 with scholia (where the king is wrongly called Amasis).

24 Xen. *Hell.* 5.1.31.

Where in this period is the production of *Ecclesiazusae* to be placed? It is clear that it postdates the outbreak of war and the formation of the anti-Spartan alliance (193-200), and equally clear that it is earlier than *Wealth*, which is known to have been produced in 388[25]. A scholion on line 193 appears at first sight to give us by implication a precise date, stating on the excellent authority of Philochorus[26] that "two years earlier" (*sc.* than the date of the play) an alliance had been made between the Spartans and the Boeotians. Unfortunately this is nonsense as it stands (no such alliance was made at any date that could possibly be relevant); and even if we substitute "Athenians" for "Spartans" it is not clear whether the reference is to the bilateral defensive alliance *before* Haliartus or to the broader league formed *after* Haliartus[27], and the interpretation, and indeed the textual accuracy, of the stated time-interval are likewise uncertain[28]. We will do better to rely on internal evidence. The most important indicators are as follows:

(*a*) There has been talk of launching a fleet, with a clear divergence of opinion between "the poor" and "the rich and the farmers" (197-8).

(*b*) Athens has recently caught a glimpse of "salvation" (or, rendering the Greek more literally, salvation has "peeped out" like a woman peeping out of a house door or window[29]), but the opportunity has been let slip owing to the attitude of Thrasybulus, who is or was "furious because *he* isn't invited to take charge" (202-3).

(*c*) Thrasybulus (whether or not on the same occasion) has made a powerful and strongly anti-Spartan speech (356-7).

(*d*) Heurippides has recently proposed a tax of $2^1/_2$ per cent, which it was claimed would yield 500 talents of revenue, but his scheme has been a failure and he has incurred derision (823-9).

---

25 The most obvious evidence for this is the deterioration, between the two plays, in the eyesight of Neocleides: in *Eccl.* he is "bleary-eyed" (254, 398), in *Wealth* he is "blind" (665, cf. 747).

26 *FGrH* 328 F 148. Philochorus will not, of course, have mentioned Ar.'s play (he will have dated the alliance by the Athenian archon in office at the time); the calculation of the interval between the alliance and the play was the work of the annotator who first wrote the note from which our scholium derives.

27 D.S. 14.81.2-82.1 dates the former to the Athenian year 396/5, the latter to 395/4.

28 Scholia were subject to rephrasing in transmission, and employed abbreviations freely, especially for numbers. Rephrasing may have carelessly substituted "two years before" for "in the second year before" (which, by our reckoning, would imply an interval of only one year); abbreviation may have resulted e.g. in the numeral δʹ "four" being taken as a contraction of δύο "two". Taking into account all these sources of uncertainty combined, our scholium is consistent with any date for *Eccl.* between 394 and 390 inclusive – or even 389 if we were to suppose that the archon of 390/89, Demostratus, had been confused with the archon of 393/2 who bore the same name.

29 Cf. 884; *Peace* 979-985; *Thesm.* 797-9.

Among these the strongest evidence is provided by (*a*) and (*d*). While Athens had available Conon's fleet and Persian money, there was no need to create a large Athenian navy or to propose special taxes; so there is a strong presumption that the play was produced after the dismissal and arrest of Conon – and, what is more, some months at least after that event, since there has been time for Heurippides' tax proposal to have been tried and to have failed; that is, in 391 at the earliest.

The same conclusion can be drawn, almost as decisively, from (*b*). In wartime, "salvation" can mean either victory or peace. Before 392 there was no moment in the Corinthian War at which Athens could have been said to have had a sudden and brief *glimpse* of either. Cnidus was certainly a great success, but it was not followed by rapid disillusionment: on the contrary, despite the setback (limited in its effects) at Coronea, the next two years, thanks mainly to Conon, were Athens' best of the whole war. But in the course of 392 any Athenian for whom, in the words of Ussher xxiv, "salvation" meant "peace, but ... peace with honour", would have had a real emotional white-knuckle ride. First comes the astonishing news that Sparta is suing for peace. Then Athenian envoys go to Sardis, only to report back that Sparta has offered terms which neither they nor any of the allies had even dared to take home for consideration. Soon things get worse still, as word comes of Conon's arrest with all that it implies, and then the Spartans break through the allies' defence system at Corinth. It seems for a moment that they may even invade Attica, and that "the safety of the City" is in the direst peril[30]. But instead they establish a couple of garrisons and go home; and then, out of the blue, comes an invitation to a new peace conference – from which, moreover, the Athenian delegation brings home *better* terms than before, and recommends their acceptance! It must have seemed like a miracle. And at this miracle, the Athenians turn up their noses – thanks to Thrasybulus. For *Eccl.* provides crucial evidence that it was Thrasybulus who made the decisive speech (*b, c*) that brought about the rejection of the peace proposals brought from Sparta, arguing (according to Andocides[31]) that acceptance would pose a serious danger to the democratic constitution – an argument so powerful that Andocides devotes nearly a third of his speech to attempting to refute it[32]. The "glimpse of salvation" has vanished. It will not reappear.

---

30 Isaeus 5.38.

31 Andoc. 3.1. Here, and throughout his speech as published, he mentions none of his opponents (nor indeed any other living Athenian) by name; but R. Seager, *JHS* 87 (1967) 107-8 (cf. also *CAH* vi^2 [1994] 108-9) rightly holds, citing *Eccl.* as evidence, that Thrasybulus is his main target.

32 With the help of wild distortions of fifth-century history (3.3-9) and a sophistic quibble designed to escape from the obvious and recent example of what happened after the peace of 404 (3.10-12).

I therefore regard it as certain that *Ecclesiazusae* was produced not earlier than 391 BC, and if in 391, more likely at the City Dionysia than at the Lenaea[33] to allow adequate time for such developments as the rejection of the peace treaty and the discrediting of Heurippides' tax scheme to find their way into the script[34]. Nothing in the play can be shown to refer to any event later than the winter of 392/1; a production-date of 390 cannot be entirely excluded[35], but if the play was produced so late it is surprising that Praxagora's impressionistic summary of current politics (193-203) *ends* with an event now a year in the past.

We do not know what other plays competed against *Ecclesiazusae*, nor the result of the contest – though we know that Aristophanes was nervous enough about the outcome, especially when *Eccl.* came out first in the draw for order of performance, to insert at the last minute an appeal to the judges for a favourable verdict (1154-62). We know too of one other comedy produced in 391, whether or not at the same festival: *Phaon* by Plato, the only other top-class comic poet of Aristophanes' generation who was still active. Phaon was a man who by Aphrodite's favour had been made irresistible to women, and the surviving fragments (Plato com. fr. 188-

33 So J.C. Carrière, *Le carnaval et la politique* (Paris, 1979) 177-182. Vetta xxx-xxxii assigns it to the Lenaea, but only on the weak grounds that (i) the action appears to be set in winter (yet cf. *Birds* 105-6, from a known Dionysia play) and (ii) the numerous references to internal Athenian affairs and Athenian personages would have been lost on the many foreign spectators at the City Dionysia (yet the surviving Aristophanic play with the greatest number of such references is again *Birds*). It is likely that by the time of the City Dionysia Thrasybulus had been elected one of the generals for 391/0, but this would not be inconsistent with the reference to him in 202-3; see n.35 below.

34 For other references which can be fruitfully interpreted on the assumption of a production in 391 (or 390), though they could not by themselves *establish* such a date for the play, see on 195-6, 200, 201, 428, 571, 810, 982-4, 1169-75. It may be added that the absence of all reference to Conon would be somewhat surprising in a play produced in 393 or early 392 – especially given that his lieutenant Hieronymus *is* mentioned (201).

35 So rightly R. Seager, *JHS* 87 (1967) 107 n.110, who disposes of the weak argument (still deployed by Vetta xxxi) that the reference to Epicrates' beard (71) must predate his exile. Funke 170 argues that it would be inappropriate to speak of Thrasybulus in 391/0, when he was almost certainly a general, as "not being invited to take charge" (203); but that passage refers to the time when the "glimpse of salvation" appeared and vanished, not necessarily to the time of performance – indeed the point being made (that Thrasybulus had opposed peace for selfish reasons) would be all the stronger if his opposition to peace had enabled him to win high office (see note *ad loc.*). Seager's own argument (*loc.cit.*) in favour of 390 – that 197-8 fits better a time closer to the beginning of "Athens' first serious naval efforts" – is also of limited cogency: 197-8 does not necessarily imply that a substantial Athenian fleet was actually in being, only that the building of one had been debated.

198) suggest that erotic themes may have been even more prominent in *Phaon* than in *Eccl.*[36]

2. *Gynaecocracy in Old Comedy*

Ecclesiazusae unites – as Crates' *Beasts* had done nearly forty years earlier – the common Old Comic theme of a Utopian society in which, as in the mythical Age of Cronus, work (for male citizens) is abolished[37] with that of a reversal of one of the established hierarchies of nature such as the animal revolutions of Crates' play, of Aristophanes' own *Birds* and of Archippus' *Fishes*. For to ancient Greeks (as to most peoples before the last few generations) the domination of men over women was part of the natural order of things[38]; and, just as the only imaginable alternative to the supremacy of humans over beasts was a fantasy of animal supremacy over humans, so the only imaginable alternative to the supremacy of men over women was a fantasy of women's supremacy over men, a "gynaecocracy"[39] – the idea of a political system in which men and women participated on equal terms was something beyond even the power of fantasy to conceive, except indeed for Plato (of whom more presently).

It is not clear whether the gynaecocracy of *Ecclesiazusae* was the first that Old Comedy had imagined; but it is not at all unlikely that it was. There had, however, been various partial precursors of it. In Aristophanes' own *Lysistrata* the heroine and her women occupy the Acropolis, forcibly prevent a state official from taking money thence for the war effort, and tell him that whereas formerly women have had to accept in silence the foolish political decisions of men, now "war [is to] be for

---

36 Plato com. fr. 195, where an old man (who may or may not be Phaon) addresses a music-girl as "my golden crown, the <delight [?]> of my voluptuous lifestyle, my sweet arm to rest on", bears a striking resemblance to *Eccl.* 973-4. On *Phaon* see R.M. Rosen in G.W. Dobrov ed. *Beyond Aristophanes: Transition and Diversity in Greek Comedy* (Atlanta, 1995) 132-5.

37 On this theme see B. Zimmermann, *WJA* 9 (1983) 57-77; B. Zimmermann in W. Rösler and B. Zimmermann, *Carnevale e utopia nella Grecia antica* (Bari, 1991) 53-101; T.K. Hubbard in G.W. Dobrov ed. *The City as Comedy* (Chapel Hill, 1997) 23-50.

38 Cf. e.g. Aristotle, *Politics* 1259b1-3, 1260a8-13 "The male is more fitted to rule than the female, unless conditions are quite contrary to nature. ... Most instances of ruling and being ruled are natural. For rule of free over slave, male over female, man over boy, are all different, because while parts of the soul are present in each case, the distribution is different. Thus the deliberative faculty in the soul is not present at all in a slave; in a female it is present but ineffective" (tr. T.A. Sinclair and T.J. Saunders [Harmondsworth, 1981]).

39 Greek *gunaikokratiā* (evidently modelled on *dēmokratiā*) and its cognates do not appear in our sources until after 350, in the titles of comedies (by Amphis and Alexis) and in Aristotle's *Politics* (1269b24, 1313b33); but since Aristotle's use of the words gives no indication that he finds them comic or novel, they may well have been in use earlier (e.g. in discussion of the vices of tyranny).

women to take care of ... we'll unravel this war, if we're allowed to, sorting it out by sending embassies, now this way, now that" (*Lys.* 537, 569-570) while *men* sit silent and listen to them (*Lys.* 527-8, 534); but the seizure of power, like the sex-strike that reinforces it, is a temporary measure only, and indeed when the peace treaty comes to be made (*Lys.* 1108-87) it is made and sworn to by the men (though Lysistrata controls the process), and when Athenians and Spartans are exhorted[40] "for the future [to] take care never to make the same mistake again" (*Lys.* 1277-8), the subject of the verb, as a participle in agreement with it reveals, is masculine.

It has often been thought that a true comic gynaecocracy was presented by Aristophanes' older contemporary, Pherecrates, in his play *Tyrannis* (which might mean "The Dictatorship" or "The Lady Dictator"). In fact only one of the fragments of this play even remotely suggests such an idea: fr. 152, in which women are apparently working as potters and, true to their comic stereotype, making "cups" for men to drink out of which are hardly more than saucers while their own are "as deep and full-bellied as cargo-ships"; but the punch-line, far from suggesting that these women now hold power in the state or even in the household, suggests they are merely playing their traditional game of underhand evasion of male control:

> Then, when we complain that they've drunk up all the wine,
> they shout and swear that they've "just drunk one cup, that's all" –
> but that one cup is bigger than a thousand ordinary ones![41]

There is, however, a lexical citation of the comic coinage *stratēgis* "Lady General" (*Eccl.* 835, 870) from an unnamed play of Pherecrates (fr. 269), and this *could* have come from *Tyrannis*; but in the absence of any other evidence it is well to be cautious[42].

Another comedy that may be seen as partially anticipating *Eccl.* is Theopompus' *Stratiotides* ("The Lady Soldiers") – probably produced within a few years of 400, for it made mention (fr. 58) of Anytus, the leader of the restored democracy in its early days and one of the accusers of Socrates. In this play women were portrayed as taking over one of the most important and defining roles of the male citizen, and probably (cf. fr. 56) as maintaining their husbands and children on their (doubled) army pay. It is not clear, though, whether the women did this on their own

---

40 By Lysistrata in my view (see my note on *Lys.* 1273-90); but most recent editors and translators have assigned the passage to a male Athenian.

41 The speech is in trochaic tetrameters, so may well be from the (ant)epirrhema of a parabasis – in which case this play will have had a chorus of males.

42 Particularly since *stratēgis* was in regular, non-comic use in the sense "flagship of a fleet", and for all we know the lexical entry (now found only in the ninth-century lexicographer Photius) may in an earlier form have read e.g. "*stratēgis*: a woman <in Aristophanes; a ship> in Pherecrates".

initiative; in the *agon* someone said to the women of the chorus "The wife of Thrasymachus will make a good overseer for *you*" (fr. 57), which implies that the leader of the women is being *appointed from outside* (by a man?) rather than emerging of her own accord as in *Lysistrata* and *Eccl.* Possibly therefore the whole idea of a women's army was in this play the invention of an ingenious male comic hero whose aim was nothing more than to avoid military service himself!

There existed, to be sure, a very celebrated mythical precedent for a band of women who did indeed on their own initiative seize control of a society that had previously been male-dominated: the women of Lemnos, who under the leadership of Hypsipyle made themselves a byword for atrocity by killing all the men on the island. And we know of two comedies of the late fifth or early fourth centuries, one by Aristophanes himself[43], named *The Lemnian Women.* Both of them, however, were set after the arrival at Lemnos of Jason and the Argonauts, whom the Lemnian women took as lovers, and seem to have centred on the relationship between Jason himself and Hypsipyle[44]. Another celebrated mythical gynaecocracy, that of the Amazons, featured in a comedy of that name by Cephisodorus, whose *floruit* seems to have fallen between 402 (when he won first prize, cf. Lys. 21.4) and the early 380s; but we know nothing of the plot[45].

Thus while several comedies before *Ecclesiazusae* did, for substantial parts of their action, show women in control of society, this control seems to have been either temporary (as in *Lysistrata*, the Lemnian plays, and probably Cephisodorus' *Amazons*) or created on male initiative (as apparently in *Stratiotides*). The idea of a permanent gynaecocratic Utopia may well in 391 have been a complete novelty, something "never ... done or said before" (579). So too may have been the new social order that the women introduce once in power; but this requires a section to itself.

---

43 The other was by Nicochares, son of the Philonides who had produced several plays on Aristophanes' behalf between 422 (or earlier) and 405.

44 In Aristophanes' play the murder of the men of Lemnos is referred to as a past event (fr. 374), the island is now "teeming with foreign men" (fr. 375), and a woman, surely Hypsipyle, is said to be "soaping herself in the bathtub" (fr. 376), no doubt in preparation for a party (cf. *Birds* 132, *Lys.* 1065-7); one of the few brief fragments that survive of Nicochares' play (fr. 15) has Jason, apparently at his first meeting with Hypsipyle, tell her "We were sailing for a fleece" – except that the Greek phrase (*epi kōs*) could also mean "to bed".

45 If Epicrates' *Amazons*, a generation later, was a reworking of Cephisodorus' play – and Epicrates does seem to have reworked another play, *Antilais*, from Cephisodorus' small output – then here too comedy seems to have concentrated on the reconquest of the rebellious female by the male: the one surviving fragment of Epicrates' play (of Cephisodorus' play no word survives) runs "It seems to me that the men have finished their dinner very opportunely" (Epicrates fr. 1, cf. *Eccl.* 691ff).

3. *Praxagora's new society*

In *Ecclesiazusae* the women of Athens are presented as conspiring successfully to take over political power in their city. They do so, in the fashion supposed to be typical of women, by deceit (see on 237-8): disguising themselves as men, they come to the Pnyx well before sunrise on the day of an Assembly meeting, hoping by a combination of numbers[46] and eloquence to secure the passage of the motion, which their leader Praxagora will propose, that control of the state be handed over to the women. The meeting itself is not presented on stage; instead we are given two distinct indirect portrayals of it – the first through a dress-rehearsal which Praxagora holds in the opening scene and which includes a full-length speech by her in support of her proposal (173-240), the second through a report given to Praxagora's husband, who had missed the meeting, by a man who had stayed to listen despite not getting a pay-ticket (394-457); from the latter we learn that the women's perception that the state of Athens is desperate (109, 174-182, 206-8) is fully shared by the men, who support the motion to put women in power "because ... this was the only thing that hadn't ever been done before" (456-7).

Praxagora has thus far given no indication of any motive for her scheme beyond that of "do[ing the City] some good" (108), and no indication of what her policy as ruler is to be[47] except for a disquisition (which proves to be highly misleading) on the inherent conservatism[48] of women (215-228). It does not, of course, follow that she *has* no hidden agenda: it is not rare for the full scope of an Aristophanic character's plans or ambitions to be revealed only when (s)he has finally attained the power necessary to realize them[49]. Much of the time in these earlier scenes Praxagora is

---

46 The women who actually appear on stage are only a small subgroup of those in the plot (cf. 280-2). The plot presupposes that most men attend the Assembly only for the sake of the three obols each is paid for doing so (as 376-393 confirms is the case; cf. on 284): hence if women pre-empt a large proportion of the 6000 pay-tickets available, those men who arrive too late to get tickets will mostly not trouble to stay for the meeting even when it is about "how to save the City" (396-7). Additionally, many a man, like Blepyrus, will be prevented from going to the Pnyx at all if he owns only one outer garment (cf. on 315-6) and his wife has taken it for her disguise.

47 For it is already clear that the new régime is to be "in name a democracy, but in reality government by the first woman" (to adapt the words of Thuc. 2.65.9 about the Athens of Pericles), and even before it is created Praxagora has already been elected (sole) general (246-7).

48 This term is not meant here to connote anti-democratic or anti-egalitarian views, only a preference for the *status quo*, whatever that may happen to be, as against innovation of any sort.

49 In *Knights* the Sausage-seller displaces Paphlagon-Cleon as steward to Demos by

either performing before an audience of men, or rehearsing for such a performance; and when she speaks as a woman among women (in 32-168 and 242-284) her colleagues show no curiosity about the ultimate aim of the conspiracy[50]. Any spectators who suspect that there is more in the scheme than meets the eye[51] will probably assume that the women plan to use power to pursue what, in comedy, are women's traditional goals of easier access to their husbands' property (above all to alcoholic drink)[52] and an unrestricted right to sexual enjoyment[53] whether with their husbands (as the elderly Blepyrus fears at 465-9) or with others; this, after all, seems to have been what women had done in earlier comedies when opportunity arose (see above).

Instead, however, in an extended speech which fills the place of the traditional comic *agōn* (583-710), Praxagora presents a blueprint for a completely remodelled society which (it has been argued) has been, whether knowingly or not, directly or indirectly the basis for every subsequent communistically organized utopia in the Western philosophical and political tradition[54]. Her innovations are, to be sure, centred on the institutions of private property and of marriage, but they go far beyond what any spectator can have anticipated. Both these institutions, in fact, are totally abolished[55]. All private property, whether in land, in chattels or in money, is to be surrendered into a common stock, from which the citizenry will be maintained; food will be provided by the labour of slaves (651) and clothing by the labour of

---

outdoing him in villainy, and only then begins to behave as a virtuous statesman seeking Demos' true well-being rather than pandering to his short-term desires. In *Clouds*, the Clouds encourage Strepsiades to put himself in Socrates' hands and learn (or later, have his son learn) rhetoric, in order to punish him for desiring to cheat his creditors; but not till nearly the end of the play (1452ff) do we, and Strepsiades, learn what they have been doing and why. In *Birds* Peisetaerus makes both the birds and the audience believe that his plan will give sovereignty over the universe to the birds, but in the end *he* becomes the "most exalted of gods" (1765), wielding the thunderbolt of Zeus (1745-53), executing and eating birds at his pleasure (1583-5).

50 We are reminded twice over (18, 59) that the conspiracy was hatched on a previous occasion (at the Scira festival), so that the women may be taken to know its aims already. At 17-18 Praxagora is just about to explain them to her lamp (i.e. to the audience) when she is sidetracked, and the promised explanation never comes.

51 As many may, particularly after the advice to the imaginary Assembly "not ... [to] inquire of [the women] what it is they actually mean to do" (230-1) has drawn their attention to the fact that they, the audience, have been given no hint of the answer to that question, and that the Assembly will be asked to give the women absolute *carte blanche*.

52 Cf. on 14-15 (general theft) and 132 (drink).

53 Cf. 225, 228, 624; *Lys.* 99-110; *Thesm.* 340-6, 400-6, 416-7, 477-501, 549-550.

54 Cf. Shafarevich 3-6 (not meaning thereby to commend Praxagora's social model).

55 Blepyrus, admittedly, still thinks of himself as Praxagora's husband (727), as does her maid (1126): old ways of thought are not that easy to discard on the instant when revolution comes.

women (653-4), leaving men with nothing to do but "to go to dinner, sleek and gleaming, when the shadow is ten feet long" (652)[56] – a system, it will be observed, that *prima facie* is of far greater benefit to men than to women[57]. Sexual enjoyment too becomes something communally available: women[58] are to be "common property, for any man who wishes, to have sex and produce children" (614-5), though if the same woman is desired by more than one man (or vice versa) preference must be given to the older or uglier claimant (615-634). This abolishes at a stroke not only marriage but the whole structure of family and of patrilineal kinship on which Greek societies had been based from time immemorial: no child will know his father, and each will regard every older man of appropriate age as a father and act accordingly (e.g. by protecting any such "father" of his from unlawful violence)[59]. This too is hardly a measure designed to benefit women at men's expense. Women gain immensely (for instead of being restricted to one legitimate partner, usually not of their own choice, they can have as many as they wish and whom they wish subject to the preference rules), but men over their whole life cycle do not lose (the abolition of prostitution, and of the right to have sex with slaves, is counterbalanced by the free availability of citizen females, again subject to the preference rules), and older men, who nearly always get the best of things in Old Comedy[60], gain considerably.

It has long been observed[61] that this new model of society is very close to that which is devised (for the Guardians only) in the third and fifth books of Plato's *Republic*,

---

56 No mention is made of other kinds of productive work, but this is not a weakness in Praxagora's scheme: there was probably no craft of which there were not slave as well as free practitioners, and in *Wealth* (517-8) Chremylus assumes that in *his* utopia, in which all (virtuous) men are rich and free from toil, all work (including e.g. carpentry, metalwork, shoemaking, as well as agriculture, cf. 512-6) will be performed by slaves.

57 Only *prima facie*, because women control the distribution process (599-600) and therefore have power in practice to favour some men at the expense of others, or each other at the expense of all men: but of this flaw – one inherent in the structure not only of Praxagora's society but of most other communist societies, imaginary or real – the play takes no notice.

58 Women of citizen status, that is; those of lower status are to be allowed to have intercourse only with men of their own class (718-724).

59 No steps are taken to ensure that children do not know their *mothers* (contrast Pl. *Rep.* 460c-d), so it is possible, indeed quite likely, that a new matrilineal family structure would soon emerge if this scheme were ever put into practice; but such a structure, though common in many parts of the world, is so alien to the ancient Greek mind that no character in *Eccl.* envisages it for a moment as a possibility.

60 See *CQ* 34 (1984) 320-1. It is true that some of them fear that at their time of life they may not be able to make much use of their new privileges (619-622, cf. 465-9); but as so often, the magic of comedy makes old men young (cf. 848-850), and Blepyrus in the final scene gives no indication of being afraid he may disappoint the two girls!

61 For discussions of the relationship between *Ecclesiazusae* and the *Republic*, see Rogers xxii-xxviii (who considers only explanation (i) below); J. Adam, *The Republic of Plato*

indeed far too close for the similarities to be coincidental. The following are the points which the two models have in common:

(1) The Guardians are to have no private property "unless absolutely essential" (416d, cf. *Eccl.* 590-610; in 464d they have "no private possessions except their bodies").
(2) Thanks to this communal ownership of property, there will be little or no litigation among them (464d, cf. *Eccl.* 655-661).
(3) They are to have no private dwelling-places or stores "that cannot be entered by anyone who wishes" (416d, cf. *Eccl.* 674-5).
(4) They will dine in communal halls (416e, cf. *Eccl.* 675-688).
(5) Their maintenance will be provided for them by those of lower status (416e, 463b, 464c, cf. *Eccl.* 651-2).
(6) At their feasts, songs will be sung in honour of brave warriors, while those who have shown cowardice will be prevented from attending (468a,d, cf. *Eccl.* 678-680).
(7) Marriage is not to exist, and all women are to be "common" to all men (457c, cf. *Eccl.* 614-5).
(8) No parent is to know who is his child, nor any child its parent (457d, cf. *Eccl.* 635-6); but ...
(9) Every person will treat as his parent every older person who *might* in principle be his actual parent (461d-e, cf. *Eccl.* 636-7)[62]; and in consequence ...
(10) Virtually any two Guardians will regard each other as close kin and behave accordingly (463c-e, cf. *Eccl.* 638-650), and in particular ...
(11) There will be no violence by the young against the old, because they will respect their "parents" and/or fear that other "children" of the victim will come to his aid (465a-b, cf. *Eccl.* 641-3).

(Cambridge, 1905) i 345-355 (favouring (ii)); David 20-29 (inclining tentatively to (ii)); and S. Halliwell, *Plato: Republic 5* (Warminster, 1993) 224-5 (sceptical of any direct connection).

62 In *Eccl.* (where only fatherhood, not motherhood, is uncertain) this means any man old enough to be his father; in *Rep.* it means anyone who had been a member of a breeding pair in the season in which he (the child) was conceived (the zoological terminology is appropriate, since Plato's scheme is avowedly modelled on the practice of animal breeders). Both systems will inevitably soon bring it about that most young men and women are socially (and do not know whether or not they are biologically) brothers and sisters, and Plato accordingly allows siblings to mate provided the Delphic oracle approves (461e); Praxagora says nothing about this matter, but she does not need to, since sexual relations between children of the same father by different mothers (the only siblings who, in Praxagora's society, would not be aware of their relationship) were not considered incestuous in classical Athens. The Oedipal incest scare raised by the Girl in 1038-42 is chimerical (see on 1042).

Of all the significant features in Praxagora's exposition of her new society, the only ones not represented in Plato are the detailed regulations governing sex (615-634) – which are too comic to be capable of adaptation for a seriously designed utopia; the assurance that women will continue to do textile work as hitherto (654); and some remarks on crime and its punishment (662-672).

In the abstract this relationship between the two texts might be explained (i) by supposing that Aristophanes is caricaturing Plato's model, or (ii) by supposing that Plato is adopting Aristophanes' comic model and putting it to serious use, or (iii) that both are dependent on a common source or sources. Of these possibilities (i) is almost certainly ruled out by chronology: *Eccl.* was produced only eight or nine years after the death of Socrates, and it is virtually out of the question that the *Republic* could be that early[63]; the suggestion[64] that Plato had already in the 390s formulated his ideas for a perfect society (of which there is no trace in any of his early dialogues), and that Aristophanes knew them through personal contact with the philosopher, is neither supported by any evidence nor probable in itself[65]. Explanation (iii), favoured by recent editors of *Eccl.*[66], runs counter to the explicit

---

63 Nothing in the *Republic* gives any direct indication of when it was composed, but on stylistic grounds it is generally agreed that except possibly for the first book (not here relevant) the dialogue must postdate *Menexenus* and the *Symposium*, both of which must themselves have been written after the peace of 387/6 (*Menex.* 245a, 245e refer anachronistically to this peace, and *Symp.* 193a to the breaking up of the city of Mantinea by the Spartans in 385/4; see K.J. Dover, *Phronesis* 10 [1965] 1-20 = *The Greeks and their Legacy* [Oxford, 1988] 86-101), and must be somewhat earlier than *Theaetetus* whose prologue (142a-b) refers to a battle at Corinth which took place in 369/8. It is therefore likely that the *Republic* was being composed during the 370s; perhaps significantly, the earliest known reference to Plato in comedy (Theopompus com. fr. 16, probably reflecting *Phaedo* 96e) appears to fall in that decade. On the sequence and chronology of Plato's dialogues, see L. Brandwood in R. Kraut ed. *The Cambridge Companion to Plato* (Cambridge, 1992) 90-120, esp. 112-5.

64 Which I once mistakenly endorsed (*Aristophanes: Lysistrata, The Acharnians, The Clouds* [Harmondsworth, 1973] 11n.)

65 Whether or not Plato is historically accurate in portraying Socrates in the *Symposium* as being on friendly terms with Aristophanes in 416 (and historical accuracy does not in general appear to have been a major concern of those who created settings for Socratic conversations), it is hard to imagine him giving Aristophanes privileged access in the 390s to ideas which he was not to publish for fifteen or twenty years and which he even then feared would incur ridicule, at a time when he had either recently written or was soon to write the *Apology of Socrates* in which Aristophanes, and Aristophanes alone, is named (19c) of those allegedly responsible for the long-standing campaign of slanderous accusation against Socrates which he regards as more dangerous to him than the actual charges made by his prosecutors – and which Plato therefore presumably wished to present as the principal cause of the unjust execution of the man he most admired in the world.

66 Ussher xv-xx; Vetta xvi-xvii.

statement of Aristotle[67] that Plato was unique among the "statesmen, philosophers and laymen"[68] who had proposed model constitutions in including in his model communism in property and communism in sex and parenthood – precisely the two features that are likewise distinctive of Praxagora's model. It is true that the late fifth and early fourth centuries were a period of luxuriant speculation on alternative orderings of society, whether hypothetical or allegedly actual in remote regions[69]; but it is a very long way from the casual remarks on the subject for which we have evidence to the two coherent, well-rounded and closely parallel blueprints that Aristophanes and Plato offer us. It is also true that Sparta provided precedents both for a form, though a strictly limited form, of licensed extra-marital procreation[70] and for a custom whereby any citizen was free to use, without seeking permission, the chattels of any other[71]; but these Spartan practices, far from abolishing property or marriage, actually presupposed both. If we posit a single common source, we have to explain how Aristotle, in his extensive researches on the subject, remained totally unaware of its existence; if we posit multiple common sources, we have to explain how Aristophanes and Plato combined and modified them in such closely similar ways. The only reasonable explanation is that the elusive common source is *Ecclesiazusae* itself[72].

It has seemed incredible to many that Plato should take such crucial features of his ideal state from so frivolous a source. It is, however, striking that it is precisely in this section of the *Republic* that Plato makes Socrates particularly anxious lest *his* proposals be taken for comic fantasy and become the object of ridicule[73]:

---

67 *Politics* 1266a31-36, 1274b9-10.

68 This listing is equivalent to "all", since *idiōtēs* "layman" in such contexts denotes anyone not included in whatever specialized category or categories have been mentioned just before.

69 Evidence of which (as regards communal sex and procreation) surfaces several times in Herodotus (4.104; 4.180.5 – with accounts of the implications for kinship that differ both from each other and from that on which Ar. and Plato agree; cf. also 1.216.1 which shows that it was already a widespread Greek belief that Scythians practised communal sex) and Euripides (fr. 653).

70 Xen. *Lac.* 1.7-9; Plut. *Lyc.* 15.12-13.

71 Xen. *Lac.* 6.3; Arist. *Pol.* 1263a35-37. The custom appears to be alluded to by the Spartan Menelaus in Eur. *Andr.* 374-7.

72 There is no need to explain Aristotle's silence on *this* precursor of Plato; it would never have occurred to him to treat an Old Comic fantasy as a serious proposal for a model constitution on a par with those he discusses, alongside Plato's, in *Politics* 1260b27-1269a28.

73 See J. Adam, *The Republic of Plato* (Cambridge, 1905) i 348-350; note that right at the beginning of the section (451c) Socrates refers to the forthcoming exposition as a "women's *drama*". All the following translations from *Republic* 5 are by S. Halliwell (Warminster, 1993).

> Perhaps many details of what we're now saying, because they contradict tradition, would seem ridiculous, if they could be realised precisely as proposed. ... We mustn't be intimidated by all the various jokes that the facetious would make against such a radical change ... . When first the Cretans, and then the Spartans, instituted naked gymnastics [sc. for men], the wits of the time were able to mock [*kōmōidein*] all these things. (452a-d)

> It is a fool who finds ridiculous anything other than bad things, as also the man who tries to arouse laughter by treating any appearance as ridiculous other than that of what is stupid and bad (452d)

These remarks would be particularly pointed if Plato were at that moment doing the reverse of what he fears may be done to him: if, rather than making comic mockery of a serious project, he were making serious use of a project[74] first conceived for comic purposes. And essentially, this is what he does – but with two important changes. In the first place, Praxagora's society had maintained most of the traditional distinctions between men's and women's spheres of activity (e.g. men go to war, women make clothes) while transferring political power from men to women and offloading all of men's economic activities on to slaves. Plato abolishes all these distinctions: in his society, or rather in its élite (with which book 5 is alone concerned), "there is no activity ... which belongs to a woman *qua* woman, nor any to a man *qua* man" (455d) except for those activities of women that are strictly necessary consequences of their reproductive role[75]. And secondly, in regard to reproduction, since this is a serious and not a comic project, Plato replaces the topsy-turvy sexual regulations of *Eccl.* with a system designed, under the appearance of fairness and randomness, to maximize breeding from the best individuals, with childbearing in principle being permitted only from (temporary) unions formed by order of the authorities (458d-461c). In crucial fundamentals, though, his scheme and Praxagora's are the same; and if so, it may well be claimed that *Ecclesiazusae* has been in the long run the most intellectually influential of all ancient comedies.

---

74 Or should we say two projects? At any rate one highly controversial element of Plato's scheme which is absent from *Eccl.* – the participation of women in military training and warfare – had been the theme of another comedy (Theopompus' *Stratiotides*, discussed above).

75 Although – rather illogically it might seem, but equal opportunities legislation has created parallels in our time – "the women must be allotted lighter tasks than the men" because of their physical weakness (457a).

Plato never abandoned his belief that the social order sketched in the *Republic* was the ideal, even if perhaps an unattainable one[76]; so presumably he at least, among those who saw *Eccl.* in 391 or 390, thought that Praxagora's society, shorn of a comic eccentricity or two, might have something to recommend it. Aristophanes can hardly have anticipated that. His comic heroes attack *real* evils (for example, a devastating war; the domination of Cleon; the threatened downfall of Athens and of tragic drama; the unjust distribution of wealth) by applying *fantasy* remedies (a private peace-treaty; a flight up to heaven; a panhellenic sexual boycott; the advance of a sausage-seller to political power; the resurrection of a dead poet; the healing of the blind god of Wealth). In *Eccl.* the evil that is being attacked might seem rather vague: Athens is "dead in the water" (109), Praxagora is "vexed and grieved at the whole situation the City is in" (174-5), no one has any practical proposals "to save the City" (396-7). But when we analyse the *causes* of this national malaise, we find that attention is repeatedly drawn to just two, which are, moreover, closely related: the *contrast of wealth and poverty*, and *selfishness* throughout society.

It is the latter which is emphasized first and most strongly, beginning in Praxagora's rehearsal-speech. Repeatedly she shows how Athenians form their views on political issues, not on the merits of a proposal, but on whether they as individuals will gain or lose by it:

> Whoever has received cash [for attending the Assembly] praises [Agyrrhius] to the skies, while whoever hasn't had any says that those who try to treat the Assembly as a wage-earning job deserve to be put to death (186-8)
>
> We need to launch a fleet: the poor man says yes, the rich and the farmers say no (197-8)
>
> We get a glimpse of salvation; but Thrasybulus is furious because *he* isn't invited to take charge (202-3)
>
> You each look out for a way to gain a profit for yourselves, while the public interest gets kicked around like Aesimus (207-8)

In subsequent scenes further stress is put on the idea that most men do indeed "treat the Assembly as a wage-earning job" and little else (282-4, 289-310, 376-393, 547-8); but when we hear about the actual Assembly meeting, selfishness shares the centre of the stage with the problem of poverty. Euaeon (408-426) combines both in his own person: clad in a cloak so threadbare that most of those present thought he was naked, he argues for ... free supplies of warm clothing and free access to warm bedding; it is not too obvious how this will save Athens, but it will certainly provide

76 Cf. *Rep.* 592b, *Laws* 739b-e.

him with his own desideratum of "something to save *me* – something weighing about eight pounds" (412-3). Yet despite the transparent self-interest of his plea it wins considerable sympathy, in particular from Blepyrus (422), and he and Blepyrus alike have harsh words for grasping tradesmen (fullers, tanners, corn-dealers): far too many Athenians are about as badly off as Euaeon is, and others are making money out of their misery. And the women – so argues the disguised Praxagora – even within the current social order suggest a better way, lending each other goods and money freely and restoring them honestly (446-451), doing of their own accord what Euaeon and Blepyrus would force the tradesmen to do under compulsion[77].

Once in power, however, Praxagora goes much further, and the abolition of poverty and inequality is placed firmly in the foreground. Before giving any details of her plan, she at once declares that there will be "no being jealous of your neighbours, nobody being naked or poor, ... no seizures for debt" (565-7); and as soon as she has laid down the basic principle of communism (590), she defines its implications as follows:

> We should not have one man being rich and another wretched, nor one farming broad acres while another hasn't enough land to be buried in, nor one man owning many slaves while another doesn't have even one attendant: I'll make it so that there is one shared livelihood for everyone, and it's equal (591-4).

The abolition of inequality will also do much to eliminate crime, which can be caused either by great poverty (note the juxtaposition of nakedness and clothes-stealing in 565-6) or by great wealth which only whets the appetite for even greater wealth (see on 608).

As to selfishness, whether or not it is possible to eradicate it from human nature, Praxagora's constant claim is that her scheme will remove all its evil consequences by making it impossible for anyone to *benefit* by behaving selfishly – and if there are flaws in her reasoning (as indeed there are), nobody is allowed to point them out except to the extent that Praxagora is provided with arguments in rebuttal, and it is asking too much of an audience not trained in political philosophy to expect them to pick holes in her case when the characters fail to do so. A man with money, she argues, will gain nothing by refusing to surrender it (603-610); the power to purchase sex is worthless when it is available free on demand (611-5); criminals will be deterred by the threat of "being punished via the stomach" (662-6); no one will steal property of which he is already part-owner (667), or snatch a cloak when he

---

77 Aristotle, while condemning Plato's abolition of private property, strongly commends the principle that individuals should make their property freely available for others to borrow and use (*Politics* 1263a26-39).

can get one from the state (668-9), or gamble when he has no money of his own to stake (672).

At this point Praxagora leaves the stage, not to return, and the two scenes that follow show aspects of her new society in operation – first of all communism in lifestyle and property (730-876), then communism in sex (877-1111). It soon becomes evident that the revolution has not immediately abolished selfishness[78], which, on the contrary, is very much alive in the persons of the Dissident in the first scene and (arguably) every character in the second. But, as we have seen, Praxagora never claimed that her revolution would of itself abolish selfishness: what she claimed was that she would take the *gain* out of it – or, otherwise put, that she would create a situation in which it was in everyone's selfish interest to be altruistic and cooperative[79].

The first of the two scenes under consideration (730-876) puts this claim to the test. The Dissident is as self-centred as the Neighbour is public-spirited. To the Dissident, the Neighbour is a fool: to the Neighbour, the Dissident is a villain. And certainly to the average spectator the Dissident will come across as a thoroughly bad citizen, particularly when he prates of obeying the City's decisions and assisting in its public activities (854, 861-2) while blatantly intent on doing so only when he gains from it[80]. Is Praxagora right in asserting that such selfishness will not pay, in this case or in any other? We may safely assume – since the Dissident himself does not deny – that the Neighbour is right to expect that the women will bar from the communal dining-halls, by force, anyone who refuses to surrender his property (855-864), and we may add that they will have the support of those men who, like the Neighbour, *have* surrendered theirs and will be eager to prevent others from sharing their reward without earning it (cf. 865-871). If the scene ended there, we could hardly doubt that Praxagora, thus far, was vindicated. But it goes on for another five lines, and the Dissident is given the last word: he devises, apparently, a brilliant scheme for having his cake and eating it – and departs without revealing what the scheme is, nor do we ever discover whether it was successful. It is not, however, credible that the play went through rehearsal without anyone asking the author "Why aren't we told what becomes of the Dissident?" if this was really a

78 On this see especially Rothwell 60-72.

79 So in *Wealth*, when the god of Wealth recovers his sight and is able to make the virtuous rich and the wicked poor, the expected consequence is that everybody will become virtuous (*Wealth* 497) and therefore (or: in order to be) rich.

80 Cf. 778-9 where the Neighbour incredulously asks if the Dissident's rule of life is "we must only take and not give", and the Dissident happily confirms that it is; contrast e.g. Pericles' description of the Athenian national character in Thuc. 2.40.4-5: "We acquire friends not by receiving favours but by bestowing them ... We are the only people who help others not from calculated self-interest but from confident, fearless liberality", and see Dover *GPM* 175-8.

problem likely to concern the audience; it follows that to an experienced theatre spectator in the 390s the answer was obvious. Possibly the Dissident's failure was predicted in a following choral song; possibly, as in several other Aristophanic scenes where a character leaves threatening action hostile to the comic project, it was simply assumed (see on 875).

Selfishness, then, has thus far failed; and we may note that according to the evidence of the Neighbour's eyes, most people are cooperating with the new order (805-6), whatever some of the rich may think of it (806-810). The basic desire for food and drink – now obtainable only by those who surrender their property – has proved too strong to resist, as Praxagora expected it would. In the following scene, however, we are shown the effects of her attempt to regulate another basic desire by law; and here anyone who thought of her scheme as a practical policy would be given considerable pause. To be sure, the outcome of the scene is the outcome which the law envisaged; but not one of those involved (except of course the ultimate winner, the Third Old Woman) has obeyed the law willingly, the First Old Woman has been tricked into abandoning what at the time was a valid legal claim, and the only concern of every character has been to get sexual satisfaction for himself or herself with the most attractive partner available or, if that is not an option, at least to avoid having to sleep with the most repulsive. It is not possible this time to control the anti-social consequences of one human desire (for possessions) by the manipulation of another (for food); so far as we are told, the new sex laws are enforced by no sanction except physical self-help (1019-20), and in the contest for the favours of Epigenes it is every woman for herself. What is more, while (as already mentioned, p. 13) the discomfiture of arrogant youth by rejuvenated age is a common feature of Aristophanic comedy, the language of rejuvenation is nowhere used of the old women in this scene; on the contrary, they are persistently associated with the idea of death (cf. on 905, 996, 1030-5, 1073, 1105-11) and, far from contact with Epigenes revitalizing them, we are given the impression that contact with them will be, almost literally, the death of him. But then we are not likely to think of *this* aspect of Praxagora's scheme as a practical policy (it is, as we have seen, the one major plank of the scheme that Plato discarded); this scene, and the whole business of the new sex laws, has no bearing whatever on the economic and political ills that the scheme was meant to cure; it is, furthermore, entirely self-contained – the only scene in the play (indeed in all surviving Greek comedy) whose entire cast is peculiar to it and includes no character appearing elsewhere – and when it is over the action proceeds as though it had never existed. The evidence of other early "gynaecocratic" comedies (above, pp. 8–10) suggests that an almost obligatory feature of such a play was a scene of some sort in which female sexuality ran riot and, as Blepyrus and Chremes had feared, women subjected men to the sexual compulsion to which in real life men had the right to subject women[81]. This is that scene. It establishes to the male audience's satisfaction, what almost all of them thought they knew already, that it is extremely dangerous to give women any control over their own sex lives; much more importantly, it begins with some lively lyrics in two or three contrasting styles, continues with some extended quick-fire dialogue that will keep any audience mentally on its toes, ends with a prolonged riot of slapstick, and is shot through with a rich variety of obscenity both direct and by innuendo (including, probably, an erect comic phallus; see on 969).

And now the play returns to Praxagora; for although she does not appear on stage, all the speaking persons in the final scene are her satellites – her husband, her maidservant, her friends and followers; and they all enjoy a typical comic triumph, with the hitherto unimpressive Blepyrus[82] even gaining the rewards traditionally assigned to comic heroes. Everyone has had a splendid dinner except for him (1132-3) – which means that he still has it to look forward to, with the food (1169-75) and the wine (1118-24, 1139) both described in mouth-watering terms, and which also means that no one in Athens is any longer going hungry; the more agreeable side of Praxagora's new sexual dispensation also now comes into view, as her elderly and previously semi-impotent husband appears with two young women, his wife invites them to dine with her, and he dances off with them and the chorus, rejuvenated as ever by the Viagra-like magic of comedy. If we leave aside the parenthesis of 877-1111, everybody's needs have been satisfied, as Praxagora said they would be; and so have the needs of the audience, both "those who are intellectual" and "those who enjoy a laugh" (1155-6; the latter will have particularly appreciated the parenthetic scene). And if some of them take away the idea that there is something wrong with a society in which everyone's first question on any issue is "what's in it for me?" and in which, since the loss of empire, too many are desperately poor, then, to say the least, no harm will have been done. Aristophanes was to revisit much of the same ground in *Wealth* two or three years later.

4. "Ecclesiazusae" and the development of comedy

In its basic story-pattern *Ecclesiazusae* is a thoroughly typical Aristophanic comedy[83]: the community is in a serious predicament, the heroine carries through against opposition a fantasy-plan to save it, and in the final stages of the play the consequences of her success are displayed. In many of its formal features, however,

---

81 The rape of a wife (let alone of a slave) was not only no crime, but among most Athenians it seems to have incurred no stigma (see on 467-9).

82 For the identity of the male character in this final scene, see on 1113.

83 See G.M. Sifakis, *JHS* 112 (1992) 123-142, and my *Aristophanes: Acharnians* (Warminster, 1980) 11-13.

it exhibits considerable changes from the patterns found in Aristophanes' fifth-century plays, particularly as regards the choral and lyrical elements.

These developments are not immediately apparent in the early scenes: the gathering of women preparing for conspiratorial action in *Eccl.* seems to differ little from the gathering of women preparing for conspiratorial action in *Lysistrata*, until we realize[84] that with the exception of Praxagora and two others who have had significant speaking parts, they are going to constitute the chorus of the play[85]. The early movements of the chorus are thus unusual: they enter without song and without being clearly identified at first as a chorus, the song (285-310) corresponding structurally to the normal choral entrance-sequence (*parodos*) accompanies not the chorus's entrance but its *exit*, and it is off stage for a considerable time (311-477) before returning in what is sometimes called an *epiparodos* (478-503). Similar patterns of choral movement, however, are found in several other plays[86], and in each case they result from dramaturgical decisions peculiar to the individual play: in this play Aristophanes had decided to have (i) an onstage Assembly rehearsal, (ii) an offstage Assembly meeting and (iii) a chorus of women supporters of Praxagora, he had also decided for the sake of simplicity that

84 It is not clear just when spectators *would* realize this. The title of the play, if announced in advance (as it probably was), would indicate to them with high probability that the chorus would consist of (some of) the women who were going to attend the Assembly, but these could still be a different group from those who are present in the prologue: in *Lysistrata* three different groups of Athenian women conspirators are identified – the younger women on stage in the prologue who swear to the sexual boycott, the older women who seize the Acropolis (175-9, 240-2) and appear on stage briefly in a later scene (439-461), and another group of old women who arrive later to support them and form (half) the chorus. In *Eccl.*, however, when eventually we hear (280-2) of "other women from the countryside", we are told that they will "come straight to the Pnyx", i.e.. in effect, that they will not be seen on stage; and when, shortly afterwards, the women who *are* on stage begin to sing, we are left in little doubt that they are the chorus of the play.

85 A fourth woman who has had a limited speaking part (30-31, 43-45, 279b) proves to be the chorus-leader.

86 A departure and return by the chorus occurs in Aeschylus' *Eumenides* (231/244) and Sophocles' *Ajax* (814/866), in Euripides' *Alcestis* (746/861) and *Helen* (385/515), in the pseudo-Euripidean *Rhesus* (564/674), and possibly in the pseudo-Aeschylean *Prometheus Bound* (283/397); see O.P. Taplin, *The Stagecraft of Aeschylus* (Oxford, 1977) 256-7, 375-386. The virtually silent initial entry of the *Eccl.* chorus is paralleled in Euripides' *Suppliant Women*, where they are present as suppliants from the very beginning of the play (their first utterance begins at line 42), and probably, again, in *Eumenides* where they, or some of them, appear asleep in a tableau after line 63, begin to make inarticulate noises at 117, and become an active chorus only at 140 (see my *Aeschylus: Eumenides* [Cambridge, 1989] 93, and A.J. Podlecki, *Aeschylus: Eumenides* [Warminster, 1989] 12-13; *aliter* Taplin *op.cit.* 369-374).

the same group of women should serve all three purposes, and this was the only way he could do it.

When the chorus return, Praxagora, now head of state, tells them that they are to be her "advisers" (518); but they never actually give her any advice[87], and from now on both she and the play almost totally ignore them until the final scene, and those components of the play in which the chorus traditionally took a major part either disappear from the script or are drastically reduced. The *parabasis*, already shortened and simplified in Aristophanes' plays of 411 and later, has now vanished altogether (though a trace of it reappears at the end of the play: see below). The *agōn* remains, as it still does in *Wealth*, but it has now lost the double, responsive structure which had been virtually unchanged from *Knights* to *Frogs*, and consists only of an astrophic choral prelude and a single long speech in anapaestic tetrameters by Praxagora (with interjected questions and criticisms by two male characters) introduced by a *katakeleusmos* from the chorus-leader (581-2) and ending with a *pnīgos* (689-709)[88]. The choral songs which separate successive episodes in every earlier play of Aristophanes are absent from the script, or at most are represented by the note *khorou* "<performance> of the chorus"; it is likely that the chorus did in fact sing at the two points where this note appears in the ms. R (729/730 and 876/7)[89], but their words were evidently not considered important enough for inclusion in the texts that went into circulation[90]. And the presence of the chorus is so completely disregarded by the characters that it has been seriously suggested that they are not present at all[91]. This ignoring of the chorus is not

87 Unless one is to count the vapid recommendations of 571-582, which can be summed up as "Say something clever and novel, and be quick about it".

88 The structural simplification is not to be explained by reference to the fact that this *agōn* consists essentially of an exposition by one character instead of a debate between two: on the one hand, Peisetaerus in *Birds* likewise has no antagonist, yet the *agon* still has a double structure complete to the last detail; on the other, the *agōn* in *Wealth* is a genuine debate yet is even more rudimentary in structure than that of *Eccl.*

89 See commentary on these passages, and also on 1111/2 where there *may* likewise have been a choral song though no ms. indicates one.

90 Or at least in those copies which survived into Hellenistic times to be commented on by scholarly annotators and to become the ancestors of our text. It has often been suggested that the words of these omitted songs were traditional and not composed by the dramatist; but one omitted song at any rate (at *Wealth* 770/1) must have contained words relevant to the play, because the next words spoken by Wealth only make sense as a reply to it.

91 T. Gelzer, *RE* Suppl. 12 (1971) 1496, following W. Schmid, *Geschichte der griechischen Literatur* iv (Munich, 1946) 365, 368. This supposition is most unlikely: (i) in 711-729 the exits of the three principals present (Praxagora, Blepyrus and the Neighbour) are carefully motivated but nothing is said about any departure of the chorus, and Praxagora speaks of the tasks awaiting her in the Agora exclusively in the first person *singular* (711, 712, 714, 718); (ii) at 1114 (when, according to Gelzer, the

without precedent in Aristophanes[92], but it has never before continued so long as here, and it is clear that the process has begun (though only begun) which will lead us eventually to the vestigial reveller-choruses of the comedies of Menander.

But there are moments at which the chorus still has considerable significance in the drama – and this applies equally to *Wealth*. These moments are its entrance and its exit (or rather, in this play, exits). In particular, it dominates the very conclusion of the play as much as that of any earlier Aristophanic comedy except perhaps *Peace*. The Maid addresses the chorus on entering, and once Blepyrus is ready to go to dinner, the chorus-leader takes charge of the action (1151ff): from that point on, of the two principals present, Blepyrus says (in the Greek) only five words and the Maid nothing. In a last-minute insertion, the chorus-leader pleads with the competition judges, in the manner of several *parabases* in earlier plays[93]: then the chorus begin a dance in which Blepyrus, the Maid and Blepyrus' two girl companions join, sing the longest known word in the Greek language (in one breath?) and depart with shouts and anticipations both of a fictive banquet (the one in the Agora) and of a real one (in honour of the expected victory of the play).

The characters, by contrast with most of those in Aristophanes' earlier plays, seem remarkably ordinary. There are no divinities like Hermes, Poseidon, Heracles, Dionysus; no famous or notorious contemporaries like Euripides, Paphlagon-Cleon, Socrates, Meton, Cinesias; no type-characters like informers, creditors, magistrates, let alone corpses; no foreigners speaking dialect or pidgin-Greek like Scythian policemen, Persian ambassadors, Spartans, Thebans or Megarians. Every male character is a fairly average Athenian citizen: none is exceptionally poor, none is rich[94], none has any unusual occupation (indeed we are not told anything at all about what occupation, if any, they do have). And every female character is the wife, or the widow, or the daughter, or the slave of a fairly average Athenian citizen[95]. So

chorus have just returned from the Agora) the Maid, who has herself come thence, addresses them as "you ladies who *are standing* near our door" and presently asks them where her mistress's husband is (1125-6); (iii) at the end of the play they go off to dine (1165, 1181) as eagerly as the so far dinnerless Blepyrus, whereas if they had been in the Agora since 729 they would have dined already.

92 A striking example is the Cinesias-Myrrhine scene in *Lys.* 870-951, where Myrrhine refuses to make love in the presence of her baby (907) but takes no notice whatever of the presence of a chorus of twelve old men and twelve old women; cf. also *Ach.* 440-4 where Dicaeopolis tells Euripides that he wants to deceive the chorus (so he calls them). I have discussed this question in *QSt* 11 (1980) 411 n.10.

93 Being in trochaic tetrameters, her speech corresponds in that respect to the *epirrhema* of a parabasis, but is considerably shorter (eight lines against the normal sixteen or twenty).

94 Nothing indicates that even the Dissident is particularly wealthy; he's mean, that's all.

95 Including the four women of 877-1111; they certainly behave like prostitutes (except that they don't charge for their services), but that is how citizen women are *expected* to

colourless are many of the characters that it is sometimes very hard to identify them within scenes (where there are two subordinate male or two subordinate female characters) or to be confident whether a character in one scene is to be identified with a character in another[96].

One character who is far from colourless is Praxagora, "the woman of effective speech" (as her name proclaims her) but equally of effective thought and effective action, who devises the scheme for a *coup d'état* and carries it through almost single-handed – for her supporters, though they are loyal and enthusiastic and their participation essential to success, have little intelligence or foresight and require the closest guidance and direction if they are not to ruin the project, as the dress-rehearsal proves: after their disastrous attempts to make speeches (129-169) they are confined to the role of a claque (189, 204, 213, 431-2) and a voting mass. Like her counterpart of twenty years earlier, Lysistrata, she has all the reach-for-the-sky idealism of the typical Old Comic hero, and a determination (by classical Athenian standards, a most unfeminine determination) to take the initiative to set right what is wrong in the public sphere[97]; like Lysistrata too, on the other hand, and probably because of her gender, she lacks the element of low-comic naughtiness (what Whitman called *ponēriā*)[98] that gives spice to characters like Dicaeopolis and Peisetaerus; but again like Lysistrata, and in spite of her gender, she is free from the vices commonly ascribed to women, and while not above the various desires of the flesh (cf. 8-11, 14-15, 525-6) she, unlike her confederates, never lets them control her or divert her from her purpose. And having succeeded in gaining power by acting the part of a male orator, she first puts on a brief but brilliant act in the totally different role of an ordinary dutiful wife unjustly accused of improper behaviour (520-550) and then suddenly produces a complete blueprint for an entirely new model of society which, like a true politician, she has kept concealed throughout the action until now.

It is all the more surprising, then, that after 729 Praxagora disappears from the action. As we have seen, she returns in spirit at the end, but she does not return in person. Few other Aristophanic hero(in)es are off stage for prolonged periods[99], and

---

behave under the new order.

96 This is, of course, a problem only for the modern reader (and the modern director); the spectator at the original production would have known immediately, by the masks, who was who. Issues of character identification are discussed in the notes on 30-284, 327-356, 372, 564, 583-729, 730, 746, 1113.

97 Athenian tragedy is full of women who take the initiative, but almost always they do so only when their personal life has been injured or disrupted, normally in connection with family, sexual or parental relationships.

98 C.H. Whitman, *Aristophanes and the Comic Hero* (Cambridge MA, 1964) 29-41.

99 In Ar.'s six surviving plays from the years 425-414, the hero is never off stage for longer than the duration of the parabasis. Lysistrata has some longer absences (*Lys.*

even they always return in the final scene[100]. Aristophanes may perhaps at one stage have intended to bring Praxagora back at the end, in the manner of Dicaeopolis or Peisetaerus, to lead her husband and her followers triumphantly to the feast in the Agora. In the end, however, he opted for a spectacular finale with plenty of dancing, in which it would be undignified for the "Lady General" to take part but from which she could not be made to stand aloof without seeming isolated from her community[101]; and he replaced Praxagora in this scene with her maid, who could also be portrayed, as Praxagora could not, as being riotously drunk.

A striking feature of *Ecclesiazusae*, compared with most Aristophanic plays of broadly similar plot structure, is the lack of divine involvement, in particular of divine support for the heroine[102]. Other Aristophanic hero(in)es who are working for the general good, rather than exclusively for their personal interests, almost always have divine assistance or signs of divine approval[103]. Dicaeopolis' peace-treaty is arranged for him by an immortal envoy, he celebrates two festivals within the play, and at the end he is invited to feast with the priest of Dionysus; the Sausage-seller is marked out by oracles (some of them Apollo's, *Knights* 220, 1229-48) as the man destined to overthrow Paphlagon-Cleon; Trygaeus rescues the goddess Peace with the help of Hermes; Peisetaerus, in his war against Zeus, wins the support first of

---

253-430, 864-1108), as does Chremylus in *Wealth* (627-781, 802-958), but there is nothing to compare with Praxagora's continuous absence for nearly half the play. Indeed she is the only Aristophanic hero(ine) who is *present* for less than half the play in total (1-284, 504-729, in all 43% of the play's length; Lysistrata is present during 55% of her play, Chremylus during 62% of his).

100 It has often been doubted that Lysistrata returns at *Lys.* 1273, and sometimes that Dionysus returns at *Frogs* 1500; but see my notes on these passages.

101 *Lysistrata* also has a dancing finale, and the heroine does not take part in the dancing; but this is much less uncomfortable dramatically, because from her entry at 1108 onwards Lysistrata has seemed to be living on a higher plane than the men and women whose movements she has controlled and indeed has been increasingly assimilated, not just as hitherto to her near-namesake Lysimache the priestess of Athena Polias (cf. *Lys.* 554), but to Athena herself (see J.J. Henderson, *Aristophanes: Lysistrata* [Oxford, 1987] xxxvii-xl; E.J.S. Sibley, *The Role of Athena in Greek Drama* [Diss. Nottingham 1995]; and note that the priestess of Athena Polias sometimes impersonated the goddess by wearing the aegis [Suda αι60] and that Athena, who has been so important in the play as a whole, is not named among the gods invoked in the song 1279-90 – because she is present already?)

102 This feature of *Eccl.* was acutely pointed out to me many years ago by an undergraduate student, the late Mrs Sylvia Warmingham.

103 Some of these (Trygaeus, Peisetaerus, Chremylus) are rebelling against Zeus, but all have the support of other gods and all are successful. Since the gods notoriously had many quarrels among themselves, it can be understood how comedy could happily envisage mortals taking sides in such quarrels and even stirring them up – even if to the Euripidean Heracles (*HF* 1341-6) or the Platonic Socrates (*Euthyphro* 7b-8b) the very existence of such quarrels was theologically unthinkable.

Prometheus and then of Heracles; Lysistrata is the servant, almost the embodiment, of Athena (see note 101) and is victorious thanks to Aphrodite (*Lys.* 551, 833-4, 1290); Chremylus is guided by Apollo to meet the god Wealth, whose sight is then restored by Asclepius; and the hero of *Frogs* is of course himself a god. When, on the other hand, the central character of a comedy is pursuing an anti-social project, he is shown as an enemy of the gods: Strepsiades, having explicitly rejected all the traditional deities (*Clouds* 423-6), is lured to his doom by the Clouds (*ib.* 1452-64, 1477), while Euripides in *Thesmophoriazusae* commits a grave act of impiety, punishable in real life by death (and very nearly so punished in the play), by sending his in-law to infiltrate the Thesmophorian sanctuary and rites from which men were strictly debarred. It is only in *Wasps* and *Ecclesiazusae* (which otherwise bear no particular resemblance to each other) that the action proceeds on an almost wholly secular level[104]. I draw attention to this fact; I do not pretend to be able to explain it[105].

5. *Staging*

Ecclesiazusae seems to have been written for a theatre of essentially the same form as that in which Aristophanes' earlier plays were staged. It makes, however, fuller use than any earlier surviving play of the three doors in the *skēnē*[106], though only two are ever in use at one time. Whenever Praxagora or a member of her household is present, one door represents their house, and we may presume that this is the central door. The following other dwellings must, at one time or another, be represented on stage[107]:

---

104 Nor is there any mention of religious matters in Praxagora's account of her new society: and in the descriptions of the communal feasting there is no reference to sacrifice or even libation. Contrast *Wealth* where Chremylus' first act on coming home with Wealth from the sanctuary of Asclepius is to sacrifice a boar, a he-goat and a ram (*Wealth* 819-820): where the Just Man, on being raised from poverty to riches, comes at once to offer prayer and make dedications (823-849): and where the play ends with a procession for the installation of Wealth in the *opisthodomos* of Athena (1191-9).

105 But it should not be used to argue that Praxagora's project is to be seen as impious: if that were the case, Ar. would have let someone make the point. The only religious argument that is used against Praxagora is the obviously absurd and anti-social argument that it is a religious duty to "only take and not give" because that is what the gods do (777-783).

106 Attested by Eupolis fr. 48 (from *Autolycus*, produced in 420) and, later, by Menander's *Dyskolos* where they represent the house of Cnemon, the house of Gorgias, and (in the centre) the shrine of Pan and the Nymphs. The only other Aristophanic play where it is likely that all three doors were used is *Peace*, where they represent the house of Trygaeus, the palace of Zeus, and (in the centre) the cave in which Peace is imprisoned (later, the shrine in which Trygaeus installs her): see Russo 137-141.

107 There is no need to suppose that the dwellings of Chremes or the Dissident are visible to the audience: see on 372 and 746.

(1) The home of the First Woman, whom Praxagora calls her neighbour (33) and on whose door she gently knocks.

(2) The home of Blepyrus' neighbour (327).

(3) The home of the man who comes on stage at 564 and who later (728-9) goes indoors to prepare his property for surrender to the state.

(4) The home of the Girl, at whose door Epigenes knocks (977, 989); she is upstairs when he arrives (cf. 962 "run down").

(5) The home of the First Old Woman, who "peeps out" at 884, 924 and 930, answers Epigenes' knock (which she professes to believe was for her) at 976, and tries to drag him inside at 1035-7.

(6) The home of the Second Old Woman, who also speaks of getting him inside (1062).

(7) The home of the Third Old Woman, towards whose door Epigenes is being dragged at 1093-4; this is the "port" into which he is about to sail at 1106[108].

Since, as already observed, the scene 877-1111 shares no characters with the rest of the play, the theatrical identification of dwellings (1-3) and of dwellings (4-7) can be treated as entirely separate problems. The identification of (1-3) depends on which if any of three persons – First Woman's husband (37-40, 76-81), Blepyrus' neighbour, and the man of 564ff – are to be identified with each other, and the conclusion to which this leads us[109] is that (1) is one house, (2) = (3) is another.

In the scene 877-1111 we appear to have *four* dwellings, but this need cause no difficulty, since once the Girl has left the scene (before 1054) her door (from which she emerged at 1037) can become that of the Third Old Woman (who appears at 1065). It is likely that the central door is that of the First Old Woman, with the Second Old Woman having one of the flanking doors and the Girl (later the Third Old Woman) the other[110]. The Girl, being upstairs during the duet 952-975, must have (re)appeared at a window at 949, and there is no reason to doubt that this is also where she was during 884-936. The First Old Woman, on the other hand, who is hoping to "snare one of [the men] as he passes by" (881-2), is probably downstairs

---

108 It is theoretically possible that these passages refer to the door of the *Second* Old Woman and that the Third lives somewhere offstage; but see on 1074-97.

109 See on 327-356 (where reasons are also given for supposing that the Neighbour in this scene appears at an upstairs window) and 564.

110 For the reasoning on which this assignment is based see on 877-1111, where it is also argued that the Girl is to be placed on the side of the *skēnē* more remote from the Agora.

at her door, to give herself the best chance of ensuring that she can grab a man before he can get away[111]; when she withdraws from sight (at 937 and again at 946), she is no doubt to be imagined as waiting just inside the door (watching through a crack, or leaving the door slightly ajar) so as to be able to intervene instantly when she judges the moment has come to do so.

In this play there are two off-stage locations of significance: in the first half of the play, the Pnyx where the Assembly meets; in the second half, the Agora to which property is taken for surrender and where the communal dinner is held. To the Pnyx go Praxagora and the women between 284 and 310, and from the Pnyx they return between 478 and 504, preceded by Chremes at 372; the other men we see – Blepyrus and his neighbour – also intend to go to the Pnyx but, being unable to find their outdoor clothes, they never get there. To the Agora go Praxagora and Blepyrus[112] at 729, the Neighbour and his slaves at 871, the Dissident a minute or two later; from the Agora come the Heraldess at 834, Epigenes at 934, the Maid at 1112; and the final *exeunt omnes* is also in the direction of the Agora and the banquet. The two offstage locations, it will be seen, are never dramatically active at the same time, and it is not therefore necessary to assume that they are represented by different directions of movement in the theatre. In fact, to go from the Theatre of Dionysus itself to either of these destinations one would first take the same direction – westwards, or stage-left[113]: the Pnyx lies nearly due west of the theatre, the Agora is behind the Acropolis and is reached by rounding its western foot. I have accordingly identified both the Pnyx and the Agora directions as stage-left, with the stage-right *eisodos* leading to the homes of those persons who do not live in the houses we see[114]; but this is a largely arbitrary decision, and there is as good a case for forgetting the real topography of the theatre-Acropolis area[115] and assuming that one *eisodos* was used for the Pnyx direction and the other for the Agora, so that the play's offstage centre of gravity, as it were, could be seen to *move* from the Pnyx (the space of politics) to the Agora (now become the space of feasting)[116].

---

111 Indeed, there is no clear evidence anywhere in Ar. that there was more than one upper window available in the *skēnē*.

112 That Blepyrus has gone there is later forgotten; see on 1113.

113 In my stage-directions, and in the Commentary, I consistently use "right" and "left" in the modern theatrical sense, which defines these directions from the *performers'* point of view: hence in the Theatre of Dionysus, where the *skēnē* was on the south side and the performers faced north, "right" means east and "left" west. Much modern writing on the ancient theatre, contrariwise, defines right and left from the *spectators'* viewpoint.

114 These persons are the chorus, the Second Woman, Chremes and the Dissident. This will also be the side on which the Heraldess exits at 852, and Blepyrus enters at 1128.

115 After all, there is no particular reason to imagine Praxagora's home as located in this area; there were many parts of Athens from which one would go in one direction to the Pnyx and in the other to the Agora.

116 If so, it is likely that the direction of the Pnyx was stage-left, since there is good

Ecclesiazusae, like most other Aristophanic plays, is written to be performed by four speaking actors[117]; there is no scene in which all four appear together, but at 1049 the Second Old Woman has an entrance only five lines after the exit of the First while Epigenes and the Girl are both on stage, which with three actors would require one of them to make a quicker change than is needed anywhere else in surviving Greek drama[118], and at 1112 the simultaneous exit of three characters is followed without a break by the entrance of the Maid.

The distribution of roles among the four actors can be established only to a limited extent; in particular, it is not possible to determine what roles were taken by the protagonist after he had finished playing Praxagora[119], though if he took the part of the Maid in the final scene (as he must have done if he appeared in that scene at all) it is tempting to suppose that he also played the Heraldess who is likewise Praxagora's spokeswoman and agent. In this case he would have had to play the First Old Woman[120] in the intervening scene, and one possible distribution of parts, giving the second actor four roles of some weight[121], would be as follows:

---

evidence, dating back to the fifth century (Cratinus fr. 229), that when a dramatic chorus entered in formation (as the chorus of *Eccl.* does at its second entrance, coming from the Pnyx, though not at its first) it always entered from the left, with the result that the left file of the marching body was nearest the audience and the best performers were placed in it (cf. Aristides 3.154 with scholia); see Csapo & Slater 353. On the significance of the opposition of the two *eisodoi* in the staging of Greek drama, see also D. Wiles, *Tragedy in Athens* (Cambridge, 1997) 134-160

117 See D.M. MacDowell, *CQ* 44 (1994) 325-335. The play could be performed by three actors if there was a choral song between 1111 and 1112, but there probably was not (see note *ad loc.*).

118 The next quickest is in Men. *Dysk.* 873-9, where, if there are only three actors, one of them must exit as Gorgias or Sostratus at 873 and reappear as Getas at 879. It is probable that by Menander's time the number of speaking actors in comedy, as in tragedy, was indeed restricted to three: the treatment of Sophrone in *Epitr.* 1062-end – when she is repeatedly addressed (1062-75, 1118-20, 1122, 1126-8), and at one point (1126-8) shows manifest signs of joy, but never says a word – is hard to account for in any other way. In the somewhat similar case of the dog Labes' silence in *Wasps* (944-9) there are *four* speaking actors on stage (playing Philocleon, Bdelycleon, Xanthias and the Hound of Cydathenaeum; see *CQ* 27 [1977] 270-1).

119 Except that he obviously could not have played Blepyrus or the Neighbour, who had been on stage with Praxagora earlier – unless we gratuitously assume that roles were routinely split between different actors.

120 Not the Second or Third, nor Epigenes, since all of these are on stage until a moment before the Maid enters; nor the Girl, since the actor playing her must double as the Third Old Woman if the scene 877-1111 is not to require five actors.

121 And giving the protagonist something of a break, after he has carried the whole central scene 504-729; that this was a matter of concern to producers at this period is suggested by the curious fashion in which Chremylus (protagonist?) and his slave Carion (deuteragonist?) are present, and take the leading role, in *alternate scenes* in the second

First actor: Praxagora, Heraldess, First Old Woman, Maid
Second actor: First Woman, Blepyrus, Dissident, Girl, Third Old Woman
Third actor: Second Woman, Chremes, Second Old Woman
Fourth actor: Neighbour, Epigenes

Ecclesiazusae does not give quite the opportunities for fanciful mask and costume design that are found in such plays as *Wasps* or *Birds*, but there is ample scope for comic exploitation of cross-dressing (in the first 519 lines of the play Chremes is the only character who appears out of doors without ever wearing the clothes of the opposite sex), of the women's half-tanned faces (126-7) and false beards, and of the old women who try to seize Epigenes with their hideous faces, caked with make-up (878, 1057, 1072), and their attempts to dress to look a quarter their age (879). And as in *Lysistrata* and *Thesmophoriazusae*, the comic phallus attracts considerable attention, whether it is hanging loose as on Blepyrus (see on 622) and Chremes (see on 470, where he apparently sucks his) or frustratedly erect as on Epigenes (see on 969); and if, as is not impossible, Blepyrus too has an erect phallus in the final scene to emphasize his rejuvenation[122], this play in which every aspect of human society, but especially those concerned with gender, has been turned topsy-turvy will end with the typically comic reassertion of masculinity triumphant as an old man, very visibly become young again, basks in freedom from toil and responsibility, in the prospect of feasting at public expense for the rest of his life, in the possession of a brilliant and powerful wife *and* of two very attractive young women on the side, and in the obliging readiness of the former, unimaginable in real life, not merely to tolerate but herself to entertain the latter!

---

half of *Wealth*, when in any of Ar.'s fifth-century plays the hero would have been on stage almost throughout.

122 Like Dicaeopolis at the end of *Ach.* (cf. 1220) and probably Trygaeus at the end of *Peace* (cf. 1351; see S.D. Olson, *Aristophanes: Peace* [Oxford, 1998] on 1318-21).

Select Bibliography

Aristophanes

Editions of the complete plays. The best complete modern edition is still that of V. Coulon (Collection Budé: Paris, 1923-30), with French translation, introductions, and brief notes by H. van Daele. A critical edition of the eleven comedies will form volume III.1 of *Poetae Comici Graeci* (see next paragraph). The edition of F.W. Hall and W.M. Geldart (Oxford Classical Texts: 2nd ed., Oxford, 1906-7) provides neither a reliable text nor a systematic apparatus. Of importance for their commentaries are the editions of J. van Leeuwen (Leiden, 1896-1909) and B.B. Rogers (London, 1902-15); Rogers' text and translation formed the basis of the very inadequate Loeb Classical Library edition (London/Cambridge MA, 1924), now being replaced by a new Loeb edition by J.J. Henderson (1998-). Two series of editions with commentary, by various editors, are currently in progress (Oxford, 1965- . 7 vols. so far published, including *Ecclesiazusae* by R.G. Ussher (1973); Milan, 1985- . with Italian translation by D. Del Corno, 4 vols. so far published, including *Ecclesiazusae* by M. Vetta (1989). For other separate editions of *Ecclesiazusae*, see below.

Fragments of lost plays. R. Kassel and C. Austin, *Poetae Comici Graeci* (Berlin, 1983-). is superseding, as its publication progresses, all previous collections of comic fragments: the fragments of Aristophanes are in volume III.2 (1984).

Scholia (ancient and medieval commentaries). The edition of all the *Scholia in Aristophanem* under the direction of W.J.W. Koster and D. Holwerda (Groningen, 1960-) is now complete for eight of the eleven plays, but for *Ecclesiazusae* the antiquated complete editions of the scholia by W. Dindorf (Oxford, 1838) and F. Dübner (Paris, 1843) have not yet been superseded. The edition by W.G. Rutherford (London, 1896) is of the scholia in the ms. R only.

There is an *index verborum* to Aristophanes by O.J. Todd (Cambridge MA, 1932).

Bibliographies. Reports on research on, and literature about, Aristophanes appeared in *(Bursians) Jahresbericht über die Fortschritte der klassischen Altertumswissenschaft* every few years from 1877 to 1939. Subsequent surveys (those asterisked also cover other writers of Old Comedy) include those by K.J. Dover, *Lustrum* 2 (1957) 52-112 (for 1938-55); W. Kraus, *Anzeiger für die Altertumswissenschaft* 24 (1971) 161-180 (for 1949-70);*H.J. Newiger, *Aristophanes und die alte Komödie* (Darmstadt, 1975) 487-510 (for 1955-73); *I.C. Storey, *EMC* 6 (1987) 1-46 (for 1975-84) and *Antichthon* 26 (1992) 1-29 (for 1982-91); and B. Zimmermann, *Anzeiger für die Altertumswissenschaft* 45 (1992) 161-184 and 47 (1994) 1-18 (for 1971-92).

General studies

W. Schmid, *Geschichte der griechischen Literatur* I.iv (Munich, 1946) 174-440.

A. Lesky, *A History of Greek Literature* (tr. J. Willis and C. de Heer) (London, 1966) 417-452.

T. Gelzer, "Aristophanes (12)", in *RE* Supplementband XII cols. 1391-1570; also published separately as *Aristophanes der Komiker* (Stuttgart, 1971).

E.W. Handley, "Comedy", in P.E. Easterling and B.M.W. Knox ed. *The Cambridge History of Classical Literature* i (Cambridge, 1985) 355-425 = *Greek Drama* (Cambridge, 1989) 103-173 (for bibliography, by M. Drury, see pp.773-9 = 189-195).

H.J. Newiger ed. *Aristophanes und die alte Komödie* (Darmstadt, 1975). An anthology of twentieth-century articles.

E. Segal ed. *Oxford Readings in Aristophanes* (Oxford, 1996). Another anthology.

K.J. Dover, *Aristophanic Comedy* (London, 1972).

A. Solomos, *The Living Aristophanes* (tr. A. Solomos and M. Felheim) (Ann Arbor, 1974).

R.M. Harriott, *Aristophanes, Poet and Dramatist* (London, 1985).

K.J. Reckford, *Aristophanes' Old-and-New Comedy I: Six Essays in Perspective* (Chapel Hill NC, 1987).

J.M. Bremer and E.W. Handley ed. *Aristophane* (*Entretiens sur l'antiquité classique* 38) (Geneva, 1993).

A.M. Bowie, *Aristophanes: Myth, Ritual and Comedy* (Cambridge, 1993).

L.K. Taaffe, *Aristophanes and Women* (London, 1993).

G. Mastromarco, *Introduzione a Aristofane* (Bari, 1994).

D.M. MacDowell, *Aristophanes and Athens: An Introduction to the Plays* (Oxford, 1995).

G.W. Dobrov ed. *Beyond Aristophanes: Transition and Diversity in Greek Comedy* (Atlanta, 1995).

P. Thiercy and M. Menu ed. *Aristophane: la langue, la scène, la cité* (Bari, 1996).

S. Halliwell, *Aristophanes: Birds, Lysistrata, Assembly-Women, Wealth* (Oxford, 1997) ix-lxxix.

G.W. Dobrov ed. *The City as Comedy: Society and Representation in Athenian Drama* (Chapel Hill, 1997).

B. Zimmermann, *Die griechische Komödie* (Düsseldorf/Zürich, 1998) 9-188.

Dramatic technique

T. Zielinski, *Die Gliederung der altattischen Komödie* (Leipzig, 1885).

P. Mazon, *Essai sur la composition des comédies d'Aristophane* (Paris, 1904).

H.J. Newiger, *Metapher und Allegorie: Studien zu Aristophanes* (Munich, 1957).

T. Gelzer, *Der epirrhematische Agon bei Aristophanes* (Munich, 1960).

C.H. Whitman, *Aristophanes and the Comic Hero* (Cambridge MA, 1964).

P. Rau, *Paratragodia: Untersuchungen einer komischen Form des Aristophanes* (Munich, 1967).

G.M. Sifakis, *Parabasis and Animal Choruses* (London, 1971).

M. Landfester, *Handlungsverlauf und Komik in den frühen Komödien des Aristophanes* (Berlin, 1977).

K. McLeish, *The Theatre of Aristophanes* (London, 1980).

B. Zimmermann, "The parodoi of the Aristophanic comedies", *SIFC* (3rd ser.) 2 (1984) 13-24; reprinted with revisions in Segal ed. *Oxford Readings in Aristophanes* 182-193.

P. Thiercy, *Aristophane: fiction et dramaturgie* (Paris, 1986).

N.J. Lowe, "Greek stagecraft and Aristophanes", in J. Redmond ed. *Themes in Drama 10: Farce* (Cambridge, 1988) 33-52.

T.K. Hubbard, *The Mask of Comedy: Aristophanes and the Intertextual Parabasis* (Ithaca NY, 1991).

G.M. Sifakis, "The structure of Aristophanic comedy", *JHS* 112 (1992) 123-142.

W.G. Arnott, "Comic openings", *Drama* 2 (1993) 14-32, with response by N. Felson-Rubin (33-38).

P. von Möllendorff, *Grundlagen einer Ästhetik der Alten Komödie* (Tübingen, 1995).

Language and style

J. Taillardat, *Les images d'Aristophane*² (Paris, 1965).

E.S. Spyropoulos, *L'accumulation verbale chez Aristophane* (Thessaloniki, 1974).

K.J. Dover, "The style of Aristophanes", in *Greek and the Greeks* (Oxford, 1987) 224-236.

K.J. Dover, "Language and character in Aristophanes", *ibid.* 237-248[123].

J.J. Henderson, *The Maculate Muse: Obscene Language in Attic Comedy*² (Oxford, 1991).

S.D. Olson, "Names and naming in Aristophanic comedy", *CQ* 42 (1992) 304-319.

A. López Eire, *La lengua coloquial de la comedia aristofánica* (Murcia, 1996).

A. López Eire, "Lengua y política en la comedia aristofánica", in A. López Eire ed. *Sociedad, política y literatura: comedia griega antigua* (Salamanca, 1997) 45-80.

A.H. Sommerstein, "The anatomy of euphemism in Aristophanic comedy", in F. De Martino and A.H. Sommerstein ed. *Studi sull'eufemismo* (Bari, forthcoming) .

Metre

J.W. White, *The Verse of Greek Comedy* (London, 1912). Still valuable on the spoken and chanted (as distinct from lyric) metres.

A.M. Dale, *The Lyric Metres of Greek Drama*² (Cambridge, 1968).

B. Zimmermann, *Untersuchungen zur Form und dramatischen Technik der aristophanischen Komödien* (3 vols., Königstein/Frankfurt, 1984-7).

L.P.E. Parker, *The Songs of Aristophanes* (Oxford, 1996).

---

123 These two articles are revised versions of papers originally published in Italian in 1970 and 1976 respectively.

Production

T.B.L. Webster, *Monuments Illustrating Old and Middle Comedy*[3] (rev. J.R. Green) (*BICS* Suppl. 39, 1978).

C.W. Dearden, *The Stage of Aristophanes* (London, 1976).

H.J. Newiger, "Drama und Theater", in G.A. Seeck ed. *Das griechische Drama* (Darmstadt, 1979) 434-503.

L.M. Stone, *Costume in Aristophanic Comedy* (New York, 1981).

A.W. Pickard-Cambridge, *The Dramatic Festivals of Athens*[3] (rev. J. Gould and D.M. Lewis) (Oxford, 1988).

J.R. Green, "On seeing and depicting the theatre in classical Athens", *GRBS* 32 (1991) 15-50.

O.P. Taplin, *Comic Angels and Other Approaches to Greek Drama through Vase-Paintings* (Oxford, 1993).

C.F. Russo, *Aristophanes: An Author for the Stage* (London, 1994).

Comedy and society

G.E.M. de Ste Croix, *The Origins of the Peloponnesian War* (London, 1972), Appendix XXIX.

P.A. Cartledge, *Aristophanes and his Theatre of the Absurd* (Bristol, 1990).

J.J. Winkler and F.I. Zeitlin ed. *Nothing to Do with Dionysos?* (Princeton, 1990), esp. chapters by Goldhill, Ober & Strauss, and Henderson.

S. Halliwell, "Comic satire and freedom of speech in classical Athens", *JHS* 111 (1991) 48-70.

A.H. Sommerstein et al. ed. *Tragedy, Comedy and the Polis* (Bari, 1993), esp. chapters by Henderson, Halliwell, Mastromarco and Handley.

A.T. Edwards, "Historicizing the popular grotesque: Bakhtin's *Rabelais* and Attic Old Comedy", in R.S. Scodel ed. *Theater and Society in the Classical World* (Ann Arbor, 1993) 89–117.

C. Carey, "Comic ridicule and democracy", in R.G. Osborne and S. Hornblower ed. *Ritual, Finance, Politics: Athenian Democratic Accounts Presented to David Lewis* (Oxford, 1994) 69-83.

E.G. Csapo and W.J. Slater, *The Context of Ancient Drama* (Ann Arbor, 1994); a sourcebook of texts and images on all aspects of the theatrical and social environment of drama.

J.R. Green, *Theatre in Ancient Greek Society* (London, 1995).

A.H. Sommerstein, "How to avoid being a *komodoumenos*", *CQ* 46 (1996) 327-356.

M. Heath, "Aristophanes and the discourse of politics", in Dobrov ed. *The City as Comedy* (Chapel Hill, 1997; see above) 230-249.

Miscellaneous

E. Fraenkel, *Beobachtungen zu Aristophanes* (Rome, 1962).

V. Ehrenberg, *The People of Aristophanes: A Sociology of Old Attic Comedy*[3] (New York, 1962).

W. Süss, *Aristophanes und die Nachwelt* (Leipzig, 1911).

Ecclesiazusae

Editions. The twentieth-century editions with commentary of *Ecclesiazusae* (all of which have formed part of complete or ongoing complete Aristophanes series, see above) have been those by B.B. Rogers (London, 1902); J. van Leeuwen (Leiden, 1905); R.G. Ussher (Oxford, 1973); and M. Vetta (Milan, 1989).

Books and articles.

C.M. Bowra, "A love-duet", *AJP* 79 (1958) 376-391; reprinted in Bowra, *On Greek Margins* (Oxford, 1970) 149-163.

H. Flashar, "Zur Eigenart des aristophanischen Spätwerks", *Poetica* 1 (1967) 154-175; for English translation see E. Segal ed. *Oxford Readings in Aristophanes* (Oxford, 1996) 314-328.

R.G. Ussher, "The staging of the Ecclesiazusae", *Hermes* 97 (1969) 22-37.

S. S. Saïd, "*L'Assemblée des Femmes*: les femmes, l'économie et la politique", in J. Bonnamour and H. Delavault ed. *Aristophane, les femmes et la cité* (Fontenay-aux-Roses, 1979) 33-69; abridged English translation in Segal ed. *Oxford Readings in Aristophanes* 282-313.

H.P. Foley, "The 'female intruder' reconsidered: women in Aristophanes' *Lysistrata* and *Ecclesiazusae*", *CP* 77 (1982) 1-21.

E. David, *Aristophanes and Athenian Society of the Early Fourth Century B.C.* (Leiden, 1984).

A.H. Sommerstein, "Aristophanes and the demon Poverty", *CQ* 34 (1984) 314-333; reprinted in Segal ed. *Oxford Readings in Aristophanes* 252-281.

S.D. Olson, "The identity of the *despotes* at *Ecclesiazusae* 1128f.", *GRBS* 28 (1987) 161-6.

S.D. Olson, "The 'love duet' in Aristophanes' *Ecclesiazusae*", *CQ* 38 (1988) 328-330.

S.D. Olson, "The staging of Aristophanes, *Ec.* 504-727", *AJP* 110 (1989) 223-6.

N.W. Slater, "Lekythoi in Aristophanes' *Ecclesiazusae*", *Lexis* 3 (1989) 43-51.

K.S. Rothwell, *Politics and Persuasion in Aristophanes' Ecclesiazusae* (Leiden, 1990).

D.F. Sutton, "Aristophanes and the transition to Middle Comedy", *LCM* 15 (1990) 81-95.

S.D. Olson, "Anonymous male parts in Aristophanes' *Ecclesiazusae* and the identity of the *despotes*", *CQ* 41 (1991) 36-40.

L.K. Taaffe, "The illusion of gender disguise in Aristophanes' *Ecclesiazusae*", *Helios* 18 (1991) 91-112.

L.K. Taaffe, *Aristophanes and Women* (London, 1993) 103-133.

A.A. González Terriza, "Los rostros de la Empusa. Monstruos, heteras, niñeras y brujas: aportación a una nueva lectura de Aristófanes 'Ec.' 877-1111", *CFC* 6 (1996) 261-300.

D. Auger, "Figures et représentations de la cité et du politique sur la scéne d'Aristophane", in Thiercy & Menu ed. *Aristophane* (Bari, 1997) 361-377.

N.W. Slater, "Waiting in the wings: Aristophanes' *Ecclesiazusae*", *Arion* n.s. 5 (1997) 97-129.

Note on the Text

The textual tradition of *Ecclesiazusae* is almost as meagre as that of *Lysistrata*. Michigan Papyrus 6649 (Π60), published in 1981[124], was the first papyrus to be identified as coming from this play; it contains portions of 32 lines from the *agon*, confirming a conjecture of Bentley's at 652. Of the seven medieval mss., three are not independent witnesses: Vb1 is a copy of Γ, and Mu1 (Monacensis 137, fifteenth century) is a copy of Λ[125]. The case of B is a little more complex.

Everything in B (which, like Γ, ends at 1135) can be accounted for either as derived from Γ, as error, or as conjecture. B is not a direct copy of Γ, since sometimes (613, 784) it emends to fill a lacuna when the text of Γ is not defective; it is therefore a copy of a copy of Γ. The intermediate copy was much more carelessly made in the second half of the play than in the first: errors present in B and absent in Γ number 24 in lines 1-568 and 61 in lines 569-1135. Some of B's emendations are perceptive (e.g. at 364, 455, 459, 611, 758, 987, 1067), but there is nothing that requires us to assume that they derive from a ms. source. That these good readings are conjectural is confirmed by the fact that in nine places (357, 359, 361, 363, 365, 398, 561, 658, 914) where Γ had left a line incomplete, B failed to fill what (except perhaps in 914) were obvious lacunae[126].

Of the other four mss., R and Λ contain the whole play[127]; Γ ends at 1135; A ends at 282. As in the other plays they both contain (*Acharnians*, *Knights* and *Birds*), AΓ are closely related to each other, forming one family as against R.

The much later ms. Λ might seem at first sight to be intermediate between the two families, but this impression is illusory. For while Λ is frequently alone with R in a true reading, it is rarely alone with R in error: it shares 11 errors with R but 87 with Γ (or, in 1-282, AΓ), including omissions at 223b and 302b. It can thus be regarded as a ms. basically of the AΓ family, an ancestor of which had been heavily – and on the whole judiciously – corrected from R or a copy of R; every omission in (A)Γ

---

124 T. Renner, *ZPE* 41 (1981) 1-12. In citations from this papyrus I use underlining, instead of the conventional subscript dots, to indicate doubtfully identified letters.

125 See Vetta lxvi, lxviii-lxix. Mu1, having nothing of significance to contribute to the text even by way of conjecture, is not mentioned in my textual notes or in the table of sigla.

126 Nor did it restore the lines omitted altogether by Γ at 559-560, 633, 802 and 988.

127 So does the Aldine edition of 1498, to which *Peace* and *Eccl.* were added at the last minute from a ms. newly come into the editor's possession. This no longer extant ms. (whose relationships in *Peace* are discussed by S.D. Olson, *CQ* 48 [1998] 62-74) seems in *Eccl.* to have had a text which stemmed originally from an ancestor (perhaps the immediate exemplar) of Λ but which had received some editorial corrections, partly overlapping those found in B; what now appear as unique good readings of the Aldine (e.g. at 26, 42, 773, 933) derive in part from these corrections and in part from lucky errors such as the omission of a letter at 26.

was made good except the two above-mentioned, which are not obvious even to a fairly careful reader (the latter leaves good grammar and sense behind, the former comes in the middle of a long sequence of lines all with the same ending). At 23, 441, 896 and 1110 Λ seems to display a blend of the readings of R and of (A)Γ.

Within the AΓ family Λ shares errors with Γ against A at 75, 131, 141 and 275. These errors do not, however, derive directly or indirectly from Γ itself, since at 72, 118 and 142, where R and Γ are both wrong, Λ agrees with A in a true reading; similarly in 283-1135 Λ is right against both R and Γ at 419, 629, 896, 920, 1086, 1087, 1111 and 1124 (in four of these places B also managed to restore the truth). In all but one of these eleven passages R and Γ have different and independent errors; the one exception, 142, is an easy minuscule corruption. The likeliest explanation is that Λ's basic ancestor was not Γ but a sister of Γ. If so, Λ is capable, after 282, of preserving the truth alone whenever R and Γ have erred independently[128].

Other notable good readings in Λ appear at 235 (above the line, with the Suda), and at 281 and 613 (both orthographic) where the truth appears to have been restored with the help of near-identical words in the immediate context. After 1135 Λ is the only ms. we have besides R (it is right against R at 1137, 1139, 1155 and 1169).

In view of the above evidence, the textual notes in this edition (which are based on Vetta's apparatus) cite Λ regularly throughout in addition to RAΓ[129], but B (and the Aldine, see note 127) only as sources of emendations.

---

128 In principle Λ could also have preserved the truth alone in passages before 282; but this would require a triple coincidence involving an error in A also, which is inherently unlikely and does not seem to have occurred in fact.

129 I am grateful to the Biblioteca Comunale di Perugia for making available to me a microfilm of Λ, thus enabling me to report the readings of its scholia for the first time. One of these reveals that a reading (in 23) which had previously been thought to be a conjecture by Bentley was in fact already a medieval, and probably an ancient, variant.

Sigla

Manuscripts		*Century*
Π60	Michigan Papyrus inv. 6649 (contains 600-614, 638-654)	4th/5th
R	Ravennas 429	10th
A	Parisinus Regius 2712 (contains 1-282)	13th/14th
Γ	Laurentianus XXXI 15 (contains 1-1135)	14th
Λ	Perusinus H56	15th
B	Parisinus Regius 2715 (contains 1-1135)	15th
Vb1	Vaticanus Barberinianus I 45 (contains 1-1135; a copy of Γ)	15th
Ald.	the Aldine *editio princeps* (Venice, 1498)	

codd. = RAΓΛ (in 1-282); RΓΛ (in 283-1135); RΛ (in 1136-end)

Other Symbols

Σ	scholion
Σ(i), Σ(ii)	separate scholia on the same passage in the same ms(s).
λ	lemma (words from the text quoted as the heading of a scholion)
γρ	reading noted in ms. or scholia as a variant
i	implied by or inferable from
ac	before correction
pc	after correction
s	above the line
vel sim.	or the like; with unimportant or irrelevant variations
A^1 (et sim.)	the hand of the original copyist
A^2 (et sim.)	any later hand
[A] (et sim.)	the reading of the ms. or hand in question cannot be determined*
ε̲ι̲ (et sim.)	these letters cannot be identified with certainty from the visible traces
[ ]	denotes portions of the text of a papyrus that are lost
< >	denotes tentative editorial supplements
{ }	denotes tentative editorial deletions
† †	denotes corrupt readings that have not been satisfactorily emended
$Suda^A$	the ms. A of the Suda lexicon
$Suda^r$	all significant mss. of the Suda except those cited for a different reading

* e.g. because it has been obliterated by a correction, or because a page has been torn. (This convention does not apply to papyri: where the text of a papyrus is wholly lost or illegible at the relevant point, the papyrus is normally not mentioned at all in the apparatus.)

ECCLESIAZUSAE

ΤΑ ΤΟΥ ΔΡΑΜΑΤΟΣ ΠΡΟΣΩΠΑ

ΠΡΑΞΑΓΟΡΑ, γυνὴ Ἀττική.
ΧΟΡΟΣ, γυναικῶν Ἀττικῶν.
ΓΥΝΗ Α, γείτων Πραξαγόρας.
ΓΥΝΗ Β.
ΒΛΕΠΥΡΟΣ, γέρων, ἀνὴρ Πραξαγόρας.
ΓΕΙΤΩΝ Βλεπύρου.
ΧΡΕΜΗΣ, γέρων.
ΑΝΗΡ οὐ βουλόμενος τὰ ἑαυτοῦ καταθεῖναι.
ΚΗΡΥΚΑΙΝΑ.
ΓΡΑΥΣ Α.
ΚΟΡΗ.
ΕΠΙΓΕΝΗΣ, μειράκιον, ἐρῶν τῆς κόρης.
ΓΡΑΥΣ Β.
ΓΡΑΥΣ Γ.
ΘΕΡΑΠΑΙΝΑ Πραξαγόρας.

Κωφὰ πρόσωπα

ΣΙΚΩΝ καὶ ΠΑΡΜΕΝΩΝ, οἰκέται τοῦ γείτονος.
ΜΕΙΡΑΚΕΣ δύο συνακολουθοῦσαι Βλεπύρῳ.

Characters Of The Play

PRAXAGORA, *an Athenian wife.*
CHORUS *of Athenian wives.*
FIRST WOMAN, *one of Praxagora's neighbours.*
SECOND WOMAN.
BLEPYRUS, *an old man, Praxagora's husband.*
NEIGHBOUR *to Blepyrus.*
CHREMES, *an old man.*
DISSIDENT, *a man who is unwilling to surrender his property.*
HERALDESS.
FIRST OLD WOMAN.
GIRL.
EPIGENES, *a youth, in love with the Girl.*
SECOND OLD WOMAN.
THIRD OLD WOMAN.
MAID *to Praxagora.*

Silent Characters

SICON *and* PARMENON, *slaves to the Neighbour.*
TWO YOUNG WOMEN *accompanying Blepyrus.*

ΠΡΑΞΑΓΟΡΑ

Ὦ λαμπρὸν ὄμμα τοῦ τροχηλάτου λύχνου,
κάλλιστ' ἐν εὐστόχοισιν ἐξηυρημένον
(γονάς τε γὰρ σὰς καὶ τύχας δηλώσομεν·
τροχῷ γὰρ ἐλαθεὶς κεραμικῆς ῥύμης ὕπο
μυκτῆρσι λαμπρὰς ἡλίου τιμὰς ἔχεις),
ὅρμα φλογὸς σημεῖα τὰ ξυγκείμενα.
σοὶ γὰρ μόνῳ δηλοῦμεν – εἰκότως, ἐπεὶ
κἀν τοῖσι δωματίοισιν Ἀφροδίτης τρόπων
πειρωμέναισι πλησίος παραστατεῖς,
λορδουμένων τε σωμάτων ἐπιστάτην
ὀφθαλμὸν οὐδεὶς τὸν σὸν ἐξείργει δόμων·
μόνος δὲ μηρῶν εἰς ἀπορρήτους μυχοὺς
λάμπεις, αφεύων τὴν ἐπανθοῦσαν τρίχα·
στοὰς δὲ καρποῦ Βακχίου τε νάματος
πλήρεις ὑποιγνύσαισι συμπαραστατεῖς·
καὶ ταῦτα συνδρῶν οὐ λαλεῖς τοῖς πλησίον.
ἀνθ' ὧν συνείσει καὶ τὰ νῦν βουλεύματα,
ὅσα Σκίροις ἔδοξε ταῖς ἐμαῖς φίλαις.
ἀλλ' οὐδεμία πάρεστιν ἃς ἥκειν ἐχρῆν.
καίτοι πρὸς ὄρθρον γ' ἐστίν, ἡ δ' ἐκκλησία
αὐτίκα μάλ' ἔσται· καταλαβεῖν δ' ἡμᾶς ἕδρας
δεῖ τὰς ἑταίρας κἀγκαθιζομένας λαθεῖν,
ἃς Φυρόμαχός ποτ' εἶπεν, εἰ μέμνησθ' ἔτι.
τί δῆτ' ἂν εἴη; πότερον οὐκ ἐρραμμένους
ἔχουσι τοὺς πώγωνας, οὓς εἴρητ' ἔχειν;
ἢ θαἰμάτια τἀνδρεῖα κλεψάσαις λαθεῖν
ἦν χαλεπὸν αὐταῖς; ἀλλ' ὁρῶ τονδὶ λύχνον

2 εὐστόχοισιν R: εὐσκόποισιν ΑΓΛ $^{i}\Sigma^{R\Gamma\Lambda}$.
2 ἐξηυρημένον (-ευρ-) Gray, cf. $\Sigma^{R\Gamma\Lambda}$ εὑρημένον: ἐξητημένον RΑΓΛ: ἐξηρτημένον Vb1^{2}: ἐζητημένον Bergler.
4 ὕπο Küster: ἄπο codd. Suda.
9 πλησίος ΓΛ: πλησίως R: πλησίον Α.
14 δὲ Blaydes: τε codd. Suda.
17 συνείσει Biset: συνοίσει codd.
23 transposed by Dover to precede 22.
23 κἀγκαθιζομένας Σ^{Λ} (on 1): πῶς κἀγαθιζομένας Λ: καθαγιαζομένας πως ΑΓ: πῶς κωλαθιζομένας R: κῶλά θ' ἱζομένας Palmer.
22 Φυρόμαχός R: Σφυρόμαχός ΑΓΛ Suda $\Sigma(i)^{R}$ $\Sigma^{\Gamma\Lambda}$: Κλεόμαχός Λ^{s} $\Sigma(ii)^{R}$+λ $^{\gamma\rho}\Sigma^{\Gamma\Lambda}$.
25 τοὺς Λ: τὰς R (ΑΓ omit 24-26).
26 ἢ θαἰμάτια Ald.: ἦσθ' αἱμάτια Λ: εἶθ' αἱμάτια R.

[*The stage-house represents three town houses. Praxagora comes out of the middle one. She is wearing man's clothes, but her pale, smooth face proclaims her a woman. In her right hand she carries a lamp, in her left hand she is clutching a walking-stick and various other objects. She holds out the lamp at arm's length and apostrophizes it, declaiming in tragic style.*]

PRAXAGORA:

O eye most radiant of the wheel-borne lamp,
Superb invention of sagacious men –
5 For I thy birth and fortunes shall declare:
Born on a wheel, by power of potter's arm,
Thou hast the sun's bright glories in thy nozzles –
Send forth the flaming signal as agreed!

[*She waves the lamp around, repeating the same pattern of movements several times.*]

To thee alone our secret we'll reveal;
And rightly, for within our bedrooms too,
When we try out new sexual variations,
10-11 Close by thou standest, and thine eye o'ersees
Our arching bodies, yet none ever shuts it
Out of the chamber; thou alone dost shine
Into the secret corners of our thighs
When singeing off the hairs that sprout from them;
14-15 By us thou standest when illicitly
We open up the brimming granaries
And stores of Bacchic juice – yet, true accomplice,
You never blab a word to other folk!
And therefore shalt thou know our present scheme,
All that my friends resolved on at the Scira. –

[*Looking off, left and right*] But none of those who were supposed to
20 come is here, although it's beginning to get light; the Assembly will be
22-3 starting very soon, and we've got to bag places and get seated there
without being noticed, acting *in the most intimate cooperation* as
Phyromachus once put it, if you remember that now. [*Looking off*
24-5 *again*] What *can* it be? Is it that they haven't got the beards sewn
together, which they were told to have? Or have they found it hard to
nick those men's cloaks unobserved? Ah, but here I see a lamp coming

προσιόντα. φέρε νυν ἐπαναχωρήσω πάλιν,
μὴ καί τις ὢν ἀνὴρ ὁ προσιὼν τυγχάνει.

ΧΟΡΟΣ

ὥρα βαδίζειν, ὡς ὁ κῆρυξ ἀρτίως
ἡμῶν προσιουσῶν δευτέραν κεκόκκυκεν.

Πρ. ἐγω δέ γ' ὑμᾶς προσδοκῶσ' ἐγρηγόρη
τὴν νύκτα πᾶσαν. ἀλλὰ φέρε τὴν γείτονα
τήνδ' ἐκκαλέσωμαι θρυγανῶσα τὴν θύραν·
δεῖ γὰρ τὸν ἄνδρ' αὐτῆς λαθεῖν.

ΓΥΝΗ Α ἤκουσά τοι
ὑποδουμένη τὸ κνῦμά σου τῶν δακτύλων,
ἅτ' οὐ καταδαρθοῦσ'. ὁ γὰρ ἀνήρ, ὦ φιλτάτη—
Σαλαμίνιος γάρ ἐστιν ᾧ ξύνειμ' ἐγώ—
τὴν νύχθ' ὅλην ἤλαυνέ μ' ἐν τοῖς στρώμασιν,
ὥστ' ἄρτι τουτὶ θοἰμάτιον αὐτοῦ 'λαβον.

Πρ. καὶ μὴν ὁρῶ καὶ Κλειναρέτην καὶ Σωστράτην
προσιοῦσαν ἤδη τήνδε καὶ Φιλαινέτην.

Χο. οὔκουν ἐπείξεσθ'; ὡς Γλύκη κατώμοσεν
τὴν ὑστάτην ἥκουσαν ἡμῶν τρεῖς χοᾶς
οἴνου 'ποτείσειν κἀρεβίνθων χοίνικα.

Πρ. τὴν Σμικυθίωνος δ' οὐχ ὁρᾷς Μελιστίχην
σπεύδουσαν ἐν ταῖς ἐμβάσιν; καί μοι δοκεῖ
κατὰ σχολὴν παρὰ τἀνδρὸς ἐξελθεῖν μόνη.

Γυ.^{a} τὴν τοῦ καπήλου δ' οὐχ ὁρᾷς Γευσιστράτην
ἔχουσαν ἐν τῇ δεξιᾷ τὴν λαμπάδα;

Πρ. καὶ τὴν Φιλοδωρήτου γε καὶ Χαιρητάδου
ὁρῶ προσιούσας χἀτέρας πολλὰς πάνυ
γυναῖκας, ὅ τι πέρ ἐστ' ὄφελος ἐν τῇ πόλει.

ΓΥΝΗ Β

καὶ πάνυ ταλαιπώρως ἔγωγ', ὦ φιλτάτη,
ἐκδρᾶσα παρέδυν. ὁ γὰρ ἀνὴρ τὴν νύχθ' ὅλην

29 τύγχάνει Naber: τυγχάνεις RΑΓΛ: τυγχάνῃ Β.
31 προσιουσῶν Le Febvre: προσιόντων codd.
32 ἐγρηγόρη Porson: ἐγρηγορεῖν codd.
34 θρυγαν- Biset, cf. Hesychius θ787: τρυγαν- Α: θρυγον- RΛ: τρυγον- Γ Suda.
40 αὐτοῦ 'λαβον (αὐτ' οὔλαβον) R^{2}: αὐτοῦ λαβών vel sim. R^{1}ΑΓΛ
42 προσιοῦσαν Ald.: παροῦσαν codd.
44-45 ἡμῶν ... οἴνου Richards: οἴνου ... ἡμῶν (ἀπο-) codd. Suda.
51 Φιλοδωρήτου Α: Φιλοδωρίτου RΓΛ.
51 γε Meineke: τε codd.

this way. Here now, let me step back again, in case by any chance the person coming is actually a man. [*She withdraws under an open wing of the stage-house, left, as several women enter from the other side – the first of the groups which will form the chorus. They are wearing women's inner (but not outer) garments, and carrying men's cloaks, shoes, walking-sticks and false beards.*]

CHORUS-LEADER [*calling back to her companions as she approaches*]: Time to be moving now, because the morning herald has just crowed for the second time as we were coming along!

PRAXAGORA [*emerging to meet the new arrivals*]: And *I've* been awake all night waiting for you lot. But look, let me call out my neighbour here, just *scratching* at her door, because her husband mustn't hear anything.

[*She taps very gently on the door to the left of her own. After a short delay a woman (First Woman) comes out; she is already wearing man's shoes.*]

FIRST WOMAN: I was putting these shoes on, you know, and I did hear the scrape of your fingers. Because I never got to sleep. My husband, my darling – because my other half comes from Salamis, you see, and all night long he was *rowing* me under the covers. So it was only just now that I was able to take this cloak of his.

PRAXAGORA [*looking off, right*]: Now I can also see Cleinarete coming – and here's Sostrate – and Philaenete.

CHORUS-LEADER [*calling out to those approaching*]: Well, hurry up, won't you? Because Glyce took an oath that the last of us to arrive would have to pay a fine of two gallons of wine and a quart of chickpeas.

PRAXAGORA [*to First Woman*]: And don't you see Smicythion's wife, Melistiche, hurrying along in his shoes? And I think she was the only one that was able to get away from her husband in her own time.

FIRST WOMAN: And don't you see the tavern-keeper's wife, Geusistrate, with the torch in her right hand?

PRAXAGORA: Yes, and I can see Philodoretus' and Chaeretades' wives coming, and a great many other women, all that's worth anything in the City. [*By now a full chorus of twenty-four has assembled.*]

SECOND WOMAN [*arriving last, breathlessly apologetic*]: Oh, darling, I really had the greatest trouble escaping and slipping along here!

ἔβηττε, τριχίδων ἑσπέρας ἐμπλήμενος.
Πρ. κάθησθε τοίνυν, ὡς ἂν ἀνέρωμαι τάδε
ὑμᾶς, ἐπειδὴ συλλελεγμένας ὁρῶ,
ὅσα Σκίροις ἔδοξεν εἰ δεδράκατε.
Γυ.α ἔγωγε. πρῶτον μέν γ' ἔχω τὰς μασχάλας
λόχμης δασυτέρας, καθάπερ ἦν ξυγκείμενον·
ἔπειθ', ὁπόθ' ἀνὴρ εἰς ἀγορὰν οἴχοιτό μου,
ἀλειψαμένη τὸ σῶμ' ὅλον δι' ἡμέρας
ἐχραινόμην ἑστῶσα πρὸς τὸν ἥλιον.
Γυ.β κἄγωγε· τὸ ξυρὸν δέ γ' ἐκ τῆς οἰκίας
ἔρριψα πρῶτον, ἵνα δασυνθείην ὅλη
καὶ μηδὲν εἴην ἔτι γυναικὶ προσφερής.
Πρ. ἔχετε δὲ τοὺς πώγωνας, οὓς εἴρητ' ἔχειν
πάσαισιν ὑμῖν, ὁπότε συλλεγοίμεθα;
Γυ.α νὴ τὴν Ἑκάτην, καλόν γ' ἔγωγε τουτονί.
Γυ.β κἄγωγ' Ἐπικράτους οὐκ ὀλίγῳ καλλίονα.
Πρ. ὑμεῖς δὲ τί φατε;
Γυ.α φασί· κατανεύουσι γοῦν.
Πρ. καὶ μὴν τά γ' ἄλλ' ὑμῖν ὁρῶ πεπραγμένα·
Λακωνικὰς γὰρ ἔχετε καὶ βακτηρίας
καὶ θαἰμάτια τἀνδρεῖα, καθάπερ εἴπομεν.
Γυ.α ἔγωγέ τοι τὸ σκύταλον ἐξηνεγκάμην
τὸ τοῦ Λαμίου τουτὶ καθεύδοντος λάθρᾳ.
Γυ.β τοῦτ' ἔστ' †ἐκεῖνο τῶν σκυτάλων ὧν πέρδεται†.
Πρ. νὴ τὸν Δία τὸν σωτῆρ', ἐπιτήδειός γ' ἂν ἦν
τὴν τοῦ Πανόπτου διφθέραν ἐνημμένος
εἴπερ τις ἄλλος βουκολεῖν τὸν δήμιον.
‹ἀλλ'› ἄγεθ', ὅπως καὶ τἀπὶ τούτοις δράσομεν,
ἕως ἔτ' ἐστὶν ἄστρα κατὰ τὸν οὐρανόν·

57 ἂν ἀνέρωμαι Dawes: ἀνείρωμαι RΛ: ἂν εἴρωμαι ΑΓ.
64 ἐχραινόμην Boissonade: ἐχλιαινόμην codd. ^{1}Suda.
69 ὑμῖν RΛ: ἡμῖν ΑΓ.
72 κατανεύουσι ΑΛ: κατανεῦσι R: κατανεῦσαι Γ.
72 γοῦν vel sim. RΛ: γάρ ΑΓ.
78 †ἐκεῖνο (ἐκείνων Suda) τῶν σκυτάλων ὧν πέρδεται† codd. Suda: ἐκεῖνο τὸ σκύταλον ᾧ π. Bothe: ἐκείνων ὧν ‹περιφέρων› π. Coulon: perh. e.g. ἐκεῖνο ‹δῆθ', ὃ› πέρδεται ‹φέρων›.
81 τὸν δήμιον ΑΓΛ: τὸν δημήμιον R: τὸν δῆμον Σ^{R}: τ δήμι $^{\lambda}\Sigma^{R}$: τὸ δήμιον Bothe.
82 ‹ἀλλ'› ἄγεθ' Dindorf: γεθ' (preceded by a space) R: λέγεθ' ΑΓΛ.

The whole night long my husband was coughing, because last evening he'd stuffed himself with anchovies.

PRAXAGORA [*to all the women*]: Well, sit down, then [*they do so*], so that now I see you're all assembled, I can ask you this: have you done all the things that we resolved on at the Scira?

FIRST WOMAN: I have. To begin with, I've got armpits that are bushier than a shrubbery, just as we agreed. Then, whenever my husband went off to the Agora, I oiled myself all over and stood in the sun all day to get a tan.

SECOND WOMAN: Me too; but the *first* thing I did was throw my razor out of the house, so that I would get hairy all over and not look like a woman at all any more.

PRAXAGORA: And have you got the beards, which you were all told to have with you when we met?

FIRST WOMAN [*displaying the false beard she has brought*]: Yes, by Hecate, I've got a lovely one here.

SECOND WOMAN [*ditto*]: And I've got one that beats Epicrates by a street!

PRAXAGORA [*to the others*]: And you, what's your answer?

FIRST WOMAN [*surveying the group*]: It's yes; at least they're nodding.

PRAXAGORA: And the other things I can see you've done; you've got Laconian shoes, and walking-sticks, and men's cloaks, just as we said.

FIRST WOMAN [*displaying a walking-stick with a knobbed head*]: I have, anyway; I brought out this cudgel of Lamius' on the sly when he was asleep.

SECOND WOMAN: So *that's* the one he goes around with, farting!

PRAXAGORA: By Zeus the Saviour, if he put on the leather coat of the All-seeing One, he, if any man, would be the proper person to be one-to-one with ... the public executioner! But come now, let's make sure we get on with our job, while there are still stars in the sky. The

ἠκκλησία δ', εἰς ἣν παρεσκευάσμεθα
ἡμεῖς βαδίζειν, ἐξ ἕω γενήσεται.
Γυ.[α] νὴ τὸν Δι', ὥστε δεῖ γε καταλαβεῖν ἕδρας
ὑπὸ τῷ λίθῳ τῶν πρυτάνεων καταντικρύ.
Γυ.[β] ταυτί γέ τοι, νὴ τὸν Δί', ἐφερόμην, ἵνα
πληρουμένης ξαίνοιμι τῆς ἐκκλησίας.
Πρ. πληρουμένης, τάλαινα;
Γυ.[β] νὴ τὴν Ἄρτεμιν
ἔγωγε. τί γὰρ ἂν χεῖρον ἀκροῴμην ἅμα
ξαίνουσα; γυμνὰ δ' ἐστί μου τὰ παιδία.
Πρ. ἰδού γέ σε ξαίνουσαν, ἣν τοῦ σώματος
οὐδὲν παραφῆναι τοῖς καθημένοις ἔδει.
οὐκοῦν καλά γ' ἂν πάθοιμεν, εἰ πλήρης τύχοι
ὁ δῆμος ὢν κἄπειθ' ὑπερβαίνουσά τις
ἀναβαλλομένη δείξειε τὸν Φορμίσιον.
ἢν δ' ἐγκαθιζώμεσθα πρότεραι, λήσομεν
ξυστειλάμεναι θαἰμάτια· τὸν πώγωνά τε
ὅταν καθῶμεν ὃν περιδησόμεσθ' ἐκεῖ,
τίς οὐκ ἂν ἡμᾶς ἄνδρας ἡγήσαιθ' ὁρῶν;
'Αγύρριος γοῦν τὸν Προνόμου πώγων' ἔχων
λέληθε. καίτοι πρότερον ἦν οὗτος γυνή·
νυνὶ δ' – ὁρᾷς; – πράττει τὰ μέγιστ' ἐν τῇ πόλει.
τούτου γέ τοι, νὴ τὴν ἐπιοῦσαν ἡμέραν,
τόλμημα τολμῶμεν τοσοῦτον οὕνεκα,
ἥν πως παραλαβεῖν τῆς πόλεως τὰ πράγματα
δυνώμεθ', ὥστ' ἀγαθόν τι πρᾶξαι τὴν πόλιν.
νῦν μὲν γὰρ οὔτε θέομεν οὔτ' ἐλαύνομεν.
Γυ.[α] καὶ πῶς γυναικῶν θηλύφρων ξυνουσία
δημηγορήσει;
Πρ. πολὺ μὲν οὖν ἄριστά που.
λέγουσι γὰρ καὶ τῶν νεανίσκων ὅσοι
πλεῖστα σποδοῦνται, δεινοτάτους εἶναι λέγειν·
ἡμῖν δ' ὑπάρχει τοῦτο κατὰ τύχην τινά.
Γυ.[α] οὐκ οἶδα· δεινὸν δ' ἐστὶν ἡ μὴ 'μπειρία.
Πρ. οὔκουν ἐπίτηδες ξυνελέγημεν ἐνθάδε,
ὅπως προμελετήσαιμεν ἁκεῖ δεῖ λέγειν;

86 γε Meineke: σε codd.
91 ἅμα Dobree: ἄρα codd.
117 προμελετήσαιμεν Kidd: προμελετήσωμεν codd.

Assembly meeting, which we've made preparations to go to, is due to begin at sunrise.

FIRST WOMAN: Yes, it is, so we really must occupy some seats, at the foot of the Rock, directly facing the Prytaneis.

SECOND WOMAN [*displaying a woman's work-basket, which she has brought along in addition to her masculine paraphernalia*]: Actually that's why I brought along this stuff, so I could do some carding while the Assembly was filling up.

PRAXAGORA [*furious*]: *Filling up*, you idiot?

SECOND WOMAN: Yes, indeed, by Artemis. I won't be any less well able to hear the speeches, will I, if I'm carding as well? And my children have nothing to wear!

PRAXAGORA: Listen to you – carding! When you ought not to be showing any part of your body to the men sitting there! Why, it would be a fine thing for us, if the Assembly was already full, and then one of us was climbing over them, lifted up her clothes and revealed her real Phorm...isius! But if we get ourselves seated *first*, nobody will see who we are if we draw the cloaks tight around us; and when we sport the long beards that we're going to have tied on there, who that sees us won't think we're men? After all, Agyrrhius has nicked Pronomus' beard without anyone noticing – and that although *he* used to be a woman; and now, do you see, he's screwing up the City with the best of them! This, I tell you, this, by the holy light of this dawning day [*she stretches out her arms towards the eastern horizon*], is the reason why we are venturing this great venture, to see if we can succeed in taking over the running of the City so that we can do it some good. Because as things are now, we're dead in the water.

FIRST WOMAN: But how will a "feminine-minded company of women" be able to make public speeches?

PRAXAGORA: Why, very well indeed, I fancy! They say, don't they, that the young men who get shagged the most turn out to be the smartest speakers? Well, by a stroke of luck, we all have that advantage!

FIRST WOMAN: I don't know about that, but inexperience is a daunting thing.

PRAXAGORA: Well, wasn't that exactly why we gathered here, in

οὐκ ἂν φθάνοις τὸ γένειον ἂν περιδουμένη
ἄλλαι θ' ὅσαι λαλεῖν μεμελετήκασί που.
Γυ.β τίς δ', ὦ μέλ', ἡμῶν οὐ λαλεῖν ἐπίσταται;
Πρ. ἴθι δὴ σύ, περιδοῦ, καὶ ταχέως ἀνὴρ γενοῦ·
ἐγὼ δὲ θεῖσα τοὺς στεφάνους περιδήσομαι
καὐτὴ μεθ' ὑμῶν, ἤν τί μοι δόξῃ λέγειν.
Γυ.β δεῦρ', ὦ γλυκυτάτη Πραξαγόρα· σκέψαι, τάλαν,
ὡς καὶ καταγέλαστον τὸ πρᾶγμα φαίνεται.
Πρ. πῶς καταγέλαστον;
Γυ.β ὥσπερ εἴ τις σηπίαις
πώγωνα περιδήσειεν ἐσταθευμέναις.
Πρ. ὁ περιστίαρχος, περιφέρειν χρὴ τὴν γαλῆν.
πάριτ' εἰς τὸ πρόσθεν. 'Αρίφραδες, παῦσαι λαλῶν·
κάθιζε παριών. τίς ἀγορεύειν βούλεται;
Γυ.β ἐγώ.
Πρ. περίθου δὴ τὸν στέφανον τυχἀγαθῇ.
Γυ.β ἰδού.
Πρ. λέγοις ἄν.
Γυ.β εἶτα πρὶν πιεῖν λέγω;
Πρ. ἰδοὺ πιεῖν.
Γυ.β τί γάρ, ὦ μέλ', ἐστεφανωσάμην;
Πρ. ἄπιθ' ἐκποδών. τοιαῦτ' ἂν ἡμᾶς ἠργάσω
κἀκεῖ.
Γυ.β τί δ'; οὐ πίνουσι κἀν τἠκκλησίᾳ;
Πρ. ἰδού γέ σοι πίνουσι.

118 περιδουμένη ΑΛ: περιδυμένη Γ: περιδομένη R.

order to rehearse what we're to say when we go there? You can't tie on your beard too soon, and likewise all the others who, I take it, have practised their talks.

SECOND WOMAN: Well, dear girl, every one of us knows how to *talk*!

PRAXAGORA: You come on, now, tie it on, and quickly turn into a man; and I'll lay down the garlands and tie one on myself together with you, in case I decide to make a speech.

[*Praxagora lays two garlands on the stage-altar. She then puts on her false beard, as do First Woman and Second Woman.*]

SECOND WOMAN [*who has been examining her new face in her mirror*]: Come here, Praxagora, my sweet! [*Praxagora goes over to her.*] Look, my dear [*offering her the mirror*], and see how really ludicrous the thing looks.

PRAXAGORA: In what way ludicrous?

SECOND WOMAN: It's as if someone tied beards on to lightly browned cuttlefish!

PRAXAGORA [*returning to the platform, and taking the role of herald*]: Purifier, please carry the ferret round the bounds. [*Loudly*] Move forward! [*Pointing to an imaginary person at the back of the meeting*] Stop talking, Ariphrades; move forward and sit down. [*After a pause*] Who wishes to speak?

SECOND WOMAN [*coming forward*]: I do.

PRAXAGORA: Then put on the garland, and may it bring you good fortune.

SECOND WOMAN [*taking a garland and putting it on her head*]: There you are. [*She takes her stand on the platform and looks inquisitively about her.*]

PRAXAGORA: Go on, speak.

SECOND WOMAN: You mean I'm to make a speech before having a drink?

PRAXAGORA: Drink indeed!

SECOND WOMAN: My good woman, what else did I put on a garland for?

PRAXAGORA: Off you go, out of the way. You'd have gone there and done the same sort of thing to us.

SECOND WOMAN [*standing her ground*]: What, don't they drink in the Assembly too?

PRAXAGORA: Listen to you – "don't they drink"!

Γυ.[β] νὴ τὴν Ἄρτεμιν,
καὶ ταῦτά γ' εὔζωρον. τὰ γοῦν βουλεύματα
αὐτῶν, ὅσ' ἂν πράξωσιν ἐνθυμουμένοις,
ὥσπερ μεθυόντων ἐστὶ παραπεπληγμένα.
καὶ νὴ Δία σπένδουσί γ'· ἢ τίνος χάριν
τοσαῦτ' ἂν ηὔχοντ', εἴπερ οἶνος μὴ παρῆν;
καὶ λοιδοροῦνταί γ' ὥσπερ ἐμπεπωκότες,
καὶ τὸν παροινοῦντ' ἐκφέρουσ' οἱ τοξόται.
Πρ. σὺ μὲν βάδιζε καὶ κάθησ'· οὐδὲν γὰρ εἶ.
Γυ.[β] νὴ τὸν Δί', ἦ μοι μὴ γενειᾶν κρεῖττον ἦν·
δίψῃ γάρ, ὡς ἔοικ', ἀφαυανθήσομαι.
Πρ. ἔσθ' ἥτις ἑτέρα βούλεται λέγειν;
Γυ.[α] ἐγώ.
Πρ. ἴθι δὴ στεφανοῦ· καὶ γὰρ τὸ χρῆμ' ἐργάζεται.
ἄγε νυν, ὅπως ἀνδριστὶ καὶ καλῶς ἐρεῖς,
διερεισαμένη τὸ σχῆμα τῇ βακτηρίᾳ.
Γυ.[α] ἐβουλόμην μὲν ἕτερον ἂν τῶν ἠθάδων
λέγειν τὰ βέλτισθ', ἵν' ἐκαθήμην ἥσυχος·
νῦν δ' οὐκ ἐάσω, κατά γε τὴν ἐμὴν μίαν,
ἐν τοῖς καπηλείοισι λάκκους ἐμποιεῖν
ὕδατος. ἐμοὶ μὲν οὐ δοκεῖ, μὰ τὼ θεώ.
Πρ. μὰ τὼ θεώ, τάλαινα; ποῦ τὸν νοῦν ἔχεις;
Γυ.[α] τί δ' ἐστίν; οὐ γὰρ δὴ πιεῖν γ' ᾔτησά σε.
Πρ. μὰ Δί', ἀλλ' ἀνὴρ ὢν τὼ θεὼ κατώμοσας,
καίτοι τά γ' ἄλλ' εἰποῦσα δεξιώτατα.
Γυ.[α] ὦ νὴ τὸν Ἀπόλλω—
Πρ. παῦε τοίνυν· ὡς ἐγὼ
ἐκκλησιάσουσ' οὐκ ἂν προβαίην τὸν πόδα
τὸν ἕτερον, εἰ μὴ ταῦτ' ἀκριβωθήσεται.
Γυ.[β] φέρε τὸν στέφανον· ἐγὼ γὰρ αὖ λέξω πάλιν.
οἶμαι γὰρ ἤδη μεμελετηκέναι καλῶς.
ἐμοὶ γάρ, ὦ γυναῖκες αἱ καθήμεναι,—
Πρ. γυναῖκας αὖ, δύστηνε, τοὺς ἄνδρας λέγεις;

141 τοσαῦτ' ἂν Hermann: τοσαῦτά γ' RA: τοσαῦτ' ΓΛ.
142 ἐμπ- ΑΛ: ἐκπ- RΓ.
146 δίψῃ B: δίψει RAΓΛ.
150 διερεισαμένη Schaefer, cf. Σ[RΓΛ]: διερεισμένη vel sim. codd.
161 ἐκκλησιασουσ' Bentley: ἐκκλησιάζουσ' R[pc]ΓΛ: ἐκκληζιάζουσ' A: ἐκκλησιάζουμπρο R[ac].

SECOND WOMAN: They *do*, by Artemis, and pretty strong stuff too! At any rate their policies, if you consider all the things they do, are crazy enough to be the work of drunkards. And what's more, they pour libations, they do; or else why would they make all those prayers, if there wasn't any wine there? *And* they rail at each other like men who've had a few, and then someone turns violent and is carried out by the archers.

PRAXAGORA: You go and sit down. You're useless.

SECOND WOMAN [*reluctantly relinquishing her garland and returning to her place*]: By Zeus, I'd have been better off staying beardless. I'm so thirsty, I think I'm going to die of dehydration.

PRAXAGORA: Is there anyone else who wants to speak?

FIRST WOMAN [*coming forward*]: I do.

PRAXAGORA: Come on, then, garland yourself; the job's been started now. [*First Woman puts on the second garland.*] Now look, make sure that you speak man's language and speak well, and lean hard with your body on your stick.

FIRST WOMAN [*taking the platform*]: I would have wished that someone else, one of the regular speakers, had given the best advice, so that I could have sat quiet. But as it is, so far as in me lies, I will not stand for the installation in taverns of storage-pits for water! I think it's wrong, by the Two Goddesses!

PRAXAGORA: By the Two Goddesses, you fool? Where have you put your brain?

FIRST WOMAN: What's wrong? I certainly didn't ask you for a drink!

PRAXAGORA: No, but you swore by the Two Goddesses when you were being a *man* – although *otherwise* you spoke very skilfully indeed.

FIRST WOMAN: Oh, yes, by Apollo—

PRAXAGORA: So stop; because I'm not going to put one foot in front of the other to go to the Assembly, unless these things are got exactly right.

[*As First Woman returns to her place, Second Woman eagerly comes forward again.*]

SECOND WOMAN: Give me the garland. I'm going to have another turn at speaking. I think I've practised it properly now. [*Mounting the platform, and putting on the first garland*] In my opinion, ladies of the Assembly—

PRAXAGORA: Again, you wretch? You're calling the men "ladies"!

Γυ.β δι' Ἐπίγονόν γ' ἐκεινονί· βλέψασα γὰρ
ἐκεῖσε πρὸς γυναῖκας ᾠόμην λέγειν.
Πρ. ἄπερρε καὶ σὺ καὶ κάθησ' ἐντευθενί.
αὐτὴ γὰρ ὑμῶν γ' ἕνεκά μοι λέξειν δοκῶ
τονδὶ λαβοῦσα. τοῖς θεοῖς μὲν εὔχομαι
τυχεῖν κατορθώσασα τὰ βεβουλευμένα.
ἐμοὶ δ' ἴσον μὲν τῆσδε τῆς χώρας μέτα
ὅσονπερ ὑμῖν· ἄχθομαι δὲ καὶ φέρω
τὰ τῆς πολέως ἅπαντα βαρέως πράγματα.
ὁρῶ γὰρ αὐτὴν προστάταισι χρωμένην
ἀεὶ πονηροῖς· κἄν τις ἡμέραν μίαν
χρηστὸς γένηται, δέκα πονηρὸς γίγνεται.
ἐπέτρεψας ἑτέρῳ; πλεῖον' ἔτι δράσει κακά.
χαλεπὸν μὲν οὖν ἄνδρας δυσαρέστους νουθετεῖν,
οἳ τοὺς φιλεῖν μὲν βουλομένους δεδοίκατε,
τοὺς δ' οὐκ ἐθέλοντας ἀντιβολεῖθ' ἑκάστοτε.
ἐκκλησίαισιν ἦν ὅτ' οὐκ ἐχρώμεθα
οὐδὲν τὸ παράπαν· ἀλλὰ τόν γ' Ἀγύρριον
πονηρὸν ἡγούμεσθα. νῦν δὲ χρωμένων
ὁ μὲν λαβὼν ἀργύριον ὑπερεπῄνεσεν,
ὁ δ' οὐ λαβὼν εἶναι θανάτου φήσ' ἀξίους
τοὺς μισθοφορεῖν ζητοῦντας ἐν τἠκκλησίᾳ.
Γυ.α νὴ τὴν Ἀφροδίτην, εὖ γε ταυταγὶ λέγεις.
Πρ. τάλαιν', Ἀφροδίτην ὤμοσας; χαρίεντά γ' ἂν
ἔδρασας, εἰ τοῦτ' εἶπας ἐν τἠκκλησίᾳ.
Γυ.α ἀλλ' οὐκ ἂν εἶπον.
Πρ. μηδ' ἐθίζου νῦν λέγειν.
τὸ συμμαχικὸν αὖ τοῦθ', ὅτ' ἐσκοπούμεθα,
εἰ μὴ γένοιτ', ἀπολεῖν ἔφασκον τὴν πόλιν·
ὅτε δὴ δ' ἐγένετ', ἤχθοντο, τῶν δὲ ῥητόρων
ὁ τοῦτ' ἀναπείσας εὐθὺς ἀποδρὰς ᾤχετο.
ναῦς δεῖ καθέλκειν· τῷ πένητι μὲν δοκεῖ,
τοῖς πλουσίοις δὲ καὶ γεωργοῖς οὐ δοκεῖ.

167 ἐκεινονί· βλέψασα Elmsley: ἐκεῖνον· ἐπιβλέψασα (εἴ τι βλ- $R^{ac}Λ^{ac}$) codd. ἐπιβλέψας (beginning of citation) Suda ε2268.
170 γ' ΓΛ: om. R: [A]
172 κατορθώσασα RΛ: κατορθώσας ΑΓ: κατορθώσασι Richards.
190 ὤμοσας Dobree: ὠνόμασας RAΛ: γ' ὠνόμασας Γ.

SECOND WOMAN [*pointing into the audience*]: That was because of Epigonus over there. I looked over that way, and it made me think I was speaking to women.

PRAXAGORA: Be off with you too, and sit down, away from here! [*Second Woman retires.*] If this is what you lot are like, I think *I'm* going to take this and speak. [*She takes up the first garland and holds it up over the altar.*] I pray to the gods that I may succeed in bringing our plans to fruition. [*Putting on the garland, and addressing both the women and the theatre audience*] I have as much of a stake in this country as you do; and I am vexed and grieved at the whole situation the City is in. I see her employing leaders who are always villains: even if one of them acts decently for a day, he then behaves wickedly for ten. You try entrusting your affairs to someone else? He'll do even more harm! Well, it is difficult to advise men who are so hard to please, men who are afraid of those who want to be their friends and are for ever on their knees to those who *don't* want to. There was a time when we didn't have Assemblies at all; but at least we thought that Agyrrhius was a villain. Now, when we do have them, whoever has received cash praises him to the skies, while whoever hasn't had any says that those who try to treat the Assembly as a wage-earning job deserve to be put to death.

FIRST WOMAN: By Aphrodite, that's well said!

PRAXAGORA: Swearing by Aphrodite, you fool? A nice thing you'd have done if you'd said that at the Assembly!

FIRST WOMAN: But I wouldn't have said it there.

PRAXAGORA: Well, don't get *now* into the *habit* of saying it. – Again, this Alliance: when we were considering making it, they said that if it didn't come off, it would mean the end of the City; then, when it did come off, they were annoyed, and all at once the politician who had induced us to make it ran off and disappeared. We need to launch a fleet: the poor man says yes, the rich and the farmers say no. Now you get

Κορινθίοις ἄχθεσθε, κἀκεῖνοί γε σοί·
νῦν εἰσὶ χρηστοί – "καὶ σὺ νῦν χρηστὸς γενοῦ".
ἀργεῖος ἀμαθής· ἀλλ' Ἱερώνυμος σοφός.
σωτηρία παρέκυψεν· ἀλλ' ὀργίζεται
Θρασύβουλος αὐτὸς οὐχὶ παρακαλούμενος.
Γυ.[a] ὡς ξυνετὸς ἀνήρ.
Πρ. νῦν καλῶς ἐπῄνεσας.
ὑμεῖς γάρ ἐστ', ὦ δῆμε, τούτων αἴτιοι.
τὰ δημόσια γὰρ μισθοφοροῦντες χρήματα
ἰδίᾳ σκοπεῖσθ' ἕκαστος ὅ τι τις κερδανεῖ·
τὸ δὲ κοινὸν ὥσπερ Αἴσιμος κυλίνδεται.
ἢν οὖν ἐμοὶ πείθησθε, σωθήσεσθ' ἔτι.
ταῖς γὰρ γυναιξί φημι χρῆναι τὴν πόλιν
ἡμᾶς παραδοῦναι. καὶ γὰρ ἐν ταῖς οἰκίαις
ταύταις ἐπιτρόποις καὶ ταμίαισι χρώμεθα.
Γυ.[β] εὖ γ', εὖ γε νὴ Δί', εὖ γε.
Γυ.[a] λέγε, λέγ', ὦγαθέ.
Πρ. ὡς δ' εἰσὶν ἡμῶν τοὺς τρόπους βελτίονες
ἐγὼ διδάξω. πρῶτα μὲν γὰρ τἄρια
βάπτουσι θερμῷ κατὰ τὸν ἀρχαῖον νόμον
ἁπαξάπασαι, κοὐχὶ μεταπειρωμένας
ἴδοις ἂν αὐτάς· ἡ δ' Ἀθηναίων πόλις,
εἰ τοῦτο χρηστῶς εἶχεν, οὐκ ἂν ἐσῴζετο,
εἰ μή τι καινόν γ' ἄλλο περιηργάζετο.
καθήμεναι φρύγουσιν ὥσπερ καὶ πρὸ τοῦ·
ἐπὶ τῆς κεφαλῆς φέρουσιν ὥσπερ καὶ πρὸ τοῦ·
τὰ Θεσμοφόρι' ἄγουσιν ὥσπερ καὶ πρὸ τοῦ·
πέττουσι τοὺς πλακοῦντας ὥσπερ καὶ πρὸ τοῦ·
τοὺς ἄνδρας ἐπιτρίβουσιν ὥσπερ καὶ πρὸ τοῦ·
μοιχοὺς ἔχουσιν ἔνδον ὥσπερ καὶ πρὸ τοῦ·
αὑταῖς παροψωνοῦσιν ὥσπερ καὶ πρὸ τοῦ·
οἶνον φιλοῦσ' εὔζωρον ὥσπερ καὶ πρὸ τοῦ·
βινούμεναι χαίρουσιν ὥσπερ καὶ πρὸ τοῦ.
ταύταισιν οὖν, ὦνδρες, παραδόντες τὴν πόλιν

199 ἄχθεσθε ΑΓΛ: ἄχθεσθαι R: ἤχθεσθε Reiske.
202 ὀργίζεται Hermann: ορείζεται R: ὁρίζεται Λ: οὐχ ὁρίζεται ΑΓ.
219 εἰ τοῦτο codd. Suda: εἴ πού τι Dobree.
220 καινόν γ' Wilson: καινὸν RΑΛ: κακὸν Γ.
227 οἶνον φιλοῦσ' εὔζωρον Hanow: τὸν οἶνον εὔζωρον φιλοῦσ' (φιλοῦσιν ΑΓ) codd.

annoyed with the Corinthians, and so do they with you; now they're decent chaps, and you're told you should be decent too now. The Argives are stupid; but Hieronymus is sensible. We get a glimpse of salvation; but Thrasybulus is furious because *he* isn't invited to take charge.

FIRST WOMAN: Smart man, this!

PRAXAGORA: Now *that's* the right way to praise the speaker. – You, the people, you are the cause of all this. You take public money in wages, and you each look out for a way to gain a profit for yourselves, while the public interest gets kicked around like Aesimus. Now then, if you listen to my advice, you will yet be able to win through. I say that we should hand over the City to the women. After all, we already employ them as managers and controllers of our households.

SECOND WOMAN: Bravo, bravo! Bravo, by Zeus!

FIRST WOMAN: More, more! Good man!

PRAXAGORA: I will also show that they have better qualities than we do. In the first place, they maintain, one and all, their ancient custom of dyeing wool in hot water, and you won't ever see them experimenting with anything different; whereas the Athenian state, if that was satisfactory, wouldn't want to preserve it – quite the contrary, they'd be pointlessly busying themselves with some innovation or other. Women parch corn sitting on their haunches, just like in the old days. They carry things on their heads, just like in the old days. They keep the Thesmophoria just like in the old days. They bake their flat-cakes just like in the old days. They make life hell for their husbands just like in the old days. They keep lovers in the house just like in the old days. They buy extra food for themselves just like in the old days. They like good strong wine just like in the old days. They enjoy getting fucked just like in the old days. So, gentlemen, let us hand over the City to them;

μὴ περιλαλῶμεν, μηδὲ πυνθανώμεθα
τί ποτ' ἄρα δρᾶν μέλλουσιν, ἀλλ' ἁπλῷ τρόπῳ
ἐῶμεν ἄρχειν, σκεψάμενοι ταυτὶ μόνα,
ὡς τοὺς στρατιώτας πρῶτον οὖσαι μητέρες
σῴζειν ἐπιθυμήσουσιν· εἶτα σιτία
τίς τῆς τεκούσης θᾶττον ἐπιπέμψειεν ἄν;
χρήματα πορίζειν δ' εὐπορώτατον γυνή,
ἄρχουσά τ' οὐκ ἂν ἐξαπατηθείη ποτέ·
αὐταὶ γάρ εἰσιν ἐξαπατᾶν εἰθισμέναι.
τὰ δ' ἄλλ' ἐάσω. ταῦτ' ἐὰν πείθησθέ μοι,
εὐδαιμονοῦντες τὸν βίον διάξετε.
Γυ.[β] εὖ γ' ὦ γλυκυτάτη Πραξαγόρα, καὶ δεξιῶς.
πόθεν, ὦ τάλαινα, ταῦτ' ἔμαθες οὕτω καλῶς;
Πρ. ἐν ταῖς φυγαῖς μετὰ τἀνδρὸς ᾤκησ' ἐν Πυκνί·
ἔπειτ' ἀκούουσ' ἐξέμαθον τῶν ῥητόρων.
Γυ.[a] οὐκ ἐτὸς ἄρ', ὦ μέλ', ἦσθα δεινὴ καὶ σοφή·
καί σε στρατηγὸν αἱ γυναῖκες αὐτόθεν
αἱρούμεθ', ἢν ταῦθ' ἁπινοεῖς κατεργάσῃ.
ἀτὰρ ἢν Κέφαλός σοι λοιδορῆται προσφθαρείς,
πῶς ἀντερεῖς πρὸς αὐτὸν ἐν τἠκκλησίᾳ;
Πρ. φήσω παραφρονεῖν αὐτόν.
Γυ.[a] ἀλλὰ τοῦτό γε
ἴσασι πάντες.
Πρ. ἀλλὰ καὶ μελαγχολᾶν.
Γυ.[a] καὶ τοῦτ' ἴσασιν.
Πρ. ἀλλὰ καὶ τὰ τρύβλια
κακῶς κεραμεύειν, τὴν δὲ πόλιν εὖ καὶ καλῶς.
Γυ.[a] τί δ', ἢν Νεοκλείδης ὁ γλάμων σε λοιδορῇ;
Πρ. τούτῳ μὲν εἶπον εἰς κυνὸς πυγὴν ὁρᾶν.
Γυ.[a] τί δ', ἢν ὑποκρούωσίν σε;
Πρ. προσκινήσομαι,
ἅτ' οὐκ ἄπειρος οὖσα πολλῶν κρουμάτων.
Γυ.[a] ἐκεῖνο μόνον ἄσκεπτον, εἴ σ' οἱ τοξόται

234 εἶτα Λ: εἰ τα R: εἰ τὰ ΑΓ: τὰ (beginning of citation) Suda.
235 θᾶττον $Λ^{s}$ Suda: μᾶλλον RΓΛ: [A].
236 πορίζειν δ' Velsen: πορίζειν codd.
239 ταῦτ' ἐὰν Bergk: ταῦτα κἂν vel sim. RΛ: κἂν Γ: [A].
244 ἔπειτ' codd.: ἐκεῖ τ' Dindorf.
255 εἶπον RΑΓΛ Σ *Ach.* 863: εἴπω Suda (τ844): εἴποιμ' B: ἂν εἴποιμ' Brunck.
256 ὑποκρου- R Suda $^{i}Σ^{RΛ}$ $^{λ}Σ^{R}$: ὑποκρούσ- ΑΓΛ.

let's not indulge in unnecessary chatter, nor inquire of them what it is they actually mean to do, but quite simply let them govern. Consider only these points: in the first place, being the mothers of our soldiers, they will be anxious to secure their safety; then again, who would be quicker than their mother to send them extra supplies? There is nothing more resourceful than a women when it comes to finding financial resources, and when in power she's never going to be deceived, because women are so used to being deceivers themselves. The rest of what I might say I will pass over. If you follow this advice of mine, you will live happily ever after. [*Acclamation.*]

SECOND WOMAN: Bravo, Praxagora, my sweet! How clever! Where did you learn that stuff so well, my dear?

PRAXAGORA: In the refugee time I lived with my husband on the Pnyx; that enabled me to listen to the speakers and learn off their tricks.

FIRST WOMAN: No wonder you were so skilful and expert, my good friend! And now [*looking round the gathering to indicate that she is seeking its support*] we women here and now elect you to be general if you succeed in this plan of yours. [*All raise their hands in approval.*] But in the Assembly, if that blasted Cephalus comes up and starts abusing you, how will you respond to him?

PRAXAGORA: I'll say he's off his rocker.

FIRST WOMAN: But everyone knows *that* already!

PRAXAGORA: Then I'll say he's completely barmy.

FIRST WOMAN: They know that as well.

PRAXAGORA: Then I'll say he makes his pots shoddily – but that he's making the City go to pot all right, good and proper!

FIRST WOMAN: But what if that bleary-eyed Neocleides abuses you?

PRAXAGORA [*making an insulting gesture*]: My advice to *him* is to look up a dog's arse!

FIRST WOMAN: What if they interrupt and try to knock you off your stride?

PRAXAGORA [*making suggestive pelvic motions*]: I'll thrust back; I've got substantial and varied experience as far as *knocking* goes!

FIRST WOMAN: There's only one thing we haven't considered: if

ἕλκωσιν, ὅ τι δράσεις ποτ'.
Πρ. ἐξαγκωνιῶ
ὡδί· μέση γὰρ οὐδέποτε ληφθήσομαι.
Γυ.[α] ἡμεῖς δέ γ', ἢν αἴρωσ', ἐὰν κελεύσομεν.
Γυ.[β] ταυτὶ μὲν ἡμῖν ἐντεθύμηται καλῶς·
ἐκεῖνο δ' οὐ πεφροντίκαμεν, ὅτῳ τρόπῳ
τὰς χεῖρας αἴρειν μνημονεύσομεν τότε.
εἰθισμέναι γάρ ἐσμεν αἴρειν τὼ σκέλει.
Πρ. χαλεπὸν τὸ πρᾶγμ'· ὅμως δὲ χειροτονητέον
ἐξωμισάσαις τὸν ἕτερον βραχίονα.
ἄγε νυν, ἀναστέλλεσθ' ἄνω τὰ χιτώνια·
ὑποδεῖσθε δ' ὡς τάχιστα τὰς Λακωνικάς,
ὥσπερ τὸν ἄνδρ' ἐθεᾶσθ', ὅτ' εἰς ἐκκλησίαν
μέλλοι βαδίζειν ἢ θύραζ' ἑκάστοτε.
ἔπειτ', ἐπειδὰν ταῦτα πάντ' ἔχῃ καλῶς,
περιδεῖσθε τοὺς πώγωνας. ἡνίκ' ἂν δέ γε
τούτους ἀκριβώσητε περιηρμοσμέναι,
καὶ θαἰμάτια τἀνδρεῖ', ἅπερ γ' ἐκλέψατε,
ἐπαναβάλεσθε, κᾆτα ταῖς βακτηρίαις
ἐπερειδόμεναι βαδίζετ' ᾄδουσαι μέλος
πρεσβυτικόν τι, τὸν τρόπον μιμούμεναι
τὸν τῶν ἀγροίκων.
Χο. εὖ λέγεις.
Πρ. ἡμεῖς δέ γε
προΐωμεν αὐτῶν· καὶ γὰρ ἑτέρας οἴομαι
ἐκ τῶν ἀγρῶν εἰς τὴν Πύκν' ἥξειν ἄντικρυς
γυναῖκας. ἀλλὰ σπεύσαθ'· ὡς εἴωθ' ἐκεῖ
τοῖς μὴ παροῦσιν ὀρθρίοις †ἐς τὴν Πύκνα†
ὑπαποτρέχειν ἔχουσι μηδὲ πάτταλον.
Χο. ὥρα προβαίνειν, ὦνδρες, ἡμῖν ἐστι· τοῦτο γὰρ χρὴ

264 -σομεν τότε codd.: -σομέν ποτε Ussher.
275 τἀνδρεῖ' ἅπερ γ' Elmsley: τἀνδρεῖά γ' ἅπερ (A: τ' ἅπερ RΓ, τἄπερ Λ) codd.
276 ἐπαναβάλεσθε B Σ^{RΛ} ^{λ}Suda^{Γ}, Zonaras: ἐπαναβάλεσθαι ^{λ}Suda^{A}: ἐπαναβάλλεσθε RAΓ: ἐπανεβάλλεσθε Λ: ἐπαναβάλησθε Denniston.
281 πύκν' Λ: πνύκ' R: πνύχ' AΓ.
283 ὀρθρίοις Γ^{pc}Λ Suda^{Γ}: ὀρθρίσιν Γ^{ac}: ὀρθίοις R Suda^{G}.
283 †ἐς τὴν πύκνα† (πνύκα Γ Suda) codd. Suda: ‹ἄρχων λέγειν› e.g. van Leeuwen, cf. 289-292.

two of the archers start dragging you off, what, may I ask, will you do then?

PRAXAGORA: I'll do the elbow trick, like this [*making a sharp sideways thrust with both elbows*]; I'll never submit to being held in the middle!

FIRST WOMAN: And if they lift you off the ground, *we'll* ... tell them to leave you alone.

SECOND WOMAN: Well, we've taken all these things into account all right, but here's something we haven't thought of. How are we going to remember, come the vote, to raise our *hands*? We're so used to raising our *legs*!

PRAXAGORA: Difficult problem! But all the same, you must put your hands up, baring one arm from the shoulder. – [*As Praxagora successively gives the following orders, all the women complete their disguises as instructed, so far as they have not already done so.*] Now come on and shorten your underdresses; and put on your Laconians, quick as you can, just as you've seen your husband do every time he was getting ready to go to the Assembly or go out anywhere. Then, when all that is in proper order, tie on your beards; and *when* you've fitted those on and adjusted them precisely, then put on your men's cloaks as well, the ones that you stole, and then move off, leaning on your sticks and singing an old men's song, imitating the way country people act.

CHORUS-LEADER: Very good.

PRAXAGORA [*to First and Second Women, who have completed their preparations*]: And let's us go ahead of them, because I expect that there'll be other women from the countryside who'll come straight to the Pnyx. [*To the chorus, some of whom are not quite ready*] Now hurry up, because the practice up there is for <the magistrate to tell> those who haven't arrived before daybreak to slink away home without getting so much as a bean. [*She goes out, left, accompanied by First and Second Women.*]

CHORUS-LEADER [*as the chorus form up for their exit*]: It's time for us to be moving, *men* – for that's what we must always remember to

μεμνημένας ἀεὶ λέγειν, μὴ καί ποτ' ἐξολίσθῃ
ἡμᾶς. ὁ κίνδυνος γὰρ οὐχὶ μικρός, ἢν ἁλῶμεν
ἐνδυόμεναι κατὰ σκότον τόλμημα τηλικοῦτον.

χωρῶμεν εἰς ἐκκλησίαν, ὦνδρες· ἠπείλησε γὰρ (στρ.
ὁ θεσμοθέτης, ὃς ἂν
μὴ πρῴ πάνυ τοῦ κνέφους
ἥκῃ κεκονιμένος,
στέργων σκοροδάλμῃ,
βλέπων ὑπότριμμα, μὴ
δώσειν τὸ τριώβολον.
ἀλλ', ὦ Χαριτιμίδη
καὶ Σμίκυθε καὶ Δράκης,
ἕπου κατεπείγων,
σαυτῷ προσέχων ὅπως
μηδὲν παραχορδιεῖς
ὧν δεῖ σ' ἀποδεῖξαι.
ὅπως δὲ τὸ σύμβολον
λαβόντες εἶτα πλη-
σίοι καθεδούμεθ', ὡς
ἂν χειροτονῶμεν
ἅπανθ', ὁπόσ' ἂν δέῃ
τὰς ἡμετέρας φίλας—
καίτοι τί λέγω; φίλους
γὰρ χρῆν μ' ὀνομάζειν.

ὅρα δ' ὅπως ὠθήσομεν τούσδε τοὺς ἐξ ἄστεως (ἀντ.
ἥκοντας, ὅσοι πρὸ τοῦ
μέν, ἡνίκ' ἔδει λαβεῖν
ἐλθόντ' ὀβολὸν μόνον,
καθῆντο λαλοῦντες
ἐν τοῖς στεφανώμασιν,
νυνὶ δ' ἐνοχλοῦσ' ἄγαν.

286 μὴ καί ποτ' Dobree: ὡς μήποτ' codd. Suda.
288 ἐνδυόμεναι Le Febvre, cf. Σ^Λ: ἐνδούμεναι codd.
291-2 στέργων σκοροδάλμῃ, βλέπων ὑπότριμμα Porson: βλέπων ὑπότριμμα· στέργων σκοροδάλμῃ codd. Suda.
293 Χαριτιμίδη Bentley: χαριτιμία ἢ vel sim. codd.
295 ἀποδεῖξαι codd. Suda: ἐπιδεῖξαι Ussher.
301-2 ἔδει λαβεῖν ἐλθόντ' Dawes: ἐλθόντ' ἔδει λαβεῖν R^pc Λ: ἐλθόντα δεῖ λαβεῖν R^ac: ἐλθόντες ἔδει λαβεῖν Γ.

say, to make sure it never slips our minds. We're running no small risk, if we're caught taking on an undercover venture of this magnitude.

CHORUS [*circling the orchestra*]:
Let's go to the Assembly, men! Because the magistrate
has issued a warning that if anyone
doesn't come good and early,
when it's still dark, covered with dust,
content with a pickled-garlic breakfast
and with a *sauce piquante* look in his eye,
he won't give him his three obols.
So, Charitimides
and Smicythus and Draces,
follow us, be quick,
and take great care to avoid
striking any wrong note
in the display you've got to make.
And when we've got our tickets,
then we must make sure
we sit close together,
so that we can vote to approve
all of the measures
our sisters may need—
only, what am I saying? I should
have called them our *brethren*.

Make sure we thrust aside these folk coming
from town, all those who previously,
when the fee due for coming along
was only one obol,
used to sit down and chat
among the garland stalls,
but who *now* make themselves a thorough nuisance!

ἀλλ' οὐχί, Μυρωνίδης
ὅτ' ἦρχεν ὁ γεννάδας,
οὐδεὶς ἂν ἐτόλμα
τὰ τῆς πόλεως διοι-
κεῖν ἀργύριον φέρων·
ἀλλ' ἧκεν ἕκαστος
ἐν ἀσκιδίῳ φέρων
πιεῖν ἅμα τ' ἄρτον αὐ-
τὸς καὶ δύο κρομμύω
καὶ τρεῖς ἂν ἐλάας.
νυνὶ δὲ τριώβολον
ζητοῦσι λαβεῖν, ὅταν
πράττωσί τι κοινόν, ὥσ-
περ πηλοφοροῦντες.

ΒΛΕΠΥΡΟΣ

τί τὸ πρᾶγμα; ποῖ ποθ' ἡ γυνὴ φρούδη 'στί μοι;
ἐπεὶ πρὸς ἕω νῦν γ' ἐστίν, ἡ δ' οὐ φαίνεται.
ἐγὼ δὲ κατάκειμαι πάλαι χεζητιῶν,
τὰς ἐμβάδας ζητῶν λαβεῖν ἐν τῷ σκότῳ
καὶ θοἰμάτιον. ὅτε δὴ δ' ἐκεῖνο ψηλαφῶν
οὐκ ἐδυνάμην εὑρεῖν, ὁ δ' ἤδη τὴν θύραν
ἐπεῖχε κρούων μοὐ Κόπρειος, λαμβάνω
τουτὶ τὸ τῆς γυναικὸς ἡμιδιπλοΐδιον,
καὶ τὰς ἐκείνης Περσικὰς ὑφέλκομαι.
ἀλλ' ἐν καθαρῷ ποῦ ποῦ τις ἂν χέσας τύχοι;
ἢ πανταχοῦ τοι νυκτός ἐστιν ἐν καλῷ·
οὐ γάρ με νῦν χέζοντά γ' οὐδεὶς ὄψεται.
οἴμοι κακοδαίμων, ὅτι γέρων ὢν ἠγόμην
γυναῖχ'· ὅσας εἴμ' ἄξιος πληγὰς λαβεῖν.
οὐ γάρ ποθ' ὑγιὲς οὐδὲν ἐξελήλυθεν
δράσουσ'. ὅμως δ' οὖν ἔστιν ἀποπατητέον.

ΓΕΙΤΩΝ

τίς ἐστιν; οὐ δήπου Βλέπυρος ὁ γειτνιῶν;
νὴ τὸν Δί' αὐτὸς δῆτ' ἐκεῖνος. εἰπέ μοι,
τί τοῦτό σοι τὸ πυρρόν ἐστιν; οὔ τί που

307 αὐτὸς Sommerstein: αὖ R: αὖ Λ: om. Γ: αὐτῷ Velsen: αὖον Reiske.
316 ὁ δ' Küster: ὅδ' codd.
317 μοὐ Κόπρειος Blaydes, cf. 912: ὁ κοπρεαῖος RΛ: ὁ κοπραῖος Γ.

It wasn't like this when the noble
Myronides was general:
no one then would have had the audacity
to draw pay for managing
the City's affairs.
No, everyone would come
bringing for himself
a drink in a little leather flask, and also
a loaf, two onions
and three olives.
But *now* they expect
to get three obols when they
do something for the common good, as if
they were builders' labourers!

[*The chorus follow Praxagora and her colleagues out. Presently Blepyrus comes out of Praxagora's house. He is wearing his wife's yellow underdress and a pair of soft woman's ankle-shoes, and is apparently in some physical distress. He looks up and down the street as if searching for someone.*]

BLEPYRUS: What's happened? Where on earth has my wife gone off to? It's getting on for sunrise now, and she's nowhere to be found. I've been lying awake for a long time, needing a crap, and trying to find my shoes and cloak in the dark. When finally, after a lot of groping around, I just couldn't find it, and meanwhile the man from Shittington kept on knocking at my door, I took this semi-foldover of my wife's and pulled on her Persian slippers. [*Looking around*] Now let me see, where will one be able to shit in privacy? Why, you know, at night *anywhere* is OK; nobody is going to see me shitting *now*! Dash it all, why did I go and get married at such an age? I really deserve a sound thrashing! She's certainly up to no good, going out like that. Anyway, I'd better relieve myself.

[*He squats down, close to the house to the right of his own. He strains hard, but succeeds only in breaking wind. At this his neighbour appears, half-dressed, at an upstairs window.*]

NEIGHBOUR [*calling down*]: Who's that? Not, surely, my neighbour Blepyrus? [*To himself*] Why, by Zeus, that's just who it is. [*To Blepyrus*] Tell me, what's that yellow you've got on you? Cinesias hasn't

Κινησίας σοι κατατετίληκεν;
Βλ. πόθεν;
οὔκ, ἀλλὰ τῆς γυναικὸς ἐξελήλυθα
τὸ κροκωτίδιον ἀμπισχόμενος οὑνδύεται.
Γε. τὸ δ' ἱμάτιόν σου ποῦ 'στιν;
Βλ. οὐκ ἔχω φράσαι·
ζητῶν γὰρ αὔτ' οὐχ ηὗρον ἐν τοῖς στρώμασιν.
Γε. εἶτ' οὐδὲ τὴν γυναῖκ' ἐκέλευσάς σοι φράσαι;
Βλ. μὰ τὸν Δί'· οὐ γὰρ ἔνδον οὖσα τυγχάνει,
ἀλλ' ἐκτετρύπηκέν λαθοῦσά μ' ἔνδοθεν·
ὃ καὶ δέδοικα μή τι δρᾷ νεώτερον.
Γε. νὴ τὸν Ποσειδῶ, ταὐτὰ τοίνυν ἄντικρυς
ἐμοὶ πέπονθας. καὶ γὰρ ᾗ ξύνειμ' ἐγὼ
φρούδη 'στ' ἔχουσα θοἰμάτιον οὑγὼ 'φόρουν.
κοὐ τοῦτο λυπεῖ μ', ἀλλὰ καὶ τὰς ἐμβάδας·
οὔκουν λαβεῖν γ' αὐτὰς ἐδυνάμην οὐδαμοῦ.
Βλ. μὰ τὸν Διόνυσον, οὐδ' ἐγὼ γὰρ τὰς ἐμὰς
Λακωνικάς· ἀλλ' ὡς ἔτυχον χεζητιῶν,
εἰς τὼ κοθόρνω τὼ πόδ' ἐνθεὶς ἵεμαι,
ἵνα μὴ 'γχέσαιμ' εἰς τὴν σισύραν· φανὴ γὰρ ἦν.
Γε. τί δῆτ' ἂν εἴη; μῶν ἐπ' ἄριστον γυνὴ
κέκληκεν αὐτὴν τῶν φίλων;
Βλ. γνώμην γ' ἐμήν.
οὔκουν πονηρά γ' ἐστίν, ὅ τι κἄμ' εἰδέναι.
Γε. ἀλλὰ σὺ μὲν ἱμονίαν τιν' ἀποπατεῖς· ἐμοὶ δ'
ὥρα βαδίζειν ἐστὶν εἰς ἐκκλησίαν,
ἤνπερ λάβω θοἰμάτιον, ὅπερ ἦν μοι μόνον.
Βλ. κἄγωγ', ἐπειδὰν ἀποπατήσω· νῦν δέ μοι
ἀχράς τις ἐγκλῄσασ' ἔχει τὰ σιτία.
Γε. μῶν ἣν Θρασύβουλος εἶπε τοῖς Λακωνικοῖς;
Βλ. νὴ τὸν Διόνυσον· ἐνέχεται γοῦν μοι σφόδρα.
ἀτὰρ τί δράσω; καὶ γὰρ οὐδὲ τοῦτό με
μόνον τὸ λυποῦν ἐστιν, ἀλλ' ὅταν φάγω,
ὅποι βαδιεῖταί μοι τὸ λοιπὸν ἡ κόπρος.
νῦν μὲν γὰρ οὗτος βεβαλάνωκε τὴν θύραν,

332 κροκωτίδιον Arnaldus: κροκώτιον R: κροκώπιον ΓΛ.
335 ἐκέλευσάς B: ἐκέλευσά RΓΛ.
354 νῦν B: νυνὶ RΓΛ.
354 μοι Meineke: μου codd.

by any chance been shitting over you, has he?

BLEPYRUS: What are you blethering about? No, I've come out wearing my wife's little saffron number that she usually puts on.

NEIGHBOUR: Why, where's your cloak?

BLEPYRUS: Can't say. I looked for it among the bedclothes, but couldn't find it.

NEIGHBOUR: So didn't you ask your wife to tell you where it was?

BLEPYRUS: Couldn't. She's not actually at home; she's sneaked out of the house without my noticing. It makes me fear she may be doing something untoward.

NEIGHBOUR: By Poseidon, then you've had exactly the same happen to you as I have. My other half's vanished too, and she's got the cloak that I always wear. And that doesn't annoy me so much, but she's taken my shoes too; at any rate I haven't been able to find them anywhere.

BLEPYRUS: I couldn't find my Laconians either, by Dionysus; so when I felt I needed a crap, I thrust my feet into her soft boots and rushed out, so as not to soil my blanket – it was fresh clean.

NEIGHBOUR: Well, what can it be? It couldn't, could it, be some woman friend of hers who's invited her for lunch?

BLEPYRUS: I expect that's it. She's not a bad type, after all, not that I know of.

NEIGHBOUR: Well, *you* seem to be shitting a cable, and it's time for *me* to go to the Assembly – so long as I find my cloak; it was the only one I had. [*He withdraws from the window.*]

BLEPYRUS [*calling up to him*]: I will too, once I've finished relieving myself; at the moment there's a sort of wild pear that's keeping my food locked inside.

NEIGHBOUR [*briefly popping his head out again*]: Not the one that Thrasybulus told the Spartans about?

BLEPYRUS: Yes, indeed, by Dionysus; at any rate it's taking a very hostile attitude to me! – But what am I to do? The thing is, what's more, it's not just *this* that's bothering me; it's that when I eat in future, where is the end-product going to *go*? At the moment this fellow from Pearswick, whoever he is, has bolted and barred the door! [*Appealing to*

ὅστις ποτ' ἔσθ', ἄνθρωπος ἀχραδούσιος.
τίς ἂν οὖν ἰατρόν μοι μετέλθοι, καὶ τίνα;
τίς τῶν κατὰ πρωκτὸν δεινός ἐστι τὴν τέχνην;
ἆρ' οἶδ' Ἀμύνων; ἀλλ' ἴσως ἀρνήσεται.
Ἀντισθένη τις καλεσάτω πάσῃ τέχνῃ·
οὗτος γὰρ ἀνὴρ ἕνεκά γε στεναγμάτων
οἶδεν τί πρωκτὸς βούλεται χεζητιῶν.
ὦ πότνι' Ἰλείθυα, μή με περιίδῃς
διαρραγέντα μηδὲ βεβαλανωμένον,
ἵνα μὴ γένωμαι σκωραμὶς κωμῳδική.

ΧΡΕΜΗΣ
οὗτος, τί ποιεῖς; οὔ τί που χέζεις;
Βλ. ἐγώ;
οὐ δῆτ' ἔτι γε, μὰ τὸν Δί', ἀλλ' ἀνίσταμαι.
Χρ. τὸ τῆς γυναικὸς δ' ἀμπέχει χιτώνιον;
Βλ. ἐν τῷ σκότῳ γὰρ τοῦτ' ἔτυχον ἔνδον λαβών.
ἀτὰρ πόθεν ἥκεις ἐτεόν;
Χρ. ἐξ ἐκκλησίας.
Βλ. ἤδη λέλυται γάρ;
Χρ. νὴ Δί' ὄρθριον μὲν οὖν.
καὶ δῆτα πολὺν ἡ μίλτος, ὦ Ζεῦ φίλτατε,
γέλων παρέσχεν, ἣν προσέρραινον κύκλῳ.
Βλ. τὸ τριώβολον δῆτ' ἔλαβες;
Χρ. εἰ γὰρ ὤφελον.
ἀλλ' ὕστερος νῦν ἦλθον, ὥστ' αἰσχύνομαι.
Βλ. μὰ τὸν Δί' οὐδέν' ἄλλον ἢ τὸν θύλακον.
τὸ δ' αἴτιον τί;
Χρ. πλεῖστος ἀνθρώπων ὄχλος,
ὅσος οὐδεπώποτ', ἦλθ' ἁθρόος εἰς τὴν Πύκνα.

362 ἔσθ' ἄνθρωπος Blaydes, ἀχραδούσιος Brunck: ἔστ' ἄνθρ. Ἀχρ. vel sim. codd.: ἐστιν ἄνθρωπος Ἀχερδούσιος Stephanus of Byzantium 153.2.
364 κατὰ πρωκτὸν B: κατὰ πρωκτῶν Γ: καταπρώκτων RΛ.
365 ἆρ' codd.: ἀλλ' Meineke.
366 Ἀντισθένη B Suda: Ἀντισθένην RΓΛ.
369 Ἰλείθυα Coulon, cf. Threatte i 342-3, ii 735, *SEG* xxxiii 167 e.ii.13: Εἰλήθυα Σ^{R}: Εἰλείθυια vel sim. codd. Suda Σ^{Λ}.
381 ἀλλ' ὕστερος νῦν (Γ: νυνὶ Λ: νὴ Δί' R) ἦλθον codd.: (Βλ.) ἀλλ' ὕστερος ἦλθες; (Χρ.) νὴ Δί' Jackson.
382 οὐδέν' ἄλλον RΓΛ: οὐδὲν ἄλλον B: οὐδὲν ἄλλο γ' Brunck: perh. οὐδένα γ' ἄλλον: Elmsley suspected a lacuna before 382 (‹ἄπρακτος ἥκων οἴκαδ'. (Βλ.) οὐδὲν οὖν ἔχεις;› e.g. van Leeuwen, giving 382 to Chremes).

the audience] Who will go and fetch a doctor for me – [*thinking aloud*] and what doctor? Who is there that's a real specialist in anal problems? Does Amynon know? But probably he won't admit it! [*Calling out again*] Someone please, at all costs, summon Antisthenes! To judge by the way he groans, that man knows the meaning of an arsehole that's desperate to unburden itself. [*Raising his arms in prayer*] O Lady Hileithya, don't stand by and let me burst or stay blocked up like this; I don't want to become a comic shitpot!

[*Enter Chremes, from the left. Just as he arrives, Blepyrus appears to have found relief at last; he has just finished wiping his bottom (with a smooth stone) when Chremes comes up to him.*]

CHREMES: Here, you, what are you doing? Not shitting by any chance, are you?

BLEPYRUS [*rising*]: Me? No, no, not any more; I'm just getting up.

CHREMES: And you're wearing your wife's underdress?

BLEPYRUS: Yes, I picked it up by mistake, inside in the dark. But where have you come from, actually?

CHREMES: From the Assembly.

BLEPYRUS: You mean it's already over?

CHREMES: Already? It was finished before daylight! And – oh, dear Zeus! – it was so funny, the way they were showering that vermilion dye at people in all directions!

BLEPYRUS: Then you got your three obols?

CHREMES: If only I had! But in fact I came too late, which makes me feel really ashamed.

BLEPYRUS: Ashamed to face who? Your shopping-bag, that's all! But what was the reason?

CHREMES: An enormous throng of people, more than ever before, came in a solid mass to the Pnyx. And actually, seeing them, we

καὶ δῆτα πάντας σκυτοτόμοις ᾐκάζομεν
ὁρῶντες αὐτούς· οὐ γὰρ ἀλλ' ὑπερφυῶς
ὡς λευκοπληθὴς ἦν ἰδεῖν ἡκκλησία.
ὥστ' οὐκ ἔλαβον οὔτ' αὐτὸς οὔτ' ἄλλοι συχνοί.
Βλ. οὐδ' ἄρ' ἂν ἐγὼ λάβοιμι νῦν ἐλθών;
Χρ. πόθεν;
οὐδ' ἂν μὰ Δί' εἰ τότ' ἦλθες, ὅτε τὸ δεύτερον
ἀλεκτρυὼν ἐφθέγγετ'.
Βλ. οἴμοι δείλαιος.
'Αντίλοχ', ἀποίμωξόν με τοῦ τριωβόλου
τὸν ζῶντα μᾶλλον· τἀμὰ γὰρ διοίχεται.
ἀτὰρ τί τὸ πρᾶγμ' ἦν, ὅτι τοσοῦτον χρῆμ' ὄχλου
οὕτως ἐν ὥρᾳ ξυνελέγη;
Χρ. τί δ' ἄλλο γ' ἢ
ἔδοξε τοῖς πρυτάνεσι περὶ σωτηρίας
γνώμας προθεῖναι τῆς πόλεως; κᾆτ' εὐθέως
πρῶτος Νεοκλείδης ὁ γλάμων παρείρπυσεν.
κἄπειθ' ὁ δῆμος ἀναβοᾷ πόσον δοκεῖς·
"οὐ δεινὰ τολμᾶν τουτονὶ δημηγορεῖν,
καὶ ταῦτα περὶ σωτηρίας προκειμένου,
ὃς αὐτὸς αὑτῷ βλεφαρίδ' οὐκ ἐσώσατο;"
ὁ δ' ἀναβοήσας καὶ περιβλέψας ἔφη·
"τί δαί με χρὴ δρᾶν;"
Βλ. "σκόροδ' ὁμοῦ τρίψαντ' ὀπῷ,
τιθύμαλλον ἐμβαλόντα τοῦ Λακωνικοῦ,
σαυτοῦ παραλείφειν τὰ βλέφαρα τῆς ἑσπέρας",
ἔγωγ' ἂν εἶπον, εἰ παρὼν ἐτύγχανον.
Χρ. μετὰ τοῦτον Εὐαίων ὁ δεξιώτατος
παρῆλθε γυμνός, ὡς ἐδόκει τοῖς πλείοσιν·
αὐτός γέ μέντοὔφασκεν ἱμάτιον ἔχειν.
κἄπειτ' ἔλεξε δημοτικωτάτους λόγους·
"ὁρᾶτε μέν με δεόμενον σωτηρίας
τετραστατήρου καὐτόν· ἀλλ' ὅμως ἐρῶ
ὡς τὴν πόλιν καὶ τοὺς πολίτας σώσετε.

385 πάντας R Suda[A]: πάντα Suda[Γ]: πάντες ΓΛ.
390 ἂν μὰ Δί' εἰ van Leeuwen: εἰ μὰ Δία codd.
397 προθεῖναι Schömann: καθεῖναι codd.
403 ὁ δ' Küster: ὅδ' codd.
404 χρὴ RΓ: χρῆν Λ.

thought they all looked like shoemakers; it really was extraordinary how full of white faces the Assembly was to look at. The result was, I didn't get anything, and nor did lots of others.

BLEPYRUS: You mean, if I went now, I wouldn't get anything either?

CHREMES: What are you blethering about? Why, you wouldn't even have got anything if you'd gone at the time of the second cock-crow!

BLEPYRUS [*devastated*]: God help me! [*Brokenly, in tragic tones*]

Antilochus, mourn rather me that lives
Than my three obols: all I had is gone! —

But what was the reason why such an enormous crowd had gathered so early?

CHREMES: Why, what else but the Prytaneis deciding to set down for debate the subject of how to save the City? First of all, straight after the preliminaries, that bleary-eyed Neocleides edged his way to the platform. At that the public cries out, you can't imagine how loud, "Isn't it shocking that this man should dare address the people, and that too when the debate is about saving the City, when he hasn't been able to save his own eyelids!" And he peered around him, lifted up his voice and said, "Well, what am I supposed to do about it?"

BLEPYRUS: "Pound together garlic and fig-juice, chuck in some spurge of the Laconian variety, and smear it on to your eyelids before going to bed"; that's what I'd have said, if I'd happened to be there.

CHREMES: After him that very clever speaker Euaeon came forward, naked – or so he seemed to most people there; *he*, however, insisted that he was wearing a cloak. And he proceeded to deliver a speech full of the democratic spirit: "You can see that I could do with something to save *me* – something weighing about eight pounds; but all the same I'll tell you the way you'll save the City and her citizens. If the

ἢν γὰρ παρέχωσι τοῖς δεομένοις οἱ κναφῆς
χλαίνας, ἐπειδὰν πρῶτον ἥλιος τραπῇ,
πλευρῖτις ἡμῶν οὐδέν' ἂν λάβοι ποτέ.
ὅσοις δὲ κλίνη μή 'στι μηδὲ στρώματα,
ἰέναι καθευδήσοντας ἀπονενιμμένους
εἰς τῶν σκυλοδεψῶν· ἢν δ' ἀποκλῄῃ τῇ θύρᾳ
χειμῶνος ὄντος, τρεῖς σισύρας ὀφειλέτω."
Βλ. νὴ τὸν Διόνυσον, χρηστά γ'· εἰ δ' ἐκεῖνό γε
προσέθηκεν, οὐδεὶς ἀντεχειροτόνησεν ἄν,
τοὺς ἀλφιταμοιβοὺς τοῖς ἀπόροις τρεῖς χοίνικας
δεῖπνον παρέχειν ἅπασιν ἢ κλάειν μακρά,
ἵνα τοῦτ' ἀπέλαυσαν Ναυσικύδους τἀγαθόν.
Χρ. μετὰ τοῦτο τοίνυν εὐπρεπὴς νεανίας
λευκός τις ἀνεπήδησ' ὅμοιος Νικίᾳ
δημηγορήσων, κἀπεχείρησεν λέγειν
ὡς χρὴ παραδοῦναι ταῖς γυναιξὶ τὴν πόλιν.
εἶτ' ἐθορύβησαν κἀνέκραγον ὡς εὖ λέγοι,
τὸ σκυτοτομικὸν πλῆθος, οἱ δ' ἐκ τῶν ἀγρῶν
ἀνεβορβόρυξαν.
Βλ. νοῦν γὰρ εἶχον, νὴ Δία.
Χρ. ἀλλ' ἦσαν ἥττους. ὁ δὲ κατεῖχε τῇ βοῇ,
τὰς μὲν γυναῖκας πόλλ' ἀγαθὰ λέγων, σὲ δὲ
πολλὰ κακά.
Βλ. καὶ τί εἶπε;
Χρ. πρῶτον μέν σ' ἔφη
εἶναι πανοῦργον.
Βλ. καὶ σέ;
Χρ. μήπω τοῦτ' ἔρῃ.
κἄπειτα κλέπτην.
Βλ. ἐμὲ μόνον;
Χρ. καὶ νὴ Δία
καὶ συκοφάντην.
Βλ. ἐμὲ μόνον;
Χρ. καὶ νὴ Δία
τωνδὶ τὸ πλῆθος.
Βλ. τίς δὲ τοῦτ' ἄλλως λέγει;

417 ἡμῶν codd.: ὑμῶν Suda.
420 ἀποκλῄῃ (ἀποκλείῃ) Le Febvre: ἀποκλίνῃ vel sim. codd. Suda.
422 ἐκεῖνό van Leeuwen: ἐκεῖνά codd.: (δὲ) κἀκεῖνα Suda.

fullers, immediately after the turning of the sun, supply warm cloaks free to those who need them, then none of us should ever get pleurisy again. And all those who don't have a bed or bedding should be allowed, after washing their hands, to go to the tanners' shops to sleep; and if the tanner shuts the door against them in winter, let him be fined three fleecy blankets."

BLEPYRUS: Good stuff, by Dionysus! And if he'd added one thing more, there wouldn't have been a hand raised in opposition – namely, that the corn-dealers should supply all the poor with three quarts of corn each for dinner, or else they'd be well and truly for it. Then the people would get at least *that* much benefit out of Nausicydes!

CHREMES: Well, after that, a good-looking, white-faced young man, rather like Nicias, jumped up to make a speech; and he set himself to argue that the City ought to be handed over to the women. At that they cheered and shouted "Well said", did the shoemaking crowd; but the folk from the countryside raised a rumble of dissent.

BLEPYRUS: Very sensible of them too, by Zeus!

CHREMES: But they were outnumbered; and he dominated the meeting with his bellowing, saying a great deal in praise of women and a great deal in condemnation of you.

BLEPYRUS: And what did he say?

CHREMES: In the first place, that you were a villain.

BLEPYRUS: And you?

CHREMES: Ask me that in a moment. Secondly, that you were a thief.

BLEPYRUS: What, only me?

CHREMES: And also, by Zeus, an informer.

BLEPYRUS: What, only me?

CHREMES: And also, by Zeus, most of these people here [*indicating the audience*].

BLEPYRUS: Well, who doesn't agree with *that*?

Χρ. γυναῖκα δ' εἶναι πρᾶγμ' ἔφη νουβυστικὸν
καὶ χρηματοποιόν. κοὔτε τἀπόρρητ' ἔφη
ἐκ Θεσμοφόροιν ἑκάστοτ' αὐτὰς ἐκφέρειν,
σὲ δὲ κἀμὲ βουλεύοντε τοῦτο δρᾶν ἀεί.
Βλ. καὶ νὴ τὸν Ἑρμῆν τοῦτό γ' οὐκ ἐψεύσατο.
Χρ. ἔπειτα συμβάλλειν πρὸς ἀλλήλας ἔφη
ἱμάτια, χρυσί', ἀργύριον, ἐκπώματα,
μόνας μόναις, οὐ μαρτύρων ἐναντίον,
καὶ ταῦτ' ἀποφέρειν πάντα κοὐκ ἀποστερεῖν·
ἡμῶν δὲ τοὺς πολλοὺς ἔφασκε τοῦτο δρᾶν.
Βλ. νὴ τὸν Ποσειδῶ, μαρτύρων γ' ἐναντίον. 451
Χρ. ἕτερά τε πλεῖστα τὰς γυναῖκας ηὐλόγει· 454
οὐ συκοφαντεῖν, οὐ διώκειν, οὐδὲ τὸν 452
δῆμον καταλύειν, ἄλλα πολλὰ κἀγαθά. 453
Βλ. τί δῆτ' ἔδοξεν;
Χρ. ἐπιτρέπειν γε τὴν πόλιν
ταύταις. ἐδόκει γὰρ τοῦτο μόνον ἐν τῇ πόλει
οὔπω γεγενῆσθαι.
Βλ. καὶ δέδοκται;
Χρ. φήμ' ἐγώ.
Βλ. ἅπαντ' ἄρ' αὐταῖς ἐστι προστεταγμένα,
ἃ τοῖσιν ἀστοῖς ἔμελεν;
Χρ. οὕτω ταῦτ' ἔχει.
Βλ. οὐδ' εἰς δικαστήριον ἄρ' εἶμ', ἀλλ' ἡ γυνή;
Χρ. οὐδ' ἔτι σὺ θρέψεις οὓς ἔχεις, ἀλλ' ἡ γυνή.
Βλ. οὐδὲ στένειν τὸν ὄρθρον ἔτι πρᾶγμ' ἆρά μοι;
Χρ. μὰ Δί', ἀλλὰ ταῖς γυναιξὶ ταῦτ' ἤδη μέλει·
σὺ δ' ἀστενακτεὶ περδόμενος οἴκοι μενεῖς.
Βλ. ἐκεῖνο δεινὸν τοῖσιν ἡλίκοισι νῷν,
μὴ παραλαβοῦσαι τῆς πόλεως τὰς ἡνίας
ἔπειτ' ἀναγκάζωσι πρὸς βίαν—
Χρ. τί δρᾶν;

444 βουλεύοντε Fracini: βουλεύονται R: δουλεύοντε ΓΛ.
448 οὐ μαρτύρων Bergk: οὐ μαρτύρων γ' RΛ Suda: γ' οὐ μαρτύρων Γ.
454 transposed by Bachmann to precede 452.
453 ἄλλα Ussher: ἀλλὰ codd.
455 γε B: σε RΓΛ.
458 ἅπαντ' ἄρ' Cobet: ἅπαντά θ' RΛ: ἅπαντά τ' Γ.
459 ἔμελεν B: ἔμελλεν R: τ' ἔμελλεν ΓΛ.

CHREMES: And he said that a woman was a being full of intelligence, and good at raising income. And he said that *they* don't leak the secrets of the Thesmophoria every time they hold it, whereas you and I, when we're on the Council, are always doing that.

445 BLEPYRUS: And, by Hermes, *that* was no lie he told!

CHREMES: Then he said that they lend each other clothes,
jewellery, money, drinking cups, when they're all on their own, not in
front of witnesses; and they give it all back and don't cheat the lender;
450 whereas most of us, he said, do do so.

451 BLEPYRUS: Yes, we do, by Poseidon, in *front* of witnesses!

454 CHREMES: And he said many other things in praise of women:
452 they don't become informers, they don't bring prosecutions, they don't
453 subvert the democracy, lots of other good things about them.

455 BLEPYRUS: So what was decided on in the end?

CHREMES: Why, to entrust the City to them; because it was thought that this was the only thing that hadn't ever been done before in Athens.

BLEPYRUS: That's actually been decreed?

CHREMES: Yes, it has.

BLEPYRUS: So all the duties that the male citizens used to be concerned with have now been assigned to the women?

CHREMES: That's right.

460 BLEPYRUS: You mean I won't even be going to court in future,
my wife will?

CHREMES: And you won't be maintaining your household any more, your wife will.

BLEPYRUS: So I don't have the bother any more, either, of getting up groaning at first light?

CHREMES: No, indeed, that's the women's concern now; you can stay farting at home, groan-free.

465 BLEPYRUS: There's one thing that folk of our age have to fear:
that when the women take over the reins of the City, they may then
compel us by force to—

CHREMES: To do what?

Βλ. κινεῖν ἑαυτάς· ἢν δὲ μὴ δυνώμεθα,
ἄριστον οὐ δώσουσι.
Χρ. σὺ δέ γε νὴ Δία
δρᾶ ταῦθ', ἵν' ἀριστᾷς τε καὶ κινῇς ἅμα.
Βλ. τὸ πρὸς βίαν δεινότατον.
Χρ. ἀλλ' εἰ τῇ πόλει
τοῦτο ξυνοίσει, ταῦτα χρὴ πάντ' ἄνδρα δρᾶν.
Βλ. λόγος γέ τοί τίς ἐστι τῶν γεραιτέρων,
ὅσ' ἂν ἀνόητ' ἢ μῶρα βουλευσώμεθα,
ἅπαντ' ἐπὶ τὸ βέλτιον ἡμῖν ξυμφέρειν.
Χρ. καὶ συμφέροι γ', ὦ πότνια Παλλὰς καὶ θεοί.
ἀλλ' εἶμι· σὺ δ' ὑγίαινε.
Βλ. καὶ σύ γ', ὦ Χρέμης.
Χο. ἔμβα, χώρει.
ἆρ' εστὶ τῶν ἀνδρῶν τις ἡμῖν ὅστις ἐπακολουθεῖ;
στρέφου, σκόπει,
φύλαττε σαυτὴν ἀσφαλῶς, πολλοὶ γὰρ οἱ πανοῦργοι,
μή πού τις ἐκ τοὔπισθεν ὢν τὸ σχῆμα καταφυλάξῃ.

ἀλλ' ὡς μάλιστα τοῖν ποδοῖν ἐπικτυπῶν βάδιζε· (στρ.
ἡμῖν δ' ἂν αἰσχύνην φέροι
πάσαισι παρὰ τοῖς ἀνδράσιν τὸ πρᾶγμα τοῦτ' ἐλεγχθέν.
πρὸς ταῦτα συστέλλου σεαυ-
τὴν καὶ περισκοπουμένη
κἀκεῖσε καὶ τἀκ δεξιᾶς
‹φύλατθ' ὅπως› μὴ ξυμφορὰ γενήσεται τὸ πρᾶγμα.
ἀλλ' ἐγκονῶμεν· τοῦ τόπου γὰρ ἐγγύς ἐσμεν ἤδη,
ὅθενπερ εἰς ἐκκλησίαν ὡρμώμεθ' ἡνίκ' ᾖμεν·
τὴν δ' οἰκίαν ἔξεσθ' ὁρᾶν, ὅθενπερ ἡ στρατηγός
ἐσθ', ἡ τὸ πρᾶγμ' εὑροῦσ' ὃ νῦν ἔδοξε τοῖς πολίταις.

473 γε Suda^{G} μ1337: τε codd. Suda^{Γ} μ1337 Suda γ195.
474 ἀνόητ' ἢ Bentley: ἀνόητα καὶ ΓΛ: ἀνόητα χὴ vel sim. R Suda.
483 ἐπικτυπῶν βάδιζε codd.: βάδιζ' ἐπικτυποῦσα Blaydes.
488 ‹φύλατθ' ὅπως› Blaydes: om. codd.: ‹τὰ τῇδε καὶ› (before τἀκ δεξιᾶς) Valckenaer: ‹τὰ πάντ' ἄθρει› (before κἀκεῖσε) Coulon.
490 ὡρμώμεθ' Biset: ὁρμώμεθ' vel sim. codd.

BLEPYRUS: To screw them; and if we're not able to, they won't give us our lunch.

CHREMES: Well then, by Zeus, you should do *this* [*bending forward and raising his long comic phallus to his lips*], to enable you to lunch *and* to screw at the same time!

BLEPYRUS: Terrible thing, though, doing it under compulsion.

CHREMYLUS: Well, if that's going to be for the good of the City, that's what every man ought to do.

BLEPYRUS: Well, there certainly is a saying that our forebears had, that all the stupid or foolish decisions we make, all of them turn out to be to our benefit in the end.

CHREMES: And may this one turn out so, Lady Pallas and all you gods! But I'll be going; good health to you.

BLEPYRUS: And to you, Chremes. [*Chremes goes out, right. Blepyrus goes into his house.*]

[*Enter, left, Chorus, cautiously, still in disguise.*]
CHORUS-LEADER:
Step out, march!
Is there any of the men that's following after us?
Turn round, look—
[*The Chorus look behind them.*]
guard yourself securely, for there are plenty of villains around,
in case there may be someone in our rear watching how we walk.

CHORUS:
So when you walk, make as much noise with your feet as you can;
it would put us all to shame
in front of the men, if this operation was detected.
So with that in mind, wrap yourself up
tight, look around you
both in that direction and on the right side—
[*They look to left and right in search of a hostile presence.*]
and take care that the operation doesn't end in disaster.
Let's hurry, though; for we're near the place now
from which we started when we were going to the Assembly;
and we can see the house that our General is from,
she who devised the plan that the citizen body has now approved.

ὥστ᾽ εἰκὸς ἡμᾶς μὴ βραδύνειν ἔστ᾽ ἐπαναμενούσας (ἀντ.
πώγωνας ἐξηρτημένας,
μή καί τις ἡμᾶς ὄψεται χἠμῶν ἴσως κατείπῃ.
ἀλλ᾽ εἶα, δεῦρ᾽ ἐπὶ σκιᾶς
ἐλθοῦσα πρὸς τὸ τειχίον,
παραβλέπουσα θατέρῳ,
πάλιν μετασκεύαζε σαυτὴν αὖθις ἥπερ ἦσθα,
καὶ μὴ βράδυν᾽· ὡς τήνδε καὶ δὴ τὴν στρατηγὸν ἡμῶν
χωροῦσαν ἐξ ἐκκλησίας ὁρῶμεν. ἀλλ᾽ ἐπείγου
ἅπασα καὶ μίσει σάκον πρὸς ταῖν γνάθοιν ἔχουσα·
καὐταὶ γὰρ ἄκουσαι πάλαι τὸ σχῆμα τοῦτ᾽ ἔχουσιν.

Πρ. ταυτὶ μὲν ἡμῖν, ὦ γυναῖκες, εὐτυχῶς
τὰ πράγματ᾽ ἐκβέβηκεν ἁβουλεύσαμεν.
ἀλλ᾽ ὡς τάχιστα, πρίν τιν᾽ ἀνθρώπων ἰδεῖν,
ῥιπτεῖτε χλαίνας, ἐμβὰς ἐκποδὼν ἴτω,
χάλα συναπτοὺς ἡνίας Λακωνικάς,
βακτηρίας ἄφεσθε. καὶ μέντοι σὺ μὲν
ταύτας κατευτρέπιζ᾽· ἐγὼ δὲ βούλομαι,
εἴσω παρερπύσασα πρὶν τὸν ἄνδρα με
ἰδεῖν, καταθέσθαι θοἰμάτιον αὐτοῦ πάλιν
ὅθενπερ ἔλαβον τἄλλα θ᾽ ἁξηνεγκάμην.

Χο. κεῖται καὶ δὴ πάνθ᾽ ἅπερ εἶπας· σὸν δ᾽ ἔργον τἄλλα διδάσκειν,
ὅ τι σοι δρῶσαι ξύμφορον ἡμεῖς δόξομεν ὀρθῶς ὑπακούειν·
οὐδεμιᾷ γὰρ δεινοτέρᾳ σοῦ ξυμμείξασ᾽ οἶδα γυναικί.
Πρ. περιμείνατέ νυν, ἵνα τῆς ἀρχῆς, ἣν ἄρτι κεχειροτόνημαι,
ξυμβούλοισιν πάσαις ὑμῖν χρήσωμαι. καὶ γὰρ ἐκεῖ μοι
ἐν τῷ θορύβῳ καὶ τοῖς δεινοῖς ἀνδρειόταται γεγένησθε.

495 ἡμᾶς ὄψεται Hermann: ὄψεθ᾽ ἡμᾶς RΛ: ὄψαιτο ἡμᾶς Γ.
503 καὐταὶ ᾽αν Leeuwen: χαὖται codd.
503 ἄκουσαι ... ἔχουσιν Agar: ἤκουσιν ... ἔχουσαι codd.: ἀλγοῦσιν ... ἔχουσαι Palmer.
508 Λακωνικάς codd.: Λακωνικῶν van Leeuwen.
509 ταύτας codd.: ταυτὶ Meineke.
514 καὶ Dobree: om. codd.

So it's best that we shouldn't waste time and hang around
with beards tied on our chins,
in case someone does see us and may possibly tell on us.
Hi there! come over here,
to the wall, into the shade,
keeping a look-out from the corner of an eye—
[*All the chorus come as close as possible to the stage-house.*]
and change yourself back again to be the person you were.
[*Looking back the way they have come*]
And don't be slow about it; for look, here we can see our General
coming from the Assembly. Hurry up now,
everyone, and don't stand for having a piece of sacking on your
cheeks; they themselves have been wearing this get-up under protest
for some time now!

[*As the women tear off and discard their beards, Praxagora re-enters, left, alone. She is wearing her own underdress, let down now to full length, and carrying her husband's cloak, shoes and stick.*]

PRAXAGORA: Well, ladies, this scheme that we planned has come off successfully. Now, as quickly as possible, before anyone sees you, cast off cloaks, get shoes out from underfoot, "let loose the knotted-up Laconian reins", throw away sticks. And actually [*to the chorus-leader*] you get this lot in order; I want to slip through inside before my husband sees me and put down the cloak back in the same place I got it from, and also the other things I took with me.

[*Praxagora goes inside. The chorus busy themselves with removing the various items of their disguise, which are left under the stage-platform. As they form up again, looking feminine once more, Praxagora comes out; she has put on her own cloak and shoes.*]

CHORUS-LEADER: Look, everything you mentioned is on the ground. Now it's your job to give us our further instructions, what you think will be the right way for us to obey your orders and do something useful; because we're not aware of ever having met a woman more astute than you.

PRAXAGORA: Well then, stay around here, so that I can make use of you all as my advisers in the office to which I've just been elected; because back there, amid the din and the danger, I think you showed yourselves full of manly courage.

Βλ. αὕτη, πόθεν ἥκεις, Πραξαγόρα;
Πρ. τί δ', ὦ μέλε,
σοὶ τοῦθ';
Βλ. ὅ τι μοι τοῦτ' ἐστίν; ὡς εὐηθικῶς.
Πρ. οὔτοι παρά του μοιχοῦ γε φήσεις.
Βλ. οὐκ ἴσως
ἑνός γε.
Πρ. καὶ μὴν βασανίσαι τουτί γέ σοι
ἔξεστι.
Βλ. πῶς;
Πρ. εἰ τῆς κεφαλῆς ὄζω μύρου.
Βλ. τί δ'; οὐχὶ βινεῖται γυνὴ κἄνευ μύρου;
Πρ. οὐ δῆτα, τάλαν, ἔγωγε.
Βλ. πῶς οὖν ὄρθριον
ᾤχου σιωπῇ θοἰμάτιον λαβοῦσά μου;
Πρ. γυνή μέ τις νύκτωρ ἑταίρα καὶ φίλη
μετεπέμψατ' ὠδίνουσα.
Βλ. κᾆτ' οὐκ ἦν ἐμοὶ
φράσασαν ἰέναι;
Πρ. τῆς λεχοῦς δ' οὐ φροντίσαι
οὕτως ἐχούσης, ὦνερ;
Βλ. εἰποῦσάν γ' ἐμοί.
ἀλλ' ἔστιν ἐνταῦθά τι κακόν.
Πρ. μὰ τὼ θεώ,
ἀλλ' ὥσπερ εἶχον ᾠχόμην· ἐδεῖτο δὲ
ἥπερ μεθῆκέ μ' ἐξιέναι πάσῃ τέχνῃ.
Βλ. εἶτ' οὐ τὸ σαυτῆς ἱμάτιον ἐχρῆν σ' ἔχειν;
αλλ' ἔμ' ἀποδύσασ', ἐπιβαλοῦσα τοὔγκυκλον,
ᾤχου καταλιποῦσ' ὡσπερεὶ προκείμενον,
μόνον οὐ στεφανώσασ' οὐδ' ἐπιθεῖσα λήκυθον.
Πρ. ψῦχος γὰρ ἦν, ἐγὼ δὲ λεπτὴ κἀσθενής·
ἔπειθ', ἵν' ἀλεαίνοιμι, τοῦτ' ἠμπεσχόμην·
σὲ δ' ἐν ἀλέᾳ κατακείμενον καὶ στρώμασιν
κατέλιπον, ὦνερ.

522 παρά του Invernizi: παρὰ τοῦ codd.
526 δῆτα, τάλαν Reiske: δὴ τάλαιν' codd.
531 γ' ἐμοί R: γέ μοι ΓΛ.
540 ἠμπεσχόμην Bekk. *An.* 381.25, *Lex. Bachm.* 73.8: ἠμπισχόμην RL Suda, Zonaras: ἠμπισχημένον Γ.

[*Blepyrus comes out of his house, fully dressed in his own clothes, and accosts Praxagora.*]

BLEPYRUS: Here, you, Praxagora, where have you been?

PRAXAGORA: What business is that of yours, my good man?

BLEPYRUS: "What business is that of mine?" How simple can you get?

PRAXAGORA: You're certainly not going to say I came from a *lover*!

BLEPYRUS: Well, perhaps not from *a* lover!

PRAXAGORA: Well, you're free to put that to the test.

BLEPYRUS: How?

PRAXAGORA: See if my head smells of perfume.

BLEPYRUS: What, can't a woman get herself fucked even without perfume?

PRAXAGORA: *I* certainly can't, my dear!

BLEPYRUS: Well, how come you went off at the glimmer of dawn, without a word, and taking my cloak?

PRAXAGORA: A woman who's a close friend of mine sent for me. She'd gone into labour during the night.

BLEPYRUS: So couldn't you have told me that before going?

PRAXAGORA: And not had a thought for the mother-to-be, dear, when she was in such a state?

BLEPYRUS: Yes, but *after telling me*! There's something fishy about this.

PRAXAGORA: No, by the Two Goddesses! I just went straight away. The girl who came for me begged me to come out at all costs.

BLEPYRUS: Well, shouldn't you have worn your *own* cloak? Instead, you stripped me, threw your mantle over me, and went off leaving me there like a laid-out corpse. I'm surprised you didn't put an oil-jar beside me and a wreath on my head!

PRAXAGORA: It was cold, and I'm not strong or well-built; so I put that cloak on to keep warm. And I left you lying warm and well covered, dear.

Βλ. αἱ δὲ δὴ Λακωνικαὶ
ᾤχοντο μετὰ σοῦ κατὰ τί χὴ βακτηρία;
Πρ. ἵνα θοἰμάτιον σώσαιμι, μεθυπεδησάμην,
μιμουμένη σὲ καὶ κτυποῦσα τοῖν ποδοῖν
καὶ τοὺς λίθους παίουσα τῇ βακτηρίᾳ.
Βλ. οἶσθ' οὖν ἀπολωλεκυῖα πυρῶν ἑκτέα,
ὃν χρῆν ἔμ' ἐξ ἐκκλησίας εἰληφέναι;
Πρ. μὴ φροντίσῃς· ἄρρεν γὰρ ἔτεκε παιδίον.
Βλ. ἠκκλησία;
Πρ. μὰ Δί', ἀλλ' ἐφ' ἣν ἐγῴχόμην.
ἀτὰρ γεγένηται;
Βλ. ναὶ μὰ Δί'. οὐκ ᾔδησθά με
φράσαντά σοι χθές;
Πρ. ἄρτι γ' ἀναμιμνῄσκομαι.
Βλ. οὐδ' ἄρα τὰ δόξαντ' οἶσθα;
Πρ. μὰ Δί' ἐγὼ μὲν οὔ.
Βλ. κάθησο τοίνυν σηπίας μασωμένη.
ὑμῖν δέ φασι παραδεδόσθαι τὴν πόλιν.
Πρ. τί δρᾶν; ὑφαίνειν;
Βλ. οὐ μὰ Δί', ἀλλ' ἄρχειν.
Πρ. τίνων;
Βλ. ἁπαξαπάντων τῶν κατὰ πόλιν πραγμάτων.
Πρ. νὴ τὴν 'Αφροδίτην, μακαρία γ' ἄρ' ἡ πόλις
ἔσται τὸ λοιπόν.
Βλ. κατὰ τί;
Πρ. πολλῶν οὕνεκα.
οὐ γὰρ ἔτι τοῖς τολμῶσιν αὐτὴν αἰσχρὰ δρᾶν
< >
ἔσται τὸ λοιπὸν †οὐδαμοῦ δὲ† μαρτυρεῖν,
οὐ συκοφαντεῖν–
Βλ. μηδαμῶς πρὸς τῶν θεῶν
τουτὶ ποιήσῃς μηδ' ἀφέλῃ μου τὸν βίον.
Γε. ὦ δαιμόνι' ἀνδρῶν, τὴν γυναῖκ' ἔα λέγειν.

551 ᾔδησθα Brunck: ᾔδεισθα vel sim. codd.
559-560 are omitted by Γ.
560 lacuna posited by Sommerstein.
561 †οὐδαμοῦ δε† codd.: οὐδάμ' οὐδὲ or οὐδαμῶς, οὐ Blaydes.

BLEPYRUS: And my Laconians and my walking-stick, why did they go with you?

PRAXAGORA: I changed shoes in order not to lose the cloak, and in imitation of you I brought my feet down with a stamp and struck the stones with the stick.

BLEPYRUS: Do you know that you've lost a quarter-bushel of wheat, which I ought to have earned from the Assembly?

PRAXAGORA: Don't worry; it was a boy.

BLEPYRUS: What, the Assembly?

PRAXAGORA: No, no, the baby I went to help with. – What, there's been one?

BLEPYRUS: Yes, indeed. Didn't you remember I told you about it yesterday?

PRAXAGORA: Oh, yes, now I recollect you did.

BLEPYRUS: So you don't even know what was decided?

PRAXAGORA: Not me, I don't.

BLEPYRUS [*as one who has the most stunning of news*]: Well, sit down, and get some cuttlefish to chew. They say that the City has been handed over to you women.

PRAXAGORA [*affecting bewilderment*]: To do what with? To weave?

BLEPYRUS: No, no, to *rule*.

PRAXAGORA: Rule over who?

BLEPYRUS: Rule over absolutely all the City's affairs!

PRAXAGORA: Then, by Aphrodite, the City will be a happy place from now on!

BLEPYRUS: Why will it?

PRAXAGORA: For all sorts of reasons! Those who dare to commit shameful crimes against it will no longer <have any opportunity to do so>; there will be no <going to law> at all in future, no bearing witness, no informing—

BLEPYRUS [*crying out in alarm*]: No, please, in the gods' name, don't do that, don't take away my livelihood!

[*In the middle of this outburst, Blepyrus' neighbour has come out of his house.*]

NEIGHBOUR: My dear fellow, do give your wife a chance to speak!

Πρ. μὴ λωποδυτῆσαι, μὴ φθονεῖν τοῖς πλησίον,
μὴ γυμνὸν εἶναι, μὴ πένητα μηδένα,
μὴ λοιδορεῖσθαι, μὴ 'νεχυραζόμενον φέρειν.
Γε. νὴ τὸν Προσειδῶ μεγάλα γ', εἰ μὴ ψεύσεται.
Πρ. ἀλλ' ἀποφανῶ τοῦθ', ὥστε σέ τέ μοι μαρτυρεῖν
καὶ τοῦτον αὐτὸν μηδὲν ἀντειπεῖν ἐμοί.

Χο. νῦν δὴ δεῖ σε πυκνὴν φρένα καὶ φιλόσοφον ἐγείρειν
φροντίδ' ἐπισταμένην
ταῖσι φίλαισιν ἀμύνειν.
κοινῇ γὰρ ἐπ' εὐτυχίαισιν
ἔρχεται γλώττης ἐπίνοια πολίτην
δῆμον ἐπαγλαϊοῦσα
μυρίαισιν ὠφελίαισι βίου· δη-
λοῦν δ' ὅ τι περ δύναται καιρός.
δεῖται γάρ τι σοφοῦ τινος ἐξευρήματος ἡ πόλις ἡμῶν.
ἀλλὰ πέραινε μόνον
μήτε δεδραμένα μήτ' εἰρημένα πω πρότερον·
μισοῦσι γάρ, ἢν τὰ παλαιὰ πολλάκις θεῶνται.

ἀλλ' οὐ μέλλειν, ἀλλ' ἅπτεσθαι καὶ δὴ χρὴ τῆς διανοίας·
ὡς τὸ ταχύνειν χαρίτων μετέχει πλεῖστον παρὰ τοῖσι θεαταῖς.

Πρ. καὶ μὴν ὅτι μὲν χρηστὰ διδάξω πιστεύω· τοὺς δὲ θεατάς,
εἰ καινοτομεῖν ἐθελήσουσιν καὶ μὴ τοῖς ἠθάσι λίαν
τοῖς τ' ἀρχαίοις ἐνδιατρίβειν, τοῦτ' ἔσθ' ὃ μάλιστα δέδοικα.
Γε. περὶ μὲν τοίνυν τοῦ καινοτομεῖν μὴ δείσῃς· τοῦτο γὰρ ἡμῖν
δρᾶν ἀντ' ἄλλης ἀρετῆς ἐστιν, τῶν δ' ἀρχαίων ἀμελῆσαι.
Πρ. μή νυν πρότερον μηδεὶς ὑμῶν ἀντείπῃ μηδ' ὑποκρούσῃ,
πρὶν ἐπίστασθαι τὴν ἐπίνοιαν καὶ τοῦ φράζοντος ἀκοῦσαι.
κοινωνεῖν γὰρ πάντας φήσω χρῆναι πάντων μετέχοντας
κἀκ ταὐτοῦ ζῆν, καὶ μὴ τὸν μὲν πλουτεῖν, τὸν δ' ἄθλιον εἶναι,

569 σέ τέ Cobet: σε γέ R: γε ΓΛ.
570 ἐμοί codd.: ἔτι Cobet: ἔχειν Nauck.
576 δ' Voss: om. codd.
576 δύναται codd.: δύνασαι C.Kock.
577 (γάρ) τι Ald.: τοι ΓΛ: τοῖ γε R.
581 χρὴ B: χρῆν RΓΛ.
581 τῆς διανοίας Le Febvre: ταῖς διανοίαις codd.
587 ἀρετῆς Bergk: ἀρχῆς codd. Suda.

PRAXAGORA: No clothes-snatching, no being jealous of your neighbours, nobody being naked or poor, no slanging matches, no seizures for debt.

NEIGHBOUR: Great stuff, by Poseidon, if she doesn't turn out to be a liar!

PRAXAGORA: Why, I'll prove it clearly, so that you'll testify for me that it's true and this one himself [*meaning Blepyrus*] won't say a word in reply to me!

CHORUS:
Now is the time when you must awaken a rich intelligence and a philosophic
mind that understands
how to help your friends.
For, to the happiness of all alike,
there is coming from your tongue an idea that will adorn
the people of the City
with countless improvements in their lives;
and it is time to reveal its capabilities.
For our City stands in some need of an ingenious discovery!
Only give them, from beginning to end,
things that have never been done or said before;
they hate it if they hear the same old stuff over and over again!

CHORUS-LEADER: You shouldn't waste time, but get started right now on your idea, because pace is what wins the most favour with audiences.

PRAXAGORA: Well, I'm confident that I'll be giving good advice. But the audience – will they be willing to accept innovation, and not stay too much with the old and the familiar? That's what I'm most afraid of.

NEIGHBOUR: So far as innovation is concerned, have no fear. For us, to innovate, and to despise what's old, takes the place of every other virtue.

PRAXAGORA: Then let none of you object or interrupt before you have understood the proposal and listened to the speaker. I am going to propose that everyone should own everything jointly together and live

μηδὲ γεωργεῖν τὸν μὲν πολλήν, τῷ δ' εἶναι μηδὲ ταφῆναι,
μηδ' ἀνδραπόδοις τὸν μὲν χρῆσθαι πολλοῖς, τὸν δ' οὐδ'
ἀκολούθῳ·
ἀλλ' ἕνα ποιῶ κοινὸν πᾶσιν βίοτον, καὶ τοῦτον ὅμοιον.
Βλ. πῶς οὖν ἔσται κοινὸς ἅπασιν;
Πρ. κατέδει πέλεθον πρότερός μου.
Βλ. καὶ τῶν πελέθων κοινωνοῦμεν;
Πρ. μὰ Δί', ἀλλ' ἔφθης μ' ὑποκρούσας·
τοῦτο γὰρ ἤμελλον ἐγὼ λέξειν. τὴν γῆν πρώτιστα ποιήσω
κοινὴν πάντων καὶ τἀργύριοιν καὶ τἄλλ', ὁπόσ' ἐστὶν ἑκάστῳ·
εἶτ' ἀπὸ τούτων κοινῶν ὄντων ἡμεῖς βοσκήσομεν ὑμᾶς
ταμιεύουσαι καὶ φειδόμεναι καὶ τὴν γνώμην προσέχουσαι.
Γε. πῶς οὖν ὅστις μὴ κέκτηται γῆν ἡμῶν, ἀργύριον δὲ
καὶ Δαρεικούς, αφανῆ πλοῦτον;
Πρ. τοῦτ' εἰς τὸ μέσον καταθήσει.
Βλ. κἂν μὴ καταθεὶς ψευδορκήσῃ; κἀκτήσατο γὰρ διὰ τοῦτο.
Πρ. ἀλλ' οὐδέν τοι χρήσιμον ἔσται πάντως αὐτῷ.
Βλ. κατὰ δὴ τί;
Πρ. οὐδεὶς οὐδὲν πενίᾳ δράσει· πάντα γὰρ ἕξουσιν ἅπαντες,
ἄρτους, τεμάχη, μάζας, χλαίνας, οἶνον, στεφάνους, ἐρεβίνθους·
ὥστε τί κέρδος μὴ καταθεῖναι; σὺ γὰρ ἐξευρὼν ἀπόδειξον.
Βλ. οὔκουν καὶ νῦν οὗτοι μᾶλλον κλέπτουσ', οἷς ταῦτα πάρεστιν;
Γε. πρότερόν γ', ὦταῖρ', ὅτε τοῖσι νόμοις διεχρώμεθα τοῖς
πρότεροισιν·
νῦν δ', ἔσται γὰρ βίος ἐκ κοινοῦ, τί τὸ κέρδος μὴ καταθεῖναι;
Βλ. ἢν μείρακ' ἰδὼν ἐπιθυμήσῃ καὶ βούληται σκαλαθῦραι,
ἕξει τούτων ἀφελὼν δοῦναι, τῶν ἐκ κοινοῦ δὲ μεθέξει
ξυγκαταδαρθών.
Πρ. ἀλλ' ἐξέσται προῖκ' αὐτῷ ξυγκαταδαρθεῖν·
καὶ ταύτας γὰρ κοινὰς ποιῶ τοῖς ἀνδράσι συγκατακεῖσθαι
καὶ παιδοποιεῖν τῷ βουλομένῳ.
Βλ. πῶς οὖν οὐ πάντες ἴασιν
ἐπὶ τὴν ὡραιοτάτην αὐτῶν καὶ ζητήσουσιν ἐρείδειν;

595, 596 πελεθ- Bothe: σπελεθ- codd.
600 ταμιεύουσαι Blaydes: ταμιευόμεναι codd.: [τ]α̣[Π60.
603 κἂν ... ψευδορκήσῃ Rogers: και ... ψευδορκη[Π60: καὶ ... ψευδορκήσει codd.: (Βλ.) καὶ μὴ καταθείς; (Πρ.) ψευδορκήσει. (Βλ.) κἀκτήσατο γὰρ διὰ τοῦτο Tyrwhitt.
611 βούληται B Suda: βούλει ταῖ R: βούλεται ΓΛ.
613 -δαρθών Λ: -δαρδων Π60: -δραθών RΓ.

from a common stock, and that we should not have one man being rich and another wretched, nor one farming broad acres while another hasn't enough land to be buried in, nor one man owning many slaves while another doesn't have even one attendant; I'll make it so that there is one shared livelihood for everyone, and it's equal.

BLEPYRUS: So how is it going to be made "shared for everyone"?

PRAXAGORA [*angrily*]: You'd want to eat shit ahead of me!

BLEPYRUS: We're going to share all the shit as well?

PRAXAGORA: No, no, you jumped in too soon with your interruption; that was just what I was going to say. In the first place, I shall make land the common property of all, and money, and everything else that every individual possesses; then, from this common stock we women will maintain you, applying our intelligence to manage it economically.

NEIGHBOUR: What about any of us that doesn't own land, but invisible wealth in the form of silver coin and gold darics?

PRAXAGORA: He will deposit it in the central store.

BLEPYRUS: And what if he doesn't deposit it, and takes a false oath that he's kept nothing back? After all, that was how he got it in the first place!

PRAXAGORA: But then, you see, it won't be any use to him at all anyway.

BLEPYRUS: Oh, why not?

PRAXAGORA: Nobody will be doing anything under the pressure of poverty, because everyone will have everything – loaves, slices of fish, barley-cakes, warm cloaks, wine, garlands, chickpeas. So what will he gain by not surrendering his money? You find an answer and state it!

BLEPYRUS: Well, even now, aren't those people who have these things bigger thieves than those who don't?

NEIGHBOUR: You mean *formerly*, my friend, when we lived under the old laws. *Now*, when we're going to live on a communal basis, what will be his gain by not surrendering?

BLEPYRUS: If he sees a girl and fancies her and wants to poke her about a bit, he'll be able to take some of his money and give it to her, and then have his share of communing – with her, in bed!

PRAXAGORA: But he'll be able to sleep with her for free! Women also [*with a gesture towards the Chorus*] I'm making common property, for any man who wishes, to have sex and produce children.

BLEPYRUS: Then surely everyone will go for the most attractive of them and try to shag her!

Πρ. αἱ φαυλότεραι καὶ σιμότεραι παρὰ τὰς σεμνὰς καθεδοῦνται·
κᾆτ' ἣν ταύτης ἐπιθυμήσῃ, τὴν αἰσχρὰν πρῶθ' ὑποκρούσει.
Βλ. καὶ πῶς ἡμᾶς τοὺς πρεσβύτας, ἢν ταῖς αἰσχραῖσι συνῶμεν,
οὐκ ἐπιλείψει τὸ πέος πρότερον πρὶν ἐκεῖσ' οἷ φῄς ἀφικέσθαι;
Πρ. οὐχὶ μαχοῦνται περὶ σοῦ· θάρρει, μὴ δείσῃς· οὐχὶ μαχοῦνται.
Βλ. περὶ τοῦ;
Πρ. τοῦ μὴ ξυγκαταδαρθεῖν· καὶ σοὶ τοιοῦτον ὑπάρχει.
Βλ. τὸ μὲν ὑμέτερον γνώμην τιν' ἔχει· προβεβούλευται γὰρ ὅπως ἂν
μηδεμιᾶς ᾖ τρύπημα κενόν· τὸ δὲ τῶν ἀνδρῶν τί ποιήσει;
φεύξονται γὰρ τοὺς αἰσχίους, ἐπὶ τοὺς δὲ καλοὺς βαδιοῦνται.
Πρ. ἀλλὰ φυλάξουσ' οἱ φαυλότεροι τοὺς καλλίους ἀπιόντας
ἀπὸ τοῦ δείπνου καὶ τηρήσουσ' ἐπὶ τοῖσιν δημοσίοισιν
†οἱ φαυλότεροι†· κοὐκ ἐξέσται παρὰ τοῖσι καλοῖς καταδαρθεῖν
ταῖσι γυναιξίν, πρὶν τοῖς αἰσχροῖς καὶ τοῖς μικροῖς χαρίσωνται.
Βλ. ἡ Λυσικράτους ἄρα νυνὶ ῥὶς ἴσα τοῖσι καλοῖσι φρονήσει;
Γε. νὴ τὸν 'Απόλλω· καὶ δημοτική γ' ἡ γνώμη, καὶ καταχήνη
τῶν σεμνοτέρων ἔσται πολλὴ καὶ τῶν σφραγῖδας ἐχόντων,
ὅταν οὑμβάδ' ἔχων εἴπῃ πρότερος "παραχώρει, κᾆτ' ἐπιτήρει
ὅταν ἤδη 'γὼ διαπραξάμενος παραδῶ σοι δευτεριάζειν."
Βλ. πῶς οὖν οὕτω ζώντων ἡμῶν τοὺς αὑτοῦ παῖδας ἕκαστος
ἔσται δυνατὸς διαγιγνώσκειν;
Πρ. τί δὲ δεῖ; πατέρας γὰρ ἅπαντας
τοὺς πρεσβυτέρους αὐτῶν εἶναι τοῖσι χρόνοισιν νομιοῦσιν.
Βλ. οὔκουν ἄγξουσ' εὖ καὶ χρηστῶς ἑξῆς †τὸν πάντα† γέροντα
διὰ τὴν ἄγνοιαν; ἐπεὶ καὶ νῦν γιγνώσκοντες πατέρ' ὄντα
ἄγχουσι· τί δῆθ', ὅταν ἀγνὼς ᾖ; πῶς οὐ τότε κἀπιχεσοῦνται;
Πρ. ἀλλ' ὁ παρεστὼς οὐκ ἐπιτρέψει· τότε δ' αὐτοῖς οὐκ ἔμελ' οὐδὲν
τῶν ἀλλοτρίων, ὅστις τύπτοι· νῦν δ', ἢν πληγέντος ἀκούσῃ,

628 †οἱ φαυλότεροι† RΛ: ‹τοῖς τ' αὐλείοις› [*sic*: better would be ταῖς τ' αὐ.] Agar: ‹καὶ τοῖς μεγάλοις› (after καλοῖς) Tyrwhitt (‹καὶ μεγάλοισιν› Naber, ‹τοῖς τ' εὐπρεπέσιν› Blaydes): Γ omits the line.

629 χαρίσωνται Λ: χαρίσονται R: χαρί Γ: χαρίσασθαι Porson.

633 οὑμβάδ' ἔχων Agar: ἐμβάδ' ἔχων R: ἐμβάδ' Λ: Γ omits the line.

636 πατέρας γὰρ Le Febvre: πατέρας RΓ: πρᾶσαν Λ.

638 †τὸν πάντα† codd.:]α̲ Π60: πάντ' ἄνδρα van Leeuwen: τότε πάντα Th.Kock.

PRAXAGORA: The plainer women, the ones with the snubbier noses, will sit beside the fine lookers; and then if he fancies *her*, he'll have to give the ugly one a knock first!

BLEPYRUS: And what about us old folk? If we have to have sex with the ugly ones, isn't our cock bound to be exhausted before we get – where you said?

PRAXAGORA: Oh, they won't fight for you! Don't worry, have no fear; they won't fight!

BLEPYRUS: Fight over what?

PRAXAGORA: The right *not* to sleep with you. And [*pointing to his phallus*] *yours* is in that state to begin with anyway!

BLEPYRUS: Well, from your point of view it makes some sense; you've planned it so that none of you will have an empty hole. But what about the men's point ... of view? What'll happen to them? Because the women will run from the uglier men and go for the handsome ones.

PRAXAGORA: Ah, but the less good-looking men will watch out for the handsomer ones as they leave dinner, and keep an eye on them in the public places <. . . . . >; and the women won't be allowed to sleep with the handsome men until they've given their favours to the uglies and the shorties.

BLEPYRUS: So Lysicrates' nose will hold itself as high as that of any young beau?

NEIGHBOUR: By Apollo, yes; and it's a truly democratic idea, and it'll make absolute fools of those stuck-up folk with signet-rings, when before he can speak a man in cheap shoes says to him "Get out of my way, and then wait for when I've quite finished and I'll hand her over to you to do the second pressing!"

BLEPYRUS: Now then, if we live in this kind of way, how will any individual man be able to distinguish who are his own children?

PRAXAGORA: Why should he need to? They will regard *all* older men as their fathers, reckoning by the age difference.

BLEPYRUS: Then won't they throttle all the senior citizens good and proper, one after another, because of not knowing who their father is? Because even now, when they know he's their father, they still throttle him; so what'll happen when they *don't* know? They'll positively *shit* on him then, won't they?

PRAXAGORA: No, the bystanders won't let them. Previously they didn't care at all who was assaulting *other* people's fathers. But now,

μὴ αὐτὸν ἐκεῖνον τύπτῃ δεδιὼς τοῖς δρῶσιν τοῦτο μαχεῖται.
Βλ. τὰ μὲν ἄλλα λέγεις οὐδὲν σκαιῶς· εἰ δὲ προσελθὼν Ἐπίκουρος
ἢ Λευκόλοφος πάππαν με καλεῖ, τοῦτ' ἤδη δεινὸν ἀκοῦσαι.
Γε. πολὺ μέντοι δεινότερον τούτου τοῦ πράγματός ἐστι–
Βλ. τὸ ποῖον;
Γε. εἴ σε φιλήσειεν Ἀρίστυλλος φάσκων αὑτοῦ πατέρ' εἶναι.
Βλ. οἰμώζοι γ' ἂν καὶ κωκύοι.
Γε. σὺ δέ γ' ὄζοις ἂν καλαμίνθης.
Πρ. ἀλλ' οὗτος μὲν πρότερον γέγονεν πρὶν τὸ ψήφισμα γενέσθαι,
ὥστ' οὐχὶ δέος μή σε φιλήσῃ.
Βλ. δεινὸν μέντἂν ἐπεπόνθη.
τὴν γῆν δὲ τίς ἔσθ' ὁ γεωργήσων;
Πρ. οἱ δοῦλοι· σοὶ δὲ μελήσει,
ὅταν ᾖ δεκάπουν τὸ στοιχεῖον, λιπαρῷ χωρεῖν ἐπὶ δεῖπνον.
Βλ. περὶ δ' ἱματίων τίς πόρος ἔσται; καὶ γὰρ τοῦτ' ἐστὶν ἐρέσθαι.
Πρ. τὰ μὲν ὄνθ' ὑμῖν πρῶτον ὑπάρξει, τὰ δὲ λοίφ' ἡμεῖς ὑφανοῦμεν.
Βλ. ἓν ἔτι ζητῶ· πῶς, ἤν τις ὄφλῃ παρὰ τοῖς ἄρχουσι δίκην τῳ;
πόθεν ἐκτείσει ταῦτ'; οὐ γὰρ δὴ 'κ τῶν κοινῶν γ' ἐστὶ δίκαιον.
Πρ. ἀλλ' οὐδὲ δίκαι πρῶτον ἔσονται.
Βλ. τουτὶ τοὔπος σ' ἐπιτρίψει.
Γε. κἀγὼ ταύτῃ γνώμην ἐθέμην.
Πρ. τοῦ γάρ, τάλαν, οὕνεκ' ἔσονται;
Βλ. πολλῶν ἕνεκεν, νὴ τὸν Ἀπόλλω· πρῶτον δ' ἑνὸς οὕνεκα δήπου,
ἤν τις ὀφείλων ἐξαρνῆται.
Πρ. πόθεν οὖν ἐδάνεισ' ὁ δανείσας,
ἐν τῷ κοινῷ πάντων ὄντων; κλέπτων δήπου 'στ' ἐπίδηλος.
Γε. νὴ τὴν Δήμητρ', εὖ γε διδάσκεις.
Βλ. τουτὶ τοίνυν φρασάτω μοι·
τῆς ᾀκείας οἱ τύπτοντες πόθεν ἐκτείσουσιν, ἐπειδὰν

643 τύπτῃ (τύπτη) ΓΛ: cf. Soph. *Trach.* 663, *OT* 747:]ηι Π60: τύπτει R.
650 ἐπεπόνθη Bentley: ἐπεπόνθην Λ: ἐπεπόνθειν RΓ: επεπονθει[Π60.
652 λιπαρωι Π60 (conj. Bentley): λιπαρῶς RΓΛ Suda: λιπαρὸν B.
656 ταῦτ'; οὐ γὰρ δὴ 'κ Jackson: ταύτην; οὐ γὰρ codd.: ταύτην· οὐ γὰρ δὴ 'κ (with γε for γ' ἐστὶ) Cobet.
657 τοὔπος σ' Hansing: τοὖπος R: πόσσ' ΓΛ.
658 ταύτῃ Toup: ταύτην codd. Suda.

if they hear the cry of someone being beaten, they'll fear that the victim may be *their* old man, and attack the perpetrators.

BLEPYRUS: Most of what you say's not at all stupid. But if Epicurus or Leucolophus is going to come up to me and call me Daddy – now *that's* a dreadful thing to hear.

NEIGHBOUR: Well, there could be something a lot more dreadful than that.

BLEPYRUS: What?

NEIGHBOUR: If Aristyllus was to kiss you, claiming that you were his father.

BLEPYRUS: He'd find himself howling and wailing if he did!

NEIGHBOUR: But meanwhile *you'd* be smelling of ...tur(d)meric!

PRAXAGORA: But he was born earlier, before the decree was passed, so there's no risk he'll kiss you anyway.

BLEPYRUS: I'd still have been mortified if he had. – But who's there going to be to cultivate the land?

PRAXAGORA: The slaves. Your sole concern will be to go to dinner, sleek and gleaming, when the shadow is ten feet long.

BLEPYRUS: Then about clothes, how will they be provided? That's another question that needs asking.

PRAXAGORA: To begin with you'll have the ones you've got, and then we'll weave you others.

BLEPYRUS: There's still one thing I want to know. How about if someone has a lawsuit with someone else before the archons and loses? Where will he get the money to pay what he owes? Surely it's not fair if he gets it from the communal funds.

PRAXAGORA: But there won't *be* any lawsuits in the first place.

BLEPYRUS: Now *that* statement will be your ruin!

NEIGHBOUR: That's how I vote too.

PRAXAGORA: Why, you poor fool, what will they be about?

BLEPYRUS: Lots of things, by Apollo; one thing, surely, to begin with, is if someone owes money and denies the debt.

PRAXAGORA: So where did the lender get the money to lend, when everything was in common ownership? He must plainly have stolen it!

NEIGHBOUR: Well explained, by Demeter!

BLEPYRUS: Well, let her explain this to me: people who beat up other people, when they're in riotous mood after a banquet, where will

εὐωχηθέντες ὑβρίζουσιν; τοῦτο γὰρ οἶμαί σ' ἀπορήσειν.
Πρ. ἀπὸ τῆς μάζης ἧς σιτεῖται· ταύτης γὰρ ὅταν τις ἀφαιρῇ,
οὐχ ὑβριεῖται φαύλως οὕτως αὖθις τῇ γαστρὶ κολασθείς.
Βλ. οὐδ' αὖ κλέπτης οὐδεὶς ἔσται;
Πρ. πῶς γὰρ κλέψει, μετὸν αὐτῷ;
Βλ. οὐδ' ἀποδύσουσ' ἄρα τῶν νυκτῶν;
Γε. οὔκ, ἢν οἴκοι γε καθεύδῃς.
Πρ. οὐδ' ἤν γε θύραζ', ὥσπερ πρότερον· βίοτος γὰρ πᾶσιν ὑπάρξει.
ἢν δ' ἀποδύῃ γ', αὐτὸς δώσει· τί γὰρ αὐτῷ πρᾶγμα μάχεσθαι;
ἕτερον γὰρ ἰὼν ἐκ τοῦ κοινοῦ κρεῖττον ἐκείνου κομιεῖται.
Βλ. οὐδὲ κυβεύσουσ' ἆρ' ἅνθρωποι;
Πρ. περὶ τοῦ γὰρ τοῦτο ποιήσει;
Βλ. τὴν δὲ δίαιταν τίνα ποιήσεις;
Πρ. κοινὴν πᾶσιν. τὸ γὰρ ἄστυ
μίαν οἴκησίν φημι ποιήσειν συρρήξασ' εἰς ἓν ἅπαντα,
ὥστε βαδίζειν εἰς ἀλλήλων.
Βλ. τὸ δὲ δεῖπνον ποῦ παραθήσεις;
Πρ. τὰ δικαστήρια καὶ τὰς στοιὰς ἀνδρῶνας πάντα ποιήσω.
Βλ. τὸ δὲ βῆμα τί σοι χρήσιμον ἔσται;
Πρ. τοὺς κρατῆρας καταθεῖναι
καὶ τὰς ὑδρίας· καὶ ῥαψῳδεῖν ἔσται τοῖς παιδαρίοισιν
τοὺς ἀνδρείους ἐν τῷ πολέμῳ, κεἴ τις δειλὸς γεγένηται,
ἵνα μὴ δειπνῶσ' αἰσχυνόμενοι.
Γε. νὴ τὸν 'Απόλλω, χαριέν γε.
Βλ. τὰ δὲ κληρωτήρια ποῖ τρέψεις;
Πρ. εἰς τὴν ἀγορὰν καταθήσω,
κᾆτα στήσασα παρ' 'Αρμοδίῳ κληρώσω πάντας, ἕως ἂν
εἰδὼς ὁ λαχὼν ἀπίῃ χαίρων ἐν ὁποίῳ γράμματι δειπνεῖ·
καὶ κηρύξει τοὺς ἐκ τοῦ βῆτ' ἐπὶ τὴν ὀτοιὰν ἀκολουθεῖν
τὴν βασίλειον δειπνήσοντας, τὸ δὲ θῆτ' εἰς τὴν παρὰ ταύτην,
τοὺς δ' ἐκ τοῦ κάππ' εἰς τὴν στοιὰν ἐλθεῖν τὴν ἀλφιτόπωλιν.

665 ταύτης R: ταύτην ΓΛ.
667 κλέψει Brunck: κλέψαι codd. Suda.
675 εἰς ἀλλήλων Dindorf: εἰς ἀλλήλους R: ὡς ἀλλήλους ΓΛ.
677 καταθεῖναι van Herwerden: καταθήσω codd. Suda.

they get money to pay the damages for their assault? I fancy you'll be baffled by that one!

PRAXAGORA: He'll pay out of the barley-cake that forms his food ration. When he's deprived of part of that, he won't commit outrages so lightly in future, after being punished via the stomach!

BLEPYRUS: And won't there be any thieves, either?

PRAXAGORA: How can anyone steal anything, when he's already part-owner of it?

BLEPYRUS: So they also won't strip off people's clothes at night?

NEIGHBOUR: Not if you sleep at home!

PRAXAGORA: Not even if you go out, like you used to; because everyone will have the means of living anyway. And if someone does try to strip someone, he'll surrender the cloak voluntarily. What good will it do him to fight for it? He can go and get another one from the communal stores, better than the first.

BLEPYRUS: So people won't, either, gamble at dice?

PRAXAGORA: No, because what will they use for stakes?

BLEPYRUS: And what kind of lifestyle are you going to create?

PRAXAGORA: A life of universal communality. I declare that I mean to convert the whole town into one residence, breaking through all the walls of the buildings and merging them into one, so that everyone can walk into everyone else's house.

BLEPYRUS: And where will you serve dinner?

PRAXAGORA I'll make all the lawcourts and colonnades into dining-rooms.

BLEPYRUS: And what use will you have for the speaker's platform?

PRAXAGORA: To put the mixing-bowls and water-jars down on. And the young boys will be able to recite poetry in honour of those who have been brave in war, and also about anyone who's shown himself a coward, so they'll be so ashamed they'll stay away from dinner.

NEIGHBOUR: Nice idea, by Apollo!

BLEPYRUS: And what will you do with the allotment machines?

PRAXAGORA: I'll put them in the Agora, and then stand them by the statue of Harmodius and put everyone into the lottery, until they're drawn and know what letter they'll be dining under and go away delighted; and the herald will proclaim that those under Beta should follow her to the Basileios Colonnade to dine, the Thetas to the one next to it, and that those under Eta should go to the Cornmarket Colonnade.

Βλ. ἵνα κάπτωσιν;
Πρ. μὰ Δί', ἀλλ' ἵν' ἐκεῖ δειπνῶσιν.
Βλ. ὅτῳ δὲ τὸ γράμμα
μὴ 'ξελκυσθῇ καθ' ὃ δειπνήσει, τούτους ἀπελῶσιν ἅπαντες;
Πρ. ἀλλ' οὐκ ἔσται τοῦτο παρ' ἡμῖν.
πᾶσι γὰρ ἄφθονα πάντα παρέξομεν,
ὥστε μεθυσθεὶς αὐτῷ στεφάνῳ
πᾶς τις ἄπεισιν τὴν δᾷδα λαβών.
αἱ δὲ γυναῖκες κατὰ τὰς διόδους
προσπίπτουσαι τοῖς ἀπὸ δείπνου
τάδε λέξουσιν· "δεῦρο παρ' ἡμᾶς·
ἐνθάδε μεῖράξ ἐσθ' ὡραία."
"παρ' ἐμοὶ δ' ἑτέρα",
φήσει τις ἄνωθ' ἐξ ὑπερῴου,
"καὶ καλλίστη καὶ λευκοτάτη·
πρότερον μέντοι δεῖ σε καθεύδειν
αὐτῆς παρ' ἐμοί."
τοῖς εὐπρεπέσιν δ' ἀκολουθοῦντες
καὶ μειρακίοις οἱ φαυλότεροι
τοιάδ' ἐροῦσιν· "ποῖ θεῖς, οὗτος;
πάντως οὐδὲν δράσεις ἐλθών·
τοῖς γὰρ σιμοῖς καὶ τοῖς αἰσχροῖς
ἐψήφισται προτέροις βινεῖν,
ὑμᾶς δὲ τέως θρῖα λαβόντας
διφόρου συκῆς
ἐν τοῖς προθύροισι δέφεσθαι."

φέρε νυν φράσον μοι, ταῦτ' ἀρέσκει σφῷν;
Βλ. καὶ Γε. πάνυ.
Πρ. βαδιστέον τἄρ' ἐστὶν εἰς ἀγορὰν ἐμοί,
ἵν' ἀποδέχωμαι τὰ προσιόντα χρήματα,
λαβοῦσα κηρύκαιναν εὔφωνόν τινα.
ἐμὲ γὰρ ἀνάγκη ταῦτα δρᾶν ᾑρημένην
ἄρχειν, καταστῆσαί τε τὰ ξυσσίτια,
ὅπως ἂν εὐωχῆσθε πρῶτον τήμερον.
Βλ. ἤδη γὰρ εὐωχησόμεσθα;

688 ἅπαντες codd. Suda: ἅπαντας Ald.
701 εὐπρεπέσιν δ' Bentley: δ' εὐπρεπέσιν codd.
710 φράσον codd.: φράσατον Reisig.

BLEPYRUS: To eta up the corn?

PRAXAGORA: Of course not! To dine there.

BLEPYRUS: And anyone who doesn't get his letter drawn to give him a dinner, everybody will force them to leavè?

PRAXAGORA: No, that won't happen with us. We're going to provide everything in abundance for all, so that everyone will go away drunk, garland on head and torch in hand. And in the alleyways the women will waylay the men coming from dinner and say this to them: "Come here to our place; there's a lovely girl in here". "And I've got another," will say a woman from an upstairs flat above, "really beautiful *and* really white-skinned! *But* you'll have to sleep with me before her." Meanwhile the less good-looking men will be following close behind the young and handsome ones, and saying something like this: "Where are you off to so fast, you? You won't achieve anything, anyway, if you do go in. It's been decreed that the snub-nosed and the ugly are to fuck first, while you lot stay outside the door, take hold of the leaves of your double-fruited fig-tree, and *wank!*" – Come on then, tell me, do you two approve of all this?

BLEPYRUS *and* NEIGHBOUR: Very much!

PRAXAGORA: Then look, I've got to go to the Agora, to receive the incoming goods, after getting myself a heraldess with a strong voice. Having been elected to office, it's essential for me to do this and to set up the communal dining arrangements, so that you can have your first feast today.

BLEPYRUS: We're going to feast, so soon?

Πρ. φήμ' ἐγώ.
ἔπειτα τὰς πόρνας καταπαῦσαι βούλομαι
ἁπαξαπάσας.
Βλ. ἵνα τί;
Γε. δῆλον τουτογί·
ἵνα τῶν νέων ἔχωσιν αὗται τὰς ἀκμάς.
καὶ τάς γε δούλας οὐχὶ δεῖ κοσμουμένας
τὴν τῶν ἐλευθέρων ὑφαρπάζειν Κύπριν,
ἀλλὰ παρὰ τοῖς δούλοισι κοιμᾶσθαι μόνον,
κατωνάκην τὸν χοῖρον ἀποτετιλμένας.
Βλ. φέρε νυν ἐγώ σοι παρακολουθῶ πλησίον,
ἵν' ἀποβλέπωμαι καὶ ταδὶ λέγωσί με·
"τὸν τῆς στρατηγοῦ τοῦτον οὐ θαυμάζετε;"
Γε. ἐγὼ δ', ἵν' εἰς ἀγοράν γε τὰ σκεύη φέρω,
προχειριοῦμαι κἀξετάσω τὴν οὐσίαν.

ΧΟΡΟΥ

Γε. χώρει σὺ δεῦρο, κιναχύρα, καλὴ καλῶς
τῶν χρημάτων θύραζε πρώτη τῶν ἐμῶν,
ὅπως ἂν ἐντετριμμένη κανηφορῇς,
πολλοὺς κάτω δὴ θυλάκους στρέψασ' ἐμούς.
ποῦ 'σθ' ἡ διφροφόρος; ἡ χύτρα, δεῦρ' ἔξιθι.
νὴ Δία, μέλαινά γ' †οὐδ' ἂν εἰ† τὸ φάρμακον
ἕψουσ' ἔτυχες, ᾧ Λυσικράτης μελαίνεται.
ἵστω παρ' αὐτήν. δεῦρ' ἴθ', ἡ κομμώτρια.
φέρε δεῦρο ταύτην τὴν ὑδρίαν, ὑδριαφόρε.
ἐνταῦθα. σὺ δὲ δεῦρ', ἡ κιθαρῳδός, ἔξιθι,
πολλάκις ἀναστήσασά μ' εἰς ἐκκλησίαν
ἀωρὶ νύκτωρ διὰ τὸν ὄρθριον νόμον.
ὁ τὴν σκάφην λαβὼν προΐτω· τὰ κηρία
κόμιζε· τοὺς θαλλοὺς καθίστη πλησίον,
καὶ τὼ τρίποδ' ἐξένεγκε καὶ τὴν λήκυθον.

719 τουτογί Bentley: τουτοτί RΛ: τοῦτο τί Γ.
724 κατωνάκην Tyrwhitt: κατωνάκη or -ῃ codd. Suda.
726 ταδὶ λέγωσί με Blaydes: λέγωσί με ταδί Λ: λέγωσί μοι ταδί RΓ.
after 729 χοροῦ R: om. ΓΛ.
735 †οὐδ' ἂν εἰ† RΓ Suda: οὐδ' ἂν εἰς Λ: οἶ' ἂν εἰ Meineke: ὡς ἂν εἰ Halbertsma: perh. e.g. {οὐδ' ἂν} εἶ ‹σύ· μῶν› (... μελαίνεται;).

PRAXAGORA: That's what I'm saying. Then I want to put all the prostitutes out of business.

BLEPYRUS: Why?

NEIGHBOUR: That's pretty obvious: so that these ones here [*indicating the Chorus*] can have the p(r)ick of the young men.

PRAXAGORA: And, what's more, slave-girls aren't to doll themselves up and rob the free women of their love-rights; they are to sleep only with slaves, and have their pussies plucked in the shaggy smock style.

BLEPYRUS [*as Praxagora turns to leave for the Agora*]: Right then, let me follow close behind you, so that eyes will turn to me and people will say this of me: "Don't you admire the General's husband there?" [*He goes out, left, following Praxagora.*]

NEIGHBOUR: And I'm going to prepare and inspect my property, ready to take my stuff in to the Agora. [*He goes into his house.*]

[*The Chorus sing a short song, whose words have not survived.*]

[*The Neighbour comes out of his house carrying a flour-sieve; subsequently, as indicated below, other utensils are brought out at his instructions by his two slaves, Sicon and Parmenon (each of whom, immediately he has handed over an item or items, goes back in to fetch more), and arranged in line as if to form a procession.*]

NEIGHBOUR: Come prettily out here, my pretty bran-sifter, first of my worldly goods, so that you can serve as basket-bearer like the well-powdered girl you are, after having emptied so many of my meal-bags! [*Calling into the house*] Where's the stool-bearer? Cooking-pot, come out here! [*Sicon brings out a pot; his master inspects it.*] By Zeus, you're black – as black as if it was you that boiled the dye that Lysicrates blackens his hair with! Stand beside her. [*He places the pot next to the sieve, and calls into the house again.*] Come here, maid-in-waiting. [*Parmenon brings out a ladle and a water-jar; his master takes the ladle and places it next to the pot.*] Jar-bearer, bring that jar here [*taking the jar from Parmenon*]. There [*setting it down*]. [*Calling*] You come out here, musician! [*Sicon brings out a hand-mill.*] How often you've roused me in the dark, at an unearthly hour, to go to the Assembly, with your song of dawning! [*The two slaves respond alternately to the following orders, with whose rapid succession they have some difficulty keeping up.*] Come forward, the man with the tray. – Bring the honeycombs. [*The honeycombs, when brought, are put on the tray, which is placed between the ladle and the jar.*] – Set the olive-branches next to them, and bring out the two tripods [*three-legged tables*] and the

τὰ χυτρίδι᾽ ἤδη καὶ τὸν ὄχλον ἀφίετε.

ΑΝΗΡ

ἐγὼ καταθήσω τἀμά; κακοδαίμων ἄρα
ἀνὴρ ἔσομαι καὶ νοῦν ὀλίγον κεκτημένος.
μὰ τὸν Ποσειδῶ οὐδέποτέ γ᾽, ἀλλὰ βασανιῶ
πρώτιστον αὐτὰ πολλάκις καὶ σκέψομαι.
οὐ γὰρ τὸν ἐμὸν ἱδρῶτα καὶ φειδωλίαν
οὐδὲν πρὸς ἔπος οὕτως ἀνοήτως ἐκβαλῶ,
πρὶν ἐκπύθωμαι πᾶν τὸ πρᾶγμ᾽ ὅπως ἔχει.
οὗτος, τί τὰ σκευάρια ταυτὶ βούλεται;
πότερον μετοικιζόμενος ἐξενήνοχας
αὔτ᾽, ἢ φέρεις ἐνέχυρα θήσων;

Γε. οὐδαμῶς.
Αν. τί δῆτ᾽ ἐπὶ στοίχου ᾽στὶν οὕτως; οὔ τι μὴν
Ἱέρωνι τῷ κήρυκι πομπὴν πέμπετε;
Γε. μὰ Δί᾽, ἀλλ᾽ ἀποφέρειν αὐτὰ μέλλω τῇ πόλει
εἰς τὴν ἀγορὰν κατὰ τοὺς δεδογμένους νόμους.
Αν. μέλλεις ἀποφέρειν;
Γε. πάνυ γε.
Αν. κακοδαίμων ἄρ᾽ εἶ,
νὴ τὸν Δία τὸν σωτῆρα.
Γε. πῶς;
Αν. πῶς; ῥᾳδίως.—
Γε. τί δ᾽; οὐχὶ πειθαρχεῖν με τοῖς νόμοισι δεῖ;
Αν. ποίοισιν, ὦ δύστηνε;
Γε. τοῖς δεδογμένοις.
Αν. δεδογμένοισιν; ὡς ἀνόητος ἦσθ᾽ ἄρα.
Γε. ἀνόητος;
Αν. οὐ γάρ; ἠλιθιώτατος μὲν οὖν
ἁπαξαπάντων.
Γε. ὅτι τὸ ταττόμενον ποιῶ;
Αν. τὸ ταττόμενον γὰρ δεῖ ποιεῖν τὸν σώφρονα;
Γε. μάλιστα πάντων.
Αν. τὸν μὲν οὖν ἀβέλτερον.

748 οὐδέποτέ γ᾽ Porson: γ᾽ οὐδέποτ᾽ codd.
756 οὔ τι μὴν Ussher: cf. Pl. *Laws* 906e: οὔ τι μὴ codd., Priscian 18.258: οὔ τί που Dobree.
758 ἀλλ᾽ ἀποφέρειν B: ἀλλὰ φέρειν RΓΛ.
762 με RΛ: om. Γ: γε B.

oil-flask. [*To both slaves, as they go inside together*] Now you can let the crowd of little pots start moving.

[*While Sicon and Parmenon are bringing out further items, and they and their master are arranging them at the rear of the "procession", another man (hereafter referred to as the Dissident) enters, right. He is talking to himself, and does not at first notice the others.*]

DISSIDENT: Me surrender my goods? Then I'll really be an absolute loser and have very little sense. Never, by Poseidon, not till I've first tested and examined the matter many times. I'm not going to chuck away, so stupidly and pointlessly, the fruits of my sweat and my thrift, until I've thoroughly ascertained the lie of the whole situation. [*Seeing the Neighbour, his slaves and his goods*] Hey, you, what's the meaning of all this gear? Have you brought it out because you're moving house, or are you taking it to pawn?

NEIGHBOUR: Certainly not.

DISSIDENT [*half to himself*]: Why is it all in single file like this? [*To the Neighbour*] You're not, are you, preparing a display for Hieron the auctioneer?

NEIGHBOUR: Not at all; I'm about to take them to the Agora to give to the state, as required under the laws that have been passed.

DISSIDENT [*incredulously*]: You mean to take them in?

NEIGHBOUR: Just so.

DISSIDENT: Then you *are* a loser, by Zeus the Saviour!

NEIGHBOUR: Why?

DISSIDENT: Why? That's easy to see—

NEIGHBOUR: What, oughtn't I to obey the laws?

DISSIDENT: What laws, you wretched fool?

NEIGHBOUR: The laws that have been passed.

DISSIDENT: Been passed? How stupid you seem to be!

NEIGHBOUR: Stupid?

DISSIDENT: Aren't you? Or rather, the biggest imbecile in the whole world!

NEIGHBOUR: Because I do what I'm instructed to do?

DISSIDENT: What, you think a sound-headed man ought to do what he's told?

NEIGHBOUR: Absolutely.

DISSIDENT: You mean a *moron* should!

Γε. σὺ δ' οὐ καταθεῖναι διανοεῖ;
Αν. φυλάξομαι,
πρὶν ἄν γ' ἴδω τὸ πλῆθος ὅ τι βουλεύεται.
Γε. τί γὰρ ἄλλο γ' ἢ φέρειν παρεσκευασμένοι
τὰ χρήματ' εἰσίν;
Αν. ἀλλ' ἰδὼν ἐπειθόμην.
Γε. λέγουσι γοῦν ἐν ταῖς ὁδοῖς.
Αν. λέξουσι γάρ.
Γε. καί φασιν οἴσειν ἀράμενοι.
Αν. φήσουσι γάρ.
Γε. ἀπολεῖς ἀπιστῶν πάντ'.
Αν. ἀπιστήσουσι γάρ.
Γε. ὁ Ζεὺς σέ γ' ἐπιτρίψειεν.
Αν. ἐπιτρίψουσι γάρ.
οἴσειν δοκεῖς τιν' ὅστις αὐτῶν νοῦν εχει;
οὐ γὰρ πάτριον τοῦτ' ἐστίν.
Γε. ἀλλὰ λαμβάνειν
ἡμὰς μόνον δεῖ;
Αν. νὴ Δία· καὶ γὰρ οἱ θεοί.
γνώσει δ' ἀπὸ τῶν χειρῶν γε τῶν ἀγαλμάτων·
ὅταν γὰρ εὐχώμεσθα διδόναι τἀγαθά,
ἕστηκεν ἐκτείνοντα τὴν χεῖρ' ὑπτίαν,
οὐχ ὡς τι δώσοντ' ἀλλ' ὅπως τι λήψεται.
Γε. ὦ δαιμόνι' ἀνδρῶν, ἔα με τῶν προὔργου τι δρᾶν.
ταυτὶ γάρ ἐστι συνδετέα. ποῦ μοὔσθ' ἱμάς;
Αν. ὄντως γὰρ οἴσεις;
Γε. ναὶ μὰ Δία· καὶ δὴ μὲν οὖν
τωδὶ ξυνάπτω τὼ τρίποδε.
Αν. τῆς μωρίας·
τὸ μηδὲ περιμείναντα τοὺς ἄλλους ὅ τι
δράσουσιν, εἶτα τηνικαῦτ' ἤδη–
Γε. τί δρᾶν;
Αν. ἐπαναμένειν, ἔπειτα διατρίβειν ἔτι.
Γε. ἵνα δὴ τί;
Αν. σεισμὸς εἰ γένοιτο πολλάκις,
ἢ πῦρ ἀπότροπον, ἢ διᾴξειεν γαλῆ,
παύσαιντ' ἂν εἰσφέροντες, ὦμβρόντητε σύ.

773 λέξουσι Ald.: λέγουσι codd.
780 γε Reiske: τε codd.

NEIGHBOUR: And you mean not to surrender yours?

DISSIDENT: I'll wait and watch until such time as I see how most people are deciding.

NEIGHBOUR: Why, they're ready to take in their property, of course.

DISSIDENT: I'll believe that when I see it.

NEIGHBOUR: Well, they are talking about it in the streets—

DISSIDENT [*mockingly*]: Oh, yes, they'll talk!

NEIGHBOUR: —and saying they're going to take their stuff and deliver it in.

DISSIDENT: Oh, yes, they'll say so!

NEIGHBOUR: You'll be the death of me, being sceptical about everything like this!

DISSIDENT: Oh, yes, they'll be sceptical!

NEIGHBOUR: Oh, Zeus blast you!

DISSIDENT: Oh, yes, they'll blast! Do you think any of them that's got any sense will hand it in? That's not our tradition.

NEIGHBOUR: You mean we must only take and not give?

DISSIDENT: Yes, by Zeus. That's what the gods do. You can tell by the hands of their statues. When we pray to them to give us blessings, they stand holding out their hands palm upwards, not in the way of someone who's going to give, but looking to *get* something.

NEIGHBOUR: My good man, let me get on with what I've got to do. These things have to be tied up. Where can I find a strap?

[*One of the slaves points to a leather strap which he has brought out earlier, and the Neighbour begins to tie the tables together with it, while the slaves begin to pack the other goods into sacks.*]

DISSIDENT: You're really going to take them in?

NEIGHBOUR: Yes, indeed – or rather, I *am* tying together these two tables at this moment!

DISSIDENT: What stupidity! Not even to wait and see what other people are going to do, and *then* at *that* stage—

NEIGHBOUR: To do what?

DISSIDENT: To hang on, and then to hang on a bit longer.

NEIGHBOUR: For what purpose?

DISSIDENT: Oh, if by any chance there was an earthquake, or a bolt of lightning, or if a ferret ran across the street, they'd stop bringing their stuff in, you moonstruck idiot.

Γε. χαρίεντα γοῦν πάθοιμ' ἄν, εἰ μὴ 'χοιμ' ὅποι
ταῦτα καταθείην.
Αν. μὴ γὰρ οὐ λάβῃς ὅποι;
θάρρει, καταθήσεις, κἂν ἔνης ἔλθῃς.
Γε. τιή;
Αν. ἐγᾦδα τούτους χειροτονοῦντας μὲν ταχύ,
ἅττ' ἂν δὲ δόξῃ, ταῦτα πάλιν ἀρνουμένους.
Γε. οἴσουσιν, ὦ τᾶν.
Αν. ἢν δὲ μὴ κομίσωσι, τί;
Γε. ἀμέλει, κομιοῦσιν.
Αν. ἢν δὲ μὴ κομίσωσι, τί;
Γε. μαχούμεθ' αὐτοῖς.
Αν. ἢν δὲ κρείττους ὦσι, τί;
Γε. ἄπειμ' ἐάσας.
Αν. ἢν δὲ πωλῶσ' αὐτά, τί;
Γε. διαρραγείης.
Αν. ἢν διαρραγῶ δέ, τί;
Γε. καλῶς ποιήσεις.
Αν. σὺ δ' ἐπιθυμεῖς εἰσφέρειν;
Γε. ἔγωγε· καὶ γὰρ τοὺς ἐμαυτοῦ γείτονας
ὁρῶ φέροντας.
Αν. πάνυ γ' ἂν οὖν 'Αντισθένης
αὔτ' εἰσενέγκοι· πολὺ γὰρ ἐμμελέστερον
πρότερον χέσαι πλεῖν ἢ τριάκονθ' ἡμέρας.
Γε. οἴμωζε.
Αν. Καλλίμαχος δ' ὁ χοροδιδάσκαλος
αὐτοῖσιν εἰσοίσει τι;
Γε. πλείω Καλλίου.
Αν. ἄνθρωπος οὗτος ἀποβαλεῖ τὴν οὐσίαν.
Γε. δεινόν γε λέγεις.
Αν. τί δεινόν; ὥσπερ οὐχ ὁρῶν
ἀεὶ τοιαῦτα γιγνόμενα ψηφίσματα.
οὐκ οἶσθ' ἐκεῖν' οὔδοξε, τὸ περὶ τῶν ἁλῶν;
Γε. ἔγωγε.

794 μὴ 'χοιμ' (μὴ'χοιμ') Λ: μήχοιμ' R: μήχ' οἴμ' Γ.
795 καταθείην Brunck: καταθείμην codd.
795 λάβῃς Heindorf: λάβοις codd.
804 ἐπιθυμεῖς εἰσφέρειν Agar: ἐπιθυμήσεις φέρειν codd.
812 δεινόν Reisig: δεινά codd.

NEIGHBOUR: Nice thing it would be for me, if I came and found no space left to deposit this stuff.

DISSIDENT: Afraid you won't find space for it, is that it? Don't worry, you'll be able to deposit it, even if you come the day after tomorrow.

NEIGHBOUR: How do you make that out?

DISSIDENT: I know these people. They vote in haste, and then turn round and renege on what they've decided.

NEIGHBOUR: They'll bring theirs in, man.

DISSIDENT: And what if they don't?

NEIGHBOUR: Don't worry, they will.

DISSIDENT [*doggedly*]: And what if they don't?

NEIGHBOUR: We'll fight them.

DISSIDENT: And what if they're too strong for you?

NEIGHBOUR: I'll go away and leave them be.

DISSIDENT: And what if they sell your stuff?

NEIGHBOUR: Oh, blast you to pieces!

DISSIDENT [*in the same tone as before*]: And what if I do blast to pieces?

NEIGHBOUR: I'll be very much obliged!

DISSIDENT: And you really want to take your stuff in?

NEIGHBOUR: Yes, I do. I see that my neighbours are taking theirs.

DISSIDENT [*with heavy sarcasm*]: Oh, I'm sure Antisthenes will take in his, for one! He'd find it much more agreeable to shit for a month or more, sooner than do that!

NEIGHBOUR: Oh, to hell with you!

DISSIDENT [*unruffled*]: And Callimachus, the chorus-trainer, is he going to bring anything in to them?

NEIGHBOUR: More than Callias!

DISSIDENT: This man wants to throw away his property!

NEIGHBOUR: That's an absurd thing to say.

DISSIDENT: What's absurd about it? As if you couldn't see that decrees like this get made all the time. Don't you remember that one that got passed, the one about salt?

NEIGHBOUR: I do.

Αν. τοὺς χαλκοῦς δ' ἐκείνους ἡνίκα
ἐψηφισάμεθ', οὐκ οἶσθα;
Γε. καὶ κακόν γέ μοι
τὸ κόμμ' ἐγένετ' ἐκεῖνο. πωλῶν γὰρ βότρυς
μεστὴν ἀπῆρα τὴν γνάθον χαλκῶν ἔχων,
κἄπειτ' ἐχώρουν εἰς ἀγορὰν ἐπ' ἄλφιτα·
ἔπειθ', ὑπέχοντος ἄρτι μου τὸν θύλακον,
ἀνέκραγ' ὁ κῆρυξ· "μὴ δέχεσθαι μηδένα
χαλκὸν τὸ λοιπόν· ἀργύρῳ γὰρ χρώμεθα."
Αν. τὸ δ' ἔναγχος οὐχ ἅπαντες ἡμεῖς ὤμνυμεν
τάλαντ' ἔσεσθαι πεντακόσια τῇ πόλει
τῆς τετταρακοστῆς, ἣν ἐπόρισ' Εὐριππίδης;
κεὐθὺς κατεχρύσου πᾶς ἀνὴρ Εὐριππίδην.
ὅτε δὴ δ' ἀνασκοπουμένοις ἐφαίνετο
ὁ Διὸς Κόρινθος καὶ τὸ πρᾶγμ' οὐκ ἤρκεσεν,
πάλιν κατεπίττου πᾶς ἀνὴρ Εὐριππίδην.
Γε. οὐ ταὐτόν, ὦ τᾶν. τότε μὲν ἡμεῖς ἤρχομεν,
νῦν δ' αἱ γυναῖκες.
Αν. ἅς γ' ἐγὼ φυλάξομαι,
νὴ τὸν Ποσειδῶ, μὴ κατουρήσωσί μου.
Γε. οὐκ οἶδ' ὅ τι ληρεῖς. φέρε σὺ τἀνάφορον, ὁ παῖς.
ΚΗΡΥΚΑΙΝΑ
ὦ πάντες ἀστοί, νῦν γὰρ οὕτω ταῦτ' ἔχει,
χωρεῖτ', ἐπείγεσθ' εὐθὺ τῆς στρατηγίδος,
ὅπως ἂν ὑμῖν ἡ τύχη κληρουμένοις
φράσῃ καθ' ἕκαστον ἄνδρ' ὅποι δειπνήσετε·
ὡς αἱ τράπεζαί γ' εἰσὶν ἐπινενημέναι
ἀγαθῶν ἁπάντων καὶ παρεσκευασμέναι,
κλῖναί τε σισυρῶν καὶ δαπίδων νενασμέναι.
κρατῆρας ἐγκιρνᾶσιν, αἱ μυροπώλιδες

822 χαλκὸν Pollux 9.93: χαλκοῦν codd. Suda.
825 τεττααρα- Brunck: τεσσαρα- ΓΛ: τεσσερα- R.
825, 826, 829 Εὐριππίδ- Bergk: Εὐριπίδ- codd.
826 κεὐθὺς Küster: καὐθὺς codd.
831 ἅς γ' ΓΛ: ἃς R.
832 κατουρήσωσί B: κατουρήσουσί RΓΛ.
836 ὑμῖν Biset: ἡμῖν codd.
837 ὅποι RΓΛ: ὅπου B.
838 ἐπινενημέναι Dindorf, cf. Phrynichus *PS* 21.6: ἐπινενασμέναι codd. Suda.
841 κρατῆρας ἐγκ- Dawes: κρατῆρα (κρατῖνα ΓΛ) συγκ- codd.

DISSIDENT: And when we voted for that copper coinage, don't you remember that?

NEIGHBOUR: Yes, and that coinage did me a bad turn. I'd been selling grapes, and I started out with a full cargo of coppers in my mouth, and then made for the Agora to buy barley meal; then, just as I was holding my bag open for it to be poured in, the herald cried out "No one to accept copper any longer! Our currency is silver!"

DISSIDENT: And just recently, didn't we all swear that the City was going to get five hundred talents from the two-and-a-half-per-cent tax that Heurippides had devised – and straight away everyone was covering Heurippides with gold? Then, when they examined it closely and it turned out to be the same old story and the thing failed to yield enough, everyone turned round and started covering Heurippides with pitch!

NEIGHBOUR: It's not the same thing, man. At that time *we* were in charge; now it's the women.

DISSIDENT: The women? I'm going to watch out, by Poseidon, in case they piss over me!

NEIGHBOUR: I don't know what you're blethering about. [*To one of his slaves, who have now completed packing and securing his goods*]: Take up the pole, boy.

[*Before the slave can obey, a Heraldess enters, left, and makes the following proclamation.*]

HERALDESS: All you citizens! – because that's the way it is now. Go, hurry, straight to where the Lady General is, so that you can be entered in the lottery in which Fortune will tell you, man by man, where you can go to dine. Because the tables are prepared and heaped high with all kinds of good things, and the couches are piled with blankets and rugs. They're mixing the wine-bowls, the women perfume-sellers are standing

ἑστᾶσ' ἐφεξῆς, τὰ τεμάχη ῥιπίζεται,
λαγῷ' ἀναπηγνύασι, πόπανα πέττεται,
στέφανοι πλέκονται, φρύγεται τραγήματα,
χύτρας ἔτνους ἕψουσιν αἱ νεώταται·
Σμοῖος δ' ἐν αὐταῖς ἱππικὴν στολὴν ἔχων
τὰ τῶν γυναικῶν διακαθαίρει τρύβλια.
Γέρων δὲ χωρεῖ χλανίδα καὶ κονίποδας
ἔχων, καχάζων μεθ' ἑτέρου νεανίου·
ἐμβὰς δὲ κεῖται καὶ τρίβων ἐρριμμένος.
πρὸς ταῦτα χωρεῖθ', ὡς ὁ τὴν μᾶζαν φέρων
ἕστηκεν· ἀλλὰ τὰς γνάθους διοίγετε.
Αν. οὔκουν βαδιοῦμαι δῆτα; τί γὰρ ἕστηκ' ἔχων
ἐνταῦθ', ἐπειδὴ ταῦτα τῇ πόλει δοκεῖ;
Γε. καὶ ποῖ βαδιεῖ σὺ μὴ καταθεὶς τὴν οὐσίαν;
Αν. ἐπὶ δεῖπνον.
Γε. οὐ δῆτ', ἤν γ' ἐκείναις νοῦς ἐνῇ,
πρὶν ἄν γ' ἀπενέγκῃς.
Αν. ἀλλ' ἀποίσω.
Γε. πηνίκα;
Αν. οὐ τοὐμόν, ὦ τᾶν, ἐμποδὼν ἔσται.
Γε. τί δαί;
Αν. ἑτέρους ἀποίσειν φήμ' ἔθ' ὑστέρους ἐμοῦ.
Γε. βαδιεῖ δὲ δειπνήσων ὅμως;
Αν. τί γὰρ πάθω;
τὰ δυνατὰ γὰρ δεῖ τῇ πόλει ξυλλαμβάνειν
τοὺς εὖ φρονοῦντας.
Γε. ἢν δὲ κωλύσωσι, τί;
Αν. ὁμόσ' εἶμι κύψας.
Γε. ἢν δὲ μαστιγῶσι, τί;
Αν. καλούμεθ' αὐτάς.
Γε. ἢν δὲ καταγελῶσι, τί;
Αν. ἐπὶ ταῖς θύραις ἑστὼς—
Γε. τί δράσεις; εἰπέ μοι.
Αν. τῶν εἰσφερόντων ἁρπάσομαι τὰ σιτία.

848 Γέρων codd.: Γέρης Dindorf: perh. Ἱέρων.
848 κονίποδας Brunck: κονίποδα codd. $^{\gamma\rho}$Suda (γράφεται δὲ καὶ κ.): κονίποδε Dindorf.
852 διοίγετε $^{\gamma\rho}\Sigma^{R}$: διοίγνετε R^{ac}ΓΛ: διοίγνυτε R^{pc}.
857 πρὶν ἄν γ' Porson: πρίν γ' RΓΛ: πρίν γ' ἂν B.
858 δαί Blaydes: δή codd.

in a row, the slices of fish are being fanned on the fire, they're putting hare on the spit, cakelets are being baked, garlands plaited, sweetmeats roasted; the juniors are boiling pots of pea-soup, and Smoeus is among them, wearing a cavalry outfit, licking the women's bowls clean. Then Geron is striding out in light sandals and fine cloak, laughing heartily with another young man; rough shoe and old coat lie discarded. So come, because the boy with the barley-cake is standing ready: get your jaws open! [*The Heraldess goes out, right.*]

DISSIDENT: Well, I'm going to go then, aren't I? If that's what the City has decided, what's the point of my standing around here?

NEIGHBOUR: And *where* are you intending to go, if you haven't surrendered your property?

DISSIDENT: To dinner.

NEIGHBOUR: Not till you've brought your stuff in, not if those women have any sense.

DISSIDENT: Oh, I'll bring it in.

NEIGHBOUR: When?

DISSIDENT: It won't be *my* delay that holds them up, man.

NEIGHBOUR: Then what will it be?

DISSIDENT: I tell you there will be others who bring theirs in even later than me.

NEIGHBOUR: And you're going to go for dinner anyway?

DISSIDENT: What else am I supposed to do? It's the duty of all loyal citizens to aid the community to the best of their ability.

NEIGHBOUR: And what if they stop you?

DISSIDENT: I'll lower my head and charge them.

NEIGHBOUR: And what if they flog you?

DISSIDENT: We'll summon them to court.

NEIGHBOUR: And what if they laugh at that?

DISSIDENT: I'll stand by the door and—

NEIGHBOUR: And do what, tell me?

DISSIDENT: And snatch the food from the people bringing it in.

Γε. βάδιζε τοίνυν ὕστερος· σὺ δ', ὦ Σίκων
καὶ Παρμένων, αἴρεσθε τὴν παμπησίαν.
Αν. φέρε νυν ἐγώ σοι ξυμφέρω.
Γε. μή, μηδαμῶς.
δέδοικα γὰρ μὴ καὶ παρὰ τῇ στρατηγίδι,
ὅταν κατατιθῶ, προσποιῇ τῶν χρημάτων.
Αν. νὴ τὸν Δία δεῖ γοῦν μηχανήματός τινος,
ὅπως τὰ μὲν ὄντα χρήμαθ' ἕξω, τοῖσδέ τε
τῶν ματτομένων κοινῇ μεθέξω πως ἐγώ.
ὀρθῶς, ἔμοιγε φαίνεται· βαδιστέον
ὁμόσ' ἐστὶ δειπνήσοντα κοὐ μελλητέον.

ΧΟΡΟΥ

ΓΡΑΥΣ Α

τί ποθ' ἄνδρες οὐχ ἥκουσιν; ὥρα δ' ἦν πάλαι·
ἐγὼ δὲ καταπεπλασμένη ψιμυθίῳ
ἕστηκα καὶ κροκωτὸν ἠμφιεσμένη
ἀργός, μινυρομένη τι πρὸς ἐμαυτὴν μέλος,
παιζουσ' ὅπως ἂν περιλάβοιμ' αὐτῶν τινα
παριόντα. Μοῦσαι, δεῦρ' ἴτ' ἐπὶ τοὐμὸν στόμα,
μελύδριον εὑροῦσαί τι τῶν Ἰωνικῶν.

ΚΟΡΗ

νῦν μέν με παρακύψασα προὔφθης, ὦ σαπρά.
ᾤου δ' ἐρήμας, οὐ παρούσης ἐνθάδε
ἐμοῦ, τρυγήσειν καὶ προσάξεσθαί τινα
ᾄδουσ'· ἐγὼ δ', ἢν τοῦτο δρᾷς, ἀντᾴσομαι.
κεἰ γὰρ δι' ὄχλου τοῦτ' ἐστὶ τοῖς θεωμένοις,
ὅμως ἔχει τερπνόν τι καὶ κωμῳδικόν.
Γρ.α τούτῳ διαλέγου κἀποχώρησον· σὺ δέ,
φιλοττάριον αὐλητά, τοὺς αὐλοὺς λαβὼν
ἄξιον ἐμοῦ καὶ σοῦ προσαύλησον μέλος.

εἴ τις ἀγαθὸν βούλεται πα-
θεῖν τι, παρ' ἐμοὶ χρὴ καθεύδειν·

873 τοῖσδέ τε Elmsley: τοῖσδέ γε codd.: τοισδεδὶ Bergk.
after 876 χοροῦ R: om. ΓΛ.
877 ἥκουσιν Brunck: ἥξουσι(ν) codd.
887 δρᾷς, ἀντᾴσομαι Portus: δράσαντ' ᾄσομαι codd.

NEIGHBOUR: Then you can come *after* me. [*To his slaves*] You, Sicon, and you, Parmenon, take up my worldly goods.

DISSIDENT [*coming up to the slaves*]: Here, let me help you carry them.

NEIGHBOUR [*forcing him away*]: No, no way! I'm afraid in case when I've deposited them, you may claim before the Lady General that my goods are yours. [*He goes out, left, followed by the slaves carrying his effects.*]

DISSIDENT: I certainly need some scheme, by Zeus, to let me, on the one hand, keep the property I've got, and also somehow share with these people in the communal meal that's being prepared. [*After a moment's thought*] That's got it right, as far as I can see. I must get into the thick of things on the dinner front, without delay. [*He goes out, left.*]

[*The Chorus sing a song, whose words have not survived.*]

[*An old woman appears at the central door. She is heavily made-up and wears a yellow dress quite unsuited to her age. She peers hopefully off, left, towards the Agora.*]

FIRST OLD WOMAN: Why haven't the men come? They were due long ago. And I'm standing here, plastered with white-lead and wearing a saffron dress, doing nothing, just warbling a little tune to myself, disporting myself in the hope that I might snare one of them as he passes by. [*Praying*] Muses, come here to sit on my lips, and find me a nice little melody in the Ionian style.

[*Before she can begin to sing, a teenage girl appears at the upstairs window, right.*]

GIRL: Just for now you got in first, you rotting hulk, and poked your head out before me! You thought that I wasn't here, and that you could strip an unwatched vineyard and lure someone to you with a song. Well, if you do that, I'll sing in competition with you. Because even if the audience find that tiresome, it still has something pleasing and comedy-like about it.

FIRST OLD WOMAN [*bending over and presenting her posterior to the Girl*]: Talk to *that*, and be off with you! [*To the piper who has been accompanying the Chorus*] And you, piper sweetie, take your pipes and play a tune to show your quality – and mine.

[*Singing with pipe accompaniment*]
If anyone wants to have a good
time, he should sleep with *me*!

οὐ γὰρ ἐν νέαις τὸ σοφὸν ἔν-
  εστιν, ἀλλ' ἐν ταῖς πεπείροις.
οὐδέ τοι στέργειν ἂν ἐθέλοι μᾶλλον ἢ 'γὼ
  τὸν φίλον ᾧπερ ξυνείην,
ἀλλ' ἐφ' ἕτερον ἂν πέτοιτο—

Κο. μὴ φθόνει ταῖσιν νέαισι·
  τὸ τρυφερὸν γὰρ ἐμπέφυκε
  τοῖς ἁπαλοῖσι μηροῖς
κἀπὶ τοῖς μήλοις ἐπάν-
  θεῖ· σὺ δ', ὦ γραῦ, παραλέλεξαι κἀντέτριψαι
  τῷ Θανάτῳ μέλημα.

Γρ.[a] ἐκπέσοι σου τὸ τρῆμα
  τό τ' ἐπίκλιντρον ἀποβάλοις
  βουλομένη σποδεῖσθαι,
κἀπὶ τῆς κλίνης ὄφιν προσελκύσαιο
  βουλομένη φιλῆσαι.

Κο. αἰαῖ, τί ποτε πείσομαι;
οὐχ ἥκει μοὐταῖρος·
μόνη δ' αὐτοῦ λείπομ'· ἡ
  γάρ μοι μήτηρ ἄλλῃ—
καὶ τἄλλα μ' οὐδὲν τὰ μετὰ ταῦτα δεῖ λέγειν.
ἀλλ', ὦ μαῖ', ἱκετεύομαι,
  κάλει τὸν 'Ορθαγόραν,
  ὅπως ἂν σαυτῆς κατόναι',
  ἀντιβολῶ σε.

Γρ.[a] ἤδη τὸν ἀπ' Ἰωνίας
  τρόπον, τάλαινα, κνησιᾷς·
δοκεῖς δέ μοι καὶ λάβδα κατὰ τοὺς Λεσβίους.

896 πεπείροις vel sim. Λ Suda: πεπείραις R: ἐμπείροις Γ.
897 τοι ... ἂν RΓΛ Suda[Γ]: τι ... ἂν Suda[G]: τις ... ἂν B: perh. τἂν ... τις.
898 ᾧπερ codd.: περη. ᾧ (giving an aristophanean, cf. comm. on 893-910).
907 ἀποβάλοις codd. Suda: ἀποβάλλου Zonaras: ἀποβάλοιο Bothe.
909 ὄφιν προσελκύσαιο Wilamowitz: ὄφιν εὕροις καὶ προσελκύσαιο (-σαι Γ) codd.
912 μοὐταῖρος Reiske: μ' οὔτ' αἶρος R: μου τοῦρος ΓΛ.
913 ἄλλῃ Jackson: ἄλλῃ βέβηκε(ν) codd.
914 τἄλλα μ' οὐδὲν τὰ μετὰ Dobree: τἄλλ' οὐδὲν μετὰ RΓ: τἄλλ' οὐδέν με Λ.
917 ἂν σαυτῆς Wilamowitz: σαυτῆς codd.: σαυτῆς ἂν Hermann.
920 καὶ codd.: κἂν Blaydes.
920 λάβδα Λ: λάμβδα R: λαύδα Γ.

For expertise is not to be found
in the young, but in the mature.
And I tell you she couldn't be more ready than I am
to cherish my boyfriend;
no, she'd fly off to another—

GIRL [*interrupting*]:
Don't be jealous of the young;
for voluptuousness has its natural abode
in tender thighs
and blooms on firm breasts;
while *you*, old woman, are plucked and plastered
to be the darling of Death!

FIRST OLD WOMAN:
May your hole fall out
and may you lose your lie-upon
when you want a shag,
and may you, on your bed, draw a snake to your arms
when you want a kiss!

GIRL: "Ah me, what will become of me?
My boyfriend hasn't come,
and I'm left alone here,
because my mother's somewhere else—"
[*speaking*] and I've no need to add what comes after that!
[*Singing again*]
"Oh, nurse, I implore you—"
[*maliciously, to the Old Woman*]
invite the Hard Man round,
so that you can give yourself some pleasure,
[*passionately again*]
"I beg of you!"

FIRST OLD WOMAN:
Already, poor soul, you've got the itch
in the Ionian fashion,
[*speaking*] and it looks to me like you've got the big L as in Lesbos too!

Κο. ἀλλ' οὐκ ἄν ποθ' ὑφαρπάσαι-
ο τἀμὰ παίγνια· τὴν δ'
ἐμὴν ὥραν οὐκ ἀπολεῖς
οὐδ' ἀπολήψει.

Γρ.α ᾆδ' ὁπόσα βούλει καὶ παράκυφθ' ὥσπερ γαλῆ·
οὐδεὶς γὰρ ὡς σὲ πρότερον εἴσεισ' ἀντ' ἐμοῦ.
Κο. οὔκουν ἐπ' ἐκφοράν γε· καινόν γ', ὦ σαπρά.
Γρ.α οὐ δῆτα.
Κο. τί γὰρ ἂν γραῒ καινόν τις λέγοι;
Γρ.α οὐ τοὐμὸν ὀδυνήσει σε γῆρας.
Κο. ἀλλὰ τί;
ἤγχουσα μᾶλλον καὶ τὸ σὸν ψιμύθιον;
Γρ.α τί μοι διαλέγει;
Κο. σὺ δὲ τί διακύπτεις;
Γρ.α ἐγώ;
ᾄδω πρὸς ἐμαυτὴν Ἐπιγένει τὠμῷ φίλῳ.
Κο. σοὶ γὰρ φίλος τίς ἐστιν ἄλλος ἢ Γέρης;
Γρ.α δείξει γε καὶ σοί· τάχα γὰρ εἶσιν ὡς ἐμέ.
ὁδὶ γὰρ αὐτός ἐστιν.
Κο. οὐ σοῦ γ', ὤλεθρε,
δεόμενος οὐδέν.
Γρ.α νὴ Δί', ὦ φθίνυλλα σύ.
Κο. δείξει τάχ' αὐτός· ὡς ἔγωγ' ἀπέρχομαι.
Γρ.α κἄγωγ', ἵνα γνῷς ὡς πολὺ σοῦ μεῖζον φρονῶ.

ΕΠΙΓΕΝΗΣ
εἴθ' ἐξῆν παρὰ τῇ νέᾳ καθεύδειν
καὶ μὴ 'δει πρότερον διασποδῆσαι
ἀνάσιμον ἢ πρεσβυτέραν·
οὐ γὰρ ἀνασχετὸν τοῦτό γ' ἐλευθέρῳ.

Γρ.α οἰμώζων ἄρα νὴ Δία σποδήσεις·

921-2 ὑφαρπάσαιο codd.: ὑφαρπάσαις Scaliger: perh. ὑφαρπάσαις σὺ.
927 καινόν Blaydes: καινά codd.
933 δείξει Ald.: δόξει RΓ: δόξῃ Λ.
939 μὴ 'δει Elmsley: μηδὲν codd. Suda.
940 πρεσβυτέραν Bothe: πρεσβύτερον codd. Suda.

GIRL: But you'll never rob me
of my playmates, and
my youth you will not destroy
nor grab a share of!

FIRST OLD WOMAN: Sing as much as you like, and peep out there like a ferret if you want! Nobody's going to go into your place before mine!

GIRL: Not to take me to the grave, anyway! [*Laughing at her own joke*] Hey, that's a new one, you rotting hulk!

FIRST OLD WOMAN: No, it isn't.

GIRL [*mockingly correcting herself*]: No, what *could* anyone say that would be new to an old crone like you?

FIRST OLD WOMAN: It's not my *age* that's going to be a pain to you!

GIRL: Then what is? Are your rouge and your white-lead going to hurt me more?

FIRST OLD WOMAN: Why do you keep talking to me?

GIRL: And why do *you* keep peeping out like that?

FIRST OLD WOMAN: Me? I'm singing to myself a song to my boyfriend Epigenes.

GIRL: *You've* got a boyfriend – apart from Geres, that is?

FIRST OLD WOMAN [*looking off, left*]: He'll show you. He's going to come to me in a moment. Because here he is himself.

GIRL: But not wanting anything from *you*, you old ruin!

FIRST OLD WOMAN: Oh, yes, he does, Miss Anorexia.

GIRL: Well, he'll soon show us himself; because I'm going. [*She withdraws from the window.*]

FIRST OLD WOMAN: And so am I, so that you can see how much more confident I am than you. [*She goes inside.*]

[*The young man Epigenes enters, left, wearing a garland and carrying a torch.*]

EPIGENES [*singing*]:
If only I was allowed to sleep with the young one
and didn't first have to screw
an old woman or one with a turned-up nose!
That's intolerable for a free man.

FIRST OLD WOMAN [*reappearing at the door*]:
You'll howl if you do screw her, by Zeus!

οὐ γὰρ τἀπὶ Χαριξένης τάδ᾽ ἐστίν.
κατὰ τὸν νόμον ταῦτα ποιεῖν
ἐστι δίκαιον, εἰ δημοκρατούμεθα.

ἀλλ᾽ εἶμι τηρήσουσ᾽ ὅ τι καὶ δράσει ποτέ.
Επ. εἴθ᾽, ὦ θεοί, λάβοιμι τὴν καλὴν μόνην,
ἐφ᾽ ἣν πεπωκὼς ἔρχομαι πάλαι ποθῶν.
Κο. ἐξηπάτηκα τὸ κατάρατον γρᾴδιον·
φρούδη γάρ ἐστιν οἰομένη μ᾽ ἔνδον μενεῖν.
ἀλλ᾽ οὑτοσὶ γὰρ αὐτὸς οὗ ᾽μεμνήμεθα.

δεῦρο δή, δεῦρο δή, (στρ.
φίλον ἐμόν, δεῦρό μοι
πρόσελθε καὶ ξύνευνέ μοι
τὴν εὐφρόνην ὅπως ἔσει.
πάνυ γάρ ‹δεινός› τις ἔρως με δονεῖ
τῶνδε τῶν σῶν βοστρύχων·
ἄτοπος δ᾽ ἔγκειταί μοί τις πόθος,
ὅς με διακναίσας ἔχει.
μέθες, ἱκνοῦμαί σ᾽, Ἔρως,
καὶ ποίησον τόνδ᾽ ἐς εὐνὴν
τὴν ἐμὴν ἱκέσθαι.

Επ. δεῦρο δή, δεῦρο δή, (ἀντ.
φίλον ἐμόν, καὶ σύ μοι
καταδραμοῦσα τὴν θύραν
τήνδ᾽ ἄνοιξον· εἰ δὲ μή,
καταπεσὼν κείσομαι.
ἀλλ᾽ ἐν †τῷ σῷ βούλομαι† κόλπῳ
πληκτίζεσθαι μετὰ σῆς πυγῆς.
Κύπρι, τί μ᾽ ἐκμαίνεις ἐπὶ ταύτῃ;
μέθες, ἱκνοῦμαί σ᾽, Ἔρως,

946 δράσει Brunck: δράσοι Γ: δράσεις RΛ.
949 ἐξηπάτηκα Blaydes: ἐξηπάτησα codd.
953 ξύνευνέ μοι Bergk: ξύνευνός μοι codd.: ξύνευνος Bothe.
954 ‹δεινός› τις ἔρως Dindorf: τις ἔρως codd. Suda: τις ἔρως ‹δεινός› Coulon.
960 φίλον ἐμόν Wilamowitz: om. codd. (but cf. on 963).
961-2 τήνδ᾽ ἄνοιξον Newiger: ἄνοιξον τήνδ᾽ codd.: ἄνοιξον Blaydes.
963 ἀλλ᾽ Wilamowitz: φίλον ἀλλ᾽ codd.
963 †τῷ σῷ βούλομαι† codd.: σῷ βούλομ᾽ ἐγὼ Wilamowitz: perh. e.g. τῷ σῷ χρῄζω.
964 σῆς Bentley: τῆς σῆς codd.

It's not the days of Charixene now.
It's right and proper for these things to be done
according to the law, if we live in a democracy.

[*Aside*] Right, I'll go, and keep watch on what he finally does. [*She withdraws again.*]

EPIGENES [*now in front of the Girl's house*]: Ye gods, if only I could have just the pretty one! I've yearned for her so long, and now, with a few inside, I've come for her!

GIRL [*reappearing at her window and looking down*]: Good, I've conned that old hag, curse her! She's gone, thinking I was going to stay inside. [*Seeing Epigenes*] Ah, here's the very man we were talking about.

[*Singing to Epigenes*]

Come hither, O come hither,
my love, come hither
to me, and be sure to be
my bedfellow through the night:
I am awhirl with fierce passion
for those locks of yours!
An extraordinary longing assails me,
it has me racked to pieces!
Release me, Eros, I beseech you,
and make him come
to my bed!

EPIGENES:
Come hither, O come hither,
you too, my love, I pray,
run down and open
this door: if you do not,
I'll fall to the ground and lie here!
Ah, I want to lie in your bosom
and exchange bonks with your bum!
Ah, Cypris, why are you making me mad for her?
Release me, Eros, I beseech you,

καὶ ποίησον τήνδ' ἐς εὐνὴν
τὴν ἐμὴν ἱκέσθαι.

καὶ ταῦτα μέντοι μετρίως (στρ.
πρὸς τὴν ἐμὴν ἀνάγκην
εἰρημέν' ἐστίν. σὺ δέ μοι,
φίλτατον, ὦ ἱκετεύω,
ἄνοιξον, ἀσπάζου με·
διά τοι σὲ πόνους ἔχω.

ὦ χρυσοδαίδαλτον ἐμὸν (ἀντ.
μέλημα, Κύπριδος ἔρνος,
μέλιττα Μούσης, Χαρίτων
θρέμμα, Τρυφῆς πρόσωπον,
ἄνοιξον, ἀσπάζου με·
διά τοι σὲ πόνους ἔχω.

Γρ.[α] οὗτος, τί κόπτεις; μῶν ἐμὲ ζητεῖς;
Επ. πόθεν;
Γρ.[α] καὶ τὴν θύραν γ' ἤραττες.
Επ. ἀποθάνοιμ' ἄρα.
Γρ.[α] τοῦ δαὶ δεόμενος δᾷδ' ἔχων ἐλήλυθας;
Επ. 'Αναφλύστιον ζητῶν τιν' ἄνθρωπον.
Γρ.[α] τίνα;
Επ. οὐ τὸν Σεβῖνον, ὃν σὺ προσδοκᾷς ἴσως.
Γρ.[α] νὴ τὴν 'Αφροδίτην, ἤν τε βούλῃ γ' ἤν τε μή.
Επ. ἀλλ' οὐχὶ νυνὶ τὰς ὑπερεξηκοντέτεις
εἰσάγομεν, ἀλλ' εἰσαῦθις ἀναβεβλήμεθα·
τὰς ἐντὸς εἴκοσιν γὰρ ἐκδικάζομεν.
Γρ.[α] ἐπὶ τῆς πρότερον ἀρχῆς γε ταῦτ' ἦν, ὦ γλύκων·
νυνὶ δὲ πρῶτον εἰσάγειν ἡμᾶς δοκεῖ.
Επ. τῷ βουλομένῳ γε, κατὰ τὸν ἐν πεττοῖς νόμον.
Γρ.[α] ἀλλ' οὐδ' ἐδείπνεις κατὰ τὸν ἐν πεττοῖς νόμον.

969 μέντοι R: μέν μοι ΓΛ.
971 με B: τε RΓΛ.
980 Σεβῖνον Bentley: σὲ βινοῦνθ' R: σὲ βινουῶνθ' Λ: σὲ κινοῦνθ' Γ.
985 πρότερον Γ: προτέρας RΛ.
987 πεττοῖς B: πετοῖς Γ: Παιτοῖς RΛ $^{i}\Sigma^{R\Lambda}$.
988 οὐδ' ἐδείπνεις Bentley: οὐδὲ δειπνεῖς RΛ (ΓB omit this line).
988 πεττοῖς Brunck: Παιτοῖς RΛ.

and make her come
to my bed!

And all of that, compared
with my state of distress,
has been putting it mildly. But now,
my beloved, oh, I implore you,
open and welcome me:
it's for you, I tell you, that I suffer so.

You golden work of art,
my darling, scion of Cypris,
honeybee of the Muses, nursling
of the Graces, the very image of Delight,
open and welcome me;
it's for you, I tell you, that I suffer so.

[*He knocks hard on the Girl's door; but it is the Old Woman who comes out of <u>her</u> door and accosts him.*]

FIRST OLD WOMAN: Here, you, why are you knocking? Not looking for me, are you?

EPIGENES: No way!

FIRST OLD WOMAN: And you really bashed on my door, too!

EPIGENES: Strike me dead if I did!

FIRST OLD WOMAN [*pointing to his erect phallus*]: Well, what were you after, coming here with a ... torch?

EPIGENES: I was looking for a man from Wanksbury.

FIRST OLD WOMAN: Who?

EPIGENES: Well, not Shagathon, which is who you seem to be expecting.

FIRST OLD WOMAN [*grabbing hold of him*]: Yes, it is, by Aphrodite – whether you like it or whether you don't!

EPIGENES [*trying to free himself*]: But we're not entering cases over sixty for trial at present; we've postponed them to a later date. We're finishing dealing with those under twenty first.

FIRST OLD WOMAN: That was under the *previous* regime, sweetie. *Now* the ruling is that you must enter *us* first.

EPIGENES: "At the player's option", as the rules of backgammon say.

FIRST OLD WOMAN: But you didn't follow the rules of backgammon when it was a question of having dinner!

Επ. οὐκ οἶδ' ὅ τι λέγεις· τηνδεδί μοι κρουστέον.
Γρ.[α] ὅταν γε κρούσῃς τὴν ἐμὴν πρῶτον θύραν.
Επ. ἀλλ' οὐχὶ νυνὶ κρησέραν αἰτούμεθα.
Γρ.[α] οἶδ' ὅτι φιλοῦμαι· νῦν δὲ θαυμάζεις ὅτι
θύρασί μ' ηὗρες. ἀλλὰ πρόσαγε τὸ στόμα.
Επ. ἀλλ', ὦ μέλ', ὀρρωδῶ τὸν ἐραστήν σου.
Γρ.[α] τίνα;
Επ. τὸν τῶν γραφέων ἄριστον.
Γρ.[α] οὗτος δ' ἐστὶ τίς;
Επ. ὃς τοῖς νεκροῖσι ζωγραφεῖ τὰς ληκύθους.
ἀλλ' ἄπιθ', ὅπως μή σ' ἐπὶ θύραισιν ὄψεται.
Γρ.[α] οἶδ' οἶδ' ὅ τι βούλει.
Επ. καὶ γὰρ ἐγὼ σέ, νὴ Δία.
Γρ.[α] μὰ τὴν Ἀφροδίτην, ἥ μ' ἔλαχε κληρουμένη,
μὴ 'γώ σ' ἀφήσω.
Επ. παραφρονεῖς, ὦ γρᾴδιον.
Γρ.[α] ληρεῖς· ἐγὼ δ' ἄξω σ' ἐπὶ τἀμὰ στρώματα.
Επ. τί δῆτα κρεάγρας τοῖς κάδοις ὠνοίμεθ' ἄν,
ἐξὸν καθέντα γρᾴδιον τοιουτονὶ
ἐκ τῶν φρεάτων τοὺς κάδους ξυλλαμβάνειν;
Γρ.[α] μὴ σκῶπτέ μ', ὦ τάλαν, ἀλλ' ἕπου δεῦρ' ὡς ἐμέ.
Επ. ἀλλ' οὐκ ἀνάγκη μοὐστίν, εἰ μὴ τῶν ἐμῶν
τὴν πεντακοσιοστὴν κατέθηκας τῇ πόλει.
Γρ.[α] νὴ τὴν Ἀφροδίτην, δεῖ γε μέντοι σ'· ὡς ἐγὼ
τοῖς τηλικούτοις ξυγκαθεύδουσ' ἥδομαι.
Επ. ἐγὼ δὲ ταῖς γε τηλικαύταις ἄχθομαι,
κοὐκ ἂν πιθοίμην οὐδέποτ'.
Γρ.[α] ἀλλὰ νὴ Δία
ἀναγκάσει τουτί σε.
Επ. τοῦτο δ' ἐστὶ τί;
Γρ.[α] ψήφισμα, καθ' ὅ σε δεῖ βαδίζειν ὡς ἐμέ.
Επ. λέγ' αὐτὸ τί ποτε κἄστι.

992 φιλοῦμαι codd.: φιλεῖς με van Leeuwen.
998 ἐγὼ σὲ (ἐγώ σε) codd.: ἔγωγε $^{i}\Sigma^{R\Gamma\Lambda}$.
1002 ὠνοίμεθ' ἄν vel sim. RΓ Suda κ2360: cf. *Birds* 1152: ὠνήμεθ' ἄν Λ· ὠνούμεθ' ἄν Suda ϵ1800: ὠνούμεθα Cobet.
1008 σ' Reisig: om. codd.

EPIGENES [*trying to turn back to the Girl's door*]: I don't know what you're talking about. I've got to knock on this door.

FIRST OLD WOMAN: Only when you've *knocked* my door first!

EPIGENES: We're not wanting to borrow a flour-sieve just now.

FIRST OLD WOMAN: I know that I'm loved; only at present you're taken aback because you found me out of doors. Come on [*offering to kiss him*], put your lips here.

EPIGENES: But, dear lady, I'm worried about your boyfriend.

FIRST OLD WOMAN: Who's he?

EPIGENES: The best painter alive.

FIRST OLD WOMAN: And which one's that?

EPIGENES: The one who paints jars for funerals. Go now, in case he sees you outside the door.

FIRST OLD WOMAN [*with affected coyness*]: I know what you're after, I know!

EPIGENES: And I know what *you're* after, by Zeus!

FIRST OLD WOMAN [*gripping him firmly, despite his continuing struggles*]: By Aphrodite, to whose allotted realm I belong, I will not let you go!

EPIGENES: Old woman, you're out of your mind!

FIRST OLD WOMAN: Nonsense! I'm going to take you under my covers.

EPIGENES [*still resisting; turning to the audience*]: Why should we buy hooks any more to haul up buckets, when we could let an old biddy like this down into our wells and grab the buckets that way?

FIRST OLD WOMAN: Stop making fun of me, you wretched man! This way – follow me – to my place.

EPIGENES: I'm not obliged to. Not unless you've paid the City 0.2 per cent of what I'm worth.

FIRST OLD WOMAN: Oh, yes, you must, by Aphrodite! I *love* sleeping with lads your age!

EPIGENES: And *I hate* sleeping with women *your* age! I'm not going to do what you want, ever.

FIRST OLD WOMAN [*producing a scroll*]: But *this* will *make* you!

EPIGENES: Oh, what is it?

FIRST OLD WOMAN: A decree that says you've got to come to me.

EPIGENES: Read it and let's see just what it does say.

Γρ.[a] καὶ δή σοι λέγω.
"ἔδοξε ταῖς γυναιξίν· ἢν ἀνὴρ νέος
νέας ἐπιθυμῇ, μὴ σποδεῖν αὐτὴν πρὶν ἂν
τὴν γραῦν προκρούσῃ πρῶτον· ἢν δὲ μὴ 'θέλῃ
πρότερον προκρούειν, ἀλλ' ἐπιθυμῇ τῆς νέας,
ταῖς πρεσβυτέραις γυναιξὶν ἔστω τὸν νέον
ἕλκειν ἀνατεὶ λαβομένας τοῦ παττάλου."
Επ. οἴμοι, Προκρούστης τήμερον γενήσομαι.
Γρ.[a] τοῖς γὰρ νόμοις τοῖς ἡμετέροισι πειστέον.
Επ. τί δ', ἢν ἀφαιρεῖταί μ' ἀνὴρ τῶν δημοτῶν
ἢ τῶν φίλων ἐλθών τις;
Γρ.[a] ἀλλ' οὐ κύριος
ὑπὲρ μεδίμνόν ἐστ' ἀνὴρ οὐδεὶς ἔτι.
Επ. ἐξωμοσία δ' οὐκ ἔστιν;
Γρ.[a] οὐ γὰρ δεῖ στροφῆς.
Επ. ἀλλ' ἔμπορος εἶναι σκήψομαι.
Γρ.[a] κλάων γε σύ.
Επ. τί δῆτα χρὴ δρᾶν;
Γρ.[a] δεῦρ' ἀκολουθεῖν ὡς ἐμέ.
Επ. καὶ ταῦτ' ἀνάγκη μοὐστί;
Γρ.[a] Διομήδειά γε.
Επ. ὑποστόρεσαί νυν πρῶτα τῆς ὀριγάνου,
καὶ κλήμαθ' ὑπόθου συγκλάσασα τέτταρα,
καὶ ταινίωσαι, καὶ παράθου τὰς ληκύθους,
ὕδατός τε κατάθου τοὔστρακον πρὸ τῆς θύρας.
Γρ.[a] ἦ μὴν ἔτ' ὠνήσει σὺ καὶ στεφάνην ἐμοί.
Επ. νὴ τὸν Δί', ἤνπερ ᾖ γέ που τῶν κηρίνων·
οἶμαι γὰρ ἔνδον διαπεσεῖσθαί σ' αὐτίκα.
Κο. ποῖ τοῦτον ἕλκεις;
Γρ.[a] τὸν ἐμὸν αὐτῆς εἰσάγω.
Κο. οὐ σωφρονοῦσά γ'· οὐ γὰρ ἡλικίαν ἔχει
παρὰ σοὶ καθεύδειν τηλικοῦτος ὤν· ἐπεὶ
μήτηρ ἂν αὐτῷ μᾶλλον εἴης ἢ γυνή.
ὥστ' εἰ καταστήσεσθε τοῦτον τὸν νόμον,
τὴν γῆν ἅπασαν Οἰδιπόδων ἐμπλήσετε.

1037 τὸν ἐμὸν αὐτῆς Hall & Geldart: τὸν ἐμαυτῆς codd.: εἰς ἐμαυτῆς Meineke.

FIRST OLD WOMAN: All right, I'm reading it to you. [*Reads*] "Resolved by the women: if a young man desires a young woman, he shall not shag her until he has first screwed her elderly neighbour; and if he refuses to perform such pre-screwing and continues to lust after the young woman, the older women shall be permitted, without penalty, to drag the young man away, taking hold of him by the peg."

EPIGENES: Help, I'm going to get screwered alive today!

FIRST OLD WOMAN: Yes; *our* laws have got to be obeyed.

EPIGENES: What if someone from my deme, or one of my friends, comes and offers to go bail for my freedom?

FIRST OLD WOMAN: No good; no *man* has power any more to make a contract over the value of a bushel.

EPIGENES: Can't I swear an oath of excusal?

FIRST OLD WOMAN: No evasive tactics, now!

EPIGENES: Then I'll claim to be a merchant.

FIRST OLD WOMAN: You'll be for it if you do!

EPIGENES: So what am I to do?

FIRST OLD WOMAN: Follow me this way to my place!

EPIGENES: I absolutely must?

FIRST OLD WOMAN: By Diomedes' compulsion! [*Still gripping Epigenes firmly with one hand, she pushes him in the back with the palm of the other.*]

EPIGENES: Then strew your bed with marjoram, break off four vine branches and lay them underneath, put on ribbons, place the flasks beside the bed, and put down the pot of water in front of your door.

FIRST OLD WOMAN: I swear you'll buy me a tiara yet, as well!

EPIGENES: I will indeed, I fancy, so long as you mean one of the wax ones! I think as soon as we're in there you'll fall to pieces!

[*As the old woman half shoves, half drags Epigenes towards her door, the Girl comes out and confronts her.*]

GIRL: Where are you dragging this lad?

FIRST OLD WOMAN: I'm taking him in here; he's *mine*!

GIRL: You're being stupid! He's not old enough to sleep with you, at his age. Why, you'd be more like a mother to him than a wife. In fact, if you establish this law, you'll fill the whole country with Oedipuses! [*In her shock at this, the old woman looses her grip on Epigenes; the Girl takes hold of him, steers him away from the old woman (down, left) and shields him from her.*]

Γρ.$^{\alpha}$ ὦ παμβδελύρα, φθονοῦσα τόνδε τὸν λόγον
ἐξηῦρες· ἀλλ' ἐγώ σε τιμωρήσομαι.
Επ. νὴ τὸν Δία τὸν σωτῆρα, κεχάρισαί γέ μοι,
ὦ γλυκύτατον, τὴν γραῦν ἀπαλλάξασά μου·
ὥστ' ἀντὶ τούτων τῶν ἀγαθῶν εἰς ἑσπέραν
μεγάλην ἀποδώσω καὶ παχεῖάν σοι χάριν.

ΓΡΑΥΣ Β

αὕτη σύ, ποῖ τονδὶ παραβᾶσα τὸν νόμον
ἕλκεις, παρ' ἐμοὶ τῶν γραμμάτων εἰρηκότων
πρότερον καθεύδειν αὐτόν;
Επ. οἴμοι δείλαιος.
πόθεν ἐξέκυψας, ὦ κάκιστ' ἀπολουμένη;
τοῦτο γὰρ ἐκείνου τὸ κακὸν ἐξωλέστερον.
Γρ.$^{\beta}$ βάδιζε δεῦρο.
Επ. μηδαμῶς με περιίδῃς
ἑλκόμενον ὑπὸ τῆσδ', ἀντιβολῶ σ'.
Γρ.$^{\beta}$ ἀλλ' οὐκ ἐγώ,
ἀλλ' ὁ νόμος ἕλκει σ'.
Επ. οὐκ ἐμέ γ', ἀλλ' Ἔμπουσά τις
ἐξ αἵματος φλύκταιναν ἠμφιεσμένη.
Γρ.$^{\beta}$ ἕπου, μαλακίων, δεῦρ' ἀνύσας καὶ μὴ λάλει.
Επ. ἴθι νυν, ἔασον εἰς ἄφοδον πρώτιστά με
ἐλθόντα θαρρῆσαι πρὸς ἐμαυτόν· εἰ δὲ μή,
αὐτοῦ τι δρῶντα πυρρὸν ὄψει μ' αὐτίκα
ὑπὸ τοῦ δέους.
Γρ.$^{\beta}$ θάρρει, βάδιζ'· ἔνδον χεσεῖ.
Επ. δέδοικα κἀγὼ μὴ πλέον γ' ἢ βούλομαι.
ἀλλ' ἐγγυητάς σοι καταστήσω δύο
ἀξιόχρεως.
Γρ.$^{\beta}$ μή μοι καθίστη.

1043 λόγον Le Febvre: νόμον codd.
1049 τονδὶ παραβᾶσα Bothe: παραβᾶσα τόνδε codd.
1060 ἐλθόντα θαρρῆσαι codd.: ἐλθόντ' ἀναθαρρῆσαι van Leeuwen.
1063 γ' ἢ R: ἢ ΓΛ: ἤπερ Σ^{R}: εἴπερ Σ^{Λ}.

FIRST OLD WOMAN [*shaking her fist at the Girl*]: You loathsome, loathsome creature, you were jealous of me – that was why you thought up that argument! But I'll get my own back on you yet! [*She withdraws into her house.*]

EPIGENES [*to the Girl*]: By Zeus the Saviour, sweetheart, you've done me a good turn, letting me escape from that old crone! So tonight, in return for your favour, I'll be giving you a reward – a long thick reward!

[*As the pair move lovingly towards the Girl's door, a second old woman comes out of the far (left-hand) door and confronts them. She is even older than the first, heavily rouged, and brandishes a copy of the decree on sexual rights.*]

SECOND OLD WOMAN [*to Girl*]: Hey, you, where are you dragging this man, in contravention of the law, when it says in black and white that he should sleep with me first? [*Epigenes starts back in fright; the Girl, even more terrified, lets go of him and flees off, left.*]

EPIGENES: God help me! Where have you popped out from, damn and curse you? This evil creature is more horrendous than the last one!

SECOND OLD WOMAN [*locking her arm round his neck*]: Come this way!

EPIGENES [*unable to turn his head, but thinking the Girl is still somewhere near*]: Don't, I beg you, don't stand by and let this woman drag me off! [*There is no reply.*]

SECOND OLD WOMAN [*waving her scroll*]: It's not *me* dragging you off, it's the *law.*

EPIGENES: No, it isn't, it's a sort of Empusa covered in bleeding blisters!

SECOND OLD WOMAN: Hurry up, softie, come with me, and stop jabbering.

EPIGENES: Then please let me first go to the bog and give myself some courage. Otherwise you'll be seeing me doing something yellow, right here, any moment, I'm that frightened!

SECOND OLD WOMAN: Don't worry about that. Come on. You can have a shit once you're in there.

EPIGENES: That's just what I'm afraid of – I may have more of one than I'd like! Look, I'll appoint two competent sureties, if you want.

SECOND OLD WOMAN: I'm not having any sureties!

ΓΡΑΥΣ Γ ποῖ σύ, ποῖ
χωρεῖς μετὰ ταύτης;
Επ. οὐκ ἔγωγ', ἀλλ' ἕλκομαι.
ἀτάρ, ἥτις εἶ γε, πόλλ' ἀγαθὰ γένοιτό σοι,
ὅτι μ' οὐ περιεῖδες ἐπιτριβέντ'. ὦ Ἡράκλεις,
ὦ Πᾶνες, ὦ Κορύβαντες, ὦ Διοσκόρω,
τοῦτ' αὖ πολὺ τούτου τὸ κακὸν ἐξωλέστερον.
ἀτὰρ τί τὸ πρᾶγμ' ἔστ', ἀντιβολῶ, τουτί ποτε;
πότερον πίθηκος ἀνάπλεως ψιμυθίου,
ἢ γραῦς ἀνεστηκυῖα παρὰ τῶν πλειόνων;
Γρ.$^{\gamma}$ μὴ σκῶπτέ μ', ἀλλὰ δεῦρ' ἕπου.
Γρ.$^{\beta}$ δευρὶ μὲν οὖν.
Γρ.$^{\gamma}$ ὡς οὐκ ἀφήσω σ' οὐδέποτ'.
Γρ.$^{\beta}$ οὐδὲ μὴν ἐγώ.
Επ. διασπάσεσθέ μ', ὦ κακῶς ἀπολούμεναι.
Γρ.$^{\beta}$ ἐμοὶ γὰρ ἀκολουθεῖν σε δεῖ κατὰ τὸν νόμον.
Γρ.$^{\gamma}$ οὔκ, ἢν ἑτέρα γε γραῦς ἔτ' αἰσχίων φανῇ.
Επ. ἢν οὖν ὑφ' ὑμῶν πρῶτον ἀπόλωμαι κακῶς,
φέρε, πῶς ἐπ' ἐκείνην τὴν καλὴν ἀφίξομαι;
Γρ.$^{\beta}$ αὐτὸς σκόπει σύ· τάδε δέ σοι ποιητέον.
Επ. ποτέρας προτέρας οὖν κατελάσας ἀπαλλαγῶ;
Γρ.$^{\gamma}$ οὐκ οἶσθα; βαδιεῖ δεῦρ'.
Επ. ἀφέτω νύν μ' αὑτηί.
Γρ.$^{\beta}$ δευρὶ μὲν οὖν ἴθ' ὡς ἔμ'.
Επ. ἤν γ' ἡδί μ' ἀφῇ.
Γρ.$^{\gamma}$ ἀλλ' οὐκ ἀφήσω μὰ Δία σ'.
Γρ.$^{\beta}$ οὐδὲ μὴν ἐγώ.
Επ. χαλεπαί γ' ἂν ἦστε γενόμεναι πορθμῆς.

1067 ἥτις B: εἴ τις RΓΛ.
1077 σε δεῖ Cobet: σ' ἔδει codd.
1084 γ' ἡδί μ' Brunck: ἡδί γ' R: νὴ Δία γ' ΓΛ: μὰ Δία μ' B.
1086 ἦστε Ald. (ἥστε Γ, ἧστε Λ): ἦσται R: ἦτε Suda.

[*As she begins to haul him towards her house, a third old woman comes out of the right-hand door, and approaches the pair from behind. She is older and uglier still, and her face is plastered with white lead.*]

THIRD OLD WOMAN [*to Epigenes*]: Where do you think you're going with this woman?

EPIGENES [*struggling, at first ineffectively, to free himself*]: I'm not going anywhere – I'm being dragged. Blessings on you, though, whoever you are, that you didn't stand by and let me be done in. [*He succeeds in wriggling free, turns, sees the Third Old Woman, and nearly collapses.*] O Heracles! O Pans! O Corybantes! O Sons of Zeus! Another evil creature, and a lot *more* horrendous than this one! Only what on earth *is* this thing, I beg you? Is it a monkey smothered in white lead, or an old hag who's risen from the ... majority?

THIRD OLD WOMAN [*laying hold of him*]: Don't make fun of me; follow me, this way.

SECOND OLD WOMAN [*laying hold of him*]: No, *this* way.

THIRD OLD WOMAN [*tugging*]: I tell you, I'm never going to let you go!

SECOND OLD WOMAN [*tugging*]: Neither am I!

EPIGENES: You'll tear me in pieces, curse and blast you both!

SECOND OLD WOMAN [*waving scroll*]: According to the law, you've got to come with me!

THIRD OLD WOMAN: No, not if another old woman turns up who's even uglier.

EPIGENES: So if I've first been massacred by you two, tell me, how will I ever get to that lovely girl?

SECOND OLD WOMAN: That's *your* look-out. *This* [*waving scroll*] you're duty bound to do.

EPIGENES: Well, which am I to thrust up first, so as to get it over with?

THIRD OLD WOMAN [*pulling harder*]: Don't you know? You're to come here.

EPIGENES [*trying to obey*]: Then let this one let me go.

SECOND OLD WOMAN [*pulling harder*]: No, come here to me.

EPIGENES [*trying to obey*]: If this one leaves hold of me.

THIRD OLD WOMAN: No, by Zeus, I'm *not* leaving hold of you!

SECOND OLD WOMAN: Neither am I!

EPIGENES: You'd be a fine nuisance, you two, if you ran ferry-boats.

Γρ.$^{\gamma}$ τιή;
Επ. ἕλκοντε τοὺς πλωτῆρας ἂν ἀπεκναίετε.
Γρ.$^{\beta}$ σιγῇ βάδιζε δεῦρο.
Γρ.$^{\gamma}$ μὰ Δί', ἀλλ' ὡς ἐμέ.
Επ. τουτὶ τὸ πρᾶγμα κατὰ τὸ Καννωνοῦ σαφῶς
ψήφισμα· βινεῖν δεῖ με διαλελημμένον.
πῶς οὖν δικωπεῖν ἀμφοτέρας δυνήσομαι;
Γρ.$^{\beta}$ καλῶς, ἐπειδὰν καταφάγῃς βολβῶν χύτραν.
Επ. οἴμοι κακοδαίμων, ἐγγὺς ἤδη τῆς θύρας
ἑλκόμενος εἰμ'.
Γρ.$^{\beta}$ ἀλλ' οὐδὲν ἔσται σοι πλέον·
ξυνεισπεσοῦμαι γὰρ μετὰ σοῦ.
Επ. μή, πρὸς θεῶν·
ἑνὶ γὰρ ξυνέχεσθαι κρεῖττον ἢ δυοῖν κακοῖν.
Γρ.$^{\beta}$ νὴ τὴν 'Εκάτην, ἐάν τε βούλῃ γ' ἤν τε μή.
Επ. ὢ τρισκακοδαίμων, εἰ γυναῖκα δεῖ σαπρὰν
βινεῖν ὅλην τὴν νύκτα καὶ τὴν ἡμέραν,
κἄπειτ', ἐπειδὰν τῆσδ' ἀπαλλαγῶ, πάλιν
φρύνην ἔχουσαν λήκυθον πρὸς ταῖς γνάθοις.
ἆρ' οὐ κακοδαίμων εἰμί; βαρυδαίμων μὲν οὖν
νὴ τὸν Δία τὸν σωτῆρ' ἀνὴρ καὶ δυστυχής,
ὅστις τοιούτοις θηρίοις συνείρξομαι.
ὅμως δ', ἐάν τι πολλὰ πολλάκις πάθω
ὑπο ταῖνδε ταῖν κασαλβάδοιν δεῦρ' εἰσπλέων,
θάψαι μ' ἐπ' αὐτῷ τῷ στόματι τῆς εἰσβολῆς·
καὶ τήνδ' ἄνωθεν ἐπιπολῆς τοῦ σήματος
ζῶσαν καταπιττώσαντες, εἶτα τὼ πόδε
μολυβδοχοήσαντες κύκλῳ περὶ τὰ σφύρα,
ἄνω 'πιθεῖναι πρόφασιν ἀντὶ ληκύθου.

1104 συνείρξομαι Bergk: συνείξομαι codd.: συννήξομαι Gelenius.
1108 τήνδ' Bergler: τὴν B: τῶν RΓΛ.
1109 καταπιττώσαντες Γ: καταπιττώσαντας RΛ.
1110 -χοήσαντες Gormont (1528): -χοήσαντας RΓ: -χοήσαντος Λ.
1111 'πιθεῖναι Λ: 'πιτιθεῖναι Γ: πιθῆναι R.
after 1111 Bergk inserted χοροῦ.

THIRD OLD WOMAN: Oh, why?

EPIGENES: You'd drag the passengers about so much, you'd bruise them to death!

SECOND OLD WOMAN: Keep quiet and come here.

THIRD OLD WOMAN: No, no, come to *me*.

EPIGENES: This business is definitely being done under the decree of Cannonus: I've got to fuck while held by two warders! How will I be able to ply the oar in both holes at once?

SECOND OLD WOMAN: Easy, once you've eaten up a potful of bulbs.

[*At this point the Third Old Woman, with a supreme heave, succeeds in pulling Epigenes away from her rival, and begins dragging him towards her house. The Second Old Woman hurries after them.*]

EPIGENES: Help! poor me! I've almost been dragged right to the door!

SECOND OLD WOMAN [*laying hold on him again, and letting herself be dragged along too*]: It won't do you any good; I'm going to tumble in there along with you.

EPIGENES: Don't, in the gods' name! Better to be tangled up with one horror than with *two*!

SECOND OLD WOMAN: Whether you want it, by Hecate, or whether you don't!

EPIGENES [*now almost on the threshold of the Third Old Woman's house*]: Oh, wretched, wretched me, if I've got to fuck a decaying old woman all the night and all the day, and then, when I've finished with her, go on to a toad with a carbuncle on her cheek! Aren't I wretched? Accursed and luckless, more like, by Zeus the Saviour, to be shut up with wild beasts like these! [*Addressing all who care to take notice*] Still, if (as may well be) something does happen to me at the hands of these whores when I sail into this port, then bury me right at the mouth of the strait; and take this woman [*gesturing with his head towards the Second Old Woman*], cover her alive with pitch, then pour molten lead over her feet right round the ankles, and put her up on top above my tomb to serve as a substitute for a monumental urn. [*Epigenes, with the Second Old Woman still clinging to him, is dragged inside by the Third Old Woman. His torch, dropped in the course of the struggle, is left lying on the ground.*]

ΘΕΡΑΠΑΙΝΑ

ὢ μακάριος μὲν δῆμος, εὐδαίμων δὲ γῆ,
αὐτή τέ μοι δέσποινα μακαριωτάτη,
ὑμεῖς θ' ὅσαι παρέστατ' ἐπὶ ταῖσιν θύραις,
οἵ γείτονές τε πάντες οἵ τε δημόται,
ἐγώ τε πρὸς τούτοισιν ἡ διάκονος,
ἥτις μεμύρισμαι τὴν κεφαλὴν μυρώμασιν
ἀγαθοῖσιν, ὦ Ζεῦ· πολὺ δ' ὑπερπέπαικεν αὖ
τούτων ἁπάντων τὰ Θάσι' ἀμφορείδια·
ἐν τῇ κεφαλῇ γὰρ ἐμμένει πολὺν χρόνον,
τὰ δ' ἄλλ' ἀπανθήσαντα πάντ' ἀπέπτατο·
ὥστ' ἐστὶ πολὺ βέλτιστα, πολὺ δῆτ', ὦ θεοί.
κέρασον ἄκρατον· εὐφρανεῖ τὴν νύχθ' ὅλην
ἐκλεγομένας ὅ τι ἂν μάλιστ' ὀσμὴν ἔχῃ.
ἀλλ', ὦ γυναῖκες, φράσατέ μοι τὸν δεσπότην—
τὸν ἄνδρ', ὅπου 'στί, τῆς ἐμῆς κεκτημένης.
Χο. αὐτοῦ μένων ἡμῖν γ' ἂν ἐξευρεῖν δοκεῖς
μάλισθ'· ὁδὶ γὰρ ἐπὶ τὸ δεῖπνον ἔρχεται.
Θε. ὦ δέσποτ', ὦ μακάριε καὶ τρισόλβιε.
Βλ. ἐγώ;
Θε. σὺ μέντοι, νὴ Δί', ὥς γ' οὐδεὶς ἀνήρ.
τίς γὰρ γένοιτ' ἂν μᾶλλον ὀλβιώτερος,
ὅστις πολιτῶν πλεῖον ἢ τρισμυρίων
ὄντων τὸ πλῆθος οὐ δεδείπνηκας μόνος;
Βλ. εὐδαιμονικόν γ' ἄνθρωπον εἴρηκας σαφῶς.
Θε. ποῖ ποι βαδίζεις;
Βλ. ἐπὶ τὸ δεῖπνον ἔρχομαι.
Θε. νὴ τὴν 'Αφροδίτην, πολύ γ' ἁπάντων ὕστατος.
ὅμως δ' ἐκέλευε συλλαβοῦσάν μ' ἡ γυνὴ
ἄγειν σε καὶ τασδὶ μετὰ σοῦ τὰς μείρακας.

1112 δὲ γῆ Dobree: δ' ἐγὼ codd.
1113 αὐτή B: αὔτη Γ: αὖτη RΛ.
1114 θ' Dindorf: δ' codd.
1116 τε δημόται Brunck: τῶν δημοτῶν codd.
1117 μεμύρισμαι Athenaeus 15.691b: μεμύρωμαι RΛ Suda: μύρωμαι Γ.
1121 πάντ' ἀπέπτατο Suda: πάντα πέπτατο codd.
1124 ἔχῃ Λ· ἔχει R: ἔχοι Γ.
1127 γ' ἂν Brunck: γὰρ codd.
1137 συλλαβοῦσάν (-αν) Λ: συλλαβοῦσα R.

[*Enter, left, Praxagora's maid, somewhat drunk.*]

MAID: Oh, happy people! Oh, blest country! And my mistress, who's happiest of all – and all of you ladies who are standing near our door – and all our neighbours and fellow-demesmen – and myself, the maidservant, as well! My head's all scented with scents, and Zeus, they're good ones! But then again, what beats the lot of them by a street is those darling jars of Thasian. They stay in your head for so long, when all the others have faded and flown away – which makes them far the best, *far* the best, ye gods! Mix it neat and it'll give you pleasure the whole night long, if you pick out the stuff with the most aroma. But, ladies, could you tell me where my master – I mean, where my mistress's husband is?

CHORUS-LEADER [*looking off right*]: I think you'll be most likely to find him if you stay right here; here he comes, on his way to dinner.

[*Enter, right, Blepyrus, garlanded, and with a girl on each arm.*]

MAID: Master! my blest, my three-times-happy master!

BLEPYRUS [*slightly taken aback*]: Do you mean me?

MAID: Yes, you, by Zeus, and beyond compare! Who could possibly be more blester than you? Of all our citizens, numbering more than thirty thousand, you're the only one who hasn't had his dinner!

BLEPYRUS: It's certainly a fortunate man that you're talking about! [*He makes to hurry off, left, without the girls.*]

MAID [*stopping him*]: Here, where are you off to?

BLEPYRUS: I'm going to dinner.

MAID: By Aphrodite, you're last of all by a long way! But all the same, your wife told me to get hold of you and bring you there, and these

οἶνος δὲ Χῖός ἐστι περιλελειμμένος
καὶ τἄλλ' ἀγαθά. πρὸς ταῦτα μὴ βραδύνετε,
καὶ τῶν θεατῶν εἴ τις εὔνους τυγχάνει,
καὶ τῶν κριτῶν εἰ μή τις ἑτέρωσε βλέπει,
ἴτω μεθ' ἡμῶν· πάντα γὰρ παρέξομεν.
Βλ. οὔκουν ἅπασι δῆτα γενναίως ἐρεῖς
καὶ μὴ παραλείψεις μηδέν', ἀλλ' ἐλευθέρως
καλεῖς γέροντα, μειράκιον, παιδίσκον; ὡς
τὸ δεῖπνον αὐτοῖς ἐστ' ἐπεσκευασμένον
ἁπαξάπασιν – ἢν ἀπίωσιν οἴκαδε.
ἐγὼ δὲ πρὸς τὸ δεῖπνον ἤδη 'πείξομαι·
ἔχω δέ τοι καὶ δᾷδα ταυτηνὶ καλῶς.
Χο. τί δῆτα διατρίβεις ἔχων, ἀλλ' οὐκ ἄγεις
τασδὶ λαβών; ἐν ὅσῳ δὲ καταβαίνεις, ἐγὼ
ἐπᾴσομαι μέλος τι μελλοδειπνικόν.
σμικρὸν δ' ὑποθέσθαι τοῖς κριταῖσι βούλομαι·

τοῖς σοφοῖς μὲν τῶν σοφῶν μεμνημένοις κρίνειν ἐμέ,
τοῖς γελῶσι δ' ἡδέως διὰ τὸν γέλων κρίνειν ἐμέ·
σχεδὸν ἅπαντας οὖν κελεύω δηλαδὴ κρίνειν ἐμέ·
μηδὲ τὸν κλῆρον γενέσθαι μηδὲν ἡμῖν αἴτιον,
ὅτι προείληχ'· ἀλλὰ πάντα ταῦτα χρὴ μεμνημένους
μὴ 'πιορκεῖν, ἀλλὰ κρίνειν τοὺς χοροὺς ὀρθῶς ἀεί,
μηδὲ ταῖς κακαῖς ἑταίραις τὸν τρόπον προσεικέναι,
αἳ μόνον μνήμην ἔχουσι τῶν τελευταίων ἀεί.

ὢ ὤ, ὥρα δή,
ὦ φίλαι γυναῖκες, εἴπερ μέλλομεν τὸ χρῆμα δρᾶν.
ἐπὶ τὸ δεῖπνον ὑπανακινεῖν· Κρητικῶς οὖν τὼ πόδε
καὶ σὺ κίνει.

1139 περιλελειμμένος Λ: παραλελειμμένος R.
1145 παραλείψεις Brunck: παραλείψῃς RΛ.
1146 καλεῖς Blaydes: καλεῖν codd.
1155 κρίνειν Λ: κρίν R.
1161 τὸν Bentley: τόν τε codd.
1163-4 ὢ ὤ ... ὦ φίλαι Dindorf: ὦ ὦ (ω ω R) ... φίλαι codd.: ὤ ... ὦ φίλαι Zimmermann.

girls with you. There's Chian wine still left, and all the other good things too. So [*including the chorus in a sweeping gesture*] don't you dilly-dally; and also [*turning to the audience*] any of the audience who may be rooting for us, and any of the judges who isn't turning his eyes away, let them come with us; we're going to lay on absolutely everything.

BLEPYRUS: Well, aren't you going to be properly generous and say it to *everyone*, not leaving anybody out, liberally inviting old men, youths and little boys alike? Because there's a dinner prepared for every single one of them – if they go off home! [*Picking up the torch which Epigenes had dropped*] But I'm going to hurry along to dinner now; I've got this torch as well, you see, conveniently enough!

CHORUS-LEADER: Well then, why are you still hanging around here, instead of taking these girls and going off there with them? And while you're making your way down there, I'll accompany you with a sort of pre-dining celebration song. [*Turning to the audience*] But I want to give a little bit of advice to the judges: [*here the piper begins to play*] to those who are intellectual, to remember the intellectual bits and vote for me; to those who enjoy a laugh, to think of the laughs they've had and vote for me; in other words, I'm asking just about *everyone* to vote for me. And don't let the lottery act to our disadvantage at all, the fact that we were drawn first: you must remember all these things, and not break your oath but always judge the choruses fairly, and not behave in the same way as those wretched supertarts, who never have a place in their memory for any man but their latest one.

[*To her colleagues*]

Hey, hey! it's time now,
dear ladies, if we're going to do the thing at all,
to get a move on towards dinner.
[*To Blepyrus, as the chorus begin to dance*] So you get your feet moving too,
in Cretan fashion.

Βλ. τοῦτο δρῶ.
Χο. καὶ τάσδε νυν < × –∪–
–∪–× –∪ > λαγαρὰς τοῖν σκελίσκοιν τὸν ῥυθμόν.
τάχα γὰρ ἔπεισι
λοπαδοτεμαχοσελαχογαλεο-
κρανιολειψανοδριμυποτριμματο-
σιλφιοπαραλομελιτοκατακεχυμενο-
κίχλεπικοσσυφοφαττοπεριστερα-
λεκτρυον†οπτεγκεφαλλιο†κιγκλοπε-
λειολαγῳοσιραιοβαφητραγα-
λοπτερυγών. σὺ δὲ ταῦτ' ἀκροασάμε-
νος ταχὺ καὶ ταχέως λαβὲ τρύβλιον·
εἶτα κόνισαι λαβὼν
λέκιθον, ἵν' ἐπιδειπνῇς.
Βλ. ἀλλὰ λαιμάττουσί που.
Χο. αἴρεσθ' ἄνω, ἰαί, εὐαί·
δειπνήσομεν, εὐοῖ, εὐαί,
εὐαί, ὡς ἐπὶ νίκῃ·
εὐαί, εὐαί, εὐαί, εὐαί.

1165-6 lacuna after *νυν* posited by Meineke (Λ leaves a space after λαγαρὰς): λαγαρὰς ‹ἄγαν | ταχὺ χορείας ὄρσον ὑπάγειν› τοῖν Coulon (partly following White) νυν ‹τὰς μείρακας | δεικνύναι κέλευε› λαγαρὰς van Leeuwen: perh. e.g. νυν ‹τὰς μείρακας | χρὴ συνυπάγειν κοῦφα› λαγαρὰς.
1169 -τεμαχοσελ- Λ Suda: -τεμαχοσσελ- R.
1171 -παραλο- Sommerstein: -παραο- codd.: -λιπαρο- Ussher: -τυρο- Blaydes.
1172 -κιχλ- Le Febvre: -κινκλ- codd.
1172 -κοσσυφοφαττο- Dindorf: -κοσσυκοφαττο- R: -κοσσυφαο- Λ.
1173 †-οπτεγκεφαλλιο-†† codd.: -οπτοκεφαλιο- Coulon (-οπτο- Meineke, -κεφαλιο- Bothe -οπτοπιφαλλιδο- Ussher: perh. -οπτοφαληριδο-.
1174 -τραγαλο- Blaydes: -τραγανο- codd.
1176 ταχὺ καὶ codd.: τρέχε καὶ Blaydes.
1177 κόνισαι λαβὼν R: λαβὼν κόνισαι Λ.
1181 δειπνήσομεν codd. Suda: δειπνήσωμεν Newiger.
1182 εὐαί ὡς ἐπὶ νίκῃ vel sim. codd. Suda: perh. ὡς ἐπὶ νίκῃ, εὐαί (cf. *Lys.* 1293).

BLEPYRUS [*beginning to dance*]:
That's what I'm doing!

CHORUS-LEADER: And these girls as well
<should join in moving lightly and> nimbly, with their slim legs, to the rhythm.

[*The Maid and the two girls join in the dance.*]

CHORUS: Because on the table there may be a
dishy-slicy-sharky-dogfishy-
heady-left-oversy-very-strong-saucy-
silphiumy-bit-salty-honey-poured-overy-
thrush-upon-blackbirdy-ringdovey-pigeony-
chickeny-roast-cooty-wagtaily-
rockdovey-haremeaty-boiled-winy-dippy-
deliciousy-wingedy thing! So you [*to Blepyrus*] listen to that
and get yourself a plate, quick and fast,
then raise the dust – but take
some porridge to dine on.

BLEPYRUS [*beginning to dance off towards the Agora*]:
But they must be shovelling it down!

CHORUS [*dancing off after Blepyrus, the Maid and the girls*]:
Raise it high, iai, evai!
We're going to feast, evoi, evai,
evai, a feast of victory!
Evai, evai, evai, evai!

Commentary

1 **PRAXAGORA** means something like "she who is effective in public meetings"; appropriately, the audience will first learn that this is the heroine's name at 124, just before the Assembly rehearsal begins. It is a genuine Athenian name, with three inscriptional attestations from the early and middle fourth century (*IG* ii^2 5378, 12508, 12508a).

1-18 The overall stylistic impression of this speech is redolent of elevated poetry; the rules of tragic metre are broken only once, and there are numerous features of syntax, vocabulary and phraseology normally alien to comedy (e.g. frequent omission of the definite article; a preposition following its noun at the end of a line; words like *domoi* "house, chamber" [11] and phrases like *Bakkhion ... nāma* "Bacchic juice", i.e. wine [14]). At the same time it is obvious from the start that the real subject-matter is homely, and from 8 the topic becomes the familiar comic theme of the vices of women; and the incongruity between style and subject is marked by the intrusion of vocabulary inappropriate to serious poetry, e.g. *keramikos* "of a potter" (4), *dōmation* "bedroom" (7), *lordoumenos* "arching, convex" (see on 10), *lalein* "talk, blab" (16), and the casual mention of an Athenian festival at 18. According to the scholia the opening line was "suspected" (by Alexandrian scholars?) of being modified from a tragedy by Agathon (active 416-c.400) or Dicaeogenes (early fourth century); the latter is known to have written a *Medea*, and conceivably Medea opened that play with an apostrophe to her grandfather, the Sun-god (see next two notes, and cf. Eur. *Phoen.* 1-3). But in addition to tragedy, the speech is probably also designed to be reminiscent of contemporary dithyramb, especially its use of "riddling, circumlocutory phraseology" (R.L. Hunter, *Eubulus: The Fragments* [Cambridge, 1983] 166); cf. Nesselrath 251, 255-266 for the popularity of this style in Middle (and early New) Comedy, e.g. Antiphanes fr. 55, Eubulus fr. 75, Xenarchus fr. 1, Men. *Dysk.* 946-953. Slater 98-99, noting that a lamp would be much better seen in the early morning than in full daylight, suggests that 1-18 were rewritten, and the lamp introduced, when Ar. knew his play would be first on the day's programme (cf. 1158-62).

1 **wheel-borne:** Greek *trokhēlatou* (genitive case), which could come either from *trokhēlatēs* "driver on wheels, charioteer" (appropriate to the Sun, cf. *Clouds* 571-4, Soph. *Aj.* 857, etc.) or from *trokhēlatos* "driven/propelled on wheels/a wheel" (appropriate to a product of the potter's art, cf. 4). The joke is recycled by Xenarchus fr. 1.9 ("the wheel-driven maiden" = a dinner plate). My English rendering of it is adapted from Barrett's.

1 **lamp** (Greek *lukhnou*): the tragic original no doubt had *theou* "god".

2 **superb invention of sagacious men:** this is the sense indicated by the scholia, and can be obtained by a fairly simple emendation (*exhēurēmenon* "discovered, invented" for the nonsensical *exēitēmenon* "?whose surrender was demanded") of the text offered by R. The other mss have *euskopoisin* ("aiming well" but also "commanding a wide view") for R's *eustokhoisin* ("aiming well" but also "clever, sagacious"), and this suggested to a Renaissance user of the late ms. Vb1 an even simpler emendation of the dubious participle, giving the sense "excellently hung up (*exērtēmenon*) in a conspicuous place" – which would imply that Praxagora's signal is to be a fixed light (say, over her door) rather than a moving one. Against this, however, note that "for" (3) indicates that the present line should be closely related to the *praise* of the lamp in 3-5: to say that the lamp is a very clever invention is a way of praising it, to say that it

has been hung in a very suitable position is not. Moreover, a hand-held lamp, unlike a fixed one, can easily be got rid of when it has ceased to be relevant (see on 28).

3 **I thy birth and fortunes shall declare:** as in a hymn to a god (Eur. *Hipp.* 61-71 gives a simple example, Artemis being first addressed as "daughter of Leto and Zeus" and then praised as the "most beauteous of maidens" who dwells in Zeus' palace; see further E. Norden, *Agnostos Theos* [Berlin, 1913] 143-176, esp. 147-9, 157-160) or an encomium (cf. especially Pl. *Symp.* 203b-e where Socrates, in the last of a series of encomia on Eros, reports how Diotima first described Eros' parentage and then his poverty, resourcefulness, desire of wisdom, etc.).

4 **born:** lit. "driven, propelled" (see on 1).

4 **by power of potter's arm:** lit. "by potter's impetus".

5 **nozzles:** lit. "nostrils", the holes through which the wicks protrude. Most lamps had only a single nozzle, but some had two, one on each side of the bowl; see e.g. *Agora* iv 57 nos. 216, 217.

6 **send forth the flaming signal:** the idea is based on the use of fire-signals of various kinds for military purposes; cf. Thuc. 2.94.1 (with scholia), 3.22.7-8, 3.80.2, 8.102.1; Aeneas Tacticus 7.4, 16.16, 26.13-14, 27.2; Arist. *On the Soul* 431b5-6; Polyaenus 6.2.1. It is clear from some of these passages that the idea of prearranged codes involving different numbers and/or types of signal was already familiar in the fifth and early fourth centuries; before 350 mechanical systems were being devised capable of sending numerous alternative messages (though Polybius 10.43-47 rates them much inferior to the system perfected, as he claims, by himself!). See further R.J. Forbes, *Studies in Ancient Technology* vi (Leiden 1958) 171-180; J. Ober, *Fortress Attica* (Leiden, 1985) 197-8. Praxagora's lamp-signal would of course be effective only in the theatre; realistically a lamp, held or hung no more than two metres above ground in front of an ordinary Athenian house, would not be seen beyond the next bend in the street.

8 **sexual variations:** lit. "styles of Aphrodite"; since the lamp is being described as sole sharer, and faithful keeper, of women's *secrets*, it is evident that the reference is to adulterous liaisons, in which comedy assumes women indulge constantly (cf. 225, 522-5, *Lys.* 107, 212, 404-419, *Thesm.* 340-5, 395-404, 477-501, 549-550, Ar. fr. 191). For the association between lamps and love cf. Hipponax fr. 17, *AP* 5.4, 5.7, 5.8, 5.165.

10 **arching:** Greek *lordoumenōn*, "bent over backwards" with convex spine and head thrown back, a posture associated either with back trouble and attempts to remedy it (cf. Men. *Dysk.* 533, Hippocr. *On Joints* 46, 48) or with sexual ecstasy (cf. Mnesimachus fr. 4.55). In Plato com. fr. 188.17 a list of erotic divinities includes Bendover (Kybdasos) and Bendback (Lordon).

13 **singeing off the hairs:** cf. *Lys.* 825-8, also *Thesm.* 236-246 (where a *man* is singed with a *torch*); see M. Kilmer, *JHS* 102 (1982) 104-112.

14-15 **when illicitly we open up ... :** cf. *Thesm.* 418-420 "we used to be able to ... take out barley-meal, oil, wine undetected", 813. The wife managed the household stores (211-2, *Lys.* 495, Xen. *Oec.* 7.36) and was therefore likely to be blamed if any commodity in them ran short; the first woman ever created, Pandora, had been the first to open a storage jar illicitly (Hes. *Works* 94-95).

14 **granaries and stores of ... :** lit. "colonnades of produce and of ...", the domestic store-chambers being grandiosely given the name of the Cornmarket Colonnade (*Stoā Alphitopōlis*, cf. 686) because both contained large amounts of grain.

14 **juice:** Greek *nāma*, lit. "flow", i.e. liquid; so in a passage of comparably elevated diction Men. *Dysk.* 947 calls water "the *nāma* of the Nymphs".

16 **yet, true accomplice, you never blab a word:** lit. "and <though> doing these things together <with us> you do not talk".

17 **and therefore shalt thou know our present scheme:** but just as Praxagora is about to tell her lamp (and the audience) what the scheme is, she breaks off to muse about the women's failure to arrive, and we are left to gather her intentions from incidental remarks; these tell us only that the women are going to disguise themselves as men (as we can already see Praxagora has done, though we may not have noticed that the items she is carrying include a false beard) and occupy seats in the Assembly (which we may also know already, if, as is not unlikely, the titles of plays were announced in advance). The objective of this operation is eventually revealed, briefly, in 107-8 and more fully in 171-240, though Praxagora's ultimate aims are kept from the audience until 590ff.

18 **my friends:** the Greek phrase is marked as feminine.

18 **the Scira:** a women's festival in honour of Demeter and Kore (or possibly of Demeter alone), held on the 12th of the month Scirophorion (roughly June) to which it gave its name. See Parke 88, 156-162; A.C. Brumfield, *The Attic Festivals of Demeter and their Relation to the Agricultural Year* (New York, 1981) 79-82, 156-175; L. Foxhall in R. Hawley and B. Levick ed. *Women in Antiquity: New Assessments* (London, 1995) 104-5. The women are imagined as having used this occasion, when they assembled together with no men present, to hatch a conspiracy, as in *Thesm.* they use the Thesmophoria to conspire against Euripides. The reference to the Scira, and the women's attempts to get themselves suntanned (63-64, 126-7), may suggest that we are to imagine the time as summer, but Euaeon's speech at the Assembly meeting (408-426) presupposes that winter has arrived or is approaching (cf. also 539); evidently consistency in such a matter was of no interest to dramatist or audience.

19 **none of those who were supposed to come is here:** Lysistrata makes the same complaint in *Lys.* 1-4 (cf. also *Ach.* 19ff).

20-21 **the Assembly will be starting very soon:** it began at sunrise (cf. 85, *Ach.* 19-20, also *Thesm.* 375).

21 **places:** since Greek *hedrai* can mean "seats", this passage, with 86 and 95-99, has been taken to indicate that in the fourth century at least a fair proportion of those attending the Assembly had benches to sit on. In the fifth century there had been benches for the presiding officers (*Ach.* 23-25), but most people had to sit on the rocky ground (*Knights* 754, 783-5; *Wasps* 42-43); since then the assembly-place on the Pnyx had been totally redesigned and reoriented (see H.A. Thompson, *Hesperia* Suppl. 19 [1982] 138-140). However, *hedrai* need mean no more than "places to sit"; see M.H. Hansen in B. Forsén and G.R. Stanton ed. *The Pnyx in the History of Athens* (Helsinki, 1996) 25-26 (modifying his earlier views).

22-23 **acting *in the most intimate cooperation*:** this renders the Greek feminine noun *hetairās*, by which Praxagora means "comrades", "conspirators" (i.e. members of a *hetaireiā*, a group of friends secretly pursuing political aims; cf. Lys. 12.43 where the anti-democratic conspirators of 405/4 are referred to as "the so-called *hetairoi*") but whose normal meaning in ordinary usage was "courtesans". The use of this word may leave the audience in considerable uncertainty as to the status of this woman and her associates: are they indeed *hetairai* (as 8-13 might also suggest), or are they the wives of citizens (as would normally be implied by Praxagora's mention of the civic festival of the Scira and her reference in 14-15 to the *secret* purloining of food and drink)? The allusion to Phyromachus' blunder (see next note) will suggest that the latter alternative is correct and the *double entendre* inadvertent on Praxagora's part, but this will not become certain until the other women arrive and it becomes clear that they are married (35, 37-38, 46-48, 51, 55) and part of the *polis* community (53).

22-23 **as Phyromachus once put it:** evidently Phyromachus had once, when speaking in public, used one of the words in this sentence – either *hetairās* (see above) or *hedrās* ("places, seats" but also "rumps, posteriors"); the Greek indicates that the word used was feminine and plural – in a context that made it risibly ambiguous. We do not, however, know who Phyromachus was, and ancient scholars – who probably could find no other reference to him in comedy – clearly did not know either. The scholia offer two accounts of him, both patently based on guesswork: in one he was a politician who "introduced a decree that women and men should sit separately, and the *hetairai* separately from the freeborn" (whoever thought of this must have forgotten that women did not attend the Athenian Assembly at all, separately or otherwise), while another identifies him with a tragic actor named Cleomachus (not otherwise known) who "apparently once said *hedrās* in a play [by mistake for *edrās* "you did"?] and was mocked for this indelicate language", presumably (though the scholiast does not make this explicit) by being nicknamed Phyromachus from *phūresthai* "to be in a muddle". Phyromachus was in fact a genuine Athenian name, but we do not know of any bearer of it who was in the public eye at this time (a Phyromachus [*PA* 15053 = *LGPN* 2] held the religious/judicial office of *basileus* towards the end of the fifth century, but this office did not normally confer any permanent prominence on those annually designated by lot to hold it; the parasite of Euphanes fr. 1.6 and Alexis fr. 223.16 lived about half a century later). The elucidation of Phyromachus' blunder is further complicated by uncertainty about the order of lines. With the order given in the mss. ("we've got to occupy seats – the ones Phyromachus once spoke of, if you remember that now – we, the *hetairai*, and settle our limbs without being noticed") it is easiest to assume that the blunder related to *hedrās*; with Dover's transposition of 22 and 23 it must almost inevitably be taken to have related to *hetairās*. I have adopted Dover's transposition because (i) without it *dei* "it is necessary" is much too widely separated from the accusative and infinitive that it governs and (ii) the transposition puts the joke about Phyromachus at the end of a sentence, making it easy for the speaker to pause and milk the laughter. Very likely Phyromachus' blunder, like the famous blunder of the actor Hegelochus (cf. *Frogs* 303-4), had to do with the placement of a pitch-accent: the genitive plural of *hetairos* "comrade, companion" was *hetaírōn*, the genitive plural of *hetairā* "courtesan" was *hetairôn*. The orator Demosthenes is said to have been jeered for mis-accenting the name of the god Asclepius ([Plut.] *Lives of the Ten Orators* 845b; cf. also schol. Dem. 18.52); but I slightly prefer the view that Phyromachus was an actor who spoke, perhaps, of how Odysseus had lost all his (not *companions*, but) *mistresses* at sea!

28 **let me step back again:** this provides an opportunity for Praxagora to get rid of her lamp, thus freeing a hand to provide gestural reinforcement for her speeches later on.

30-284 Who are the speakers (other than Praxagora) in this scene, and with how much assurance can the lines be apportioned between them? Three individual entries are clearly indicated: (*a*) the first arrival (30), who encourages others to come along quickly (so again in 43-45); (*b*) Praxagora's neighbour (33-34), who comes out of her house at 35 (whereas all the others appear to enter by the side-passages); (*c*) the speaker of 54-56, who is distinguished from (*a*) by the fact that she is late enough to need an excuse and from (*b*) by having a different excuse. Nothing in the scene requires us to assume that any other individual speaks. It is likely that (*a*) is the leader of the chorus, since (i) expressions like "time to get moving", "follow me quickly", etc., typically accompany the entry and exit of choruses (cf. 285, *Ach.* 204, *Clouds* 1510, *Peace* 301-3, *Lys.* 254-5, 319-320, *Thesm.* 1228-9, *Wealth* 1208-9) and (ii) in the subsequent Assembly rehearsal only *two* women other than Praxagora attempt to give speeches

(131-146, 147-160) – indeed the third attempt at a speech (163-8) is made by one of those who have spoken before – indicating that there are only three speaking *actors* present and that (in accordance with the usual conventions both of comedy and of tragedy) the *chorus-leader* does not make a set speech. Probably (cf. Russo 223-4), having fulfilled her function of getting the chorus on stage, the chorus-leader plays no further active role until the chorus as a whole are brought into the action again in 268ff in preparation for their exit-song (285ff) which fills the place in the dramatic structure normally occupied by a choral entrance-song; note that at 72, after two individuals have confirmed that they have brought their beards, the chorus are also asked about this but reply only with nods. It is more difficult to distinguish between (*b*) and (*c*), who are here labelled First Woman and Second Woman respectively. One possibility would be to assume that the character who appears first, and who is associated with one of the houses on stage, will be regarded as the more important, will normally speak before the other, and in the rehearsal-scene will be the one who volunteers first to speak and later offers to do so again without being asked. Vetta, on the other hand, following V. Coulon, *REG* 36 (1923) 374, claims (on 76-78) that Second Woman "is consistently the maker of clownish interjections and witty remarks" while First Woman "more than once echoes the seriousness and solemnity of Praxagora"; and while both of them certainly make ludicrous blunders in the Assembly rehearsal, it is *possible* to assign lines in such a way that all the serious comments and inquiries come from First Woman, and this is what I have tried to do. First Woman is never named, nor perhaps is her husband (see on 77); Second Woman *might* be one of the two whose husbands are named in 51-53, but it is more likely that she is one – indeed the very last – of the "great many other women" who follow these two.

30 **the morning herald** (the Greek merely says "the herald"): i.e. the cock (cf. Herodas 4.12-13).

31 **as we were coming along:** in the mss. the Greek participle is masculine, and one might be tempted to suppose that the speaker was already practising her skills in passing as a man; but this issue of gender identification by language is not otherwise addressed by anyone until 155-9, and it is more likely that the word is corrupt, probably under the influence of the masculine participles of the same verb that were used (correctly) in 28 and 29.

37 **my darling** (Greek *philtatē*) is vocative and feminine, i.e. it denotes Praxagora; cf. 54, and for the frequency of this and similar forms of address among women see my discussion in F. De Martino and A.H. Sommerstein ed. *Lo spettacolo delle voci* (Bari, 1995) ii 70-73, and *MCr* 25-28 (1990-3) 71-76.

38 **my other half:** lit. "the one that I am with".

38 **comes from Salamis:** the Salaminians, as the only Athenians who were islanders, had a nautical reputation, but they also had a reputation for high sexual stamina; there is a similar play on this double connotation of the name "Salamis" in *Lys.* 59-60, where, as here, it is assumed that Salaminians keep their wives busy (almost) all night.

39 **he was *rowing* me:** for this sexual metaphor cf. Plato com. fr. 3.3-4 "two divinities will destroy him [Adonis], she whom he rows, and he who rows him, with hidden oars" [i.e. Aphrodite, and Apollo or Dionysus]; in *Frogs* (49, 430) *naumakhein* "fight a sea-battle, row at battle speed" is used in the same sense.

41-42 **Cleinarete ... Sostrate ... Philaenete:** Sostrate was a very common woman's name at Athens and a favourite name for a married woman in comedy (cf. *Clouds* 678, *Wasps* 1397, *Thesm.* 374; three of Terence's six comedies feature a *matrona* named Sostrata). The other two names happen not to be attested elsewhere in Athenian literary or inscriptional texts, but they are regular and uncomic in formation and meaning.

43 **Glyce:** the Glyce of *Frogs* 1343 appears to be a poor woman, probably living alone and probably not of citizen status, but the name could also be borne by women of affluent citizen families (cf. *IG* ii^2 7424, 7702, 7717). I do not know why Ussher asserts that Glyce is "not a member of the chorus": she could hardly, except as a comic absurdity, have sworn to see that the last person to come to Praxagora's meeting would be punished if she wasn't meaning to come to it herself at all -- and if the idea *is* meant as a comic absurdity, why is attention not drawn to her absence? We are probably meant to assume that Glyce was one of the group who arrived first, with the chorus-leader.

43 **took an oath:** since the oath was taken by Glyce alone, Ussher is probably right to understand it as a threat ("I swear I'll make sure that the last one pays"; cf. *Birds* 630) rather than a promise.

44-45 **two gallons of wine:** lit. "three *khoes* of wine", a *khous* (of twelve *kotylai*) being rather more than three litres or rather less than three-quarters of a gallon. The fine is expressed in terms of wine because wine is assumed to be the most precious of all commodities to a woman: cf. 132-146, 153-5, 227, *Lys.* 194-236, *Thesm.* 347-8, 393, 630-2, 733-756.

45 **a quart:** lit. "a *khoinix*", a dry measure equivalent to four *kotylai* (see above).

45 **chickpeas:** to nibble with the wine (cf. 606, *Peace* 1136, Ephippus fr. 13.2, Xenophanes fr. 22.3 D-K). Since *erebinthos* "chickpea" can also mean "penis" (e.g. *Frogs* 545), there may be a *double entendre* involving dildoes (on which cf. Ar. fr. 592.16-28 and Herodas 6).

46 **Smicythion:** the joke about this man's impotence (see on 48) will be more effective if he is a real person known to the Athenian public, presumably an elderly man. A Smicythion of Halae (*PA* 12769 = *LGPN* 12) was secretary to the board of control for Eleusis in 407/6, and sixteen years earlier a Smicythion is mentioned in *Wasps* 401 in a context that implies he often appeared as a prosecutor in the courts: if these two and our man are all the same person, he would now be at least sixty, and if he was notably frail in appearance it would explain the joke. That Smicythion is a real person is also perhaps suggested by his wife's name **Melistiche**; this name is neither attested otherwise at Athens, nor of a common Athenian pattern, nor obviously funny, and its use is therefore best explained by the assumption that it actually was the name of the real Smicythion's wife.

47 **in his shoes:** the Greek does not explicitly state whose the shoes were, but it does call them *embades*, and *embades* were men's shoes (cf. 507); there is some tendency for *embades* to be associated especially with old and/or poor men (314, 633, 850, *Clouds* 719, 858, *Wasps* 103, 275, 447, 600, 1157, *Wealth* 759, 847). See Stone 223-5. Probably, when this woman came on stage, her gait was made comically ungainly as befitted one who had never worn *embades* before and/or had feet much too small for a man's shoe; cf. the comic exploitation of Philocleon's unfamiliarity with "Laconian" shoes in *Wasps* 1157-72.

48 **able to get away ... in her own time:** because her husband (unlike e.g. First Woman's), being impotent, has been asleep for many hours; but though Melistiche has thus had plenty of time to get to the meeting-place she has still been slow arriving, because she unwisely put on her husband's shoes before coming. This implies, of course, that the other women are *carrying* their men's shoes (except First Woman who is lucky enough to live right next to the meeting-place); they put them on only after 269.

49 **Geusistrate:** the name seems to be an invented one meaning "she who gives a taste to the army/multitude", an appropriate name for the wife of a tavern-keeper if she ran the

shop together with her husband (some women ran them alone, cf. *Thesm.* 347, *Wealth* 435, 1120), referring to the practice of allowing customers to taste samples of wine free of charge (cf. *Ach.* 186-200 where Dicaeopolis is invited to taste three alternative vintages/peace-treaties before choosing one). Neither this name nor any other derived from *geuein* "give a taste", *geuesthai* "taste", is attested at Athens. There may again be a *double entendre* insinuating that women of Geusistrate's profession (who inevitably came much into contact with strange men – and indoors too) often invited their customers to sample not their wine but their bodies (cf. Aesch. fr. 243 "a young woman who has tasted man").

50 **with the torch in her right hand:** why a torch rather than a lamp? Probably because wine-shops sold torches (Nicostratus fr. 22, Lys. 1.24), which were an essential for the nocturnal reveller (cf. 692, 978, 1150, *Wasps* 1331, *Lys.* 1217, *Wealth* 1041).

51 **Philodoretus' and Chaeretades' wives:** men speaking of women normally referred to them not by their own names but as X's wife or daughter (see *QSt* 11 [1980] 393-418 and D.M. Schaps, *CQ* 27 [1977] 323-330). Ar. usually represents women, when among themselves, as referring to each other by their own names, but here he makes the speaker follow the usual male practice. Either (i) Ar. has erred here, or (ii) women did sometimes speak of each other as "X's wife" (cf. *Thesm.* 605 where Mica, asked who she is – admittedly by a man, if a very effeminate one – replies "Cleonymus' wife"), or else (iii) Philodoretus and Chaeretades were real people of distinctive appearance (e.g. very tall/short/fat) and Ar. is making fun of them by creating "wives" for them with exaggeratedly similar characteristics (as perhaps he had done in the case of Mica, Cleonymus having been a very fat man). The names Philodoretus and Chaeretades are not otherwise attested at Athens, and the latter is reminiscent of several fictitious names in comedy (e.g. Charitimides, 293; Charinades, *Wasps* 232 and *Peace* 1155; Chaerippus, *Clouds* 64; Chaereas, Chaerestratus and Charisius in various plays of Menander), so (iii) is perhaps the least likely of these alternatives.

53 **all that's worth anything in the City:** this phrase shows that the speaker here must be Praxagora. In terms of the audience's present knowledge, it means no more than "every decent woman in Athens"; but, as they will soon discover, Praxagora believes that there are *no* decent *men* in Athens and that the women are the city's sole hope (105-9, 176-240).

56 **he'd stuffed himself with anchovies:** sc. and swallowed several fishbones (so Ussher).

59 **all the things that we resolved on at the Scira:** the repetition of 18 will raise expectations that we will now learn more about the women's plan; but in the next 45 lines we learn only marginally more than we knew already.

61 **bushier:** Greek *dasus* means both (of skin) "covered with hair" and (of ground) "covered with shrubs or trees".

63 **I oiled myself:** to protect her skin against drying and wrinkling.

64 **to get a tan:** free men, who spent most of their daylight hours out of doors, were expected to be deeply tanned; free women, who (ideally) stayed in the home, were expected to be pale; the conventions of art emphasized this contrast, and both men (735-6) and women (878, Xen. *Oec.* 10.2) might use cosmetics to make their faces darker or lighter, respectively. The Greek verb, which is imperfect not aorist, does not imply that the speaker's attempt to give herself a convincing tan was successful (cf. 126-7); later the men at the Assembly will notice the "white" complexions of the mysterious newcomers (385-7, 427-8).

65 **razor:** another item (cf. 12-13) in a woman's armoury for removing superfluous hair; in Ar. fr. 332 it stands first in a list of fifty-two feminine accessories. For a man to use

(or be said to use) a razor was proof of effeminacy (e.g. Agathon, *Thesm.* 191, 217-9; Cleisthenes, *Ach.* 119).

70 **by Hecate:** a regular woman's oath (1097, *Thesm.* 858, *Wealth* 764), though it could also be used by men (*Wealth* 1070).

71 **one that beats Epicrates by a street:** lit. "<one> not a little finer than <that of> Epicrates"; the meaning is probably (see below) that the beard is outstanding in size and/or thickness (rather than in aesthetic appeal). Epicrates (*PA* 4859 = *LGPN* 70), of the deme Cephisia, was a leading politician of the 390s. He had fought on the democratic side in the civil war of 403 (Dem. 19.277), and in 396/5 he had been among the strongest advocates of war with Sparta, some asserting that he was in Persian pay (*Hell.Oxy.* 7.2, cf. Paus. 3.9.8); there is evidence that he tried to present himself as a champion of the poor (Plut. *Pelop.* 30.12). In or about 393 (so Jacoby on Philochorus *FGrH* 328 F 149) he and Phormisius (see on 97) served on an embassy to Persia and were accused of receiving bribes (Plato com. fr. 127; Plut. loc.cit., Hegesander ap. Ath. 6.251a); about the same time he held a financial office and was charged first with bribery and then with embezzlement (Lys. 27.3-6), but all these trials ended in acquittal. In 392 he was one of the delegates to the Sparta Conference (Philochorus *FGrH* 328 F 149; see Introduction), and after the Assembly, despite the advocacy of his fellow-envoy Andocides (3 *On the Peace*), had rejected the peace terms there agreed, he and his colleagues were prosecuted by Callistratus (nephew of Agyrrhius, for whom see on 102) for disobeying their instructions, accepting bribes, and making a false report to the Council; they fled into exile to avoid trial and were condemned to death in their absence (Dem. 19.277-280; Philochorus loc.cit.). His exceptionally long beard (Plato com. fr. 130) led to his being nicknamed *sakesphoros* "bearer of a giant shield" (cf. Soph. *Aj.* 19).

74 **Laconian shoes:** cf. 269, 345, 508, 542, and see Stone 225-7. They seem to be regarded in this play as a particular type of *embades* (see on 47; in 314 and 345 Blepyrus uses both terms in referring to what must be the same pair of shoes), but in *Wasps* (1157-8) "Laconians" are clearly more expensive and dressy than *embades*; probably *embades* had both a generic and a specific sense, the latter denoting the cheaper varieties. The comic evidence suggests that "Laconians" were the regular everyday footwear of a well-dressed male town-dweller (cf. *Thesm.* 141-2). "Laconians" were tied on with a leather strap (508), and could be of various colours (red, Pollux 7.88; white, Ath. 5.215c).

74 **walking-sticks** were used mainly, as might be expected, by old men (cf. 276-8), but seem to have been used by men of a broader age range when attending the Assembly (cf. *Wasps* 33); when Praxagora in her male disguise addresses the people, Chremes takes her for a young man (427) but does not find it surprising that she has a stick. See Stone 246-8.

76 **cudgel:** Greek *skutalon*, a stick with a knobbed or twisted end, used by Spartans (*Lys.* 991, Plut. *Nic.* 19.6) and by people in Athens or elsewhere who aped Spartan ways (*Birds* 1283). To judge by the context, with its allusions to the monsters Lamia and Argus, this particular specimen should be very large and approximate more to a club than a walking-stick (the word is applied to the club of Heracles in Pind. *Olymp.* 9.30).

77 **Lamius:** we must be meant to take this as either the name or the nickname of the speaker's husband; and since mention of the name is unnecessary and even unnatural (a woman would normally say "my husband", as in 37 and 55) it is probably the name or nickname of a real person. The text actually gives the name in the genitive case (*Lamiou*) and the nominative might thus theoretically be either *Lamios* or *Lamiās*, but only the former is actually – though rarely, and not before about 300 – attested as a

name at Athens. Ancient commentators (and the lexicographers Hesychius and Photius) make four assertions about Lamius/Lamias: (i) that his real name was Mnesitheus (or Gnesitheus – but this name is otherwise unknown at Athens); (ii) that he was referred to in comedy as a jailer; (iii) that he was nicknamed "Saw" or "Axe"; (iv) that he was a poor man who lived by carrying loads of wood. Of these (i) and (iii) are associated, in the Hesychius lexicon entry (λ251), with a reference to comedy (*com. adesp.* 382), yet are not derivable from Ar.'s text, while (iv) fits well with (iii); all these three statements, then, are probably based ultimately on references to our man in another comedy or comedies, and they combine to suggest the figure of a man in public life who was accused of having risen from poverty and menial employment to wealth by means of embezzlement and bribe-taking (cf. *Wealth* 567-570, Lys. 25.26, 27.9, 28.1, [Lys.] 20.11-12, Aeschines 3.173, Dem. 18.129-131). Statement (ii), on the other hand, does not match this pattern, even though the formula "he is referred to in comedy as ..." normally indicates that the source is a treatise on victims of comic satire (*kōmōidoumenoi*); the idea that Lamius was a jailer could easily be based on a misinterpretation of 79-81 below, and the author of the treatise probably relied solely on this "evidence". Evidently our man habitually carried a stout stick (like an earlier politician, Cleigenes; cf. *Frogs* 715-7), and this may have earned him his nickname through an association with the child-eating ogress Lamia (cf. Duris, *FGrH* 76 F 17; D.S. 20.41.3; Heraclitus, *On Incredible Stories* 34; Hor. *AP* 340), who was said (Crates fr. 20, cf. *Wasps* 1177) to carry a *skutalē* (a synonym of *skutalon*) and (cf. 78) to use an evil-smelling fart as a defensive weapon. Beyond what can be gleaned from the above evidence and from Ar.'s text, we know nothing about this man; the name Mnesitheus was a very common one, but no bearer of it is known to have been even moderately prominent in public life in the 390s.

78 **So *that's* the one he goes around with, farting!:** the transmitted text is unintelligible; its literal meaning, if it can be said to have one, is "This is that one of the cudgels which he farts" (mss.) or "This is one of those cudgels which he farts" (Suda). The joke is evidently based on the assimilation of "Lamius" to Lamia (cf. previous note): not only does he resemble Lamia in carrying a big stick, he also resembles her in breaking malodorous wind (cf. *Wasps* 1035 = *Peace* 758 which describes Cleon as having "the smell of a seal, the unwashed balls of a Lamia, and the arse of a camel"; see G. Mastromarco, *RFIC* 117 [1989] 419-421). Numerous emendations have been proposed, but none (including my own suggestion, on which my translation is based, but which is offered merely *exempli gratia*) has succeeded in combining appropriate sense, adequate comic force, and a plausible explanation of the assumed corruption. Coulon's proposal ("That is one of those which he carries around, farting") perhaps comes closest; its only important shortcoming is that it envisages "Lamius" as owning *several* stout sticks, for which neither he nor Lamia would have any need.

80 **if he put on the leather coat of the All-seeing One:** having dwelt on and amplified the already established comparison of Mnesitheus to one monster, Lamia, Ar. now compares him to another, Argus "the All-seeing" (so called e.g. in Aesch. *Supp.* 304, Eur. *Phoen.* 1115), the many-eyed giant set by Hera to guard Io when she had transformed Io into a heifer to frustrate the amorous intentions of Zeus, and ultimately slain by Hermes. The word *diphtherā* "leather coat" suggests (i) a rough working garment suitable for a herdsman (cf. *Clouds* 72, *Wasps* 444, Men. *Dysk.* 415, *Epitr.* 229, 328; see Stone 166-7) and therefore also for Argus the "herder of one cow" (Aesch. loc.cit.) and more specifically (ii) Argus' own distinctive garment, the hide of the Arcadian bull that he had killed (Apoll. 2.1.2); it *may* also suggest (iii) the skin of Argus himself (in classical red-figure art often shown spangled all over with numerous

eyes), imagined as being converted after his death into a garment for someone else. Argus is described as fierce of temper ([Aesch.] *Prom.* 678) and of great strength ([Hes.] fr. 294, Apoll. loc.cit.), and – crucially – is sometimes, from about 440 onwards, shown armed with a club or stick (cf. *LIMC* s.v. Io #33-35 and 57); so "Lamius", given that he already has a cudgel (and also – one may reasonably guess – a powerful frame and irascible temperament), would only need one or two of Argus' other attributes to do Argus' job as well as he had done it himself!

81 **to be one-to-one with:** Greek *boukolein*, lit. "to tend (as a cowherd)". We expect the sentence to end with "Io", but instead it ends with **the public executioner** (Greek *ton dēmion*), no doubt as an unsubtle hint that "Lamius" deserves to make his acquaintance (cf. *Knights* 973-6, 1362-3; *Frogs* 684-5, 1504-14). It is not, however, altogether easy to find a sense in which a person could be said to *boukolein* the executioner, and for this reason (and others less persuasive) Bothe's simple emendation *to dēmion* "the public, the people" has found wide support: *boukolein* can then be taken to mean either "shepherd, lead" or (better) "cheat, deceive" (cf. Men. *Sam.* 530, 596). However, *to dēmion* in this sense (for which cf. Aesch. *Supp.* 370, 699) is not found in prose or comedy, and it is preferable to suppose that *boukolein*, like its near-synonym *boskein*, was capable of meaning "maintain, (help to) provide with a living": "Lamius", it may be hoped, will soon be providing (becoming) a day's work for the executioner.

82 **get on with our job:** lit. "do the things after these". As will later become clear, she is thinking mainly of the dress-rehearsal which is part of her plan (cf. 116-7); merely to put on the male disguises would not require so early a start (**while there are still stars in the sky**).

86 **so we really must:** the mss. read "so you [singular] must", but (1) Praxagora cannot herself occupy a whole block of seats (contrast 21-23 "*we've* got to occupy seats", 98) and (2) it is not she who needs to be reminded that time is of the essence – on the contrary she has just reminded the others, and First Woman, who is on the whole serious and helpful (see on 30-284), is reinforcing this admonition. Meineke's one-letter emendation replaces the second-person pronoun (*se*) by a particle of emphasis (*ge*), leaving the subject of "must occupy" to be understood.

87 **at the foot of the Rock:** the speaker's platform at the Pnyx, usually called the *bēma*, was sometimes (cf. *Knights* 956, *Peace* 680) referred to as "the Rock" (*petrā* or *lithos*) Probably it actually was a platform of natural rock, both before and after the redesign of the Pnyx (see on 21); its successor, the *bēma* of "Pnyx III" (second half of fourth century), certainly was cut out of the "living rock" (H.A. Thompson, *Hesperia* Suppl. 19 [1982] 141; no trace of the *bēma* of Pnyx I or II survives).

87 **the Prytaneis:** the business committee of the Council of Five Hundred, comprising all the fifty councillors from one of the ten tribes, which held office for one-tenth of the year and which at this time presided over any meetings of the Assembly held within that period (cf. *Ach.* 23, 40, 56, 167, 173; Xen. *Hell.* 1.7.14-15), sitting, as our passage shows, on benches of their own, facing the public, just below the speaker's podium. Probably about a decade later, between 384/3 and 379/8 (see F.X. Ryan, *JHS* 115 [1995] 167-8), the presidency of the Assembly (and of the Council) was transferred from the Prytaneis to a panel of nine *proedroi* chosen by lot, for one day only, from councillors of the nine tribes *not* currently prytanizing (see Arist. *Ath.Pol.* 44.2-3).

88 **this stuff:** the wool and carding-combs in the basket.

89 **while the Assembly was filling up:** it was customary for women, whenever not engaged in other work, to busy themselves with the preparation of clothing materials (in Homer even queens regularly do so, cf. *Od.* 4.121-136, 6.304-7, 17.96-97), and this woman had planned to use the time of the Assembly for this purpose, beginning as soon

as she arrived and continuing through the debate (91-92). She mentions the matter now to show that she has remembered the women must come early to the Pnyx: she has brought along enough wool for a long session! This is the first of many indications that the women other than Praxagora are still in the grip of traditionally feminine patterns of thought, speech and action, which could endanger the success of her scheme.

90 ***Filling up*, you idiot!:** Praxagora's point, which she does not need to spell out, is that women, when carding wool (in the home), often sat with one foot up on a stool and with their clothes raised above the knee, as shown e.g. on a kylix by Duris, Berlin F2289 (see E. Fantham et al., *Women in the Classical World: Image and Text* [Oxford, 1994] 105 fig. 3.18). It.would be foolish enough for a woman wishing to pass as a man to adopt a posture like this at any time, and doubly so when men were passing by to take their seats and when there were no speeches to distract them.

95 **it would be a fine thing for us:** spoken sarcastically. The train of thought has been: it is dangerous to expose our bodies by carding wool → it is dangerous to risk exposing our bodies → it is dangerous to risk exposing our bodies by arriving late; thus Praxagora is able to revert to what is her main concern at present, the need to get to the Pnyx as soon as possible (82-85).

96 **was climbing over them:** to reach one of the seats still vacant (for Assembly meetings were crowded, if only because those attending now received pay; cf. 183-8, 282-4, 289-292, 302-310, 389-393, 547-8).

97 **Phorm...isius:** Phormisius (*PA* 14945; *LGPN* 1 = 6) first appears in our sources in 406/5 (*Frogs* 965). Before the installation of the Thirty in 404 he, like Theramenes, attempted to steer a middle course between democracy and oligarchy (Arist. *Ath.Pol.* 34.3); under their rule he joined the democrats in exile, and after the fall of the oligarchy he unsuccessfully proposed that full political rights should be withheld from citizens who did not own land (D.H. *Lysias* 32). About 393 he was a colleague of Epicrates (see on 71) on the embassy to Persia which resulted in their being accused of corruption. He may still have been active in 378, if he was the Phormisius who joined in urging Athenian action in support of Theban independence from Sparta (Dein. 1.38); sexually, or so it was said, he remained active to the moment of his death (Philetaerus fr. 6). Either Phormisius' bushy beard (cf. *Frogs* 966) here serves as a metonym for the women's pubic hair, or else "Phormisius" is substituted for "cunt" in order to label Phormisius as a former male prostitute (like Agyrrhius, cf. 103): according to Hesychius (α7248 = *com. adesp.* 283) two other men's names (Basileides and Lachares) were used by comic poets in the same way, just as "Aristodemus" and two other names were used to mean "anus".

102 **Agyrrhius,** of the deme Collytus (*PA* 179; *LGPN* 1), was one of the most prominent political leaders of the 390s and early 380s. He is not known to have been politically active before 404 (unless schol. *Frogs* 367 is right in associating him with measures to reduce festival expenditures in 406/5), but immediately after the restoration of democracy in 403 he appears as secretary to the Council (*IG* ii^2 1.41); in 402/1 he was head of a tax-farming syndicate (Andoc. 1.133), and in 400 he took part in the prosecution of Andocides (ibid.). In the 390s he proposed the introduction of Assembly pay, and later increased the fee to three obols (Arist. *Ath.Pol.* 41.3; cf. 183-6 below). Possibly helped by an alliance with Conon (see Strauss 137-8), he was a powerful figure by 394/3, when his friends included the wealthy freedman banker Pasion and the son of the chief minister to the king of Bosporus (Crimea) (Isoc. 17.31-32); he was himself reputed to be a very rich man (*Wealth* 176). In 392, when Conon led the Athenian delegation at the Sardis Conference, his colleague Callimedon (Xen. *Hell.* 4.8.13) may have been a relative and agent of Agyrrhius (cf. below), but after the failure of the conference and Conon's arrest by the Persians Agyrrhius seems to have turned against peace negotiations, and the prosecution of the Sparta Conference delegates, including Epicrates (see on 71) and Agyrrhius' old enemy Andocides, was conducted by his nephew Callistratus. Probably in 389 he succeeded Thrasybulus (see on 203) in command of the Athenian fleet then off southern Asia Minor (cf. Plato com. fr. 201), but is not known to have achieved anything in this capacity; later, probably after the unsatisfactory peace of 387/6, he was prosecuted (officially for embezzlement, really no doubt for alleged political and/or military failures; cf. Strauss 160-1) and imprisoned for many years until he paid off what he had been adjudged to owe the state (Dem. 24.135). Eventually, however, he was released and returned to public life, no doubt under the wing of his nephew who by the mid 370s was the most powerful man in Athens; an inscription (*American School of Classical Studies at Athens, Newsletter*, Spring 1987, 8) shows Agyrrhius still active in politics as late as 374/3. He was almost certainly the grandfather of Callimedon "the Crayfish", a politician of the later fourth century who was mentioned in comedy (mainly for his gastronomic rather than his political activities) more often than any other man of his time (e.g. Eubulus fr. 8, Alexis fr. 57, Menander fr. 224.14; we know of fourteen comic references to him, including nine in Alexis alone).

102 **has nicked Pronomus' beard:** Pronomus is unidentifiable (*LGPN* knows no other Athenian of this name); possibly he had been a politician whose sudden disappearance from the public eye (through death or exile) had coincided with a marked increase in the length of Agyrrhius' beard, leading to the joking suggestion that Agyrrhius' beard really belonged to Pronomus.

103 ***he*** [sc. Agyrrhius] **used to be a woman:** for this kind of gibe see on 112-4, and cf. Eupolis fr. 171 (Alcibiades), Aeschines 1.111 (Hegesander and Timarchus).

104 **he's screwing up the City with the best of them:** lit. "he is doing the greatest things in the city", i.e. is a major political figure; but *prāttein ta megista* "do the greatest things" can also be a euphemism for "have sexual intercourse" (cf. Theocr. 2.143 and, for other double-entendres built around the phrase, *Thesm.* 813 and perhaps *Birds* 708). Agyrrhius may once have been a "woman", but Pronomus' beard has turned him into a real "man" both in the political sense (cf. *Knights* 179, Pl. *Symp.* 192a) and in the sexual sense!

105-6 **this ... is the reason:** viz. the fact that men like Agyrrhius are running, and ruining, the city (cf. 176-182).

105 **by the holy light of this dawning day:** lit. "by the approaching day", an unusual oath (though Hes. *Thg.* 124 does make Day a goddess, daughter of Night) designed to stress the importance of the coming day for the women and for Athens and probably to suggest that it will mark a new dawn in the City's fortunes. For such rhetorical oaths cf. Eur. *Hipp.* 306-8 "Your children will have no share in their patrimony, *by the horse-riding Amazon queen*, who has borne a son to be their master", Eupolis fr. 106 (Miltiades speaking) "*By my battle at Marathon*, none of these people is going to get away with giving pain to my heart".

107 **taking over the running of the City:** now at last we know why the women are going to the Assembly – though we are still kept in the dark as to what Praxagora means to do with power when she has it, and when some indications do begin to appear of her intentions (from 210) they will prove in the end to have been systematically misleading.

109 **we're dead in the water:** lit. "we are neither running [i.e. making headway under sail] nor rowing", clearly a current idiom both in nautical and in other contexts (the scholia cite a proverb "Where there is money, everything runs and rows", i.e. money gets things moving). At present, says Praxagora in effect, the ship of state (cf. *Wasps* 29; Aesch. *Seven* 2, 62-64, 652, 758-762, etc.; Eur. *Supp.* 473-5) is going nowhere.

110 **a "feminine-minded company of women":** even without the help of the scholia we could be fairly certain that this phrase was quoted or adapted from a tragedy (*trag. adesp.* 51). In the tragic context *xunousiā* "company" may have meant "companionship", in the mouth of a character deploring the evil effects on a young man (Achilles on Scyros?) of being brought up among women (contrast Men. *Dysk.* 384-9 where Sostratus opines that, contrariwise, a girl who has *not* been brought up among women will make an exceptionally desirable wife); Ar. reuses the phrase taking *xunousiā* in the rarer sense "band, group" (cf. Soph. *Phil.* 936). To be "feminine-minded" was, in the opinion of most men (and of women who accepted men's estimate of them), to be incapable of rational thought (note the antithesis in *Lys.* 1124 = Eur. fr. 483 "I am a woman, *but* I have got a mind"; cf. Dover *GPM* 99-100).

112-3 **the young men who get shagged ... the smartest speakers:** it is a standing joke in comedy that all the most successful politicians were once male prostitutes (cf. 102-4, *Knights* 423-8, 878-880, 1242; *Clouds* 1093-4; Pl. com. fr. 202.5), and Plato (*Symp.* 192a) makes Ar. cite this, as an accepted truth, in support of his (fantastic) theory of the origin of sexual orientations.

114 **by a stroke of luck:** ironic, since extremely powerful (though unwritten) social rules ensured that virtually every citizen woman was made a wife at an early age.

115 **inexperience is a daunting thing:** this may be another tragic quotation (*trag. adesp.* 51a); the negation of nouns ("inexperience" translates Greek *mē (e)mpeiriā*, lit. "not-experience") is alien to comedy but found in Euripides, Thucydides, and philosophical texts (see Barrett on Eur. *Hipp.* 196).

118 **you can't tie on your beard too soon:** i.e. tie it on quickly!

119 **all the others:** over-optimism on Praxagora's part: only two women even offer to speak, and one of these virtually admits (cf. 164) that she has not put in any serious practice.

119-120 **their talks ... how to *talk*:** Praxagora here uses *lalein* "talk" merely as a colloquial synonym of *legein* "speak" (cf. *Clouds* 1394; *Thesm.* 138, 267); but Second Woman takes it in the (commoner) pejorative sense "talk to no good purpose, chatter". Garrulity was one of the vices stereotypically ascribed to women (cf. *Thesm.* 393; Alexis fr. 96; Semonides fr. 7.10; Theocr. 15.87-89; Lucian, *The Rhetoric Teacher* 23).

122 **the garlands:** to be worn by the speakers, as was the custom in the real Assembly (cf. *Thesm.* 380); similarly in *Birds* (463) Peisetaerus, about to make a speech to the birds, calls for a garland. Ar. has provided Praxagora with two garlands, rather than one as might be expected, to ease the transitions from one speaker to the next (there will always be a garland ready to hand for the new speaker to put on).

125 **look, my dear:** Second Woman can hardly be inviting Praxagora to stare at her face, and I therefore assume that she has brought along a mirror (a typically feminine accessory, like her work-basket; cf. *Thesm.* 140, Ar. fr. 332.1, Eur. *Hipp.* 429), has viewed herself in it, and is asking Praxagora to do likewise.

126-7 **as if someone tied beards on to lightly browned cuttlefish:** her point is that beards are normally associated with a dark, firm, "masculine" face, and look incongruous against the background of the soft and (despite all efforts, cf. 63-64) pale complexions of the women; she compares the latter to the colour of a cuttlefish (by nature soft-fleshed and white) that has been "not very much roasted" or "roasted only on the surface" (scholia), rather like the squid of Antiphanes fr. 216.20-22 which "with the fiery lashings of the coals has changed the brilliant white nature of its flesh, and [whose] whole body rejoices in a golden-brown aura".

128-130 To create the appropriate atmosphere for her rehearsal, Praxagora quickly and sketchily runs through some of the preliminaries of an Assembly meeting; cf. *Ach.* 43-45. This is pure simulation: the (male) "purifier" is not really present any more than Ariphrades is, and there is no need for anyone to "move forward and sit down" because everone but Praxagora is seated already (57). The full procedure included elaborate prayers coupled with curses on those who did or wished ill to the people; these are parodied in *Thesm.* 295-371.

128 purifier: Greek *peristiarkhos*, the officiant responsible for making the purificatory sacrifice before meetings of the Council and Assembly (and other public gatherings, including those in the Theatre of Dionysus); cf. Aeschines 1.23, Ister *FGrH* 334 F 16, Harpocration κ4, schol. *Ach.* 44). The slaughtered victim was carried round the meeting-place, demarcating a purified area within which all those taking part in the meeting had to remain (cf. *Ach.* 44).

128 the ferret (strictly "polecat"): in reality the purification-sacrifice was a young pig. Praxagora, unlike the other women, does not elsewhere make stupid mistakes about the substance and procedure of Assembly debates, so a joke regarding women's ignorance of these matters would be inappropriate here. More likely the idea of carrying out a solemn purification ritual with an undignified and evil-smelling animal (cf. *Ach.* 255, *Wealth* 693) is evoked purely for its comic absurdity and is not designed to have any wider relevance to the drama.

129 Ariphrades can hardly be the son of Automenes (*PA* 2201; *LGPN* 1) who is several times attacked in Ar.'s early plays for his addiction to cunnilingus (*Knights* 1274-89; *Wasps* 1280-3; *Peace* 883-5; Ar. fr. dub. 926), for he is never heard of after the 420s. All we can gather about the present Ariphrades is that he was a man who could be expected to hold up the start of Assembly meetings by chatting to his friends instead of taking his seat; perhaps he had recently been publicly rebuked, or even fined, for doing this repeatedly.

132-168 On the identification of speakers, see on 30-284. Here two women make (or attempt to make) a total of three speeches; the deliverers of speech 1 (132-146) and speech 2 (147-160) are obviously different persons, and in 163 *au* (approximately "in turn") indicates that speech 3 (163-8) is given by a different person from speech 2 and therefore by the same person who made speech 1. Given this, it is clearly best, in accordance with the principles indicated on 30-284, to assign speech 2 to First Woman (who is fairly competent, using a genuine orator's opening gambit – see on 151-2 – and winning praise from Praxagora) and speeches 1 and 3 to Second Woman (who never actually starts her first speech at all, and blunders on the fourth word of her second).

132 before having a drink: women in Aristophanic comedy are insatiable lovers of wine; cf. 227, 1118-24, *Lys.* 194-239, 466, *Thesm.* 347-8, 393, 628-632, 733-757.

133 what else did I put on a garland for?: because garlands were worn at symposia; similarly in *Birds* 463-4 Peisetaerus' request for a garland (and for water to pour over his hands) leads Euelpides to ask "Are we going to have a dinner, or what?"

137 and pretty strong stuff too: despite LSJ, Greek *euzōros* means "strong" (i.e. mixed with relatively little water), not "neat" (for which the Greek word is *akrātos*), as witness its frequent use in the comparative (Antiphanes fr. 137; Ephippus fr. 3.11; Diphilus fr. 57; cf. Phryn. *Ecl.* 114).

140 they pour libations ... or else why would they make all those prayers?: important prayers were often accompanied by libations (cf. *Wasps* 863-4, *Peace* 435); hence (Second Woman reasons) if there are prayers at Assembly meetings (cf. on 128-130) there must be libations, if there are libations there must be wine, and if there is wine someone must be drinking it!

143 **someone turns violent:** the Greek verb is *paroinein*, which strictly means "behave violently or obstreperously *when drunk*" but can be used to refer to any violent behaviour whether or not alcohol-related (cf. Men. *Dysk.* 93).

143 **the archers:** public slaves purchased from Scythia, who carried out police duties under the instructions of various magistrates (cf. *Lys.* 433-462, *Thesm.* 923ff, 1001ff), including keeping order at Council and Assembly meetings and removing trouble-makers (cf. 258-9, *Ach.* 54-58, *Knights* 665, Pl. *Prot.* 319c). They are usually said to *drag* offenders off, but 261 ("if they lift you off the ground") shows that "carry" here is not necessarily an exaggeration.

144 **useless:** lit. "nothing".

145 **I'd have been better off staying beardless:** not because the beard itself has made her thirsty (Rogers, Ussher), but because she was led to expect a drink and then did not get it.

148 **the job's been started now:** lit. "the thing is being worked", "the job is (in course of) being done". Second Woman's incompetence and frivolity have discouraged Praxagora, but having set her hand to the task she will not now abandon it (so rightly Ussher).

149 **man's language:** Greek *andristi*, exactly parallel to the normal formation of adverbs meaning "in the X language" (*hellēnisti* "in Greek", *persisti* "in Persian", etc.). The word is not Ar.'s invention, Crates (fr. 24) having used it in reference to a woman imitating a man's *voice*, and it is possible that it bears the same meaning here (cf. in reverse *Thesm.* 267-8 "make sure you put on a good, convincing *woman's* voice"); but in ancient drama, where all the performers were male anyway, little comic effect could be produced by a woman character imitating a male voice, and since both Ar. and Praxagora are clearly aware of the importance of using appropriately masculine phraseology (155, 165, 189, 204) and grammar (299) I have preferred to assume that *andristi* here refers to this.

150 **lean hard with your body on your stick:** there may well be a *double entendre* (cf. Rothwell 84 n.21), since *skhēma* "shape, configuration; body" can denote the female genitals (cf. LXX *Isaiah* 3.17 – and perhaps 482 below), *diereidesthai* "lean hard" suggests *ereidesthai/ereidein* "knock, copulate" (cf. 616, *Thesm.* 488, Ar. fr. 715), and any word denoting a stick or other hard elongated object may acquire a phallic connotation in an appropriate context (see Henderson 120-4).

151-2 **I would have wished ... I could have sat quiet:** a conventional opening for a speaker who has not (or not often) previously addressed the Assembly: cf. Thrasymachus fr. 1 D-K, Isoc. 6.2, Dem. 4.1.

153 **so far as in me lies:** lit. "according to my own single <opinion> at any rate".

154 **storage-pits:** Greek *lakkoi*, pits dug in the ground and sealed with cement, either (1) for the storage of wine or oil (Xen. *Anab.* 4.2.22; Suda l60) or (2) as water-cisterns (Thphr. *Char.* 20.9, Anaxilas fr. 3, Alexis fr. 179.9). At first the mention of "taverns" suggests that the speaker means (1), and "for water" (at the end of the sentence, and at the beginning of a new verse) comes as a surprise twist. The speaker's indignation over the sale of diluted wine (cf. on 132) might be thought to come dangerously close to betraying her true gender, but Praxagora apparently does not find it objectionable (cf. 159).

155 **by the Two Goddesses:** "the Two Goddesses" are Demeter and Persephone (Pherrephatta, Kore), the goddesses of the women's festival of the Thesmophoria, who in comedy, and doubtless in real life, were invoked in oaths exclusively by women.

160 **by Apollo:** this is normally a man's oath, but is used by women at *Lys.* 917 and probably at *Frogs* 508. First Woman is not here *correcting* her mistake (that would

require the oath-particle *ma* "no, by ...", as in 155, not *n–* "yes, by ..."); rather she is *admitting* it, and possibly meaning to offer an excuse or explanation (cf. 167-8) which Praxagora forestalls.

165 **ladies of the Assembly:** lit. "women who are sitting".

167 **Epigonus:** evidently a man who looked like a woman, i.e. who did not wear, or could not grow, a beard – the same abnormality for which Agathon is satirized in *Thesm.* and Cleisthenes in almost every surviving fifth-century play of Ar. (cf. e.g. *Knights* 1373-4, *Clouds* 355, *Thesm.* 574ff). According to the scholia Epigonus was satirized (sc. elsewhere) in comedy as "soft" (i.e. a passive homosexual) and as one who was always found among women. We may have an inscriptional reference to him. *IG* ii^2 2346 (first half of fourth century) is apparently a list of the members of a cult-association (*thiasos*); fragments *a,b,c* list men's names (almost all with patronymics), while on fragment *d* the names seem all to be female – except that among them (line 109) is that of [Epi]gonus! The name is so rare in classical Athens (though extremely common in Roman times) that it must be highly probable that this man (*LGPN* 107) is identical with our Epigonus who "was always found among women" – though one would like to know whether it was with his consent that he was listed publicly in the women's section of the *thiasos* register!

167-8 **I looked over there:** Greek *blepsāsa ... ekeise*; the transmitted reading is *epiblepsāsa*, but that would imply that the speaker deliberately glanced at Epigonus, whereas her whole point is that he just happened to be the person on whom her eye fell.

170 **if this is what you lot are like:** lit. "on account of *you*". Initially Praxagora had been uncertain whether she would speak at the rehearsal (123), but the complete failure of the other women has decided her to do so. In itself the Greek phrase could also mean "for your sake, in your cause", particularly if the particle *ge* is omitted (with R); but this gives less good sense: the women are planning to take over power not in their own interests but in that of the whole community (105-9).

171-2 **I pray to the gods ...:** at first sight this seems parallel to a solemn exordium like Dem. 18.1 "First of all, Athenians, I pray to all the gods and goddesses that I may have as much goodwill from you in this trial as I have consistently shown to the City and to all of you ... [etc. etc. for another six lines]" or Lyc. *Leocr.* 1-2 (cf. also *Knights* 763-8); but Praxagora's prayer is not part of her speech (see next note), and it is rather to be compared to Pericles' practice of making a private prayer "while going up to the platform ... that not a word might inadvertently escape him that was unsuited to the business in hand" (Plut. *Per.* 8.6, cf. *Mor.* 803f) and to the Sausage-seller's prayer before he confronts Paphlagon-Cleon in the Council chamber (*Knights* 634-8).

172 **that I may succeed in bringing our plans to fruition:** since this sentence is linked to the next (173-4) by the antithetical particles *men* (171) ... *de* (173), many have supposed that Praxagora has already begun her practice Assembly speech; but in that case, if the transmitted text is correct, she would, most uncharacteristically, be making a serious blunder at the outset, since the participle *katorthōsāsa* "bringing to fruition", which is nominative singular and refers to the speaker, is feminine. Accordingly van Leeuwen, Coulon, and Vetta have accepted Richards' emendation *katorthōsāsi* (dative plural, masculine), giving the sense "I pray to the gods that *they* may succeed in bringing my/our plans to fruition". This, however, is unacceptable, since one does not pray to the gods that *they* may succeed (*tukhein* "hit the mark, be fortunate") in an enterprise: in prayer one normally assumes that the gods can effect whatever they desire (that, indeed, is what makes them worth praying to). The transmitted text should therefore be retained, and it follows that Praxagora's prayer is not part of her speech but a preliminary to it; see previous note.

173-240 We now hear the kind of speech that Praxagora means to give at the Assembly meeting. It is not precisely *the* speech that she means to give, since from Chremes' report of the meeting (427-454) we learn that she used some arguments not employed here; but being actually delivered on stage, not merely narrated, the "rehearsal" speech will have a much stronger impact on the theatre audience than the actual "performance", and Ar. takes advantage of this by making the present speech concentrate on criticism, in considerable detail, of the current Athenian political scene, which takes up more than half the speech (the positive proposal to give power to the women is introduced at 210, having till then not even been hinted at). He also makes the "rehearsal" resemble the "performance" as closely as possible by having Praxagora make the speech already wearing her false beard (cf. 118-123); realistically, from the conspirators' point of view, this was hardly necessary, but it creates precisely the situation (woman, posing as man, addressing the citizen body, here represented by the theatre audience) which will exist at the meeting on the Pnyx and which Ar. will not then be able to bring on stage. The structure of the speech is: introduction (173-5); analysis of current situation (bad leaders, 176-188; vacillating policies, 193-203; selfishness as the underlying problem, 205-8); proposal for change, with reasons (women's role as household managers, 211-2; women's conservatism, 215-228; miscellaneous arguments, 232-8); peroration (239-240). Since Praxagora is making this speech in the persona of a man, I shall for the duration of the speech (and of her actual Assembly speech, 427-454) designate this persona by the masculine name "Praxagoras" and use masculine pronouns in reference to it; "Praxagora" and feminine pronouns will denote the woman behind the false beard.

173-4 **I have as much of a stake in this country as you do:** sc. and therefore, despite my apparent youth (cf. 427) and obscure standing, I am as entitled as anyone to express a view on how it should be run. [Arist.] *Rhet. ad Alex.* 1437b13-16 recommends that a person who is not a regular Assembly speaker should excuse his intervention by arguing that in a dangerous situation "it is imperative for everyone who has a stake in the city to give an opinion on the issue now before us".

175 **at the whole situation the City is in:** i.e. my unhappiness is not primarily with particular policies but (as the sequel indicates) with the general pattern of political behaviour and attitudes.

176 **I see:** a formulaic expression in Athenian oratory for introducing the speaker's analysis of the current situation; cf. *Thesm.* 386, Thuc. 6.20.1, Dem. 5.1, 9.1, 14.3, 16.2, Dem. *Prooem.* 5.1, 6.1, 44.1.

176-7 **employing leaders who are always villains:** in *Frogs* both the chorus (718-737) and Dionysus (1455-7) make the same complaint; cf. too *Knights* 736-740.

179 **you try entrusting your affairs to someone else?:** "you" here is singular (so again 199, 200), denoting the typical citizen (cf. 435-9). This use of the 2nd person singular is not found in surviving Athenian oratory, but cf. *Birds* 586 where Peisetaerus, having addressed or referred to the birds in the plural consistently ever since the beginning of his speech (465), uses the 2nd person singular of them five times in one line, and *Wasps* 552-572 where Philocleon, describing the ways in which defendants truckle to jurors, shifts between 3rd plural and 3rd singular no less than seven times.

181 **afraid of those who want to be their friends:** cf. *Knights* 734-8 "[I am] one who has long desired you and wanted to do things for your good, as have many other good and decent people; but we can't do them, because ... you don't accept those who are good and decent".

182 **are for ever on their knees to:** lit. "are every time beseeching".

182 **those who *don't* want to:** these are not, of course, Platonic saints who can only with difficulty be persuaded to take part in politics at all, but men like Agyrrhius who *say* they are devoted to the people (cf. *Knights* 732, 1341-2; *Wasps* 592-3, 666-8) but are *really* only interested in their own power and profit.

183-4 **a time when we didn't have Assemblies at all:** this can hardly refer to the rule of the Thirty (404-403), since no fourth-century Athenian speaker or writer ever suggests that their rule, when compared with the restored democracy, had significant redeeming features, and the whole subject (like the plague of 430-426) appears to have been considered too painful ever to be mentioned in comedy. Rather it is an exaggerated description of the period immediately preceding the introduction of Assembly pay, when despite "many contrivances by the Prytaneis" it was sometimes impossible to secure (or at least to secure without undue delay) the quorum of 6,000 necessary for certain Assembly votes to be legally valid (cf. Arist. *Ath.Pol.* 41.3 and, for the quorum, Andoc. 1.87, Dem. 24.45, [Dem.] 59.89); this crisis had become particularly acute after the rejection of an initial attempt to introduce payment for attending the Assembly (*ibid.*), which may well, like the subsequent successful proposal to the same effect, have been made by Agyrrhius. On the introduction of Assembly pay see P.L. Gauthier in M. Piérart ed. *Aristote et Athènes* (Fribourg/Paris, 1993) 231-250, and M.H. Hansen in B. Forsén and G.R. Stanton ed. *The Pnyx in the History of Athens* (Helsinki, 1996) 29-30.

184 **Agyrrhius:** see on 102.

187 **whoever hasn't had any:** because he was unable to attend Assembly meetings through illness, infirmity, residence in a remote part of Attica, the nature of his work, etc. Such people, Praxagoras asserts, pretend to object to Assembly pay in principle, but really only oppose it because none of it is going to *them* (cf. 206-7).

188 **to treat the Assembly as a wage-earning job:** lit. "to get wages in the Assembly".

189-213 Praxagora's colleagues have not been very good as speakers themselves, but her speech gives them an opportunity to practise giving a speaker vocal support – in doing which, however, they must still remember that both they and the speaker are supposed to be male. As Praxagora's comment at 204 shows, the same person intervenes at 204 as at 189; the fact that she apologizes at once for an error without making any comic excuses for it (192) and that her second intervention is a perfectly correct one (two of its three Greek words are distinctively masculine) suggests that she is First Woman rather than Second Woman. It is possible that the cheers at 213 come from all (or several) of the women present (so Cobet, followed by van Leeuwen, Coulon and Vetta); since however there are *two* clearly different things being said in the line (*eu ge* "bravo!" "well <said>!" and *lege* "more!" [lit. "speak!"]) I have preferred, with Ussher, to divide it between the *two* individuals who have been the only speakers besides Praxagora since 45, and have assigned to First Woman, as the more intelligent, the only distinctively masculine word the line contains.

189 **by Aphrodite:** nearly always a women's oath, though it is used by a male character in *Thesm.* 254 – significantly, just when he is putting on a woman's garment.

193-203 Praxagoras cites, with allusive brevity, five recent instances demonstrating how frequently Athenian policy is stultified by inconsistency (193-6, 199-200, 201) or by internal divisions due to sectional or individual selfishness (197-8, 202-3).

193 **this Alliance** has been identified (1) with the Athenian-Theban alliance which led to the Haliartus campaign of 395 (Lys. 16.13, Andoc. 3.25) or (2) with the wider alliance formed after Haliartus, involving Corinth, Argos and other states (D.S. 14.82.1-3, cf. Andoc. 3.22, Xen. *Hell.* 4.2.1); the latter is more probable, since this alliance had absorbed and superseded the earlier one, was in being at the time of production, and

was engaged in war with Sparta. Vetta, however, may well be right to suggest that Praxagoras is, reasonably enough, conflating the two alliances (since the second grew out of the first) and harking back to the Assembly debate on the first alliance described by Xen. *Hell.* 3.5.7-17, according to whom no voice was raised against support for Thebes. See Introduction, pp. 2, 5.

195 they were annoyed: Haliartus was a success, and a bloodless one for the Athenians, but the first two major battles of the grand alliance, at Nemea and Coronea in 394, both ended in defeat (the Athenian army being particularly roughly handled at Nemea) and were followed by divisions and recriminations (cf. Xen. *Hell.* 4.2.18-23, 4.3.17-23; Dem. 20.52; Lys. 16.15; see Strauss 122-5 and R.J. Buck, *Thrasybulus and the Athenian Democracy* [Stuttgart, 1998] 101-6).

195-6 the politician ... ran off and disappeared: the scholia wrongly identify this politician as Conon, who was in Persian service when the two alliances of 395 were made and did not return to Athens until 393 (Xen. *Hell.* 4.8.9). The only Athenian whom we positively know to have spoken in support of either alliance was Thrasybulus (Xen. *Hell.* 3.5.16), but far from "running off and disappearing" in 394 he took the political offensive after Nemea, "accusing everyone of cowardice" (Lys. 16.15), and although he may during much of the next two years have been overshadowed by Conon (see on 202-3), he was clearly influential again by 392/1 (cf. 202-3, 356) and still a supporter of the alliance and the war. The reference may rather be to Epicrates (see on 71), who had been in favour of war with Sparta even earlier, when Thrasybulus had been against it (cf. *Hell.Oxy.* 6.2, 7.2), but had later become an advocate of peace (running off and disappearing, that is, not from Athens but from the pro-war faction).

197 we need to launch a fleet: Athens had had no effective navy since the defeat of 404, and while Conon commanded the Persian fleet she had not needed one; but Conon's disappearance from the scene had changed the situation completely. An Athenian navy was now a necessity, but it would be expensive, and it appears that no significant fleet was sent out before 390 (Xen. *Hell.* 4.8.24-25).

197-8 the poor man says yes, the rich and the farmers say no: in principle all classes might be expected to support this partial reversal of the humiliation of 404, but their particular material interests might make them think differently. If a large fleet was built, poorer Athenians could expect remunerative employment in the dockyards and/or as rowers; the rich, on the other hand, would have to bear most of the cost, partly as trierarchs (bearing individual financial responsibility for the maintenance of a particular ship) and partly through special property taxes (*eisphorai*), which were probably levied in 391 and 390 (cf. Lys. 28.3-4; see also on 821-2). The phrase here translated "the rich and the farmers" could also mean "the rich farmers" or "the rich, especially <rich> farmers" (Strauss 61-63); in any case Strauss is probably right to argue that the point of the reference to farmers is that land was the hardest kind of property to conceal from the taxman (cf. on 601-2). Thus although the policy division in the citizen body (the urban poor hawkish, the rich and the farmers dovish) is reminiscent of that evidenced by Ar.'s plays of the 420s (cf. also [Xen.] *Ath.Pol.* 2.14), many of the underlying interests that gave rise to it were different: in the 420s the urban poor will have been largely concerned to maintain the Athenian empire and its revenues (which funded not only the navy but also the pay of office-holders and jurors and, in peacetime, state building projects), and the rural population resented having their property devastated by invading Peloponnesian armies while the city people's assets were safe behind their walls (a consideration irrelevant in the 390s, when Athens had not yet fully rebuilt her walls but had acquired Argos and Corinth as allies and so made invasion of Attica virtually impossible).

199 **you get annoyed with the Corinthians ...:** this probably refers to the aftermath of the battle of Nemea in 394, when the anti-war faction at Corinth refused to admit the retreating allied forces into the city (Xen. *Hell.* 4.2.23; Dem. 20.52); the continuing strength of this faction later caused the other allies to fear that Corinth might join the Spartan side (Xen. *Hell.* 4.4.1-2).

200 **now they're decent chaps:** in 393/2 there had been a revolution at Corinth and the strongly anti-Spartan democrats had taken power with Argive support (Xen. *Hell.* 4.4.1-6 – who is bitterly hostile to the democrats); shortly afterwards (see C.J. Tuplin, *CQ* 32 [1982] 75-83) Corinth merged itself with Argos in a united state, which (not surprisingly) opposed the peace terms that emerged from the Sparta Conference, under which the union would have been broken up (cf. Andoc. 3.24-27, 32). Athenian politicians opposed to the terms will of necessity have spoken favourably of Argos-Corinth, the only major ally wholly committed to fighting on (for the Sparta proposals had satisfied Thebes by offering her control of most of Boeotia (Andoc. 3.13, 20)); and their view prevailed.

200 **you're told you should be decent too now:** lit. "'You [singular] be decent too now'", quoting (or paraphrasing) the words of a pro-Corinthian orator without any preamble.

201 **The Argives are stupid; but Hieronymus is sensible:** the context indicates that whatever these two enigmatic statements mean, they must refer to two mutually contradictory Athenian attitudes, whether held simultaneously or successively: in other words, Athenians thought "stupid" a certain opinion or proposal advanced by the Argives, but they thought very much the same opinion or proposal "sensible" when it was advanced by Hieronymus. Since the core Argive policy in 392/1 was opposition to any peace terms that did not leave Argos in control of Corinth (see previous note), it is likely that the reference is to the Sparta Conference. Argos, though presumably represented at the conference, can hardly have been eager to attend it, and may well have tried, without success, to dissuade Athens from accepting her invitation. Hieronymus was almost certainly the man (*PA* 7552; *LGPN* 3) who had been vice-admiral to Conon when the latter had been commanding the Persian fleet in 395 (*Hell.Oxy.* 15.1; D.S. 14.81.4); we know he eventually came to Athens, because at some time during the Corinthian War he became an Athenian general, probably twice (Lysias ap. Harpocration ι9; Ephorus *FGrH* 70 F 73, 74 – which cannot, *pace* Jacoby and Develin, refer to 395/4 since Hieronymus was then not an Athenian but a Persian officer). Presumably he came with Conon in 393, stayed, and was elected a general after Conon's death – together perhaps with Nicophemus, his colleague in 395, whom we find in 390 leading an expedition to Cyprus (Lys. 19) which was, so far as we know, the very first independent Athenian naval expedition since the end of the Peloponnesian War. Our passage indicates that Hieronymus was against peace in 392/1, just as Nicophemus evidently was; its probable interpretation is that, having rejected the Argive arguments against going to the Sparta Conference, the Athenians not long afterwards accepted Hieronymus' arguments against agreeing to the peace terms there proposed. Cf. Strauss 132-3, 138.

202 **we get a glimpse of salvation:** lit. "salvation (*sōtēriā*) has peeped out". As this is the last item in Praxagoras' list, it probably refers to very recent events, viz., once again, the rejection of the Sparta Conference terms, seen now as Athens' best hope of escaping from a war in which her prospects had been seriously damaged by the loss of Conon and the Persian fleet, the recent Spartan success at the Isthmus, and the threatened defection of Thebes (though in the end this did not happen), and in which, since Haliartus, the Spartans had won every major land battle; see Introduction, pp. 2–6. In commending the terms to the Assembly, Andocides (3.12) had said that "peace means safety (*sōtēriā*) and power for the democracy".

202-3 Thrasybulus, son of Lycus, of the deme Steiria (*PA* 7310; *LGPN* 22) was perhaps the nearest thing Athens had to a living national hero. He had been one of the more successful naval commanders in the later years of the Peloponnesian War, having first come into prominence in 411 when he took a leading role in the suppression of an oligarchic movement in the fleet at Samos and was irregularly elected a general (Thuc. 8.73-76), and soon afterwards promoted the recall of Alcibiades to take command of the fleet (Thuc. 8.81.1). He remained a general until 406 when, probably in consequence of his close association with Alcibiades, he failed to secure re-election; at Arginusae that summer he was a trierarch, and in the dispute which arose afterwards over the fleet's failure to pick up shipwrecked men he was among those who did most to divert public anger from the trierarchs to the generals and thereby bring about their condemnation (cf. D.S. 13.101.2-4, Xen. *Hell.* 1.7.5-6). Under the Thirty he was exiled (Xen. *Hell.* 2.3.42), went to Thebes, and from there, with a handful of followers, seized Phyle on the Attic-Boeotian border and began the revolt that led to the overthrow of the Thirty and the restoration of democracy. This naturally made him "one of the most powerful men in the state" (Isoc. 18.23), but as a peacetime politician he seems to have been ineffective: between 403 and 396 we only know of one political action by him, an unsuccessful attempt to give citizenship to all who had fought for the democracy (Arist. *Ath.Pol.* 40.2; a modified version of the same measure was later carried [*IG* ii^2 10], whether again on Thrasybulus' initiative we do not know). In 396 Thrasybulus was one of those who persuaded the Assembly to disown an unauthorized attempt to make, through Conon, an alliance with Persia against Sparta (the Demaenetus incident: *Hell.Oxy.* 6.2). In 395, however, he supported the alliance with Thebes, regarding it as dangerous but politically necessary (Xen. *Hell.* 3.5.16), and he was in command at Haliartus (Plut. *Lys.* 29.1) and probably at Nemea the following year (cf. Lys. 16.15). In 393/2 his popularity seems to have been eclipsed by that of Conon, who was no great friend of his (cf. Arist. *Rhet.* 1400b20); but after Conon's death he apparently returned to favour (a contemporary funeral oration has a strong anti-Conon and pro-Thrasybulus slant [Lys. 2.59-66]). In 390 Thrasybulus was put in command of the main Athenian fleet (Xen. *Hell.* 4.8.25) and gained several military and diplomatic successes (*ibid.* 26-30; D.S. 14.94.2-4, Dem. 20.59-60; *IG* ii^2 21, 24), but was killed in a night raid on his camp at Aspendus in Pamphylia (Xen. *Hell.* 4.8.30). His main aim on this last expedition had clearly been to acquire allies (and revenues) for Athens in key areas of the old Athenian empire; and whether or not he aspired (as many scholars believe; see e.g. R. Seager, *JHS* 87 [1967] 107-113, Strauss 152-4) to restore that empire or something like it, it is evident that he was strongly committed to the war against Sparta and, with limited resources, was ready to adopt a bold and imaginative strategy. Our passage, with 356, shows that he had been one of those who argued strongly against peace in 392/1. Like many a leader of the past, he is treated more favourably in comedy after his death (*Wealth* 550, cf. 1146) than he had been during his lifetime. See R.J. Buck, *Thrasybulus and the Athenian Democracy* (Stuttgart, 1998).

203 because *he* isn't invited to take charge: lit. "not himself being invited". The accusation against Thrasybulus is that (like Alcibiades after the Peace of Nicias, cf. Thuc. 5.43.2) he has opposed peace for the selfish reason that others, and not he, will have the credit of making it. It would gain additional force if after, and partly as a result of, his opposition to the peace proposals, and before the production of *Eccl.* at the City Dionysia, he had been elected to a generalship for 391/0 (see Introduction, pp. 6–7 and note 33); cf. *Peace* 450-2 where a curse is pronounced on anyone who "fails to assist [in rescuing Peace] because he wishes to be a general".

208 gets kicked around: lit. "rolls"; the metaphorical sense here assumed for Greek *kulindesthai* is not exactly paralleled, but the context shows Praxagora must be saying that individuals' concern for private advantage has resulted in the public interest being neglected.

208 Aesimus (*PA* 311; *LGPN* 1) was a significant figure in Athenian politics from 403 (when he had commanded the democratic forces in the civil war: Lys. 13.80) until 377 or later. In 396 he had joined his old comrades Thrasybulus and Anytus in opposing war over the Demaenetus incident (*Hell.Oxy.* 6.2). He served on an embassy to Chios, as a colleague of Cephalus (see on 248), in 384 (*IG* ii^2 34.36), and headed a commission that toured the Aegean on behalf of the Second Athenian League in 378/7, *inter alia* swearing in new members (*IG* ii^2 42.19-20); but except for the present passage he is never mentioned during the Corinthian War and may well, for whatever reason, have been in political eclipse for most of its duration (cf. Strauss 96). It therefore seems most probable that *kulindetai* (cf. previous note), as applied to Aesimus, means much the same as it does in relation to "the public interest", viz. "gets kicked around; is ignored, neglected, despised". The scholia assert that Aesimus was "lame, disfranchised [or dishonoured] and stupid", apparently taking *kulindetai* to mean "reels about like a cripple, drunkard or idiot"; but this sense of the verb is not otherwise attested.

211-2 managers and controllers of our households: it was the wife's traditional duty to be the manager (the Greek words used here are *tamiās* "treasurer" and *epitropos* "person to whom something is entrusted") of the money and chattels within the home; cf. *Lys.* 495; Lys. 1.7; Pl. *Meno* 71e; Xen. *Oec.* 3.10-15, 7.3-10.13.

215-228 Praxagoras argues that giving political power to women will benefit Athens because women, with their inherent conservatism, will refrain from the unnecessary and capricious policy changes that have recently been so frequent (cf. 193-203). That women *were* inherently conservative seems to have been taken for granted by fourth-century Athenians; Pl. *Crat.* 418b-d makes Socrates base an etymological argument on the assumption, for which he offers no evidence but which his interlocutor does not question, that where men and women differ in their pronunciation of a word, it is the women's pronunciation that is archaic and the men's that is innovative (see my discussion in F. De Martino and A.H. Sommerstein ed. *Lo spettacolo delle voci* [Bari, 1995] 81-83). The actual examples of women's conservatism presented here are comic in tone, and many of them are far from creditable to women, but they do include reminders of women's crucial contribution in three important areas of life – clothes-making (214-7), food preparation (221, 223b) and religion (223a) – to add to the references elsewhere in the speech to their roles as household managers (211-2, 236) and as child bearers and carers (233-5).

216 dyeing wool in hot water: to ensure that the dyestuff dissolves well and is absorbed thoroughly and evenly.

219 if that was satisfactory: i.e. if the (male) Athenian state was responsible for dyeing wool, and if the traditional process was (as in fact it is) satisfactory. The expression is slightly clumsy, since it might be taken to imply that the traditional process is actually *not* satisfactory, and Dobree's conjecture ("if by any chance something was satisfactory") has been adopted by most editors – but in general for the mistaken reason that *touto* "that" has no clear antecedent.

219-220 wouldn't want to preserve it – quite the contrary, they'd be ...: so these words are understood by N.G. Wilson, *CR* 26 (1976) 13, who takes *esōizeto* as middle ("preserve for themselves", cf. 402) rather than passive ("be saved"), inserts the particle *g'(e)* in 220 and takes the sentence as an instance of the idiom whereby "not A *ei mē* B *ge*" (literally "not A if not emphatically B") means "not A but, on the contrary, B" (Denniston 121; cf. *Knights* 185-6, *Birds* 1680-1, *Lys.* 942-3, *Thesm.* 897-8). The transmitted text, without *ge*, is least unsatisfactorily understood to mean that the Athenians "would be <sure they were> not on the way to being safe, if they weren't" making some innovation; but the words in angled brackets are not easy for a hearer to supply.

221-8 For the refrain "just like in the old days" cf. *Birds* 974-989 ("here, have the book") and *Frogs* 1198-1247 ("mislaid his oil-flask") – though in these scenes the refrain is uttered by one character in response to, or to cap, the words of another – and, on a smaller scale, 1155-7 and *Birds* 114-6. A similar device, though with more variation among the successive repetitions, appears three times in the scene between the Neighbour and the Dissident (773-6, 799-803, 862-4).

221 **women parch corn sitting on their haunches:** lit. "they (fem.) parch sitting"; the posture meant is described more explicitly in Pherecrates fr. 80 (also of a woman preparing food) and illustrated on an early fifth-century terracotta (see V. Ehrenberg, *The People of Aristophanes*^{2} [Oxford, 1951] pl. XIb).

222 **they carry things on their heads:** as in countless vase-paintings (and cf. *Wealth* 1198); Herodotus (2.35.3) asserted that in Egypt, where "most of the customs and usages [are] entirely opposite to those of other people", men carried loads on their heads and women on their shoulders.

223a-b The irregular line-numbering is due to the fact that the second of these lines ("They bake their flat-cakes ...") was not included in a printed text until the edition of Invernizi (1794), who inserted it from R, the only ms. in which it survives.

223a **the Thesmophoria:** a festival of Demeter and Kore, held by women only (men being forbidden on pain of death to enter the precinct in which it was held) in the month of Pyanopsion (roughly corresponding to October); see Parke 82-88; Burkert 242-6; E. Simon, *Festivals of Attica* (Madison WI, 1983) 18-22; L. Foxhall in R.G. Hawley and B. Levick ed. *Women in Antiquity: New Assessments* (London, 1995) 97-110. The festival provided the setting for Ar.'s *Thesmophoriazusae* (and for another, lost play of his, of the same name).

224 **they make life hell for their husbands:** since this was one of the great clichés of Greek popular misogyny (cf. *Thesm.* 394, 737, 786-799; Eur. *Hipp.* 627, *Andr.* 353; Hes. *Thg.* 590-602; Semonides fr. 7 passim) there is no reason to take it here (with Ussher and Vetta) in a specifically sexual sense which would not be apparent to an audience that had yet to hear 225 and 228.

225 **they keep lovers in the house:** normally an adulterer is thought of as visiting the wife clandestinely in her house when her husband is absent (cf. *Thesm.* 395-7, 493-501, *Birds* 793-6, Lys. 1.15-29). Sometimes, however, it is the wife who slips out of the house at night and goes to him (cf. 520-7, *Thesm.* 479-489); and sometimes, as here, her lover is an inmate of the house itself, whether a slave (cf. *Thesm.* 491; Ar. fr. 592.29-30, 715; Eupolis fr. 192.102) or a relative or guest of the husband's (as in the mythical cases of Helen, Phaedra and Stheneboea; cf. *Thesm.* 401-4, Semonides fr. 7.106-7). On adultery in classical Athens see D. Cohen, *Law, Sexuality and Society* (Cambridge, 1991) ch.5-6, and J. Roy, *G&R* 44 (1997) 11-22.

226 **they buy extra food for themselves:** i.e. they buy (or instruct their personal slaves to buy) more food than is required to replenish the household stores, and keep the extra in a secret cache (contrast 14-15 and *Thesm.* 419-420 where the accusation is that wives purloin food and drink from the stores themselves).

230-1 let's not ... inquire of them what ... they actually mean to do: thus the Assembly will be made to give Praxagora *carte blanche* to do as she pleases, by this simple device of having a proposal to this effect come from an apparently disinterested party. Some astute spectators will possibly suspect at this point that Praxagora's actual plans may prove to be very different indeed from what 215-228 might seem to imply (cf. on 107).

233-4 being the mothers of our soldiers, they will be anxious to secure their safety: or "being mothers, they will be anxious to secure the safety of our soldiers" (so Vetta); but the next clause indicates that it is the soldier's *own* mother who is thought of as being solicitous for his welfare.

236 finding financial resources: budgeting was a vital part of the wife's role as household manager (see on 211-2), and it was recognized that control of expenditure was crucial to the economic well-being of a household (cf. especially Xen. *Oec.* 3.15, 7.36).

237 she's never going to be deceived: sc. by foreign states or their diplomatic representatives (cf. *Ach.* 308, 634-640, *Peace* 215-9, 623, 1064-8; Andoc. 3.2) such as those from Sparta, Argos and Corinth who had recently been trying to persuade the Athenians to make or not to make peace (cf. Andoc. 3.41).

238 women are so used to being deceivers themselves: another misogynist cliché; cf. *Thesm.* 493-516; Aesch. *Ag.* 1636; Eur. *Med.* 422, *Hipp.* 480-1, *Andr.* 85, 911, *Hec.* 884, *IT* 1032; *Odyssey* 11.456; Hes. *Works* 375.

239 the rest of what I might say I will pass over: "of what I might say" is added by the translator for clarity. The sentence corresponds to a common conclusion-formula for both political and forensic speeches, whereby the speaker implies that he has many further arguments but evades actually producing them; cf. Lys. 31.34 "I think I have said enough, despite having left out a great deal", Dem. 10.75 "Though I have many things still to say about many matters, I will now end".

240 you will live happily ever after: lit. "you will pass your life being happy".

241-2 The speaker could be either of the two women: with Vetta, I have preferred Second Woman on account of the gushing address to "Praxagora my sweet" (lit. sweetest), which Second Woman employed at 124.

243 in the refugee time: lit. "in the flights". This might refer to the evacuation of the Attic countryside consequent on the Spartan occupation of Deceleia in 413; but except in 303ff (when the chorus are pretending to be old men) retrospective references in this play do not go that far back, and more probably the reference is to the aftermath of Aegospotami in 405 when Lysander deliberately sent all Athenians in the former subject/allied states back to Athens to increase crowding and shortages there (Plut. *Lys.* 13.3-4, Xen. *Hell.* 2.2.2). The scholia absurdly take the reference to be to the time of the Thirty, when refugees were not entering Athens but leaving it, and when there were no Assembly speeches on the Pnyx for Praxagora to listen to.

244 to listen to the speakers: her house was so close to the Assembly place that she could hear the speeches from the window or roof.

246-7 we ... elect you ... if you succeed: i.e. we declare now that if your plan is successful, you will hold the office of general.

246 general: rather a surprising choice of title (though intelligible, given that the generalships were the only important magistracies in Athens that were filled by election rather than by lot), and possibly designed by Ar. to mislead spectators into expecting that the new feminine government will display an Amazon-like bellicosity. It was not till the Hellenistic period that Athenian generals, or some of them, acquired significant administrative responsibilities outside the military/naval sphere; on the other hand Dionysius had made himself tyrant of Syracuse after being elected "general with sole power" (*stratēgos autokratōr*, D.S. 13.95.1), and it is *possible* that Praxagora's position as *sole* general (whereas the male Athenian generals served as a board of ten) might seem to some spectators a sinister feature of her government.

248 **Cephalus,** of the deme Collytus (*PA* 8277; *LGPN* 5), was one of the most durable politicians of the early fourth century. He first appears in our sources as a supporter of Andocides in the Mysteries trial of 400 (Andoc. 1.115, 150), when Agyrrhius was one of those who spoke on the other side. In 396 he, like Epicrates, was a supporter of war (*Hell.Oxy.* 7.2) and was accused of being in Persian pay (*ibid.* and Paus. 3.9.8). We hear little of him during the Corinthian War, but there is no reason to doubt that he remained a hawk throughout (so Strauss 142); it is significant that soon after the war ended he was active in criticizing the generals who had allegedly lost it and asserting that the defeat could have been avoided (*IG* ii^2 29). In 384 he led the embassy which sealed the alliance with Chios (see on 208); in 378, true to his policy of eighteen years earlier, he successfully proposed that an army be sent to aid Thebes' rebellion against Spartan domination (Dein. 1.39; cf. *IG* ii^2 40 Addenda, a rider to a decree regarding the treaty of alliance). Plato com. fr. 201 calls him "evil-smelling Cephalus, a most hateful plague"; but posterity thought rather better of him, Aeschines (3.194), Demosthenes (18.219, 251) and Deinarchus (1.38-39, 76) all referring to him with respect as a great democrat and patriot – and even in his lifetime Cephalus was able to boast that though he had proposed more Assembly decrees than any other man, not one of them had ever been objected to as illegal (Aeschines *loc.cit.*).

251 **he's completely barmy:** Greek *melankholān* means literally "to suffer from black bile". Fifth-century medical theory seems to have recognized a specific syndrome of bodily and mental disturbances which it ascribed to a morbid darkening of the bile (cf. Hippocr. *Airs* 10, *Epid.* 3.17.2); but in popular usage "black-biled" merely meant "utterly insane" (cf. *Birds* 14; *Wealth* 12, 366, 903; Pl. *Phdr.* 268e; Dem. 48.56; Men. *Dysk.* 89). See generally H. Flashar, *Melancholie und Melancholiker in den medizinischen Theorien der Antike* (Berlin, 1966).

252 **pots:** Greek *trublia,* strictly "bowls", especially for soup or broth (cf. *Ach.* 278, *Knights* 905, Ar. fr. 136, Diphilus fr. 64.2). For disparaging references to the trades and businesses of disliked politicians, cf. Cleon the "tanner" (*Knights* passim), Hyperbolus the "lamp-seller" (*Clouds* 1065, *Peace* 681-692), Cleophon the "lyre-maker" (Arist. *Ath.Pol.* 28.3), and Anytus the "cobbler" (Archippus fr. 31, cf. Pl. *Men.* 90c); see H. Lind, *Der Gerber Kleon in den "Rittern" des Aristophanes* (Frankfurt, 1990), esp. 247-8. We can normally assume that these men's association with the trades in question took the form of owning a business staffed by slaves, like the cutlery and furniture workshops which another politician, Demosthenes, ought to have inherited from his father (Dem. 27.9). For the accusation of bad workmanship cf. *Knights* 315-321; here Ar. disparages Cephalus' business (or rather, according to the scholia, his father's) further by choosing to refer to what must have been one of its cheapest products (cf. *Frogs* 985-6 where the breaking of a year-old *trublion* is a mishap on the same level of triviality as the illicit eating of the head of a sprat).

253 **he's making the City go to pot all right, good and proper:** lit. "he is potmaking (*kerameuein*) the City well and finely". This has been taken to mean that Cephalus was a bad potter but a good statesman (so e.g. D.M. MacDowell, *Andokides: On the Mysteries* [Oxford, 1962] 144) or as a sarcastic way of saying the exact opposite (so N.G. Wilson, *CR* 26 [1976] 13); but both these interpretations are inconsistent with the previous statements that "everyone knows" Cephalus is a madman – Ar. does not elsewhere revile and praise contemporary political leaders in the same breath. Rather, as van Leeuwen saw, we should follow the scholia, which assert that "they used to call the mishandling of public affairs *kerameuein*"; this wording implies that ancient commentators knew of other occurrences of this metaphor (though none has survived). The metaphor may refer to the potter's strong hands forcibly kneading and moulding the clay (cf. perhaps Pl. *Euthyd.* 301d with its fantasies of roasting a cook, hammering a blacksmith and "potting" a potter), to his rapid spinning of the wheel (as if he was disorienting the state and making it giddy), to the messiness of the work, to the high rate of breakage during or after firing, or to several or all of these.

254 **that bleary-eyed Neocleides:** we know nothing of this man (*PA* 10631, *LGPN* 4) outside Ar., in whose later plays he figures as a well-known Assembly speaker (398-407; *Wealth* 665-6, 716-726, 747; Ar. fr. 454) and is accused of being an embezzler (*Wealth* 666) and a professional prosecutor (*sūkophantēs*) (scholia), of using obstructive procedural tactics in the Assembly (*Wealth* 725), and of having foreign ancestry (scholia). By 388 his eye disease had progressed to the point of virtual blindness (*Wealth* 665), but this had not ended his political activity.

255 **my advice to *him* is:** lit. "I hereby tell that man" (aorist indicative denoting an action performed by the very fact of uttering the word, cf. Soph. *Aj.* 536); rather than saying what she intends to do in the future tense (as in 250, 256, 259) Praxagora gives the actual words with which she means to do it – very likely speaking straight at Neocleides in the audience. Brunck's conjecture *an eipoim'* ("I would tell him"; potential optative mood) is an attempt to restore a verb with some kind of future meaning; but the potential optative gives only a rather weak statement of intention compared with the surrounding future indicatives, and this does not suit well the earthy downrightness of Praxagora's actual message (see next note).

255 **to look up a dog's arse:** "a children's saying in relation to those with bad eyes, that they should 'look up the arse of a dog and of three foxes'" (scholia), probably with the implication "you'll see nothing there, but then you can see nothing anyway". The saying in its longer form has a regular, simple metrical structure (two *lekythia*) and was no doubt chanted rather than spoken; in *Ach.* 863 a visitor from Boeotia (in Athenian eyes a land of uncultured boors) asks the pipers who have come with him to play the "Dog's Arse" tune. In classical Athens adults might evidently be as cruel to those with disabilities, physical or mental, as children can still sometimes be (cf. *Wasps* 1491, *Birds* 149-154, 524-5, 1292-4); see Dover *GPM* 127, 201. In this at least we have progressed: such insults are now socially acceptable only when directed at (sighted) football referees.

256 **interrupt and try to knock you off your stride:** this renders (expansively, for the sake of preserving the pun) the single Greek word *hupokrouōsin*, which means both "interrupt" and "penetrate sexually" (cf. 618); the latter sense can also be borne by the simple verb *krouein*, lit. "strike, knock" (cf. 990, and *pro-krouein* in 1017-8), a derivative of which (*kroumata* "knockings", i.e. "sexual methods/positions") is used by Praxagora in her reply.

257 **I've got substantial and varied experience as far as *knocking* goes:** lit. "I'm not inexperienced in many knockings" (cf. previous note).

258 **two of the archers:** cf. on 143. "Two of" is not in the Greek, but I have added it to clarify the scenario envisaged; as police forces the world over demonstrate daily, it takes two men to drag away an offender who refuses to submit voluntarily to arrest or removal. As Praxagora's response indicates (cf. next note), the archers are imagined as gripping her by the shoulders and "frogmarching" her away.

259-260 **I'll do the elbow trick ... being held in the middle:** both expressions pun on wrestling terms. "Doing the elbow trick" (*exankōnizein*, lit. "to out-elbowize") in later Greek normally means "tie someone's hands behind his back" (e.g. D.S. 13.27.6,

34.2.13), and this is plausibly explained by F. García Romero, *Nikephoros* 8 (1995) 57-76, at pp.65-66, as a metaphor from a known wrestling manoeuvre whereby one combatant held his opponent round the back with his left arm (an "underhook" in modern wrestling terminology); cf. *POxy* 466.21-24 and schol. bT *Iliad* 23.711, and see M.B. Poliakoff, *Combat Sports in the Ancient World* (New Haven, 1987) 34-38 and fig. 30. This manoeuvre, however, while highly effective against a single wrestling opponent, would be useless to someone being hustled off between two policemen, and Rogers is right to assume that Praxagora re-etymologizes *exankōnizein* as "put my elbows out", though his interpretation of this ("stand with my arms akimbo") makes her rather too passive. What Praxagora means to do, and what she doubtless here mimes doing, is to elbow the two archers in the ribs (which, as a matter of fact, seems to be how the scholiast understood the expression; his gloss is "I will put the elbows under the ribs"). "Being held (or gripped) in the middle" (*mesos ekhesthai* or *lambanesthai*), i.e. round the waist (a "waistlock", see Poliakoff *op.cit.* 40 and figs. 31-36), was a phrase in common metaphorical use to mean "virtually defeated" (*Ach.* 571, *Knights* 387, *Clouds* 1047, *Frogs* 469), this wrestling hold being one that greatly facilitated a subsequent lift and a winning throw; but here the phrase simultaneously means "being held by two archers, one on each side of me". The words *helkein* "drag" (259) and *airein* "lift off the ground" (261) are also wrestling terms; cf. García Romero *op.cit.* 60-66.

261 if they lift you off the ground: see on 143.

261 *we'll* ... tell them to leave you alone: anticlimax; we would have expected the women to promise to use the force of their numbers to rescue their leader (cf. the confrontation in *Lys.* 433-462 where the women not only prevent a posse of archer-policemen from arresting Lysistrata and others but put the archers to flight). Possibly the point of the anticlimax may be that the women are (to be assumed) helpless if male Athens is prepared (as it will prove not to be) to use its superiority in physical force; but a stronger comic point is achieved if, with Rogers, we assume a metatheatrical joke on the notorious incapacity of most *dramatic choruses* to take effective action (even in the *Lysistrata* passage referred to, the chorus do not do anything; the archers are defeated by Lysistrata, two or three of her colleagues, and a band of women, who are *not* the chorus, coming out of the stage-house/Acropolis).

264 come the vote: Greek *tote* "then", i.e. "when the Assembly is held" or "when a vote is taken"; but Ussher's tentative suggestion *pote* ("How are we ever going to remember to raise ... ?") is very tempting.

265 raising our *legs*: in the sexual posture forsworn in *Lys.* 229-230 "I will not raise up my Persian slippers ceilingwards"; cf. *Birds* 1254, Eupolis fr. 54, Thphr. *Char.* 28.3, and see K.J. Dover, *Greek Homosexuality* (London, 1978) 101, and J. Boardman, *Athenian Red-figure Vases: The Archaic Period* (London, 1975) fig. 302.

268 underdresses: Greek *khitōnia*, plural of *khitōnion*, the inner of the two garments that a woman would normally wear (the word is a diminutive; the non-diminutive form *khitōn* usually denotes the equivalent garment for a man). The women are evidently wearing their own *khitōnia*, and these must be shortened (probably by pulling up the mid-section under the belt, cf. Stone 433 n.26) so as not to show below the hem of the short male *himatia*.

269 Laconians: cf. on 74.

275-6 then put on your men's cloaks as well ... and then move off: the emendation of J.D. Denniston, *CR* 47 (1933) 215 ("and when you've put on your men's cloaks ... then move off"), gives the sentence a tighter structure, building up to a climax at "move off". Praxagora, however, is not composing a polished oration, but giving instructions to a group of women for a job which they have never done before and which it is vital that they should do correctly, and in the transmitted text she proceeds step by step, with pauses: shorten underdresses; put on shoes; when that is properly done, tie on beards; when that is properly done, put on cloaks; then move off. See V. Coulon, *REG* 50 (1937) 31.

275 **the ones that you stole:** the implicit contrast with the inner garments, which are the women's own (see on 268), accounts for the slight emphasis given, in the Greek, to the relative pronoun by the particle *ge*.

277-9 **an old men's song ... the way country people act:** why are the women instructed to masquerade specifically as *old* men *from the country*? From Ar.'s point of view the answer may be that both old men and country people were normally sympathetic characters in comedy (cf. the heroes and/or choruses of *Acharnians*, *Peace*, *Birds* and *Wealth*), and that it enabled him to write the song 289-310, contrasting the "good old days" with the "degenerate" modern era; from Praxagora's, probably that old men from the country would attend the Assembly less often than other citizens (since they would find the long walk difficult) and therefore would not be well known to regular participants. The false beards of the chorus are presumably white, but Praxagora's own must be dark, since she is taken for a young man (427).

279-284 In the allocation of lines to speakers here I follow P. Händel, *Formen und Darstellungsweisen in der aristophanischen Komödie* (Heidelberg, 1963) 26 n.16, and Vetta. In 279c-280 the speaker turns from the women in general ("they") to two or more whom she includes with herself as "we" and who are to go to the Pnyx ahead of the others. "They" must be the chorus, who cannot leave until they have completed their song, and "we" must be Praxagora and the only other women present who are not members of the chorus, viz. First and Second Women. It follows that the instructions of 268-279a were addressed to the chorus, and therefore the assenting response ("Very good", 279b) must come from them or their representative. The speaker of 279c-282a must be Praxagora, since we would otherwise have to assume, contrary to the whole pattern of this scene, that she, the leader of the conspiracy and General-designate, complies without a word with the suggestion of a subordinate. It is possible that 282b-284, which has a comic twist in the tail (see on 284), is spoken by one of the other women (cf. *Lys.* 252-3), but there is no strong reason to suppose so, and the virtual repetition of the warning by the chorus a moment later (289-292) indicates that it has made a deep impression on them, suggesting that it was made in earnest mode by someone they greatly respect.

280-1 **other women from the countryside:** we hear of these only now. They are mentioned (1) to give Praxagora a reason for hurrying off ahead of most of her followers (she will need to get to the Pnyx before the country women do, so that she can organize and instruct them), and (2) to still any scepticism we may have felt about the ability of the rather small band of women we have seen to carry the day in an Assembly which – as we will shortly be reminded – is now usually well filled thanks to the three-obol attendance payment. Rogers wrongly supposed that these country women appeared on the scene at 300 and sang the antistrophe 300-310, only half the chorus having till then been present; if Ar. had done that, he would have left his audience wondering why Praxagora had gone off to the Pnyx to meet the newcomers, instead of staying and waiting for them.

282-4 **the practice ... is for <the magistrate to tell> those who ... to slink away:** I translate the text as tentatively emended by van Leeuwen. The transmitted text is bad in grammar and sense: (1) *eiōthe* "is accustomed" has no subject, and would have to be understood as an impersonal verb meaning "it is the custom" and governing a dative and infinitive, for which there is no parallel; (2) *e(i)s tēn Pukna* "to the Pnyx" is redundant after *ekei* "there", and anyway is inappropriate after *tois ... parousi* (lit. "those who are present" which requires an adverbial phrase of place *where*, not *whither*. It is likely therefore that *e(i)s tēn Pukna* has intruded into the text from the margin (the same phrase appears, correctly, in 281); in such a case the transmitted words give no help in restoring the true text, but van Leeuwen's supplement produces perfect grammar and excellent sense. It assumes that the *thesmothetēs* in charge of Assembly pay (cf. 290), being one of the nine archons, could be informally referred to as "the <relevant> archon" (*arkhōn* being the word I have translated "magistrate" here), as the *thesmothetēs* in charge of a particular jury-court is in *Wasps* 304 (cf. *Wasps* 775, 935).

282 up there: lit. "there", i.e. at the Pnyx.

284 to slink away does not necessarily imply that late-comers were not admitted to the Assembly; it may mean only that many felt there was no reason to stay if they were not going to be paid (cf. M.H. Hansen in B. Forsén and G.R. Stanton ed. *The Pnyx in the History of Athens* [Helsinki, 1996] 31).

284 without getting so much as a bean: lit. "not having even a peg (*pattalos*)", i.e. not receiving even the tiniest amount; cf. Ar. fr. dub. 939, Callim. fr. 196.43. Since the women must be encouraged to think of themselves as men, they are reminded that if they do not hurry they will lose the three obols which, we are given to understand, are the only reason why most men bother to attend the Assembly (cf. 289-292, 296, 300-310, 380-2, 388-393, 547-8); it is evident, especially from 377-391, that only the first *n* (perhaps 6,000, cf. on 183-4 and 296) persons to arrive at any given meeting were given pay tickets. But there may be a suggestion, via a *double entendre*, of an incentive more appropriate to women; for *pattalos* can also mean "penis" (cf. 1020, *AP* 5.129.5).

285-310 corresponds structurally to the normal choral *parodos*, but accompanies not the *entry* but the temporary *exit* of the chorus. At Aesch. *Eum.* 229-231 and Soph. *Aj.* 813-4 choruses leave the scene with only a few, spoken words from their leader; at Eur. *Hel.* 330-385 the chorus's exit is marked by a long lyric number which, however, has no strophic structure and is sung almost entirely by Helen with only four short responses by the chorus. In all these plays there has earlier been a *parodos* of normal type. See further Introduction, pp. 23–24.

285-8 Metre: iambic tetrameters, which in Aristophanic *parodoi* tend to be associated with choruses of old men (*Wasps* 230-247, *Lys.* 254-5, 266-270, 281-5, 306-318, *Wealth* 253-289).

285-8 for that's what ... of these dimensions: these words are spoken, as it were, "privately" to the women, and refer to them (in the Greek) in the feminine gender. The words of the following song, on the other hand, are "for public consumption", and in it the chorus speak of themselves exclusively in the masculine except for the self-corrected slip at 298.

286 remember to say: lit. "remembering say".

288 taking on an undercover venture: lit. "entering upon a venture in darkness [= in secret, cf. Soph. *Phil.* 578, Eur. *Phoen.* 1214]".

289-310 Metre: strophe and antistrophe open with a syncopated iambic tetrameter (four full iambic *metra* except that the first syllable of the third *metron* is suppressed) and continue in aeolics, comprising sequences of two or three telesilleans (x–∪∪–∪–) mostly followed by a reizianum (x–∪∪– –) whose end marks a brief pause. Sequences of this type are prominent in the latter part of *Peace* (856-862 = 909-915; 1329-end), when the end of war enables the country folk to return to their old homes and way of life, and it is possible that the rhythm was perceived as having associations with rusticity (cf. Zimmermann i 136).

290 **the magistrate:** the Greek specifies the magistrate as a *thesmothetēs*, one of the six junior members of the college of nine archons. The functions of the *thesmothetai* were principally judicial (cf. Arist. *Ath.Pol.* 59.1-6), but not exclusively so; in the 330s, and probably earlier, they conducted the selection by lot of office-holders for the ensuing year (Aeschines 3.13), and our passage shows that in the 390s they were in charge of arrangements for the distribution of Assembly pay. This function may have been allocated to the *thesmothetai* because it was not too dissimilar to another of their duties, the selection of the jurors who were to serve on any given day (cf. on 681-8), which was also done on a first-come first-served basis and also involved the marshalling of large numbers of persons (cf. Arist. *Ath.Pol.* 59.7, 63-66); at some time between 391 and 375, however, probably no later than 380, it was transferred to thirty members of the Council designated as "collectors of the people" (*syllogēs tou dēmou*) (cf. for their main duties *Agora* xv 38.78-82 and Pollux 8.104, for the earliest record of them *SEG* xxvi 72 which already shows them being given additional functions).

291 **covered with dust:** i.e. having got himself dusty by running or rapid walking (cf. 1177, Aesch. *Ag.* 495).

291 **a pickled-garlic breakfast:** garlic was a very cheap food (cf. *Wasps* 679, *Frogs* 987; when the hero of *Wealth* becomes rich his slaves no longer eat garlic but wipe their bottoms with it, cf. *Wealth* 817-8) and in Ar. seems sometimes to be particularly associated with old men (*Ach.* 164-5, *Lys.* 689). In addition, because garlic was fed to fighting-cocks to make them more ferocious, to be a garlic-eater might suggest an irascible disposition (cf. *Ach.* 166; *Knights* 494, 946); thus this phrase leads on to the next one.

292 **with a *sauce piquante* look in his eye:** lit. "looking *hupotrimma*". We know that *hupotrimma* was a sauce (cf. Antiphanes fr. 221.3, Nicostratus fr. 1.3), but we are not directly informed what kind of sauce it was (see Dalby 245 n.1). However, there is a whole series of Aristophanic phrases of the form "looking X" where X is the name of some article of food of acrid taste or smell, e.g. the herb savory (*Ach.* 254), mustard (*Knights* 631), cress (*Wasps* 455), fig-juice (*Peace* 1184), marjoram (*Frogs* 603), and the phrase denotes a mordant, irate facial expression; we can thus safely conclude that in the 390s *hupotrimma* meant a sauce with a fairly pungent flavour. It is not entirely clear why citizens coming to the Assembly are expected to be in a fierce mood (like, say, the jurors of *Wasps*, devotees of Cleon, who are horrified at the very thought of acquitting a defendant); the context makes it unlikely that we are to think of political zeal, and probably the idea is that they are expecting, and prepared, to engage in considerable pushing and shoving to improve their place in the queue for pay-tickets (cf. 300-3, *Wealth* 329-330).

292 **his three obols:** see on 102, 183-4, and 284.

293 **Charitimides and Smicythus and Draces:** for the name "Charitimides" see on 51; but the name may also have been chosen because it was that of an Athenian hero of bygone days who had led, and been killed in, the Egyptian expedition of 459-454 (*PA* 15497; see Ctesias *FGrH* 688 F 14; he is the only real Athenian of this name known to us). Now that even the oldest Athenians were too young to remember the Persian invasions, the age of martial glory, as remembered by the old in comedy, has moved down to the 450s when Athenians campaigned on three continents simultaneously and built a short-lived land empire in Greece itself (cf. on 303); veterans of these campaigns would by now be in their mid-eighties at least. "Smicythus", though a very common name among real fourth-century Athenians, does not appear elsewhere as a fictional name in

comedy (for the Smicythus alluded to at *Knights* 969 appears, like the Smicythion of 46 and *Wasps* 401, to have been a real person), but cf. "Smicrines" in Menander's *Aspis* and *Epitrepontes* (both miserly, selfish old men; cf. also *com. adesp.* 1142). For "Draces" cf. *Lys.* 254 and "Dracyllus" in *Ach.* 612 (both old men from a chorus); we know of no real Athenian of the name.

296 our tickets: evidently those entering the Assembly place were issued with a ticket (*sumbolon*) by the staff of the *thesmothetai*, which at the end of the meeting they could exchange for their pay (there was a similar but more complex arrangement in the lawcourts, cf. Arist. *Ath.Pol.* 68.2). If the total number of tickets available for issue was exactly 6,000 (cf. on 183-4 and 284), then once the supply of tickets ran out, it would be known, without the necessity for a head-count, that the Assembly was quorate for all purposes.

296-7 we sit close together: a common practice, designed to make the support for a particular leader or point of view seem greater than it was; cf. *Knights* 852-3, Thuc. 6.13.1, Dem. 18.143, Plut. *Per.* 11.2, and see P.J. Rhodes, *JHS* 106 (1986) 139. The practice has recently been revived in the British House of Commons, for the benefit of the television cameras, under the name of "doughnutting".

298 the measures our sisters may need—: in the Greek the relative clause as it stands makes no sense, and it is evident that the women interrupt themselves on realizing their error, leaving the sentence unfinished; it is not clear how it would have finished, and Ar. may not have given any thought to the matter.

298-9 sisters ... brethren: Greek *philās* "friends (fem.)" ... *philous* "friends (masc.)".

300-1 these folk coming from town: only here do the chorus give verbal expression to their assumed role as old men *from the country* (cf. 279).

301 when the fee ... was only one obol: this was the level at which Assembly pay was first introduced (on the proposal of Agyrrhius); it was then successively increased to two obols (Heracleides) and to three (Agyrrhius again) (Arist. *Ath.Pol.* 41.3).

302 among the garland stalls: lit. "in the garland(-stuff)s", i.e. in that part of the Agora where flowers and leaves were sold for making into festal, ritual and symposiac garlands; cf. Pherecrates fr. 2 which also, like Pherecrates fr. 70 and *Knights* 1375-6, mentions "in the perfume(-market)" as a place where men often sat gossiping. It is probably significant that in these sections of the Agora the stallholders were virtually all women (cf. 841, *Thesm.* 443-458, Athenaeus 13.612a, 15.687a), so that small groups of men could talk without risk of being eavesdropped by other men.

303 make themselves a thorough nuisance: the Greek verb, being derived from *okhlos* "crowd", probably in itself suggests that the nuisance takes the form of jostling (cf. Arist. *Ath.Pol.* 66.3, of jurors crowding and pressing to get their pay after a court session).

303 Myronides, son of Callias (*PA* 10509; *LGPN* 1), was an outstanding Athenian general between the 470s and the 450s. In 479 he was both an ambassador to Sparta (Plut. *Arist.* 10.10) and one of the generals at the battle of Plataea (*ibid.* 20.1); but his greatest fame came twenty years later. In 460 or 459 he led a scratch force of under- and over-age troops in a successful campaign in the Megarid (Thuc. 1.105.4-106); in 457 he defeated the Boeotians at Oenophyta and occupied Boeotia and Phocis (Thuc. 1.108.2-3). The old men of the chorus in *Lysistrata* (801-3) recall him as a model of manly prowess.

304 was general: lit. "held office".

304-5 no one then would have had the audacity to draw pay ... : the introduction of pay for office-holders, councillors and jurors (but not for attending the Assembly) had been the work of Pericles (Pl. *Gorg.* 515e, Arist. *Ath.Pol.* 24.3, 27.3; cf. *IG* i[3] 32.8-9, 82.20,

Thuc. 8.69.4), and occurred at latest in the early 440s (*IG* i^3 32.8-9). Ar. is most unlikely to have had any detailed knowledge of the relevant chronology, and our passage should not be taken as evidence that political pay was introduced only after the end of Myronides' career. Rather, Myronides is here being thought of as senior to, and a predecessor of, Pericles, who achieved nothing significant as a *military* leader until 454 (Thuc. 1.111.2).

306-7 bringing for himself ... a loaf: the manuscript readings here are unmetrical, and the most popular restoration has been Reiske's *(h)auon* "bringing a dry (stale) loaf". This, however, is unacceptable, for it would incongrously suggest that the ordinary citizen's diet in these "good old days" was not merely simple and frugal but *bad* and potentially unhealthy. Rather, a restoration is required that stresses the contrast between the past, when citizens willingly gave *their own* time to perform a public duty (and walked several miles into Athens, and several miles back on a very modest lunch), and the present when they expect to *be paid* for it. This contrast seems to be further marked by the use of the same word, *pherōn*, twice in close succession (305, 306) in equally valid but diametrically opposite senses, "drawing (pay)" and "bringing (food)": a people of givers has become a people of takers (cf. 777-9).

307 a drink: no doubt wine.

310 builders' labourers: lit. "carriers of clay" for making bricks and/or mortar; cf. *Birds* 1142-3. The point is that a self-respecting free man would avoid, whenever possible, doing a job for someone else for which he was paid by the day; cf. *Wasps* 712 where jurors are said to be "like olive-pickers, going at the beck and call of the man who has your wages".

311 BLEPYRUS: for other comic characters' names derived from *blepein* "look" cf. "Blepsidemus" in *Wealth* and "Blepes" in Menander's *Sikyonios* (188). The name Blepyrus itself (not rare in Athens in real life; *LGPN* cites nine fifth- and fourth-century instances) is a dissimulated form of **Blepylos*, itself a formation parallel to the synonymous *Derkylos* (cf. *Wasps* 78) and to *Chremylos*, *Meidylos*, etc.; the dissimilation itself is paralleled by *Melanthyros* (see *LGPN* s.v., and for *r/l* dissimilation generally see Schwyzer i 258-9), and there is no known Athenian name formed with the undissimilated suffix *-ylos* (or, in the feminine, *-ylē*) following an *-l-* in the stem. L. Paganelli, *MCr* 13/14 (1978/9) 231-5, argues that the name is designed to indicate the personality of its bearer, contrasting him as the *viewer* of events with Praxagora as the *doer*; but seeing that this play contains two old men called Blepyrus and Chremes, while *Wealth* contains two old men called Chremylus and Blepsidemus, it is more likely that we are merely dealing here with typical names for old men in comedy. "Blepyrus" may have been perceived as meaning "he who peers", suggesting an old man with poor eyesight (cf. 403).

312 getting on for sunrise: but still fairly dark (cf. 321), given the comparative shortness of the Mediterranean twilight. The Assembly meeting was due to begin at sunrise (85), and the women were anxious to get to the Pnyx early (95-99, 282-4, 289-292).

315-6 I just couldn't find it: it is here taken for granted that Blepyrus has only one *himation*; his neighbour, on the other hand, explicitly mentions (353) that the cloak his wife has taken is his only one. This suggests that whether one owned one such garment at a time for ordinary wear, or more than one, was a matter of choice (nothing indicates that either of these two men is especially poor or especially rich); cf. *Birds* 715 which implies that it was a common practice even for a well-to-do man to buy a new cloak every six months *and sell his old one*, and see MacDowell 310.

317 **the man from Shittington:** lit. "the man from Coprus" (= Dung), the name of a deme on the shore of the Bay of Eleusis just east of Eleusis town (Traill 52) whose inhabitants must have become very tired of being the subject of feeble jokes (cf. *Knights* 899). The "man" is, of course, a bowel-motion.

316-7 **knocking at my door:** for "door" or "gate" = a bodily orifice cf. (anus, as here) 361, *Lys.* 1162-3, Apollodorus com. fr. 13.9, and (vulva) 990, Archilochus fr. 196a.21.

318 **semi-foldover:** Greek *hēmidiploidion*, lit. "little half-twofold"; later the same garment is called a *khitōnion* (374; cf. on 268) and a *krokōtidion* (332, where see note), i.e. it is a woman's inner garment coloured saffron yellow. The particular type mentioned here must have been somehow related, probably in shape, to the *diploïs* ("twofold"), a man's outer garment that was worn folded double (cf. *AP* 7.65.3, Hesychius d1946); see W. Amelung, *RE* 3 (1899) 2342.

319 **Persian slippers:** *Persikai* were soft ankle-shoes worn by women (cf. *Lys.* 229, *Thesm.* 734); see Stone 227-9.

320 **in privacy:** lit. "in a clear <place>", i.e. away from other people.

322 **nobody is going to see me shitting *now*:** in fact Blepyrus will be seen (1) within the dramatic fiction, very shortly, by his neighbour and later by Chremes, and (2) outside it, by the entire theatre audience!

323 **at such an age:** lit. "being an old man". He has been married for thirteen or fourteen years at least, if we are entitled to require consistency with 243, and if he was already an old man then, he must be well in his seventies now. At this age he finds it difficult to satisfy his much younger wife's sexual appetite (cf. 467-8, 526, 619-622), and he fears she may be seeking solace elsewhere (cf. 325-6, 520-3); Vetta well cites [Theognis] 457-460 "A young wife is not a good match for an old man; like a boat, she does not obey the steering-oar ... but often by night breaks her cables and enters another harbour".

324 **I really deserve a sound thrashing!:** lit. "How many blows I deserve to receive!"

327-356 The character who converses with Blepyrus in this short scene is his next-door neighbour (327). We know that one of Blepyrus' neighbours is the husband of First Woman (cf. 33-40), but what we have heard about him (his sexual stamina, 37-39; his big stick, 76-77; his possible identification with a known public figure, see on 77) finds no echo in the quite colourless character we now meet, and to avoid any risk of an incongruity being perceived, it is preferable to assume that the character of 327-356 is Blepyrus' *other* neighbour (the third house is not, as many have supposed, needed for Chremes; cf. on 372 and 564). He is not wearing his wife's clothes (otherwise either he or Blepyrus would have said something about it) and is still hoping to find his own (only) *himation* (353); hence he is not at present fully dressed, and since he, unlike Blepyrus, is not given any motive to come out of his house in a state of undress, it is best to assume that he does not come out but appears at a window, like e.g. the girl at 884 and 949, and Philocleon in *Wasps* 316ff. (On the position of this window in the stage-house building, see on 877-1111.) Philocleon's attention was attracted by the singing of his fellow-jurymen; this man's attention has been attracted either by Blepyrus' groans as he strains to relieve himself (but since these would be vocalizations, one would have expected there to be some indication of them in the text) or, as I have assumed, by the loud noise of his breaking wind (cf. *Knights* 639, *Clouds* 293-4, 385-394, *Wealth* 698-703, Eur. *Cycl.* 328).

328 **why, by Zeus, that's just who it is:** RΛ (Γ has virtually no speaker indications in this part of the play) treat these words as Blepyrus' reply, but one would have expected him to show some sign of annoyance at being interrupted; rather, the Neighbour is

confirming his own identification of the man he has seen, as one of the innkeepers in *Frogs* (551-2) confirms the other's identification of the supposed Heracles.

329 **that yellow you've got on you:** men did not normally wear yellow garments; therefore if a man's clothes looked yellow, the only possible explanation (especially in comedy!) was that they had been soiled with faeces (cf. 1061, *Peace* 1176, *Frogs* 308). Blepyrus' garment, which is bright yellow all over, must on this logic have been soiled by someone with very severe diarrhoea – like Cinesias (see next note).

330 **Cinesias,** son of Meles (*PA* 8438; *LGPN* 2), was a dithyrambic poet, much satirized in comedy ever since the 420s for his empty sesquipedalian diction (*Clouds* 333-9, *Peace* 827-831), his musical innovations (Pherecrates fr. 155.8-13), his alleged impiety (Strattis fr. 18, cf. Lys. fr. 53 and probably *Frogs* 366), the emaciated body that made him look like a victim of chronic tuberculosis (*Birds* 1378, *Frogs* 1437, Ar. fr. 156.11, Plato com. fr. 200; cf. Lys. 21.20; Strattis fr. 17 calls him "Achilles of Phthi-a" with a pun on *phthi-sis* "consumption") – and his proneness to attacks of diarrhoea (Ar. fr. 156.13; cf. schol. *Frogs* 366, Lys. fr. 53); in *Birds* (1372-1409) he is one of the unwelcome visitors to Cloudcuckooville, and not long afterwards (see *CQ* 46 [1996] 334 n.52) Strattis had made him the central figure of a comedy. He was, however, successful as a poet for at least twenty years (*IG* ii^2 3028 is a dedication by a victorious *chorēgos* whose chorus he had trained), and in the 390s he took part in politics, proposing in early 393 a decree in honour of Dionysius I of Syracuse (*IG* ii^2 18; the decree was displayed in the Theatre of Dionysus) and prosecuting one Phanias for moving an illegal decree (Lys. fr. 53). On Ar.'s portrayal of him see C. Kugelmeier, *Reflexe früher und zeitgenössischer Lyrik in der alten attischen Komödie* (Stuttgart, 1996) 208-248; here he is probably alluding to an alleged occasion when Cinesias had defaecated on a shrine of Hecate (*Frogs* 366), a story now at least fifteen years old but one which he was never allowed to forget (cf. Lys. fr. 53 "Is not this the man who commits crimes against the gods which most people are ashamed even to mention but *which you hear about from the comic poets year after year*?")

330 **what are you blethering about?:** Greek *póthen?*, lit. "from where?" (possibly = "where did you get that idea from?"), an idiom for contemptuously dismissing a suggestion (cf. 389, 976, *Frogs* 1455). Some editors, following Brunck, treat *pothen* (without an accent, meaning "from somewhere") as the last word of the Neighbour's question; this would in itself be possible (with "Cinesias" as a surprise substitute for "a bird", cf. *Birds* 1117), but it is unlikely that an ancient editor would have inserted by conjecture an indication of change of speaker (present in RΛ) when the text was intelligible without it.

332 **little saffron number:** Greek *krokōtidion* (cf. on 318), a diminutive of *krokōtos*; this saffron-yellow inner garment was normally worn only by women and was regarded as their "most attractive and dressy costume" (Stone 175; cf. *Lys.* 44-51, 219-220). In *Thesmophoriazusae* Euripides' in-law wears one when he infiltrates the celebration of the Thesmophoria disguised as a woman. It is also a regular attribute of Dionysus (cf. Cratinus fr. 40.2, and see on 346), and he wears one in *Frogs* (46). Praxagora herself will have worn, under Blepyrus' *himation*, the ordinary underdress that she would have for everyday use (cf. on 268).

334 **among the bedclothes:** he was using it as an extra blanket (cf. 536-7).

338 **it makes me fear ...:** the Greek expression (lit. "in regard to which indeed I fear ...") is alien to colloquial Attic and probably intended to give a tragic colour to the sentence (cf. Eur. *Phoen.* 155, 263).

338 **untoward:** Greek *neōteron*, lit. "rather new", a common euphemism for "bad" (cf. [Eur.] *Rhes.* 590, Hdt. 5.93.2, Thuc. 2.6.2, Pl. *Prot.* 310b "you are not, are you, reporting something *neōteron*?" = "no bad news, I hope?"). He speaks more truly than he knows, for *neōteron* can also bear a political sense, "revolutionary" (cf. Hdt. 5.35.4, 6.74.1, Xen. *Hell.* 5.2.9 and the verb *neōterizein* "take revolutionary action").

341 **that I always wear:** lit. "that I used to wear", not implying that the cloak is a discarded one but only that its owner is not at present in possession of it.

345 **Laconians:** see on 74.

346 **soft boots:** Greek *kothornō*, dual of *kothornos*, properly a high, loose, soft boot which fitted either foot equally well, generally worn by women (cf. *Lys.* 657) but in comedy also by effeminate males (cf. *Birds* 994) and in art often by Dionysus (cf. e.g. Pickard-Cambridge[3] 206-8 and figs. 68, 70, 71), who wears them too in *Frogs* (47, 557); see Stone 229-232. Here the term appears to be applied loosely to what were earlier (319) called *Persikai*: I suspect that this is designed to draw attention to the fact that Blepyrus, in *krokōtos* (see on 332) and woman's shoes, looks like a grotesque version of Dionysus (by whom, be it noted, he has just sworn).

347 **blanket:** Greek *sisurā*, a cloak made of goatskin or sheepskin with the hair or fleece left on; it was worn as a garment by rustics (Stone 165-6; cf. *Wasps* 1138, *Frogs* 1459 with scholia), but in Ar. it is usually thought of as a blanket for beds or dining-couches (cf. 421, 840, *Clouds* 10, *Birds* 122, *Lys.* 933), and here Blepyrus evidently did not for a moment think of dressing himself in it even in an emergency.

348-350 Who asks the question, and who gives the answer? The solution depends on the following considerations: (1) the speaker of 349b-350 is speaking of *his own* wife, since for a man to express an informed opinion about the character of another man's wife would suggest undue familiarity with her; (2) the speaker of 348-349a is making a suggestion about *Blepyrus'* wife, since he uses the particle *dēta* which shows that his question "springs out of something ... just said" (Denniston 269), and it was the loss of Blepyrus' shoes, not of his Neighbour's, that was being spoken of just before. It follows that the Neighbour asks the question and Blepyrus answers it. Blepyrus seems to be thinking more favourably of his wife here than in 325 or 338, but there is no actual inconsistency: those earlier judgements were based on standard male assumptions about the behaviour of women in general, whereas his present view is based on what he (thinks he) knows about this particular woman – and also, we may suppose, on the reluctance that any husband would feel to admit that he had suffered the shame of being cuckolded (cf. D. Cohen, *Law, Sexuality, and Society* [Cambridge, 1991] 185).

348-9 **some woman friend ... who's invited her for lunch:** such visits were evidently a normal and accepted part of a married woman's life, particularly at times when the adult males of the family were out of the house so that there was no risk of improper contact between them and the female visitor(s); see Cohen *op.cit.* 154-6 for other evidence. It is, however, obviously absurd to suggest that it is for this purpose that Praxagora has left home *before daybreak* (and wearing her husband's clothes!); the two men are clutching at straws in order not to have to believe the worst (cf. previous note).

351 ***you* seem to be shitting a cable:** in fact, as Blepyrus explains in 354-5, it is for exactly the opposite reason that he has been squatting for so long.

355 **a sort of wild pear:** eating raw pears, especially wild ones, was thought to cause constipation, and the decoction of dried pears was a recommended remedy for diarrhoea (cf. Hippocr. *On Diet* 2.55.1, Diosc. 1.116).

356 **not the one that Thrasybulus told the Spartans about?:** it is abnormal, as Vetta notes, for a character to re-engage in dialogue, as the Neighbour is apparently made to do here, after announcing that it is time for him to go (351-3); but the deliberate misunderstanding involved in identifying the (probably literal) "wild pear" in Blepyrus' alimentary canal with the (certainly metaphorical) one that figured in a speech by

Thrasybulus becomes hopelessly artificial if, as Vetta proposes, the identification is suggested by Blepyrus himself, and it is best to accept the abnormality, parallels for which are hardly to be expected given the tiny number of cases in which characters make an exit by withdrawing from a window. The meaning of the political allusion (which was already found baffling in antiquity, to judge by the far-fetched explanation offered in the scholia) is best sought through a consideration of Blepyrus' comment on it: he says (357) that his "wild pear" resembles that of Thrasybulus in that it "*enekhetai* in/towards me very much". The mediopassive verb *enekhesthai* does not appear to be used elsewhere governing a dative case that denotes a person, and while one could reasonably assume that in reference to his own bowels Blepyrus has re-etymologized it as meaning "is held within me", that makes no sense as applied to a political speech or speaker. However, the active voice of the same verb (*enekhein*) is used in the Septuagint and New Testament (e.g. *Gen.* 49.23, *Luke* 11.53) in the sense "press hard upon, assail" (a person), and this sense, though nowhere attested for the mediopassive, would be very appropriate here: Blepyrus will be saying (1) that his constipation is giving him great trouble and (2) that Thrasybulus delivered a violent invective against the Spartans (probably during the recent debate on the Sparta Conference peace terms; cf. on 202-3). At some point in that speech he must have made mention of a wild pear (Greek *akhras*). Possibly this was an earthy metaphor or simile to emphasize an important point (perhaps e.g. Thrasybulus asserted that one or another Spartan or Persian demand was blocking the path to peace as firmly as a wild pear blocks up the bowels; cf. the vivid metaphors of Demosthenes mocked by Aeschines 3.166); alternatively, as suggested by M. Golden, *Hermes* 115 (1987), it may have been a slip of the tongue (cf. on 22-23), Thrasybulus saying *akhras* when he meant to say e.g. *akrās* "top" or *arkhās* "beginning".

358 ***this*:** viz. my immediate discomfort.

362 **this fellow from Pearswick** (cf. "a sort of wild pear", 355) represents constipation personified. Like "the man from Shittington" (317) with whom he is, as it were, doing battle, he derives his appellation from one of the demes of Attica; in this case the deme in question is Acherdûs (a small deme of unknown location), whose name is here modified to Achradûs for the sake of a pun on *akhras* (cf. on 356).

364 **a real specialist in anal problems:** Greek doctors, unlike Egyptian ones (cf. Hdt. 2.84), normally held themselves out as healers of all kinds of ailments, but there were some specialists (thus Morsimus, the tragic poet, was an eye-doctor [schol. *Frogs* 151]), and doubtless particular practitioners acquired exceptional reputations in particular areas of medicine. The present phrase, however (lit. "clever in the craft of matters relating to the anus"), will make a comic audience think not of doctors but of passive homosexuals.

365 **does Amynon know?:** or, with Meineke, "Ah, I know: Amynon". The reading of the mss., which I have retained, could mean either "does Amynon know who is a good anal specialist?" or "does Amynon know a lot about anal problems?". Whichever reading and interpretation is correct, the insinuation is the same: Amynon is a passive homosexual. The scholia assert more specifically that he was "a politician who had been <accused of being> a male prostitute" (cf. on 103 and 112-3); this suggests that ancient commentators knew of other comic references to him, but he is not now identifiable (indeed our passage is the only known reference to *any* Athenian of this name).

365 **probably he won't admit it:** for if he did, he would be barred from public life, like Grypus in the 420s (*Knights* 877) and Timarchus in 346/5 (Aeschines 1).

366 **Antisthenes** is clearly the same man who in 806-8 (where, as here, his name and the idea of defaecation seem to call each other to mind) is by implication characterized as rich and selfish. We have good information about two very rich fourth-century Athenians named Antisthenes. One (*PA* 1186, *LGPN* 1) was a banker (Dem. 36.43) who had apparently retired by 394/3, when the bank previously owned by himself and his partner Archestratus was in the hands of their former slave Pasion, either as owner or lessee, although Archestratus at least was still alive (Isoc. 17; see J.C. Trevett, *Apollodorus the Son of Pasion* [Oxford, 1992] 2, 18 n.2). The other was Antisthenes son of Antiphates of Cytherrus (*PA* 1194 = 1196 = 1197, *LGPN* 25), whose activities as landowner, priest, *chorēgos* and trierarch are abundantly attested by inscriptional evidence from the 370s to the 320s (see D.M. Lewis, *ABSA* 50 [1955] 21-22, and Davies 38-39). In addition Xenophon (*Mem.* 3.4.1-4) refers to an Antisthenes (*PA* 1184), many times a victorious *chorēgos*, who "knew about nothing except amassing money" but was at least once elected a general despite never having served as a hoplite; Davies, Develin and *LGPN* identify him with the younger of the two men above, but this requires us to assume a gross anachronism on Xenophon's part, and while that cannot be ruled out *a priori* there seems no good reason to accept it when an easy alternative is available. I suggest therefore that Xenophon, Demosthenes and Ar. are all referring to the same person; since *LGPN* 25 was probably born between 420 and 410 (see Davies *loc.cit.*), our man might well be his grandfather, who would have been aged about eighty in 392/1. The present passage indicates that he had recently made himself conspicuous by groaning with pain in public; to make fun in this way of an old and sick man may seem heartless, but this avaricious draft-dodger had evidently long been unpopular (and cf. on 255). He may have had to retain control of the family fortune longer than he would have wished, for his son Antiphates had perished in a naval battle, probably Arginusae in 406 (*IG* ii^2 1951.99), and his grandson will have been little if at all over twenty years old in 392/1.

369 **Hileithya:** the goddess of childbirth. On the spelling of her name, see my note on *Lys.* 742 (adding that the same form is now attested inscriptionally at Eretria: see *SEG* xl 760-2); the mss. here, as there, have the Homeric *Eileithyia*, a form virtually unknown in inscriptions before the Hellenistic period. It is likely, though not certain, that Blepyrus' prayer proves effective; at any rate he shows no further sign of distress after Chremes' arrival. He cannot of course actually produce a motion (apart from anything else, he, like all actors, is wearing an all-over bodysuit), but Athenian audiences were probably as used to simulated defaecation or urination (cf. *Frogs* 308, 479; *Wasps* 935-940, *Thesm.* 610-7) as modern film audiences are to simulated sex. We shall discover in a moment that during the same time that Blepyrus has been struggling with his bowels, the Assembly meeting has begun and ended on the Pnyx; thus while Blepyrus after much labour has "given birth" to a quantity of excrement, the Assembly under his wife's guidance has been giving birth (cf. 549-550) to a new Athens.

371 **a comic shitpot** is "precisely what [Blepyrus] is in this scene" (Henderson 102)! The point of the comparison is that a slop-bucket, like Blepyrus' lower bowel at this moment, receives excrement but cannot discharge it.

372 **CHREMES** ("Throat-clearer"): we will learn this character's name only at the moment of his departure (477). Even more than "Blepyrus" (see on 311), this name (attested for eight real Athenians between *c.*510 and 280 BC) is of a type that was to become standard for old men in comedy (cf. Antiphanes fr. 189.22, Alciphron 4.2.5); four of the six comedies of Terence include a character of this name (though in one of them, *The Eunuch*, he is a *young* man). The hero of Ar.'s *Wealth* bears the similar name Chremylus. As a *dramatis persona* here, Chremes appears to exist only for the purpose of reporting the Assembly debate, like the messenger in Euripides' *Orestes* (852-956) or Blepes in Menander's *Sikyonios* (150-271): he is apparently not an inhabitant of any of the houses visible on stage (for in his exit-line he says "I'm going" [*eimi*] not "I'm going inside" [*eiseimi*]) and he therefore cannot be the man who appears at 564 and is later (730ff) seen bringing his property out of his house for surrender to the state, while his loyal acceptance of the community's decisions whatever they may be (471-2) distinguishes him equally clearly from the Dissident of 746ff.

375 **by mistake:** lit. "by chance". This is a lie, but Blepyrus can be assumed to have had time to think of this way to avoid further unnecessary embarrassment, while the author wants to avoid repetition.

377 **it was finished before daylight:** an exaggeration, since the meeting had been scheduled to start at sunrise (84-85) and could not begin before the Prytaneis had arrived to preside (cf. *Ach.* 23-26, 40; Dem. 18.169-170).

378 **the vermilion dye:** we know (cf. *Ach.* 22 with scholia, Plato com. fr. 82) that in the fifth century (before the days of Assembly pay), in order to secure a good attendance at Assembly meetings, "two slaves, carrying a rope covered with vermilion dye stretched between them, used to go through the Agora and chase the crowd into the Assembly place, and all who were smeared with the dye had to pay a fine". Here, however, the dyed rope is being used at the end of the meeting, not the beginning, and its purpose must therefore be different. It cannot be to drive away latecomers from the Assembly itself (the view of M.H. Hansen, *GRBS* 23 [1982] 243-4), since Chremes himself, though a latecomer, was present throughout the debate and is able to say with confidence why the Assembly voted as it did (456-7); an alternative suggestion by Hansen *op.cit.* 243 n.11 that the rope was used "to prevent participants from stealing away ... only to return just before the session ended" does not fit our passage, since on that view the rope would no longer be needed once the meeting was over. Rather the object must be to clear the Pnyx, after the meeting ended, of all except those who have to stay behind for the time-consuming business of cashing in their pay-tickets (see on 296); possibly, once all 6000 pay-tickets for a meeting had been issued, the rope or ropes were drawn around the area occupied by the ticket-holders (thus clearly separating them from those who had arrived too late) and then, at the end of the meeting, shaken outwards to drive the late-comers away (cf. G.R. Stanton in B. Forsén and G.R. Stanton ed. *The Pnyx in the History of Athens* [Helsinki, 1996] 20). On this occasion the procedure was particularly funny (lit. "provided much laughter") because the meeting ended so early that while some non-ticketholders were trying to get away unsmeared, they were impeded by others who were only just arriving for the first time!

380 **then you got your three obols?:** Blepyrus deduces this (wrongly) from the fact that Chremes was amused by the vermilion-dye incident, supposing that he would have been in no laughing mood had he been departing empty-handed.

381 **but in fact I came too late:** too late to get a pay ticket, though not too late for the beginning of the proceedings (cf. 395-8); in the old days, by contrast, it had been common for someone arriving at the Pnyx to ask his neighbour "Has anyone spoken yet?" (*Ach.* 45). For "in fact" (Greek *nūn*, lit. "now") R reads (unmetrically) *nē Di(a)* "by Zeus", and this led J. Jackson, *Marginalia Scaenica* (Oxford, 1955) 48-49, to emend the text, combining suggestions by Bentley and Reisig, to make Blepyrus ask "You mean you came too late?" and Chremes reply "Yes, by Zeus, which makes me ..."; but R's reading may be due to a scribe's eye or mind having wandered to *nē Di(a)* in 377 (so N.G.Wilson, *CR* 26 [1976] 13).

381 **which makes me feel really ashamed:** Vetta suggests that Chremes is ashamed of having failed in his civic duty and that the materialistic Blepyrus jumps wrongly to the

conclusion that he is ashamed of having lost his three obols; but Chremes has in fact no reason to be ashamed of himself as a citizen, since he had actually arrived in good time for the meeting, and 380 ("If only I had") shows that he deeply regrets having missed his pay.

382 **Ashamed to face who? Your shopping-bag, that's all!:** lit. "<ashamed to face,> by Zeus, no one other than your bag", the point being that the (personified) bag, into which Chremes would have put the purchases he was going to make in the Agora with his three obols, has been cheated of its expectations owing to his tardiness and is now having to go home empty; cf. *Wasps* 314 where the chorus-leader's son, fearing that the court may not sit and his juryman father may therefore receive no pay, sings in shock and sorrow "Then, O my bag, I had thee but as a useless ornament!" The text, however, is problematic:

(1) The mss. continue 382 to Chremes, but that gives feeble sense ("I came too late, which makes me feel ashamed to face – no one, by Zeus, other than my bag"); see Jackson *loc.cit.*).

(2) Hesitantly following Ussher and Vetta, I have transferred 382 to Blepyrus without altering its wording; but this is not fully satisfactory either, since a qualified assent to, or a qualified denial of, another speaker's statement is normally marked by the restrictive particle *ge* or the denial particles *men oun.*

(3) It is possible to insert *ge* without any further alteration to the text (see apparatus); this creates a metrical feature (word-boundary within an anapaestic foot) which has traditionally been frowned on by editors but is actually not very rare in Ar. (see White 44-48), especially when, as here, the boundary is blurred by a vowel-elision.

(4) Editors wishing to find space for *ge* have generally, following Brunck, altered the masculine phrase *ouden' allon* "no one" to the neuter *ouden allo* "nothing"; this involves assuming a complex, and possibly hard-to-understand, play on two senses of the verb *aiskhūnesthai*, (i) "be ashamed to face (a person)" and (ii) "be ashamed of (a fault or misfortune)", the effective sense being approximately "Ashamed of what? Only of what your shopping-bag will think of it all!".

(5) It is possible that the difficulties of the text are due to the loss of one or two lines; thus van Leeuwen's supplement (see apparatus) has Chremes saying he feels ashamed "to be coming home unsuccessful", Blepyrus asking him "You mean you've not got anything?", and Chremes replying "No, by Zeus, nothing but my bag".

385 **we thought they all looked like shoemakers:** or, with ΓΛ, "we all thought they looked like shoemakers". Shoemakers, because they worked indoors, were commonly thought of as pale-faced (a proverb to this effect is quoted in a scholium to *Peace* 1310); it is not entirely clear why this stereotype was so firmly attached to shoemakers and not to other craftsmen (e.g. potters, smiths) who also normally worked indoors, but part of the explanation is probably that shoemaking was a physically undemanding craft whose main operations, cutting and sewing, were not very dissimilar to those of the textile crafts that were regarded as women's work. In Pl. *Charm.* 163b shoemaking is the first example that comes to the mind of the future oligarch Critias of a lowly and degrading occupation (he couples it with salt-fish selling and prostitution).

387 **full of white faces:** cf. on 64.

390-1 **if you'd gone at the time of the second cock-crow:** an even grosser exaggeration than that at 377, since at second cock-crow the women had not even assembled for their practice session (cf. 30-31), much less gone to the Pnyx.

392-3 **Antilochus ... all I had is gone!:** quoted, with the substitution of "my three obols" (*tou triōbolou*) for "my dead comrade" (*tou tethnēkotos*), from Aeschylus' *Myrmidons* (Aesch. fr. 138), where the lines were spoken by Achilles on receiving the news that his beloved friend Patroclus had been killed; as in the *Iliad* (18.2-34), the news had been brought to him by Antilochus, son of Nestor.

396-7 to set down for debate: lit. "to propose <that speakers offer> opinions regarding", a standard formula for placing a matter on the Assembly agenda (cf. Thuc. 1.139.3, 6.14.1). For *protheinai* "propose" (cf. 401 *prokeimenou*, in practice if not in the lexicon the passive participle of the same verb) the mss. have *katheinai* "let down, drop"; this verb has no known sense that would be relevant here, and probably *ka-* derives from a misplaced marginal correction of 399 (whose first word is *kāpeita* "and then").

396-7 the subject of how to save the City: "a recognized formula ... which would permit any proposal for the general good of the state" (P.J. Rhodes, *The Athenian Boule* [Oxford, 1972] 233); it is found being employed in emergency situations such as the constitutional crisis of 411 (Arist. *Ath.Pol.* 29.2 with 29.4) and the aftermath of the battle of Chaeronea in 338 (Dem. 18.248). The Assembly agenda was published several days in advance (Arist. *Ath.Pol.* 45.4, cf. Photius s.v. *propempta*), and Praxagora would therefore have known in good time that this was the meeting at which the women must stage their coup; that Chremes seems to have been taken by surprise, while Blepyrus was not even aware of the special importance of the meeting till this moment, is probably meant to be seen as evidence of their political apathy – they never trouble to read the agenda, and to them every Assembly meeting is exactly the same as every other, their sole object in attending it being to draw their pay.

397-8 first of all, straight after the preliminaries: lit. "and then immediately first", i.e. as soon as the herald had said "Who wishes to speak?" (130).

398 that bleary-eyed Neocleides: see on 254.

400-2 isn't it shocking ... save his own eyelids: applying (a comic extension of) the principle behind the law whereby a man who had squandered his inherited property was forbidden to speak in the Assembly; cf. Aeschines 1.30 "[The lawgiver] thought that one who had mismanaged his own household would also mismanage the public affairs of the City". Similarly in *Acharnians* (558, 578, 593) Lamachus and his supporters claim that Dicaeopolis, being supposedly a beggar, has no right to offer political advice or criticism.

404 what am I supposed to do about it? (i.e. how can I possibly now *cure* myself?): or, with Λ, "what should I have done about it?" (i.e. how could I have *prevented* the deterioration of my eyesight?), in which case Blepyrus' prescription (404-6) is being offered retrospectively (the Greek text of 404-6 neither excludes nor requires such an interpretation).

404-6 This prescription is very similar to that described in *Wealth* 716-725, where Neocleides (by now totally, or almost totally, blind) has gone to the temple of Asclepius in the hope of a cure, and the god pounds up garlic, fig-juice, squills and vinegar and – going one better than Blepyrus – applies the mixture to the *inside* of Neocleides' eyelids, with results agonizing for Neocleides but gratifying for others who saw or heard of it (*Wealth* 726, 745-7).

404 fig-juice: Greek *opos*, the acid latex of the fig-tree, used as rennet in the making of cheese (*Iliad* 5.902-3; Arist. *HA* 522b2-5).

405 spurge (*Euphorbia peplus* and other spp.) was likewise notorious for the pungency of its fluid extracts; cf. Galen 12.141.7 Kühn. Several species and varieties were known to ancient botanists and doctors (see Thphr. *HP* 9.11.5-11, Diosc. 4.164-5), but they do not refer to a "Laconian" variety; we can safely assume, however, that it was the strongest with which classical Athenians were familiar!

408 **Euaeon** (*PA* 5253, *LGPN* 1) is not otherwise known, but evidently he was conspicuously poor, like Lysistratus (*Ach.* 857-9, *Knights* 1268-73, *Wasps* 1311-3), Amynias (*Wasps* 1267-74), or Pauson (*Thesm.*949-952, *Wealth* 602). Like Neocleides he is advising the City on how to manage its affairs when he has shown himself a poor manager of his own; but he gets much more sympathy from Chremes and Blepyrus, because his misfortune is one which either afflicts or threatens a large proportion of the population.

412-426 Euaeon's speech, and Blepyrus' rider to it, show us graphically, just before Praxagora's own motion is proposed and carried, how desperate the state of Athens is, with large numbers of ordinary citizens in need of the simplest necessities of life – winter clothing, bedding, basic food – and threatened with serious damage to their health through cold and undernourishment, while (as they see it) those to whom they pay money for goods and services (fullers, tanners, corn-dealers ...) grow rich at their expense. If the report of Euaeon's speech had stood alone, we might have thought that his own distress was making him exaggerate the distress of Athenians in general; but Blepyrus' view that Euaeon erred only in not going far enough, and that "there wouldn't have been a hand raised in opposition" had he gone even further, shows that many Athenians are indeed in dire poverty (cf. *Wealth* 219, 253, 535-547) and are ready to take drastic steps to deal with it. Thus the ground is prepared in our minds for Praxagora's revolutionary proposals, which will *inter alia* abolish the money-economy and make the necessities of life freely available to all.

413 **something weighing about eight pounds:** lit. "of four staters". "Stater" was the name both for coins (of widely varying composition and value) and for a unit of weight, which in Athens, as inscribed weights show, was normally equal to about 900 grams (see M. Chambers, *CSCA* 6 [1973] 10-16). What Euaeon can be seen by all to be in need of is a new cloak, and in theory the reference here could be either to the value of such a cloak or to its weight (and therefore warmth); but in practice "stater" as a unit of value is meaningless unless qualified by "Aeginetan", "Cyzicene", "of gold" (cf. *Wealth* 816-7), etc., and cloaks are described by the weight of wool used to make them in Eupolis fr. 270 ("five staters") and, with gross exaggeration, in *Wasps* 1147 ("a talent", i.e. thirty staters).

415 **the fullers:** since an individual, even a rich man, might well have only one winter cloak of his own (cf. on 315-6), the only places where such garments could be found in quantity would be the fullers' shops where they were taken for cleaning. Note that the fullers would be required to lend out garments that did not even belong to them!

416 **the turning of the sun:** the winter solstice.

416 **warm cloaks:** Greek *khlainai*, heavy (and expensive) woollen winter garments; cf. *Wasps* 1132, *Birds* 712, 715, and see Stone 160-2.

417 **none of us:** or, with the Suda, "none of you"; it is normal for Assembly speakers to refer to the Athenian people as "you" rather than "we", but here "we" is particularly appropriate because the speaker himself so obviously stands to benefit personally from the proposed measure.

419 **after washing their hands:** this has usually been taken to mean "after dinner" (cf. *Wasps* 1217); but the persons spoken of here are hardly likely to have had much to dine on. Ussher put forward, and Vetta was attracted by, the suggestion that the paupers are imagined as visiting the public bath-houses to warm themselves (cf. *Wealth* 535, 952-4); but (i) to wash in a bath-house was not *aponiptesthai* (the verb used here) but *lou(e)sthai*, (ii) the paupers would not trouble to warm themselves at a bath-house if warm blankets were awaiting them at a tanner's shop. I suggest that those wishing to use the free sleeping facilities are being required to wash their hands so as to avoid soiling the blankets – not so much for the benefit of the tanners as for that of the next night's dossers.

420 **the tanners' shops:** since *sisurai* (see on 347; this is the word rendered "fleecy blankets" in 421) were made of skin.

424 **the corn-dealers:** for their unpopularity cf. Lysias 22 (387 BC?), a rabble-rousing prosecution speech against a group of metic corn-dealers for allegedly forcing up prices, demanding the death penalty (§19) and assuring the jury (§22) that if the accused are convicted and executed, corn will be cheaper in future.

424 **quarts:** Greek *khoinikes* (see on 45). The ration is presumably to be in barley, since wheat, being more valuable, would not be supplied by the corn-dealers unless the decree explicitly required it. One *khoinix* of barley a day was a minimum ration for a male slave (Thuc. 4.16.1), though a soldier was thought to require at least a *khoinix* of wheat (Hdt. 7.187.2). Thus, bearing in mind that women as well as children were fed less than men, a daily distribution of three *khoinikes* would be enough to support a family of four or five persons.

425 **or else they'd be well and truly for it:** lit. "or howl loudly", threatening an unspecified but very unpleasant punishment (cf. *Peace* 255, *Birds* 1207).

426 **Nausicydes** (*PA* 10567; *LGPN* 5) is mentioned by Xenophon (*Mem.* 2.7.6) as a miller who had grown rich enough to become a large rearer of livestock and to have performed several liturgies. He is probably identical with the Nausicydes of Cholargus (*PA* 10571) mentioned in Plato's *Gorgias* (487c) as believing, like Socrates' interlocutor Callicles, that the study of ethical philosophy ought to be kept within strict bounds and not allowed to impede the pursuit of self-interest; if Nausimenes of Cholargus (*PA* 10578), who died, probably in his thirties, between c.405 and c.385 (cf. Isaeus 8.8, 14), was this man's son (as is likely since a later Nausimenes son of Nausicydes is known from the same deme), then Nausicydes will have been at least sixty years old in 391. On the family and its connections see Davies 314-5.

427-8 **a good-looking, white-faced young man:** this is of course Praxagora(s).

428 **rather like Nicias:** the reference is generally taken to be to Nicias, son of Niceratus, of the deme Cydantidae (*PA* 10809, *LGPN* 96), grandson of the famous general Nicias. He was a small child in 403 (Lys. 18.10) and can hardly have been more than twenty, if that, in early 391; but he was certainly in the public eye either then or soon afterwards, for by the summer of 390 he was married, at an unusually early age, to the daughter of Thrasybulus (deduced from *IG* ii^2 2409.21-22 and Dem. 19.290 by D.M. Lewis, *ABSA* 50 [1955] 30). If this marriage was in part designed as the foundation of a political career, the design failed, perhaps because Thrasybulus perished so soon after; Nicias appears subsequently only as holder of his family's silver-mining interests and (by lot) of some minor public offices (see Davies 406). If he is the person referred to here, then in view of his youth he is more probably being complimented for his good looks (cf. Demos, son of Pyrilampes, in *Wasps* 98) than disparaged for effeminacy. But the reference may be to another person altogether; the name is an extremely common one.

428 **jumped up:** showing far greater vigour than Neocleides (398 "edged his way") or even Euaeon (409 "came forward").

432 **the folk from the countryside:** these are the *real* countrymen, as distinct from the women-impersonating-countrymen (279, 300-1) whom Chremes has taken for shoemakers. It is probably to be understood that they are hostile to Praxagoras' proposal because it violates the traditional norms of society, of which country people were thought of as staunch upholders (see L.B.Carter, *The Quiet Athenian* [Oxford, 1986] 76-98).

435 you: Chremes means "you as a typical male", but Blepyrus, until 440, takes him to mean "you as an individual".

437 ask me that in a moment: lit. "don't ask that yet". Chremes has realized Blepyrus has misunderstood him, and takes advantage of his error to tease him, making him imagine as long as possible that he alone has been publicly denounced as a criminal.

438 a thief: most Athenians did not steal each other's property, but they were very ready to believe that almost anybody (else), if given the opportunity, would steal *public* assets; cf. *Knights* 258, 296, 1127-8, 1145-50, *Wasps* 554-7, 894-981, *Birds* 1111-2, *Lys.* 490, *Thesm.* 811-2, *Wealth* 569.

439 an informer: Greek *sūkophantēs*, a man who brings prosecutions for personal gain (e.g. by blackmail) or from other unworthy motives. Although the volunteer prosecutor was indispensable to Athenian law enforcement (as one of them cogently but unavailingly argues in *Wealth* 907-919), the *sūkophantēs* was nevertheless a hate-figure; the two sides of this paradox are respectively stressed by R.G. Osborne and F.D. Harvey in P.A. Cartledge et al. ed. *Nomos: Essays in Athenian Law, Politics and Society* (Cambridge, 1990) 83-102 and 103-121.

440 most of these people here: "the audience ... were always delighted with a general charge of this kind, which each individual would clearly see exactly applied to his neighbours, and had not the slightest application to himself" (Rogers); cf. *Clouds* 1096-9, *Thesm.* 814-829, *Frogs* 274-6, 783.

442 good at raising income: cf. 236.

442-3 leak the secrets of the Thesmophoria every time they hold it: lit. "carry out the secrets every time from <the sanctuary of> the two Thesmophoroi" [= Demeter and Kore]. For the Thesmophoria see on 223a; for the secrecy of (some of) its rituals cf. *Thesm.* 626-633 where a "woman" suspected of being a man in disguise is tested by questioning her about "last year's rituals", while another (undisguised, effeminate) man is asked to "stand away ... so that you don't overhear".

444 you and I, when we're on the Council: since there were five hundred councillors, all aged over thirty, and no one could serve more than two annual terms, a high proportion of Athenians could expect to become councillors at some time in their lives; M.H. Hansen, *The Athenian Democracy in the Age of Demosthenes* (Oxford, 1991) 249, calculates that two-thirds of all citizens reaching the age of forty would eventually become councillors. Aristophanes himself served as a councillor about this time (*Agora* xv 12.26).

444 doing that: i.e. leaking secrets. The Council sometimes held secret sessions (cf. *Knights* 648, Andoc. 1.45, 2.19, Lys. 13.21, 31.31, *Hell.Oxy.* 6.1, Aeschines 3.125, Theopompus *FGrH* 115 F 30a), when non-members were excluded from the Council chamber unless invited to make a report, and members were forbidden to divulge the proceedings; but secrecy, though presumably enforced by a clause in the councillors' oath of office, will have been hard to maintain (cf. *Hell.Oxy.* 6.2). See P.J. Rhodes, *The Athenian Boule* (Oxford, 1972) 42-44. Our passage probably alludes to a specific recent case.

446-9 they lend each other ...: for a similar argument to demonstrate the honesty of women as a sex cf. Iamblichus, *On the Pythagorean Life* 55, which is thought to be based on a work written about 400 BC; see N. Demand, *GRBS* 23 (1982) 179-184. These informal everyday loans of personal and household goods or of small sums of money, or gifts of perishables on the understanding that an equivalent would be given back later, were extremely common among men also (cf. *Peace* 1154, *Thesm.* 219, 250-1, *Frogs* 1158-9), and it was considered improper to refuse, or haggle over, a reasonable request for one (cf. Men. *Dysk.* 456-518, Thphr. *Char.* 10.13, 18.7); see P.C. Millett, *Lending and*

Borrowing in Ancient Athens (Cambridge, 1991) 38-39. Women, however, being in the home a greater proportion of the time and being in charge of the household chattels (cf. 211-2), were more likely than men to be faced with the short-term domestic emergencies that made such loans necessary; and relatively few of them were in a position to make the kinds of large-scale loans that required witnesses and contracts (though cf. *Thesm.* 840-5; D.M. Schaps, *Economic Rights of Women in Ancient Greece* [Edinburgh, 1979] 63-66; E.M. Harris, *Phoenix* 46 [1992] 309-321).

452-3 **they don't become informers ... they don't subvert the democracy:** the fallacy is obvious, since women have not hitherto had any opportunity to do any of these things – and what is more, the speaker is him/herself engaged in subverting the democratic system (the sovereignty of the [male] citizen body) at this very moment!

456-7 **this was the only thing that hadn't ever been done before:** a combination of the themes "Athenians innovate for the sake of innovating" (cf. 218-220) and "every policy tried so far has been a failure" (cf. 108-9, 174-9, 193-203, 208). During the previous twenty years Athens had been ruled by democracy, the Four Hundred, the Five Thousand, democracy restored, the Thirty, the Ten, and democracy restored again.

460 **going to court:** to serve as a juror; jurors in comedy are thought of as typically old men (cf. *Wasps* passim, also *Knights* 255, 977-9, *Peace* 349, *Lys.* 380, *Wealth* 277-8), so much so that "old man" and "juror" are sometimes virtually synonymous (e.g. *Ach.* 375-6).

461 **your household:** lit. "those whom you have", i.e. wife, children, and slaves if any.

462 **getting up groaning:** lit. "groaning"; for the theme cf. *Birds* 487-492 (the cock bids men rise to work), *Wealth* 537-9 (insects buzz around one's head and rouse one from sleep with the message "get up or go hungry").

464 **farting** is similarly used as a virtual synonym for "sleeping <at a time when working folk have to be awake>" in *Clouds* 9.

467-8 **compel us by force ... to screw them:** inverting an unpleasant, and little-discussed, reality of Athenian conjugal life; *Lys.* 160-6 and 225-7 show that it was nothing out of the ordinary for wives to be coerced into sexual submission and beaten if they persisted in refusing. See A.H. Sommerstein in L. Foxhall and J.B. Salmon ed. *Thinking Men* (London, 1998) 106-9.

468-9 **and if we're not able to, they won't give us our lunch:** no doubt in real life another sanction available to husbands for punishing wives who said "no"; it was commonly used for disciplining slaves (cf. *Wasps* 435). Praxagora will in fact introduce deprivation of food as a punishment for crimes of violence (663-6). Manuscripts and editors differ on the assignment of this sentence to a speaker or speakers: following Velsen and van Leeuwen, I have given it all to Blepyrus, since he, not Chremes, is the person who finds the implications of the new order worrying (Chremes is optimistic, cf. 464, 471-2) and who is elsewhere conscious of his own fading virility (cf. 323-6, 619-622).

470 **you should do *this*:** what is "this"? It must be something that can be said to make it possible to lunch and to copulate simultaneously (that sentence is designedly ambiguous: "simultaneously" may modify either "make it possible" or "to lunch and to copulate"). Most editors and translators are unable, or too embarrassed, to make any intelligible suggestion at all, or else take *drā tauta* "do this" in the sense "obey", which the phrase can indeed bear but which is quite inappropriate here, since Blepyrus' problem is not that he is *unwilling* to obey commands of the kind envisaged, but that he fears he will be *unable* to. Henderson 186 noted that in appropriate contexts (and this is surely one), "breakfast" and "lunch" could refer to oral sexual activity (cf. *Wealth* 295, Cantharus fr. 10), and suggested that the reference here was to cunnilingus; but

while this could certainly be called "lunching", it could not be called "screwing". I suggest that what Chremes suggests Blepyrus should do is *fellate himself* (cf. *Knights* 1010 "may he bite his prick!", *Wealth* 295 with scholia, Artemidorus 1.80, Catullus 88.8, *CIL* iv 2360.3, 8512); this would both enable him to "lunch" (in the sense previously indicated) and enable him to copulate (by giving himself the erection that he normally finds it so difficult to attain). Combining as it did the opprobrious connotations of masturbation ("he can't find a partner", cf. 707-9) and of submission to oral penetration ("he/she behaves like a whore": *laikastria* "fellatrix" was a virtual synonym of *pornē* "prostitute", cf. *Ach.* 529, 537), self-fellation seems to have been thought so utterly gross an act that in the heyday of Attic erotic vase-painting, even satyrs were not depicted doing it (M.F. Kilmer, *Greek Erotica on Attic Red-figure Vases* [London, 1993] evidently did not find it anywhere in his material); Artemidorus loc.cit. classifies it as "against nature" (whereas oral sex with other persons is merely "against convention"), and Catullus loc.cit. implies that it is the worst imaginable perversion (or was, before the days of Gellius!). Both here and in *Wealth* 295 the act was doubtless mimed with the aid of the large comic phallus, without which, here at any rate, the joke would probably have been unintelligible (and without which it would be very hard for Blepyrus to carry out Chremes' suggestion!).

471-2 if that's going to be ... what every man ought to do: it is tempting to see this as a declaration of loyalty to the Athenian civic ideal, contrasting with the selfishness condemned in 205-8; but the context is strongly averse to such an interpretation. What, after all, is it that Chremes is saying "every man ought to do"? He is probably *meaning* to refer to the compulsory copulation envisaged in 467-8, a "duty" to which most men (including Chremes himself, if as is likely he is rather younger than Blepyrus) are not likely to be averse anyway (cf. 861-2 where the Dissident claims that it is his civic duty to ... eat a free dinner). After 469-470, however, he is likely to be *understood* as referring to self-fellation, than which nothing could be more alien to the status and dignity of a male citizen (see above); if that is what Chremes' declaration means, then to make it is effectively to abdicate from being a free man.

474-5 all the stupid or foolish decisions ... turn out to be to our benefit: cf. *Clouds* 587-9, where the scholia narrate the myth on which the saying is based: "When Poseidon and Athena were disputing possession of Attica, and Athena won, Poseidon was so vexed that he cursed the city, saying 'The Athenians will always make the wrong decision'; but Athena, hearing him, added the words '... and yet be successful'." It is thus appropriate that Chremes should pray especially to Pallas Athena for a successful outcome to the new political experiment.

478-509 This re-entry song or *epiparodos* is wholly in iambic metre, except for the opening line which consists of a single anapaestic *metron*; it is as if the chorus-leader wished to set a regular, even march-rhythm but was unable to impose it on her colleagues. In choral *parodoi*, iambic rhythm is characteristic of old men moving slowly (cf. on 285-8); here, in addition to its appropriateness to a chorus of women masquerading as old men, it may suggest (i) that they are moving cautiously and stealthily for fear of discovery and/or (ii) that they are fatigued through having worn heavy and unfamiliar clothing and footwear for a considerable time (cf. Parker 531-2).

482 watching how we walk: lit. "closely watching the/our configuration" (Greek *skhēma*, cf. on 150); as Vetta points out, a woman dressed as a man, and viewed from behind, would be much more likely to betray herself by her manner of walking (her hip movements and/or the delicacy of her steps) than in any other way.

483 make as much noise with your feet as you can: cf. 544-6 for a noisy footfall as a gender marker. In the transmitted text, the participle *epiktupōn* "making a noise" is masculine (cf. 289-299), whereas everywhere else in this song the women refer to themselves in the feminine gender; possibly there has been corruption (see apparatus, and cf. on 31), a simplification of word-order (*badiz' epiktupousa* → *epiktupousa badize*) having been followed by a misguided attempt to restore metre.

486 **wrap yourself up tightly:** cf. 99, which is also concerned with concealment. Ussher and Vetta take the Greek phrase *sustellou seautēn* in the quite different sense "close up your ranks"; but the verb and pronoun are *singular*, and closing ranks, unlike wrapping oneself up, is something that can only be done by a *group*.

486-8 **look around you ... end in disaster:** in the mss. the strophe is one *metron* shorter than the antistrophe, and while this would not in itself be certain proof of corruption, the sentence is also incomplete grammatically. Many supplements have been suggested, to be inserted at various different points; I have adopted that proposed by Blaydes (adding *phulatth' hopōs* "take care that"), which removes from the text the rare (though not unexampled, cf. 495, Pl. *Rep.* 451a, Xen. *Cyr.* 2.3.6) construction of *mē* "in order that ... not, for fear that" with the future indicative.

491 **our General:** cf. 246-7: with the success of Praxagora's plan, the women's decision to elect her general has now taken effect.

496 **to the wall, into the shade:** the *skēnē* in the Theatre of Dionysus faced north, so its front ("the wall") was normally in shadow. If, as is likely, there was a raised platform in front of the *skēnē*, the chorus could not come right up to its wall, but on a winter or early spring morning (for *Eccl.* was the first of the competing plays to be performed, cf. 1158-9) the shadow may have extended some way beyond the platform edge to cover the nearer part of the *orchēstrā*, at least on its western side – and anyway the platform did not necessarily stretch across the full width of the building. Alternatively "the wall" may be the front edge of the stage-platform itself (so N.W.Slater, *LCM* 13 [1988] 105); but that could not be called a "wall" unless the platform was a solid structure, which it is unlikely to have been so early as the 390s.

502 **don't stand for:** lit. "hate".

502 **a piece of sacking:** the false beards are referred to in this pejorative way to encourage the women to get rid of them as quickly as possible.

503 **they themselves** (i.e. the cheeks) **have been wearing this get-up under protest** (lit. "unwillingly"): the emended text here adopted was proposed by T.L. Agar, *CQ* 13 (1919) 15, and independently by Ussher; an earlier suggestion by A. Palmer, *Quarterly Review* 158 (1884) 370, gives the similar sense "they (the cheeks) have been hurting for some time with wearing this get-up". The mss. read "for these women have come, having had this get-up (for a long time now)", which is doubly unsatisfactory: (1) in 500-1 only Praxagora was mentioned as approaching, and her ensuing speech gives no indication of the presence of the First and Second Women of 35-284 (on the person addressed in 509-510, see below); (2) "this get-up (*skhēma*)" is not a natural way of referring to the state of *not* having an artificial beard (contrast *Ach.* 64, *Knights* 1331, *Frogs* 463).

504 What is Praxagora now wearing? Does she go inside after 513, and if so, is she differently dressed when she reappears? And what does Blepyrus wear when he appears at 520? These issues have been well discussed by S.D. Olson, *AJP* 110 (1989) 223-6, though as will be seen I disagree on some matters (cf. also previous note). The most important pointer to a solution is that after 520 both Praxagora and Blepyrus remain on stage continuously until the end of the act (729), when Praxagora goes off to the Agora (711-6) to perform her first official duties as the new chief magistrate, and Blepyrus follows her (725-7) in order to be admired as "the General's consort"; when eventually he returns to the vicinity of his home (1129) he never gets a chance to go inside but departs almost at once for the banquet. Both, therefore, must by 520 be wearing clothes in which they are happy to be seen in public, and Praxagora in particular must be dressed as befits a high (female) officer of state, i.e. in a full-length woman's *chitōn* and *himation*. She had probably been wearing the former, suitably shortened, all the time (cf. on 268 and 332), but the latter she had left at home; hence she must go in and put it on between 513 and 520. She may enter at 504 still wearing her disguise (except for the beard) and take it off along with the rest of the women, but (as in 268-279) she speaks of the costume-change in terms of "you", not "we", and it is likely (and suits her new dignity) that just as she was not seen putting on the disguise, so she should not be seen taking it off; she certainly cannot enter the house still disguised, insistent as she is that both she and the other women must waste no time in removing all trace of their plot (506, 511-2). To leave herself, then, with as little as possible to do indoors, she must arrive carrying, rather than wearing, the articles of her disguise (hence when she goes in, all she needs to do is "put [them] down" in their proper places), and with her *chitōn* readjusted to its normal length; the appearance of the other women, once they have obeyed her orders, will be similar. As to Blepyrus, we can hardly suppose that he, highly conscious as he is of his new-found status as Praxagora's husband, goes off barefoot and half-clothed to the Agora and later to the banquet; having therefore no opportunity to change after 520, he must be wearing his own shoes, and presumably therefore also his own *himation*, when he comes out of the house. It might seem that the interval between 513 and 520 is hardly enough for Praxagora to deposit the cloak, shoes and stick (as well as putting on her own outer garment) and then for Blepyrus to be assumed to find them and put them on; but the interval is actually longer than the text might suggest. By the time the first words after her exit are spoken (514), Praxagora *has already returned*, because these words are addressed to her, announcing that her orders have been fulfilled and asking for more. Hence her absence, which since it involves putting on a garment must be more than momentary, has been filled not by speech but by silent action – evidently the business of "get[ting] this lot in order" (510), i.e. the chorus restoring their feminine appearance and resuming their proper place in the *orchēstrā*. Thus between 500 and 520 the whole theme of cross-dressing, which has dominated the early part of the play, is rapidly closed down. From now on men will look like men and women will look like women; only their social (and also, as we shall discover, their sexual) roles will be turned topsy-turvy.

507 get shoes out from underfoot: lit. "let (the) shoe go out of the way", with a pun on *ekpodōn* "out of the way" and *ek podōn* "from feet".

508 "let loose the knotted-up Laconian reins": or, with van Leeuwen, "let loose the knotted reins of thy Laconians"; in either case the "reins" are the straps of the "Laconian" shoes (see on 74). Two oddities in this line (it is illogical that the undoing of the straps should be mentioned *after* the removal of the shoes; and the verb is singular, whereas the other imperatives in this sentence are plural) are probably both to be explained by supposing the line to be quoted or adapted from a tragedy (Rau 207 finds the whole of 504-511 mildly paratragic, but 508 slightly more so; for the phrase *khalā ... hēniās* "let loose the reins" cf. Eur. fr. 409).

509-510 you get this lot in order: the pronoun rendered as "this lot" is feminine, and must refer to the women. It has been alleged that *(kat)eutrepizein* "make ready, get in order" cannot take an object denoting persons, and Meineke's emendation, making the pronoun neuter (so that it refers to the discarded items of disguise), has been adopted by Vetta; but in the derived sense "win over to one's own side" *eutrepizein* has no difficulty taking a personal object (cf. Xen. *Hell.* 4.8.6, 12; Dem. 18.175). Vetta takes the addressee here to be First Woman (who in strict logic should indeed be present, since her house is next door to Praxagora's) and supposes that she is being asked to do "what [Praxagora] herself would have the intention of doing, viz. to go into her house and quietly put everything back in order [there]"; but if Praxagora were asking her addressee to do in one house exactly what she herself was going to do in another, she would continue "I *also* want to slip through inside ...". Rather, First Woman and her house have by now been forgotten (as Calonice – also a neighbour of the heroine, cf. *Lys.* 5 – is forgotten after line 253 of *Lysistrata*), and we should keep the transmitted text: Praxagora is simply delegating responsibility for the chorus's costume-change to their leader.

514-9 Metre: anapaestic tetrameters. T. Gelzer, *EH* 38 (1993) 60-61, suggests that the audience will perceive these lines as the beginning of an *agon*, in which one or both of the main speeches are often in this metre; and certainly 517-9 seems to promise a continuation (e.g. Praxagora putting forward policy proposals and seeking advice or approval from the chorus) which does not occur. If Gelzer is right, the appearance of Blepyrus will be perceived as an interruption that cuts the incipient *agon* short; when it resumes (571ff) the chorus merely introduce the *agon* and then remain silent, their anticipated role being taken over by Blepyrus and the Neighbour (see on 564) who are even asked at the end if they approve (710), despite being men and therefore (now) political nonentities.

515 **what you think ... do something useful:** the Greek is distinctly clumsy, lit. "doing what that is advantageous (?to you) we will seem (?to you) to be rightly obeying (?you)" (the syntactic connections of the pronoun *soi* "(to) you" are hopelessly ambiguous, though the general sense is clear enough).

517 **stay around here:** in effect the chorus is here instructed to remain in being as a chorus; for a less obtrusive instance of a similar instruction cf. Soph. *Phil.* 1075-7.

519 **amid the din and the danger:** "din" appropriately describes an Assembly meeting (*com. adesp.* 809 speaks of "the din of the Pnyx" using the same Greek word *thorubos*), but "danger" better suits a battlefield (cf. "full of manly courage"); possibly the phrase is a quotation from an anapaestic passage in a tragedy.

519 **full of manly courage:** Greek *andreiotatai* "very courageous"; the derivation of this adjective from *anēr* "man, adult male" was transparent, and reinforced the male stereotype whereby courage was considered something not to be expected in a woman. For the paradox cf. *Lys.* 549, 1108; *Thesm.* 656.

521 **how simple can you get?:** lit. "how simply/naively" (sc. you speak!). On Blepyrus' suspicions cf. on 323 and 348-350.

522 **from a *lover*:** or "from my lover"; Greek *tou* can be either (if accented) the definite article or (if unaccented) the equivalent of an indefinite article; the latter more usually follows than precedes its noun, but cf. *Wealth* 674. I prefer, with Vetta, to take it as unaccented, because of Blepyrus' reply; compare the following two exchanges, of which (1) makes sense and (2) does not:

(1) A: Did you bring a bottle of champagne? B: Two, actually.

(2) A: Did you bring the bottle of champagne? B: *Two, actually.

522-3 **perhaps not from *a* lover:** i.e. perhaps from two or more!

524 **see if my head smells of perfume:** for the association between perfume and sex cf. *Ach.* 1091, *Clouds* 51, *Lys.* 47, 938-947, Achilles Tatius 2.38.2; according to Plut. *Mor.* 990b "most men" insisted that their wives should scent themselves before intercourse.

526 ***I* certainly can't:** Praxagora counter-attacks, saying in effect "you're so old and feeble that without perfume I'd never be able to arouse you"; cf. Archilochus fr. 48.5-6 which speaks of a woman whose hair and breast were so well perfumed "that even an old man would have desired her".

526 **my dear:** Greek *talan*, lit. "unfortunate one", a vocative (used in this form only by women) which frequently functions as a "mild rebuke" (see Dickey 162-3).

528 **a close friend:** lit. "a companion and friend".

528-9 **during the night:** the Greek does not make it clear whether this should be attached to "gone into labour" or to "sent for me". The latter, however, would make Praxagora say something that was obvious in any case, and the former, despite involving a slight abnormality of word-order, is to be preferred. The imagined scenario is that the mother-to-be had been in labour "during the night", probably for some hours, but had not at first wished to disturb her friend's sleep, doing so only when it became clear that the baby would be born before morning. The friend is probably not being summoned to act as an amateur midwife, but to provide, with others, moral support (and, if necessary, physical assistance) under the (professional) midwife's direction; cf. Soranus 2.5, Hippocr. *On Cutting Up the Foetus* 4, and see R. Garland, *The Greek Way of Life* (London, 1990) 61-64.

531 **dear:** lit. "husband"; so also in 542.

534 **the girl who came for me:** the Greek gives no explicit information about this person except that she was female, but she would undoubtedly have been the personal maidservant of the mother-to-be.

536 **stripped me, threw your mantle over me:** Blepyrus had been using his *himation* as a blanket (cf. on 334); Praxagora covered him with hers instead, "fearing that he might get cold and fearing even more that the cold might wake him" (van Leeuwen).

537 **like a laid-out corpse:** an important part of Greek funerary ritual was the laying out (*prothesis*) of the corpse on a bier in the house; see R. Garland, *The Greek Way of Death* (London, 1985) 23-31. Blepyrus will not have *looked* more like a laid-out corpse than any other old man in bed alone; rather his point is that Praxagora has been *treating* him as if he were dead by taking his property, changing his bedclothes, and going out at night without saying a word to him, in short by ignoring his existence as a person. The equation here implied between male disempowerment and death will reappear in 994-7, 1030-3, 1105-11; cf. *Lys.* 599-607.

538 **I'm surprised you didn't put:** lit. "only not putting", i.e. "doing everything but put".

538 **an oil-jar ... a wreath:** regular features of the *prothesis* layout. The head of the corpse was adorned either with a metal crown or with a wreath of flowers (real or wax) or of leaves: cf. 1034-5; *Lys.* 602; Eur. *Tro.* 1223; Bion 1.75; J. Boardman, *ABSA* 50 (1955) 60-63 nos. 14, 17, 25. The oil-jar (*lēkuthos*) was ubiquitous in rituals for the dead; *lēkuthoi* were placed around the body at the *prothesis* and were deposited at the tomb both at and after the time of the funeral (Garland *op.cit.* 36-37, 108). In this play the *lēkuthos* is the prime symbol of death (996, 1032, 1111).

541 **warm and well covered:** lit. "in warmth and bedclothes".

544 **in order not to lose the cloak:** i.e. as a protection against nocturnal footpads (*lōpodutai*) who ambushed pedestrians in the streets or outside the city walls (cf. 565; *Birds* 497-8, 713, 1490-3; Antiphon 2.2.5) and who might well pick on a woman as a victim thinking her less likely to put up a fight.

545 **I brought my feet down with a stamp:** cf. 483.

547 **you've lost:** implying that it is primarily Praxagora, with her special responsibility for the household stores (211-2), who has suffered by preventing her husband from attending the Assembly and earning his three obols.

547 **a quarter-bushel:** a *hekteus*, equal to eight *khoinikes* (see on 45), i.e. between eight and nine litres, or just under two (UK) gallons. Since a *hekteus* was one-sixth of a *medimnos* (the standard measure for large quantities of grain), this passage implies that the current price of wheat was eighteen obols (three drachmas) per *medimnos*; sixty years later the normal price had risen to five drachmas (Dem. 34.39).

549-550 it was a boy ... no, no, the baby I went to help with: I have adopted Barrett's rendering of a joke which in the Greek is based on the grammatical feminine gender of *ekklēsiā* "assembly" (lit. "she gave birth to a male child. – The Assembly did? – No, by Zeus, the woman to whom I went"). The fact, at first sight surprising, that Praxagora expects her husband to be pleased with this news about someone else's baby is probably to be explained by supposing that, as in rural Greece today, the midwife (and doubtless also her volunteer assistants) received special presents if the child proved to be male; see C.W. Müller, *RhM* 131 (1988) 98.

554 sit down, and get some cuttlefish to chew: lit. "sit down chewing cuttlefish". This injunction has baffled interpreters. According to the scholia "chewing cuttlefish" means "enjoying luxury because of your power"; but this interpretation does not cohere with 434-464 where the object of the handover is partly to increase honesty and altruism in political life and partly to give *men* a more leisured lifestyle, and is probably a mere guess. Presumably the phrase is a proverbial one; it has been suggested that it expresses contempt for the addressee's ignorance (Rogers), but Ussher seems to me to be on the right track in seeing it as "a formula to use when introducing some unexpected news": it is still thought desirable, when breaking startling (especially bad) news to a person, to ask the addressee to sit down first, particularly if (s)he is of a nervous disposition. Ussher suggests that "chew cuttlefish" means "go on with what you are doing at the moment", but he has to posit an "old and long-forgotten story" for the proverb to be based on. More probably the phrase means either (i) "calm yourself" in preparation for a shock (as today someone about to receive bad news might be urged to have a cup of tea or to light a cigarette) or (ii) "mind you don't bite your tongue": having something soft on which to chew rhythmically (especially something rather thicker than most chewing-gums) would serve either purpose well, and small cuttlefish were cheap (cf. Ar. fr. 258.2, Eubulus fr. dub. 148.6, both mentioning them together with the despised *mainis* or blotched picarel).

555 they say reminds us that Blepyrus himself knows of the decision only at second hand.

555 to you women: the word "women" is not in the Greek, nor is there any explicit indication of the gender of "you"; but since Praxagora does not pretend to be baffled about the reference of the plural pronoun, Blepyrus probably makes it clear by a gesture towards the women of the chorus.

556 to weave?: since one cannot "weave" a city-state, we are probably meant to suppose that Praxagora is pretending to have misheard *tēn polin* "the City" as e.g. *ton peplon* "the robe".

558 by Aphrodite: with this feminine oath (cf. 189) Praxagora abruptly throws off all disguise and pretence, and reveals herself as the leader of a new régime with a radical, and distinctively feminine, programme. Ar. now wants to proceed rapidly (cf. 582) to the exposition of this programme, and does not waste time by allowing Blepyrus to express surprise at the way his own wife, of all people, is suddenly taking personal charge of the City's affairs; rather he is tacitly assumed to know what the audience know (similarly at 727 he refers to Praxagora as "the General" although this title has never been applied to her in his presence).

560-1 those who dare ... no bearing witness: the text appears to be defective here. As transmitted in RΛ (Γ omits 559 and 560, doubtless by an oversight due to the fact that 559 and 561 begin with the same words) it means literally "for no longer, for those who dare to do shameful things to it [the City], will it be (possible) in future, and nowhere to bear witness", which is objectionable in three ways: (1) *aiskhra drān* "to do shameful things" has to do double duty and be governed both by *tois tolmōsin* "those who dare" and by *estai* "it will be possible", and, to make this construction even clumsier, *estai* itself also governs *tois tolmōsin* as indirect object; (2) the conjunction *de* "and" makes the series of specific evils to be abolished, beginning with *marturein* "to bear witness", *parallel to* the very general expression *aiskhra drān*, when they ought logically to be presented as *examples of* the "shameful things" that people do in present-day Athens; (3) *marturein* is a bizarre way to begin a catalogue of evils, for bearing witness, unlike informing, clothes-snatching, jealousy, etc., is not in itself an evil – between friends and relatives, indeed, it was regarded as a duty (cf. Lys. 1.41-42, Isaeus 3.19, Dem. 29.22; in [Dem.] 49.37-38 it is claimed to be a strong sign of the weakness of Timotheus' case that none of his relations has testified in his favour on certain issues, even though none of them has testified against him either). Emendation of *oudamou de* "and nowhere (to bear witness ...)" to e.g. *oudamōs, ou* "in any way: not (to bear witness ...)", solves (2) but leaves (1) and (3) untouched. I suggest that a line or two has been lost between 560 and 561, which contained a main verb to govern *tois tolmōsin ... aiskhra drān* (probably meaning something like "there will be opportunity") and at least one example of an evident evil that Praxagora means to do away with. The most likely evil for her to mention, given that witnessing and informing come next on the list, is the prevalence of lawsuits, of which there is constant complaint throughout Old Comedy and whose total abolition is announced at 657 (cf. *Ach.* 676-718, 847, 937; *Clouds* 34, 206-8; *Wasps* passim; *Peace* 505; *Birds* 39-41, 109-111): if there are no lawsuits, there will be no need for witnesses to perform a function which was regarded as disagreeable (cf. *Clouds* 1218) and might easily expose an unoffending citizen to a vindictive prosecution for allegedly giving false evidence. Cf. generally *Knights* 1316-7 where on an occasion of public rejoicing all are bidden to "abstain from giving evidence and close the courts of law". Without knowing precisely what was in the lacuna, it is not possible to emend *oudamou de* with confidence, though a simple redivision of words (*oudam' oude*, giving the sense "there will in future be no <   > at all, nor witnessing ...") may very well be correct.

563 **don't take away my livelihood** (lit. "life"): not that Blepyrus is himself a *sūkophantēs* (despite 439), but his prospects of earning regular pay as a juror (cf. 460) depend on a constant supply of cases to try (cf. *Wasps* 303-311), which *sūkophantai* were very good at providing, and it was furthermore a common ploy of *sūkophantai* to tell juries that if they did not convict a defendant (and sentence him to a heavy fine, or to death with confiscation of property) there would not be enough money in the treasury to pay the jurors (cf. *Knights* 1358-60 and Lys. 27.1 – the latter from a speech delivered about 393, see on 71). Blepyrus forgets that even if trials were not going to be abolished, men would not be serving as jurors any more anyway! There may be parody of Soph. *Phil.* 931-3 "By taking my bow you are depriving me of my life ... In the name of your ancestral gods, don't take my life from me!".

564 It is very unusual for a new character to intervene in dialogue like this without any indication of who he is or where he has come from, and indeed without any recognition by others on stage that a new character has entered (one would at least have expected Blepyrus to make some response, probably unfriendly, when an outsider presumes to tell him how to behave to his wife). Nevertheless, this appears to be what Ar. has done, probably in order to provide continuity between this act and the following one: he will soon be removing both Praxagora and Blepyrus from the scene, and he wants another man to have heard Praxagora's exposition of her new social order, to have approved of it, and to be ready to obey immediately her orders for the surrender of private property.

Who, though, is this man, and where has he come from? He could be Chremes (372-477; so Rogers, Coulon, Dover *AC* 196, Ussher), or the Neighbour of 327-353 (so van Leeuwen, Vetta; S.D. Olson, *CQ* 41 [1991] 36-40), or conceivably an entirely new character (Olson *op.cit.* 38 n.12); but since he lives in one of the houses represented by the *skēnē* (728ff), which Chremes does not (see on 372), it is most likely that he is the Neighbour (we need not ask how he has recovered the *himation* that he could not find earlier; that phase of the play is over now, cf. on 504 and 558). We are probably meant to suppose that he has come out of his house drawn by the sound of loud voices outside (cf. *Wealth* 641, Soph. *OT* 631ff; for other examples in tragedy see O.P. Taplin, *The Stagecraft of Aeschylus* [Oxford, 1977] 220).

565 clothes-snatching: cf. on 544.

567 seizures for debt: the seizure of a debtor's chattels as security (*enekhura*) for a debt or for interest on it; cf. *Clouds* 34-35, 241, and see P.C. Millett, *Lending and Borrowing in Ancient Athens* (Cambridge, 1991) 77. Sometimes (755, *Wealth* 451) the debtor handed over the pledge at the time when the loan was made; sometimes, as in *Clouds* and as envisaged here, the creditor had the right to seize pledges to an appropriate value if the debtor defaulted on repayment or interest (cf. *IG* ii^{2} 2492.5-9).

570 in reply to me: the Greek uses the emphatic pronoun *emoi* rather than the unemphatic *moi*, and if this text is correct, Praxagora is thinking back to the days when her husband exercised the masculine right to silence her if she contradicted him (cf. *Lys.* 507-520, Soph. *Aj.* 293) and is implying that now it will be *her* turn to silence *him* (cf. *Lys.* 527-538) – though by the force of argument rather than by the argument of force. Praxagora will pay off other old scores against her husband at 621-2 (his impotence) and possibly at 669 (his habit of not coming home at night), and will grossly insult him at 595. It is possible, however, that *emoi* is a stopgap inserted after another word had been lost.

571-709 This passage corresponds to the formal debate (*agon*) which appears in most of Ar.'s earlier plays, though like the *agon* of *Birds* (451-626) it is not a contest between two speakers but an exercise in persuasion by a single speaker. In *Birds*, however, the *agon* had retained its traditional double structure, Peisetaerus' speech being divided into two halves introduced by separate choral songs (in strophic responsion) and separate couplets (*katakeleusmoi*) by the chorus-leader; here, for the first time in Ar.'s surviving work, the *agon* is reduced to a single structure consisting of a choral song (571-580), a *katakeleusmos* (581-2), and a speech (with interruptions) by Praxagora (583ff), in anapaestic tetrameters, ending with a *pnīgos* (689-709). In *Wealth*, where the *agon* (487-618) is a two-sided debate between Chremylus and Poverty, the structural pattern is the same except that there is no introductory choral song.

571-580 Metre: dactylo-epitrite, based on various sequences of the units –⏑⏑–⏑⏑– (*D*), –⏑– (*e*), and occasionally –⏑⏑– (*d*), preceded, separated or followed by single "link" syllables, and sometimes, in this song, by spondees (– –) (*sp*). The first line of the song does not fit the most common patterns of dactylo-epitrite, and Zimmermann (ii 139) and Parker (532-4) explain it quite differently (earlier scholars had suggested various implausible emendations); but it can be analysed as *sp D* ⏑ *d* – (so in effect Ussher).

571 philosophic: the only known occurrence in Ar. of the word *philosophos* or its derivatives, and its first known occurrence in poetry of any kind. In its earliest appearances (Hdt. 1.30.2, Thuc. 2.40.1) the word bears the broad sense of "seeking after knowledge"; but the sense later dominant, "systematic intellectual activity", was already in use before 400 (Gorgias, *Encomium of Helen* 13; Hippocr. *On Ancient Medicine* 20), and was familiar enough in the 390s to be used in lawcourt speeches (Pl.

Apol. 23d, 28e; Lys. 24.10). *Philosophos* was being made a buzz-word in the late 390s by Isocrates, who was just beginning his career as a teacher of rhetoric and politics, and who from the start, like his rival Plato, called himself and his students *philosophoi* and educators of other types *sophistai* (cf. Isoc. 13.11, 14, 18, 21, from his early work *Against the Sophists*; see C. Eucken, *Isokrates* [Berlin, 1983] 5, 14-18 and S. Usher, *Greek Orators III: Isocrates* [Warminster, 1990] 5); this may explain why Ar. uses the word here in a song introducing an extended, coherent and sophisticated piece of political rhetoric which, like many writings by Isocrates' teacher Gorgias and other *philosophoi*, stands conventional ethical and social assumptions on their heads.

572 your friends: feminine, giving the impression that the chorus expect Praxagora's policy to be designed exclusively in the interests of women. The next sentence will correct that impression, but spectators will still be on the alert for proposals that benefit citizen women at the expense of other sections of the population – and some such proposals there will be, at least in the sexual field (cf. 623-4, 718-724).

576 its capabilities: or, with C. Kock's one-letter emendation, "your capabilities"; but the near-personification of the "idea" in the transmitted text coheres well with the whole thrust of 571-589, where the chorus and Praxagora alike repeatedly emphasize the novelty and power of Praxagora's as yet unrevealed plan.

579 things that have never been done or said before: this does not necessarily prove that no one had ever before expounded a plan for a communistic society (though cf. Introduction, pp. 15–16); the next sentence, "they hate it if they hear (lit. spectate) the same old stuff over and over again", indicates that what is being claimed is that the idea is completely new *in comedy* (cf. *Clouds* 546-8; *Wasps* 1044, 1053, 1535-7; Metagenes fr. 15; Pherecrates fr. 84).

583-729 It is often not possible to allocate the interventions in Praxagora's speech with certainty between the two men present (Blepyrus and the Neighbour). Once or twice, however, Praxagora seems to go out of her way to humiliate one of the men (cf. on 570), and this man is almost certainly Blepyrus who not long ago was claiming the right to control her movements (520ff); there is thus a degree of hostility between Blepyrus and Praxagora, whereas the Neighbour has already shown himself favourably disposed towards her (564). Accordingly, essentially in agreement with Ussher (though he identifies the second man as Chremes; cf. on 564), I have followed the principle of giving to Blepyrus those interventions which are designed to undermine or ridicule Praxagora's plan, and to the Neighbour those which give her support; similarly where one man makes fun of the other (as in 646-8) I have assumed Blepyrus to be the victim. Where an intervention is neutral in tone I have assigned it in such a way as to maintain the coherence of the dialogue. Thus in 657-8, when *both* men condemn the abolition of lawsuits, the second speaker, whose intervention here is unexpected, must be the hitherto supportive Neighbour, and the first therefore Blepyrus; this makes it likely that the original question about lawsuits (655-6) was also asked by Blepyrus, and since he signals that it is the last of a series ("There's still one thing I want to know", 655), the two preceding questions (651, 653) are probably his as well.

586-7 For the alleged Athenian tendency to innovate for the sake of innovating, cf. 218-220, 456-7.

587 takes the place of every other virtue: lit. "is instead of other virtue", reading *aretēs* with Bergk. The mss. have *arkhēs* which gives no satisfactory sense; proposed interpretations of it include "empire" (Rogers; but Athenians had been notoriously given to innovation long before they lost their empire, cf. Thuc. 1.70.2), "principle" (Van Daele; a sense hardly attested outside philosophical writings), "form of government" (Vetta, comparing 985; but innovation is not a form of government). The corruption will have been due to the presence of *arkhaiōn* "what's old" three words later.

589 **the speaker:** the Greek word is masculine in gender, because Praxagora is reminding her audience of the general principle that "it is proper to listen to the person who stands up to speak, and unseemly to interrupt him" (*Iliad* 19.79-80).

590 **everyone should own everything jointly together:** cf. Pl. *Rep.* 416d-417b, 464b-c (though the Guardians will live not on their own pooled property but on resources contributed by the rest of the community).

592 **hasn't enough land to be buried in:** for this tear-jerking theme of an old man so poor he cannot even afford to die cf. *Wealth* 556, *Ach.* 691 "The money that should have paid for my coffin, I leave the court condemned to pay it as a fine!"

593 **doesn't have even one attendant:** if a citizen did not own even one slave he was very poor indeed (like the chorus of *Wasps*, whose *sons* light them on their way through the streets at night): even the Honest Man of *Wealth* 823-958 has one, though he has not been able to afford a new cloak for thirteen years. The speaker of Lysias 24 tries to give the impression (§6) that the purchase of a slave is beyond his means, but even he does not actually say he possesses none; another client of Lysias (5.5) says that "everyone in the City" is a slave-owner, which shows not only what most people liked to believe, but also that Lysias did not expect there to be very many non-slaveowners on the jury who might feel excluded. On the other hand the median price of an unskilled adult slave in the late fifth century was 150-175 drachmas (cf. *IG* i³ 421.34-49). Most probably (though the matter is highly controversial) most Athenians who cultivated their own land would own at least one slave; see N.R.E.Fisher, *Slavery in Classical Greece* (London, 1993) 34-57, esp. 44-45.

595 **you'd want to eat shit ahead of me:** Praxagora's next words (596-7) explain why she said this: she was annoyed by Blepyrus' asking for an explanation that she was just about to give anyway. Hence these words mean in effect "You always want to be ahead of me; even if I was about to eat dung, you would want to eat it first".

600 **applying our intelligence to manage it economically:** lit. "stewarding and economizing and applying our intelligence", i.e. doing what we have always done so well (cf. 211-2, 236, 441-2).

601-2 **what about any of us that doesn't own land, but invisible wealth ...:** it might seem that the speaker has failed to notice that Praxagora had already mentioned money (598), but his point is that it is one thing to say "I shall make [money] the common property of all" and quite another thing actually to achieve this, since money, unlike land, can be retained in private possession simply by hiding it. He is actually contrasting classes of assets, but speaks as if he were contrasting classes of persons: in actual fact many rich people are known to have owned substantial wealth in both forms (and others). The distinction between "visible" (*phanerā*) and "invisible" (*aphanēs*) wealth is frequently made in lawcourt speeches from the late fifth century onwards; the terms had no strict or legal definition, but normally visible wealth meant land, buildings and physical chattels (slaves, animals, furniture, stored produce, stock-in-trade, etc.) while invisible wealth meant money and claims to money (bank deposits, loans). See Harrison i 230-2.

602 **gold darics:** the Greek has simply "darics", Persian gold coins worth twenty drachmas (cf. Xen. *Anab.* 1.7.18); Athens, except briefly in the last years of the Peloponnesian War (cf. *Frogs* 720), had no gold coinage of its own. When Lysias was arrested by the Thirty in 404, the money seized from him included 100 darics (i.e. 2000 drachmas' worth, out of a total of about 30,000) (Lys. 12.11).

603 **and what if he doesn't ... kept nothing back?:** the words "that he's kept nothing back" are added by the translator for clarity. If the text and speaker-assignments

assumed here are correct, Blepyrus takes it for granted that everyone will be required to swear that he has surrendered all his property (cf. *Iliad* 22.119-121). This text involves two small emendations; the manuscripts' text can be retained by dividing these words, with Bentley, between Blepyrus and Praxagora, in which case Blepyrus asks "And what if he doesn't deposit it?" and Praxagora replies "Then he'll have to perjure himself" (sc. and will therefore be punished by the gods). Such a rejoinder by Praxagora, however, would be inconsistent with her immediately following argument (604-7) that it would anyway be pointless to hold on to one's money.

603 that was how he got it in the first place: as in *Wealth* (30-31, 36-38, 49-50, 96-98, 502-3) it is assumed that men who have great wealth have probably acquired it by criminal means. Blepyrus may be thinking especially of *sūkophantai* (see on 439), in *Wealth* the classic type of self-enriching villain (*Wealth* 31, 850-957, 970), who, each time they brought a prosecution, would have had to make a sworn statement (*antōmosiā*) that their accusation was true (cf. *Wasps* 1041, Isoc. 16.2; see Harrison ii 99-100).

605 nobody will be doing anything under the pressure of poverty: Ar. could have given Praxagora either of two arguments to support her claim that money "won't be any use": (1) the ex-rich man will have all his wants supplied free and will not need to spend money on satisfying them; (2) the ex-poor will no longer be compelled by poverty to produce goods and services, so there will be nothing that money can purchase (cf. *Wealth* 507-534). In fact he seems to waver between these alternatives; as was pointed out by Douglas Olson in an unpublished paper which he has kindly allowed me to cite, the present sentence makes sense only as part of argument (2), but on the other hand 608 is a rejoinder to argument (1).

606 loaves, slices of fish ... garlands, chickpeas: this short list neatly demonstrates how Athenians thought of the good things of life in terms of consumables, not of possessions that last (cf. Davidson *passim*, esp. 213-249); every item on it, except "warm cloaks" (*khlainai*, cf. 416), is something whose enjoyment lasts, at most, for the duration of a banquet. On the other hand, they are not luxuries either; even the fish (on which see Davidson 3-35) are only in "slices", not the whole large fish that a gourmet would seek to buy (cf. *Ach.* 880-894, *Wasps* 493, *Peace* 810-3, Eupolis fr. 160), and all the other items are the plainest of everyday fare and are indeed included in the provision initially made for the citizens of Plato's ideal state (*Rep.* 372a-d), which Glaucon complains is fit only for pigs. The first communal dinner will actually, or so we are later told, be rather less Spartan than this preview suggests (cf. 834-852, 1168-75); but Praxagora's present exposition is of a state that will simply provide its citizens with their bodily *needs* in food, sex and clothing (cf. 653-4), and presumably also with military equipment (cf. 679-680), and Ar., unlike Plato, does not allow her interlocutors to complain about this.

606 chickpeas: cf. on 45.

608 aren't those people who have these things bigger thieves: for example (1) men like Nausicydes (cf. 426) and (2) most politicians (cf. *Wealth* 567-570); but quite generally, as Chremylus tells Wealth, "no one has ever had his fill of you" and a man who has thirteen talents wants sixteen, a man with sixteen wants forty, and so on (*Wealth* 188-197; cf. Solon fr. 13.71-73, Arist. *Pol.* 1267a2-16, b3-5).

609-610 The only ms. that identifies the speaker of these two lines (Λ) gives them to Praxagora; but she would not address her husband as *ō hetaire* (in a man's mouth "my friend"), since "my *hetairos*", when used by a woman of a man, means "my lover" (cf. 912, Semonides fr. 7.49). The speaker is therefore the Neighbour, whom Praxagora has apparently already thoroughly convinced (cf. 631-4).

611 **if he sees a girl and fancies her ...:** Blepyrus has now thought of a possible use for hoarded money: sex, he presumes, unlike food, drink and clothing, is not something that can be deposited in a common store and shared out, and will therefore still be a purchasable commodity (and the archetypal rich man's extravagance; cf. Davidson 194-205). Being mentally still of the old world, he envisages the girl in the case as a professional sex-worker (*hetairā*); Praxagora, who plans to abolish *hetairai* (718-720), thinks of her as a woman of citizen status (cf. 614).

612 **he'll ... have his share of communing – with her, in bed:** lit. "he will share in the-things-on-a-communal-basis, sleeping with her": Blepyrus picks up the phrase *ek koinou* "on a communal basis" from 610 and applies it to the *shared* pleasures of sex.

613 **sleep with her:** this passage, down to 629, includes an unusual concentration, for Ar., of polite euphemisms for sexual activity ((*sun*)*katadarthein* "sleep (with)" four times, *sunkatakeisthai* "lie with", *suneinai* "be with", *kharizesthai* "give one's favours to"); cf. Henderson 160-1. The phenomenon cannot be entirely accounted for by the fact that this is a mixed conversation: elsewhere in Ar. men freely use the crudest obscenities in the presence of women (see my article in F. De Martino & A.H. Sommerstein ed. *Lo spettacolo delle voci* [Bari, 1995] 79), and here Praxagora herself is prepared to use the earthy verb *hupokrouein*, lit. "knock from below" (618, cf. 256-7). Possibly Ar. is here reflecting the usage of a written source (an account of Spartan wife-lending practices? cf. Xen. *Lac.* 1.5-9).

614 **women:** lit. "these", i.e. the chorus as representing all citizen women.

614 **common property:** lit. "common"; cf. Pl. *Rep.* 457c-d "All these women shall be the common possession of (lit. common of) all these men, and no woman shall live privately with any man" (but the Guardians' matings are to be strictly controlled by the authorities through a carefully rigged lottery, cf. *Rep.* 459c-460c). By Aristotle's time a modified form of sexual "common property" actually existed in Athens: no one was allowed to pay more than two drachmas for the hire (for one night) of a music-girl (i.e. a high-grade slave sex-worker), and if the demand exceeded the supply, the girls were allocated by lot (Arist. *Ath.Pol.* 50.2).

614-5 **to have sex and produce children:** the Greek is ambiguous as to whether the subject of these infinitives is the women, the men, or both.

617 **the ones with the snubbier noses:** for the perception of snub-nosedness as ugly cf. 705, Pl. *Theaet.* 143e (though in Xen. *Symp.* 5.6 Socrates tries to argue the contrary).

617 **will sit beside the fine lookers:** hardly in public view (there is no indication anywhere in the play that women will sit in the street hoping to be picked up, and a woman appearing at an upstairs window would be standing, not sitting); probably then the scenario envisaged is that when a man goes indoors to the young woman of his choice he will find her sitting there waiting for him – with an unattractive woman next to her.

618 ***her*:** referring back to "the most attractive of them" (616).

618 **he'll have to give the ugly one a knock first:** Praxagora does not explain how it will be decided who is the uglier of two or more contenders, and in a comedy her omission is nothing to cavil at; it is another matter when her methods are applied in all seriousness by modern social engineers, in fields like education and employment, under such euphemistic labels as "affirmative action", when often there is no objective means of determining whether or not an individual falls into one of the favoured groups.

620 **where you said:** presumably referring to Praxagora's words "beside the fine lookers" (617).

621-2 Praxagora reassures Blepyrus that he will not suffer the fate he fears, because (1) not even the ugliest of women would demand the right to sleep with *him* and (2) even if one did, she couldn't drain his virility further than age has drained it already.

622 **the right *not* to sleep with you:** the point is that *that*, in view of Blepyrus' well-proven impotence (cf. 323-6, 465-9, 526), would be the prize awaiting any woman foolish enough to fight for the possession of him.

622 ***yours* is in that state anyway:** lit. "for you it is-from-the-beginning of-that-kind". The Greek leaves the subject unexpressed but indicates that it is of neuter gender, which takes us back to *peos* "cock" in 620, showing in turn that *toiouton* "of that kind" means "exhausted"; but here, as in 470, gesture helping out the words is probably essential to ensure that everyone understands what is meant.

624 **none of you will have an empty hole:** the language, whose meaning as applied to women is obvious, was more commonly applied to warships (also feminine, grammatically speaking). The trierarch of a ship (the wealthy citizen appointed to command it and be responsible for its maintenance) received pay for his crew in a lump sum from the state, and it was for him to distribute it to the men; he might thus attempt to defraud the state by undermanning his ship and keeping the surplus money for himself, in which case some oars would be out of use and some oarholes therefore empty (cf. *Peace* 1232-4). The same word-play had been used by Eupolis (fr. 192.48) as long ago as 421.

624 **what about the men's point ... of view? What'll happen to them?:** lit. "But the thing of the men, what will it do?". The meaning of a phrase like *to tōn andrōn* "the thing of the men" is largely determined by its context; here one expects it to mean something like "the men's point of view, the men's side of things", but these abstract entities cannot in ordinary language be described as "doing" anything, and this phrase (especially since it directly follows "none of you will have an empty hole") should therefore probably be added to the long list of comic designations of the male organ (for which see Henderson 108-130).

626 **the less good-looking men will watch out ...:** cf. 702-9 where these men are envisaged as dogging the footsteps of the young and handsome, and ordering them to stop when about to enter a woman's house. In Pl. *Phdr.* 227c-d Socrates, hearing that Lysias had written an essay "proving" that a boy ought to grant his favours to a man who is not in love with him rather than to one who is, wishes he had likewise proved that a poor man should be preferred to a rich man, an old man to a young man, etc., which would have made his essay "a great service to democracy" (cf. 631).

628 The text of this line is defective. Those mss. which have the line (Γ omits it) meaninglessly repeat *hoi phauloteroi* "the less good-looking men" in the place where I have marked a lacuna in the translation: either these words were inserted, not very intelligently, to fill a gap, or they entered the text from the margin and displaced part of the genuine text. In either case the lost words may, but need not, have stood in the same place ("in the public places <and at the house doors>", T.L. Agar, *CQ* 13 [1919] 16); most scholars have preferred to insert supplements later in the line ("with the handsome <and tall> men" Tyrwhitt, Naber; "with the handsome <and good-looking> men" Blaydes).

629 **the shorties:** tallness was considered beautiful and shortness ugly, both in men and in woman; cf. *Birds* 1678, Arist. *Eth.Nic.* 1123b6-8, *Iliad* 21.108, *Odyssey* 5.217, 6.107, 13.289, Hdt. 1.60.4. Hence to draw attention to a man's shortness was in itself an insult (cf. *Frogs* 709).

630 **Lysicrates** (*LGPN* 44) is mentioned again in 737; from these two passages we know that he was short, with a snub nose and grey hair which he dyed black. The added detail that he was a "thief" (Apostolius 10.97), i.e. an embezzler of public funds, does not come from either passage but cannot be relied on, since it may derive from the scholia on *Birds* 513 where the reference is probably to an entirely different person; if,

however, the statement is based ultimately on another (lost) comic reference to our Lysicrates, it would indicate that he had been a holder of public office, though no office-holding Lysicrates of suitable date is otherwise known.

630 hold itself as high as that of any young beau: lit. "pride itself equally with <the noses of> the handsome"; my rendering is based on Rogers' note ad loc.

631-4 has generally (despite the oath by Apollo, on which cf. on 160) been assigned to Praxagora, but Vetta has rightly given it to the Neighbour. Before the *pnīgos*, we get no graphic word-pictures from Praxagora, only exposition and explanation; and the language of 631-2 is not that of the proposer of a scheme defending it, but that of a hearer enthusiastically approving (cf. 411, *Clouds* 205).

631 a truly democratic idea: because the poor age, and lose their looks, more quickly than the rich (who, apart from not having to spend such long hours working in the sun, can afford more and better unguents to keep their skins in good condition).

631-2 it'll make absolute fools of: lit. "it will be a great mockery (*katakhēnē*) of"; the rare word *katakhēnē* appears in a rather similar context at *Wasps* 575 where Philocleon claims that his position as a juryman, with power of life and death over the greatest men in Athens, is "a great ... *katakhēnē* of wealth".

632 signet-rings: cf. *Clouds* 332, where signet-rings are associated with long hair, in the 420s (cf. *Knights* 580) as in the 390s (cf. Lys. 16.18) an affectation of wealthy and leisured youth whose attachment to democracy was thought dubious by some.

633 before he can speak: lit. "first": "emboldened by the new law, [the poor man] will speak first, as he would not to his social superiors before" (Ussher). In a democracy all male citizens were theoretically equal, but it was recognized that "it is typical of wealth to behave arrogantly" (*Wealth* 563), and an elderly working man would certainly think it foolhardy to accost, and give orders to, a wealthy youth, especially when, as envisaged here, the latter was on his way from a drinking-bout to an assignation.

633 cheap shoes: Greek *embade*; see on 47 and 74.

634 to do the second pressing: this is probably the actual literal meaning of Greek *deuteriazein*, for *deuterios oinos* was inferior wine made from the second pressing of the grapes (Nicophon fr. 11, cf. Hesychius δ743, Pollux 1.248, 6.17).

635-643 Here Plato follows in Ar.'s footsteps more closely than ever, though with refinements and extensions. A male Guardian's "children" will be all those born in the community in the seventh or tenth month after one of his temporary "weddings" (*Rep.* 461c-e); they will be raised in communal nurseries, and precautions will be taken to ensure that even their mothers cannot identify them (460c-d); thus every Guardian will think every other Guardian a close relation, and they will be trained to behave accordingly (463c-d), and no younger man will ever assault an older one (except, Socrates is chillingly made to add, by order of the government) since he will both respect him as a "parent" and fear retaliation by other "sons" and "brothers" of the victim who are bound to be in the vicinity (465a-b).

637 reckoning by the age difference: lit. "by the times".

639-640 even now ... they still throttle him: i.e. there are *some* cases of violence by sons against fathers (something of a preoccupation in Aristophanic comedy, cf. *Clouds* 911, 1321-1451, *Wasps* 395-402, *Birds* 757-9, 1337-71, *Frogs* 149-150 – though Ar. never accuses any *individual* of having beaten his father, perhaps because of the risk of prosecution for slander, cf. Lysias 10). For "throttling" a father cf. *Birds* 1348, 1352; the expression seems to equate rebellious sons with the nightmare-demon Epioles or Epiales who suffocated his father and was later himself strangled by Heracles (Sophron fr. 68, 70 Kaibel; cf. *Wasps* 1038-9). Note that for Blepyrus, as in 608, "now" refers to the old order of society, and the new order is "then" (*tote*); whereas for Praxagora (641-3) the old order is "previously" (*tote*) and the new order "now".

640 ***shit*** **on him:** it is not clear whether this is to be taken literally or metaphorically, but in any case it implies adding insult to injury. Demosthenes' client Ariston alleges (Dem. 54.4) that when he and others had been assaulted by the sons of Conon "they beat us, threw the contents of their chamber-pots over us and also urinated on us themselves" (cf. 832).

641-3 The expression is very elliptical in the Greek, and comprehensibility is further hindered by shifts from singular to plural and back; lit. "But the bystander will not permit. Then they did not care at all about those of others, who was striking. But now, if he hears one struck, fearing lest he may be striking that man himself (Greek *autos ekeinos* "the person who really matters, the person one is most concerned about"; see R. Janko, *CQ* 35 [1985] 20-30, esp. 26-27), he will fight those doing that".

643 **they'll fear that the victim may be *their* old man:** Praxagora, or Ar., forgets that the idea of a unique father would be meaningless to those brought up in her new society: a young man in this situation would assume, not that the victim had (say) a one-in-a-thousand chance of being his (unique) father, but that the victim, if old enough, *was* his father – or rather, one of his (thousand) fathers. Plato recognized (*Rep.* 463c-e) that it is one thing to extend the label "father" to a whole generation and quite another to make the young actually behave filially towards all their elders, and prescribed educational and propaganda measures to bridge the gap; Aristotle (*Pol.* 1261b38-1262a14) argued that the attempt was foredoomed to failure.

644-5 **if Epicurus or Leucolophus is going to ... call me Daddy:** the point could be either that these two men are disreputable individuals, or that they are the sons of disreputable fathers. The latter is made likely by the probability that Leucolophus (*LGPN* 2) was the son of Adeimantus of Scambonidae (*PA* 202; *LGPN* 19), named as was customary after his paternal grandfather, whom Ar. (*Frogs* 1512) calls Leucolophus though other sources call him Leucolophides (a name that will not fit into anapaestic verse). Adeimantus had been one of the Athenian commanders at Aegospotami in 405, and he was the only Athenian prisoner not put to death after the battle (Xen. *Hell.* 2.1.32), with the result that many Athenians believed him to have betrayed the fleet (Xen. *loc.cit.*; Lys. 14.38; possibly *Frogs* 1512, if the reference to Adeimantus was added at the time of the second production in early 404). In 393 he was prosecuted by his former colleague Conon (Dem. 19.191); we do not know the charge, but Adeimantus' alleged treason will in any case have been much spoken of by the prosecution. His son was very likely the Leucolophus of Scambonidae who was one of a group of officials crowned in 352/1 for unknown services to the Athenian-settled island of Imbros (*IG* xii[8] 63a.13). See C.J. Tuplin, *GRBS* 23 (1982) 325-7. Tuplin also suggests (327-330) that Epicurus (*PA* 4853; *LGPN* 3) was the son of Paches son of Epicurus (*PA* 11746; *LGPN* 1), the Athenian commander in the Mytilene campaign of 428/7, who committed suicide in court when convicted of misconduct in office (Plut. *Arist.* 26.5, *Nic.* 6.1); Paches, however, had been dead over thirty years (his death seems to be alluded to in *Wasps* 522-3), and the identification of our Epicurus as his son must remain highly speculative.

647 **Aristyllus** (*PA* 2126; *LGPN* 2) is also mentioned in *Wealth* 314 and Ar. fr. 551; he is not known outside Ar. The pun in 648 (see below), taken together with *Wealth* 313-4, indicates that when one thought of Aristyllus one thought of a face smeared with dung, and when we add (i) that in both passages we find the Greek root *minth-* and (ii) that the scholia on both say Aristyllus was a sexual pervert (*aiskhropoios*), it is likely that he was (alleged to be) a *minthōn* (Lucian, *Lexiphanes* 12; cf. Philodemus *On Vices* p.37

Jensen, Hesychius k2652), i.e., probably, a coprophiliac (cf. *minthos* "excrement") who kissed or licked anuses (see J.F.Gannon, *Thesmophoriazusae Restitutae* [Diss. Yale 1982] 127 n.81). Hence Blepyrus' objection to being kissed by him!

648 tur(d)meric: Greek *kalamintha* "catmint", a surprise substitute for *minthos* (see above); the translation substitutes a different spice and a different pun.

650 I'd still have been mortified: most of the mss. have a third person form, which Ussher understands as "he'd have suffered for it"; but (i) this would be a repetition of Blepyrus' last remark (648), (ii) the Greek phrase *deinon/deina paskhein*, lit. "suffer a terrible thing/terrible things", is used only when the speaker either is (one of) the sufferer(s) or wants to excite sympathy for the sufferer(s) (cf. e.g. *Ach.* 323, *Clouds* 610, *Birds* 1171, Eur. *Ba.* 642) – indeed *deina paskhō* is sometimes the nearest Greek equivalent to that untranslatable English locution "It's not *fair*".

651 the slaves: so at Sparta, where the full citizens were supposed to be estate managers, soldiers and nothing else, the agricultural work was done by the serf-like Helots, who were called *douloi* "slaves" in official documents such as the Athenian-Spartan alliance of 421 (Thuc. 5.23.3); in Plato's *Laws* too (806d-e), though not in the *Republic*, slaves are to do the farm work. In *Wealth* (517ff), when Chremylus makes the same suggestion (covering all crafts as well as agriculture), Poverty asks how the slaves will be procured, and Chremylus can find no satisfactory answer; here, contrariwise, no one is allowed to raise an objection.

652 sleek and gleaming: Greek *liparos* "gleaming with oil", bathed and anointed for the feast (cf. *Knights* 536, *Wealth* 616).

652 when the shadow is ten feet long: times of day late in the afternoon were often expressed in these terms, especially in dinner invitations (*IG* xii[5] 647.16; "seven feet" Ar. fr. 695, "twelve feet" Men. fr. 265, "twenty feet" Eubulus fr. 117 = 119 Hunter). The consensus of astronomical and anthropological opinion (see O. Neugebauer, *A History of Ancient Mathematical Astronomy* [Berlin, 1975] ii 737-8; Hunter on Eubulus *loc.cit.*) is that the shadow meant is "one's own shadow measured with one's own feet" (Hunter on Eubulus *loc.cit.*), but while this is certainly true of the "shadow-tables" discussed by Neugebauer (which were designed to enable the user, *at any given time of year,* to determine the hour of the day from the length of his shadow) it cannot satisfactorily account for the usage here under discussion, which is *independent of the time of year* (as is shown by our passage, which does not relate to a particular occasion but lays down a permanent, general rule) and refers only to times of day close to sunset (or sunrise). The evidence of Eubulus fr. 117.9-10 is decisive: a 22-foot shadow, if taken as that of a man whose height is six times his foot-length, corresponds to a solar altitude of over 15° (cof^{1} 22/6) and a time at least an hour after sunrise or before sunset – which would mean that Eubulus' parasite, who left home at sunrise in response to an evening dinner invitation which he perversely interpreted as a morning one, took more than an hour to get to his unwilling host's house. At certain times of year, moreover, references to a 7-foot or 10-foot shadow would actually be meaningless; for seven weeks in the winter (roughly 27 November to 16 January at present) the sun at Athens (38° N) never reaches the altitude (31°) at which a man's shadow would be ten times as long as his foot, let alone seven. It is therefore likely that in these time-designations "the shadow" is the shadow of a one-foot stick; this would be ten feet long when the altitude of the sun was $\cot^{-1} 10 = 5.7°$, and twenty-two feet long when it was 2.5° – so that Eubulus' parasite would have turned up for the party (with apologies for lateness) ten or fifteen minutes after sunrise, and the men both of Praxagora's Athens and of third-century Coresia on Ceos (*IG* loc.cit.) would have begun feasting some half an hour before sunset. To begin dinner by day at all, it should be remembered, was something which, in the old order of society, a working man could normally have afforded to do only on festival days (though cf. *Peace* 1140-58 where farmers decide to feast during the day because it is too wet to work).

654 **we'll weave you others:** this aspect of women's life will thus remain unchanged; it is also taken for granted, and does not even need to be mentioned, that they will be responsible for the rearing of children. Men, we see, will be wholly supported (at least as to essentials, cf. on 606) by the labour of women and slaves, and can if they wish lie in bed (cf. on 464) until it is time to prepare for dinner!

655 **before the archons:** each of the nine archons presided over a jury-court. Blepyrus, still thinking in old-society terms (cf. on 639-640), forgets that, assuming courts continue to exist, the male *arkhontes* will presumably be replaced by female *arkhousai.*

656 **there won't *be* any lawsuits:** cf. Pl. *Rep.* 464d "Will not lawsuits and mutual accusations virtually disappear from among them [the Guardians], because they will have no private possessions except their bodies, everything else being common property?"

657-8 Not only Blepyrus but even the hitherto enthusiastic Neighbour find it impossible to imagine an Athens without lawsuits (cf. 560-3).

662-4 **let her explain this ... I fancy you'll be baffled:** both "her" and "you" refer to Praxagora: without there being any precise point of transition, Blepyrus begins by addressing the Neighbour and ends by addressing his wife.

663-4 **when they're in riotous mood:** the Greek verb is derived from the noun *hybris* (it is the same verb rendered "commit outrages" in 666) and means something like "be in a state of mind conducive to the perpetration of acts of wanton and contemptuous violence" – a state here, as often, induced by drink (cf. *Wasps* 1252ff, 1299ff; Eubulus fr. 93.6-7; Alexis fr. 112; Arist. *Probl.* 953b4); see N.R.E.Fisher, *Hybris* [Warminster, 1992] 99-102. Blepyrus rightly perceives that the abolition of private property will not in itself abolish crimes of violence. Plato (*Rep.* 464e-465a) deals with such crimes by inculcating into his Guardians the belief that it is their duty to give immediate assistance to anyone being attacked (which, by implication, may include the infliction of punitive as well as protective violence on the attacker).

663-4 **assault:** Greek *āikeia* (for the long initial vowel see M.L.West, *Aeschyli Tragoediae* [Stuttgart, 1990] xlv), lit. "unseemliness", the rubric under which charges of assault were normally brought when (as in Ariston's case against Conon, Dem. 54) it was not thought safe to bring the more serious charge of *hybris* (for the difference between the two cf. Arist. *Rhet.* 1374a11-15) even though the plaintiff might believe and assert (as do Ariston and the speaker of Isoc. 20) that *hybris* had in fact been committed against him. The penalty, in money payable to the successful plaintiff, would be decided by the jury choosing between proposals by plaintiff and defendant (cf. Isoc. 20.19).

665 **he'll pay out of ... his food ration:** this method of punishment has been reinvented over and over again in theoretical and actual socialist and communist societies; we find it, for example, in the Qumran community (cf. 1QS VI 25-27 = G. Vermes, *The Dead Sea Scrolls in English*[4] [Harmondsworth, 1995] 78), in the "platform" of the seventeenth-century English revolutionary Gerrard Winstanley (cf. G. Winstanley, *The Law of Freedom and Other Writings* [Harmondsworth, 1973] 335), and in the labour camps of the twentieth-century Soviet Union (for whose ration schedules in Stalin's time see R. Conquest, *The Great Terror: A Reassessment* [London, 1990] 334). In Athens such a punishment was imaginable only for slaves (cf. *Wasps* 435), children, and women (cf. on 468-9).

667 **how can anyone steal ...?:** or "why should anyone steal ...?"; in the former case Praxagora is saying that stealing will be impossible as a matter of logic, in the latter that no one could have a motive to steal communal property; a minute's thought would reveal the fallacy in either assertion (especially to Athenians all too familiar with allegations of the theft of public funds; cf. on 438), so we are hurried on to the next point.

668 **strip off people's clothes at night:** cf. on 544.

668 **not if you sleep at home:** this means of avoiding the attentions of *lōpodutai* and other malefactors is mentioned also in [Dem.] 58.65.

670-1 **what good ... better than the first:** there may be a reminiscence of the coward's apologia in Archilochus fr. 5.3-4 "I saved my own life. What do I care about that shield [which I threw away]? Let it go hang; I can get another just as good".

672 **so people won't, either, gamble at dice?:** between 663 and 667 the theme tacitly shifted from litigation to crime; now it shifts, briefly, from crime to vice. Gambling was seen as one of the quickest and deadliest ways of squandering one's property; cf. *Wasps* 74-76 with 1267-74, *Wealth* 243, Lys. 14.27, Isoc. 15.287, Aeschines 1.42, 95.

673 **what kind of lifestyle are you going to create?:** a feeble and implausible question whose sole function is to motivate Praxagora's account of the communal living and feeding arrangements.

673-4 **to convert the whole town into one residence:** in effect turning the *polis* into an *oikos* (cf. H.P. Foley, *CP* 77 [1982] 14-21). Plato's Guardians too will have no separate dwellings "into which anyone who wishes may not enter" (*Rep.* 416d, cf. 458c, 454b), and similar rules reappear in later socialist/utopian thought from More (*Utopia* ed. J.C. Collins [Oxford, 1904] 55) to the twentieth century; cf. Shafarevich 198-9.

675 **so that everyone can walk into everyone else's house:** Dindorf's conjecture is necessary: R's reading makes no sense at all, and that of the other mss. means merely "everyone can walk to everyone else" which would be nothing new. In real-life Athens it was a heinous wrong to enter another man's house without his consent and without legal excuse (cf. Lys. 1.38, 40 where this offence seems to be regarded as almost worse than adultery; in [Dem.] 47.60 a man who refuses to help when a neighbour's house is being pillaged and his servants assaulted, because "he did not think it right [to enter] in the owner's absence", is subjected to no criticism).

675 **where will you serve dinner?:** the point is that in an ordinary house dinner would normally be served in the *andrōn* ("men's room"), a room with a ledge round almost its whole circumference which served as a base for the diners' couches, of which there were usually either seven or eleven each of which could accommodate two men; the diners were always close enough together to converse as a single group, and when buildings were designed for large communal banquets the normal practice was to divide them into numerous *andrōnes* of (usually) eleven couches each. See P.S. Pantel, *La cité au banquet* (Rome/Paris, 1992) 304-313; B. Bergquist in O. Murray ed. *Sympotica* (Oxford, 1990) 37-65. Thus a dining-room large enough to accommodate the entire population of a city "convert[ed] into one residence" would be inconceivable; hence Praxagora's expedient (676-687) of dividing the citizen body into groups who will dine in existing buildings (though the new *andrōnes* will still be vast by all normal standards – the reference to "the speaker's platform" in 677 indicates that there is no thought of dividing up "the lawcourts and colonnades" into dining-rooms of normal size).

676 **colonnades:** Greek *sto(i)ai*, long structures with a roof, a solid back wall (often with enclosed rooms abutting on it), and an open, columned front. In Athens there were several of these clustered around the Agora, used for various purposes both of public and of private business; see *Agora* iii 20-47, xiv 74-78, 82-110.

676 **dining-rooms:** Greek *andrōnes* (see last note but one).

677 **speaker's platform** (Greek *bēma*): Blepyrus is thinking of the lawcourts, his own spiritual home (cf. 562-3); there were no *bēmata* in colonnades, except when they were used as lawcourts as they sometimes were (cf. *IG* ii^2 1641.28-30). Speakers in trials "go up" to the platform to speak and "come down" when they have finished (*Wasps* 905, 944, 979-981; Dem. 21.205; Aeschines 2.183).

678 **the young boys will be able to recite poetry:** sc. from the *bēma.* For boy singers at banquets cf. *Peace* 1265-1304; the themes of their songs reflect Spartan practice (Plut. *Lyc.* 21.2, cf. Philochorus *FGrH* 328 F 216).

678-9 **in war:** it may seem surprising that the blessings of Praxagora's new order apparently do not include peace. But the title of the office she holds is a martial one (cf. 246, 500, 727), and it seems to be simply taken for granted that there will be wars as there always have been – and that men will fight them. Plato's ideal state too will fight wars against Greeks as well as barbarians (*Rep.* 469b-471c), though he has both men and women serving in the army (457a, 466c); brave soldiers, in addition to many other rewards, will be praised in poetry (468d), while cowards will be demoted to the lower classes of society (468a).

681 **allotment machines:** Greek *klērōtēria,* devices for carrying out the lot-drawing by which, at Athens, most public offices were filled and jurors assigned to their courts, with the maximum possible openness, randomness and freedom from suspicion of interference. The later procedure for empanelling jurors (involving the use of twenty machines) is described in Arist. *Ath.Pol.* 63-66; for accounts based on this and on the study of surviving specimens, see S. Dow, *Hesperia* Suppl. 1 (1937) 198-215 and *HSCP* 50 (1939) 1-34; J.D. Bishop, *JHS* 90 (1970) 1-14; E.S. Staveley, *Greek and Roman Voting and Elections* (London, 1972) 61-72.

682 **by the statue of Harmodius:** the bronze statues of Harmodius and Aristogeiton (who assassinated Hipparchus, brother of the tyrant Hippias, in 514), made by Critius and Nesiotes in 477/6, stood near the centre of the Agora; see *Agora* iii 93-98, xiv 155-160. This will thus be a convenient point for would-be diners to gather round the allotment machines, more or less equidistant from the various *stoai* and other buildings where the dinners will be held.

683 **what letter they'll be dining under:** the system envisaged is adapted from that used in the empanelment of jurors. In Aristotle's time each juror had a permanent personal ticket (*pinakion*), inscribed with his name, his deme, and one of the ten letters from *alpha* to *kappa* (Arist. *Ath.Pol.* 63.4; many such tickets have been found, usually buried with their owners, see J.H. Kroll, *Athenian Bronze Allotment Plates* [Cambridge MA, 1972]). The required number of jurors were selected from those who presented themselves by means of the allotment machines, the fall of each white dice choosing (and the fall of each black dice rejecting) one person from each of the letter-classes that were using that particular machine; each of those chosen then drew by hand a lettered token entitling him to sit that day in a specific court, the courts open on the day being randomly assigned letters from *lambda* onwards. That lettered *pinakia,* or their equivalent, were in use by c.390 is confirmed by *Wealth* 1166-7 (cf. *Wealth* 277, 972). In our passage the dining-halls, which replace the courts as destinations, are directly associated with the early, not the later, letters of the alphabet, and this might suggest (see D.M. MacDowell, *The Law in Classical Athens* [London, 1978] 36-38) that at this time jurors were not assigned individually to courts, but a single allotment was held which assigned a whole letter-class to a particular court (or to no court, if some courts were not sitting that day, cf. 687-8). This, however, would require only one machine, whereas 681 envisages several, and I would propose that MacDowell's single allotment was made, not for the entire corps of jurors at once, but for each of the ten tribes

separately on a separate machine (so that the jury in a given court might comprise e.g. the whole *alpha* class from Tribe I, the whole *delta* class from Tribe II, etc.); the proclamations of 684-6 are then envisaged as being made to the men of a particular tribe. If the allotment is to be repeated daily, as that of jurors was, this would mean that any individual would be dining each evening, not only in fresh surroundings, but also with mostly fresh companions.

684 the herald will proclaim ... should follow her: in the Greek the subject of "will proclaim" and the object of "follow" are left unexpressed, and it is not till 713 that it is made explicit that heralds, like other public officials, will be female.

685 the Basileios Colonnade, situated at the north-west corner of the Agora, contained the office of the *basileus* ("king"), the second of the nine archons, with responsibility for religious affairs; see *Agora* iii 21-25, xiv 83-90, and T.L. Shear, *Hesperia* 40 (1971) 243-260, 44 (1975) 365-370.

685 the one next to it: this must be the colonnade of Zeus Eleutherios (*Agora* iii 25-30, xiv 96-103), which directly adjoined the Basileios colonnade on the south. It is not clear why it should be associated with the letter *theta*: its painting of Theseus with Democracy and Demos (Paus. 1.3.2, cf. Plin. *NH* 35.129) is irrelevant, since this mural was painted, with others, by Euphranor after the battle of Mantinea in 362 (Paus. 1.3.4, cf. Plin. *loc.cit.*).

686-7 Eta ... tó eta up the corn?: the Greek has *kappa* ... *kaptōsin* ("eat greedily", usually implying that food is taken directly into the mouth without the use of hands, cf. *Knights* 493, *Wasps* 791, *Peace* 7, *Birds* 245, 579, Ar. fr. 314).

686 the Cornmarket Colonnade (*Sto(i)ā Alphitopōlis*) has not been securely identified; it has been suggested that it may have been (part of) the "South Stoa I" at the south end of the Agora (see *Agora* xiv 76 n.216). It is to be distinguished from the colonnade of the same name in the Peiraeus (cf. *Ach.* 548 with scholia, Thuc. 8.90.5; also called the "Long Colonnade", Paus. 1.1.3), for Blepyrus would hardly have allowed it to pass without comment if Praxagora were expecting one letter-class to walk several miles in order to get their dinner.

687-8 anyone who doesn't get his letter drawn to give him a dinner: corresponding to those letter-classes of jurors for whom a black dice came out of the allotment machine, meaning that they would not sit in any court that day.

688 everybody will force them to leave: the reading of the Aldine edition, "they will force all of them to leave", has something to be said for it. The whole imagined scenario is modelled on the familiar one of the selection of jurors, and jurors unlucky in the selection would be driven away from the court area, if at all, not by "everybody", i.e. the lucky jurors, but by Scythian archers (cf. on 143) or other servants of the magistrates in charge of the proceedings; the vague subject "they" (which in the Greek, if Ald. is right, is not even expressed) would refer aptly enough to these public slaves. The reading of Ald., however, is most unlikely to derive from any authoritative source, and may well be a mere slip.

691-2 garland on head and torch in hand: for these attributes of the reveller (*kōmastēs*) cf. *Wealth* 1041, Antiphanes fr. 197, Men. *Dysk.* 964, *Mis.* 459-460 (= 989-990 Arnott), *Sam.* 731, *Sik.* 418-9.

693-701 No doubt men coming away from a real-life symposium might well be thus beset by prostitutes or their madams – but the difference now will be (cf. 613-8) that they will not have to *pay* for their pleasures, except in the manner indicated in 700-1. In addition – though the point will not be fully clarified until 718-724 – the women soliciting them will henceforth be women of citizen status.

699 really white-skinned: cf. *Birds* 668, *Thesm.* 191.

701-9 repeats the substance of 626-634, but now it is Praxagora who, at the climax of her speech, reminds the two old men of the privileged status they will have under the new sex laws, emphasizing the completeness of their triumph over the young and handsome with two highly obscene, and contrasting, words never normally used by women in the presence of men (see my article in F. De Martino and A.H. Sommerstein ed. *Lo spettacolo delle voci* [Bari, 1995] 78-80), *bīnein* "fuck" (706) and *dephesthai* "wank, masturbate" (709).

705 **the snub-nosed:** cf. 617, 630.

707-8 **the leaves of your double-fruited fig-tree:** the tree is the penis (cf. *Ach.* 996), its two fruits the testicles, and the leaves the foreskin (cf. *Ach.* 158); the whole phrase "double-fruited fig-tree" appears again, unfortunately without helpful context, at Antiphanes fr. 196 (cf. Pherecrates fr. 103). See Henderson 117-8.

712 **to receive the incoming goods:** there has never been any mention of the actual procedure by which the community will take possession of all private property; it was said that everyone would have to hand in his money (601-610), but of other chattels it was only said that they would become common property (598) without any indication of how this would be effected. Now both Praxagora and the Neighbour (728-9) speak as though they, and we, already knew that all property was to be taken forthwith to the Agora. The present phrase is evidently considered by Ar. sufficient to put the audience in the picture, and we are probably meant to imagine that the first job of the "heraldess" will be to proclaim the edict throughout the city.

713 **a heraldess with a strong voice** will certainly be needed to direct the thousands of men milling about the Agora to their proper dining-halls (cf. 684-6); but both the word *kērūkaina* "heraldess" (cf. *alektruaina* "female domestic fowl" *Clouds* 666, *mageiraina* "female cook" Pherecrates fr. 70) and the very idea of a female herald are creations of fantasy (the speaker in *Thesm.* 295ff is not a herald but a priestess; see my note *ad loc.*).

719-720 The cynical explanation of Praxagora's motive for abolishing prostitution, incorporating a word-play (see next note but one) of a type that we have heard in this scene from the male characters (624, 634, 648, 687) but never from Praxagora, must certainly come from one of the men, but it is not clear from which: one might assign it to Blepyrus because of its cynicism (so R. Seager, *LCM* 10 [1985] 121) or, as I have marginally preferred, to the Neighbour because the tendency has been for him to correct or enlighten Blepyrus rather than vice versa (cf. 609-610, 646-8, 668).

720 **these ones here:** cf. on 614 ("women").

720 **the p(r)ick of the young men:** for *tōn neōn ... tēn akmēn* "the best of the young men" (cf. [Demades] *On the Twelve Years* 12) is substituted the plural form of the same phrase which means literally "the tips (extremities) of the young men" (cf. Henderson 114).

721 **slave-girls:** many prostitutes too were slaves, but Praxagora is here thinking of female *household* slaves, whom wives could regard as rivals (Lys. 1.12, Xen. *Oec.* 10.12), sometimes with good reason (cf. *Peace* 1138-9).

722 **love-rights:** Greek *Kypris* "the Cyprian goddess", i.e. Aphrodite, i.e. sex; cf. *Thesm.* 205 where the male invert Agathon says the women hate him for (lit.) "stealing female Kypris".

724 **pussies:** Greek *khoiros* (collective singular), lit. "piglet", i.e. vulva; cf. *Ach.* 771-796, *Wasps* 1353, 1364, *Thesm.* 538, 540.

724 **plucked in the shaggy smock style:** plucking the pubic hair was an alternative, for cosmetic purposes, to singeing it (see on 13, and cf. *Lys.* 89, 151, 827-8, *Frogs* 516); but the slave-girls are to have theirs plucked like a *katōnakē*, a slave's or peasant's over-garment (cf. *Lys.* 1151) made of, or hemmed with, hairy or woolly goat- or sheepskin (*nakē*) – or, in other words, not plucked at all (so D.M. Bain, *LCM* 7 [1982] 8; M. Kilmer, *JHS* 102 [1982] 106).

727 **"Don't you admire the General's husband there?":** the idea is that whereas formerly a citizen woman had had no public existence except as someone's (daughter or) wife (and, as a corollary, could not normally even be referred to by name in public; cf. D.M. Schaps, *CQ* 27 [1977] 323-330), in future a citizen man will have no public existence except as someone's husband – with the result that the hitherto obscure Blepyrus has suddenly become, as it were, the First Gentleman of Athens! Before the revolution, for a man to be called "X's husband" had been an insult, implying that he let his wife rule him (cf. Eur. *El.* 930-7). Blepyrus forgets, and is not reminded, that marriage no longer exists (cf. on 1125-6).

729 **inspect:** Greek *exetazein*, which the audience will probably understand as "enumerate, list, inventory" (cf. Dem. 20.52, 58; *IG* ii^2 333.11), but which, when the Neighbour appears again, will prove to bear its military sense "parade and review" (cf. Thuc. 7.35.1, Xen. *Anab.* 1.2.14).

729/730 Between these two lines in R stands the word *khorou*, an abbreviation of *khorou melos* "song of the chorus"; this indication also appears in R at 876, in R and/or V at several points in *Wealth* (321/2, 626/7, 770/1 *kommation khorou* "short stanza by the chorus", 801/2) and one in *Clouds* (888/9), and in many papyri of fourth-century and later drama, including those of Menander where it invariably marks the breaks between the five acts of which each play is composed. It is now generally accepted that in later drama these breaks were filled by choral performances of some kind whose words, if any, were not considered worth recording as part of the play-script; and if this was true of Menander and his contemporaries, it may be taken *a fortiori* that it was true of Aristophanes. It is still necessary, however, to consider the following questions:

(1) Is our manuscript evidence as to the placement of these choral interludes complete and accurate? Of the four *khorou* markings that survive in *Wealth* R has only two, and there are several points later in that play (958/9, 1096/7, 1170/1) where the action pauses, the stage is empty, and a *khorou* marking may (or may not) have been lost (some 14th- and 15th-century mss. actually insert *khorou* at the first two of these places); on the other hand we know from the later scholia on *Wealth* (on 1, 252/3, 619, 626/7, 641, 771, 802, 850, 1042) that by the Middle Ages the meaning of *khorou* was not properly understood, and the word might therefore have been wrongly inserted. In the present passage one might argue (as I did in *BICS* 31 [1984] 144) that the Neighbour "sets himself immediately to do his duty [so that] even the suggestion of delay would be misleading ... [and] any substantial choral performance would be out of place"; but this leaves open the possibility of a short choral song (as in *Ach.* 358-365, *Peace* 950-5, where likewise a character has gone inside to fetch something and left the chorus alone), and there is therefore not sufficient justification for rejecting the evidence of R here (cf. R. Hamilton, *CQ* 41 [1991] 347, 352-3). On 876/7 and 1111/2, see notes *ad locc.*

(2) What was the nature of the choral performances? Song is positively attested where *melos* "lyric" or *kommation* "short stanza" is added to *khorou*, i.e. at *Wealth* 770-1, Astydamas fr. 1h.10, *trag.adesp.* 625.8/9, and probably *com.adesp.* 1056.12; moreover several Aristophanic comedies appear to end with choral exit-songs which are announced in the concluding words of the surviving text but whose own lyrics were apparently never included in the script (cf. *Ach.* 1231-4, *Lys.* 1320-1, *Wealth* 1209), and Menander's choruses of "drunken youths" are unlikely to have danced in silence. The probability is overwhelming that in fourth-century comedy, as in fourth-century tragedy (cf. Arist. *Poet.* 1456a29-30), the chorus always sang as well as dancing.

(3) Why are choral songs included in the script in the first half of this play and at its end, but not in between? In part this must be because the entrance and exit of the chorus were, and always remained, vital features of the comic entertainment; in Menander the chorus's first entrance (at the end of Act I) is the only moment at which the characters always take notice of its existence, and its exit (at the end of the play) typically takes the form of a procession of revellers with garlands and torches (see the passages cited on 691-2). In *Wealth*, apart from two short exclamations within a spoken scene (637-640), the only lyrics included in the script are (some of) those that formed part of the *parodos* (290-321). In *Eccl.* all but one of the preserved choral songs are associated with an entrance or exit of the chorus; the exception (571-580) is the introduction to the *agon*, which even in *Wealth* is marked by a couplet from the chorus-leader (487-8) whose insertion is entirely due to structural convention rather than dramatic logic.

See generally on this subject E.W. Handley, *CQ* 3 (1953) 55-61; E. Pöhlmann, *WJA* 3 (1977) 69-81; R.L. Hunter, *ZPE* 36 (1979) 23-38; A.H. Sommerstein, *BICS* 31 (1984) 139-152; F. Perusino, *Dalla commedia antica alla commedia di mezzo* (Urbino, 1987) 61-72; R. Hamilton, *CQ* 41 (1991) 346-355; and A.H. Sommerstein in J.A. López Férez ed. *Estudios actuales sobre textos griegos: Comedia* (Madrid, forthcoming).

730 Since the character who now appears is doing precisely what the Neighbour said in 728-9 that he was going to do, it can be taken as certain that he is the same person. Vetta has objected that the man of the present scene, who has two slaves (cf. 867-8), seems less poor than the Neighbour, who had only one cloak (353); but to have two slaves did not necessarily mean one was well off (see on 593; Chremylus in *Wealth*, who complains bitterly of his poverty, has at least three, cf. *Wealth* 26-27), and to have only one cloak did not necessarily mean one was poor (see on 315-6).

730-745 In this speech the Neighbour's household utensils are intermittently addressed, and spoken of, as if they were the personnel of a ritual procession at a festival, almost certainly the Panathenaea – for the roles they are made to play can in general be identified with those of participants in the Panathenaic procession as known from literary and grammatical sources and from the north and east friezes of the Parthenon (see S.I. Rotroff, *AJA* 81 [1977] 379-382 – who makes a detailed comparison between the evidence of our passage and that of the friezes – and I. Jenkins, *The Parthenon Frieze* [London, 1994]), though in this mock procession each role has only one representative rather than several as at the real Panathenaea. In accordance with the pretence, the utensils are asked to come out of the house themselves (730, 734, 737, 739), and if 730-741 had survived as an isolated fragment one might have thought that, as in *Wasps* 936-966, they were impersonated by silent performers; but 742-4 (where instructions are given to "bring" other items) and later references to the goods being tied up and carried (785-7, 833, 867-8) show that the utensils are inanimate (though, for easy visibility, some of them may be of outsize dimensions). Fetching and carrying goods was slaves' business, and Vetta is doubtless right to assume that the utensils are brought by Sicon and Parmenon alternately (cf. 757, where those arranging the "procession" are addressed by the Dissident in the second person plural); but the first item, the sieve, which in the "procession" plays the role of a cherished daughter (see notes below), may have been lovingly carried by the Neighbour himself.

730 **prettily ... pretty:** the Greek has the jingle *kalē kalōs*, an expression particularly appropriate to *kanēphoroi* (see below; cf. *Ach.* 253) and brides (cf. *Peace* 1330-1); its near-antonym *kakos kakōs* serves to condemn or to curse (*Knights* 2, *Clouds* 554, *Wealth* 65).

730 **bran-sifter:** i.e. a sieve that separates bran from flour.

732 **basket-bearer:** Greek *kanēphoros*, a maiden (approaching the age for marriage, i.e. probably between twelve and fifteen) chosen to carry a ritual basket (*kanoun*), containing the knife and other requisites of a sacrifice, in a festal procession; cf. *Ach.* 242-262, *Lys.* 646, 1194, and see Parke 22-23, 43-44, 109, 127, and A. Brelich, *Paides e parthenoi* (Rome, 1969) 279-290. On the Parthenon frieze, what appear to be a group of *kanēphoroi* head the procession, and are the only members of it who have, as it were, turned the corner from the north to the east side.

732 **well-powdered:** Greek *entetrimmenē* normally means "rubbed with cosmetics" (cf. 904, *Lys.* 149, Xen. *Oec.* 10.2), as a *kanēphoros* would be – but in reference to the sieve it will be understood as "covered in flour-dust". The same joke had been used a generation before by Hermippus (fr. 25, "[I was] *entetrimmenos* with white barley-meal, like the *kanēphoroi*"; to take this as evidence that *kanēphoroi* themselves were ritually sprinkled with barley-meal subverts the humour of both passages – they are more likely to have been well covered with white *lead*, cf. 878, Ar. fr. 332.3, Lys. 1.14, Xen. *loc.cit.*).

733 **after having emptied** (lit. "turned upside down") **so many of my meal-bags:** literally true of a sieve, into which the contents of the bag would be emptied for sifting; figuratively true of a *kanēphoros*, for to have one's daughter chosen to perform this function was not only an honour but also expensive (cf. *Lys.*1188-94 [fine clothing and jewellery], also *Ach.* 253-8, *Birds* 670; for the empty meal-bag as a symbol of impecuniosity cf. 382).

734 **stool-bearer:** Greek *diphrophoros*, a girl (of non-citizen birth, according to Aelian *VH* 6.1) who carried a stool for the *kanēphoros* to sit on, presumably so that she should not have to stand throughout the (often prolonged) sacrificial rites that followed the procession (so L. Ziehen, *RE* xviii[3] 465-6): cf. *Birds* 1552. The stool-bearers (and the parasol-bearers, see on 737) are absent from the Parthenon frieze, doubtless because they and the objects they carried had no *ritual* significance (cf. S.I. Rotroff, *AJA* 81 [1977] 381).

735-6 **as black as if it was you ... blackens his hair with:** for Lysicrates see on 630; the pot, evidently an old one, is black from scorching (cf. *Wasps* 828, 939). The transmitted text ("nor, if it had been you ...") can be made meaningful only by assuming a highly improbable ellipsis ("nor <would you have been any blacker> if it had been you ...") which is not made any less improbable or any more intelligible by calling it, with Vetta, "affectionate" or "emotional" (anyway the speaker is not at this moment expressing his affection for the pot; he is making a joke at the expense of Lysicrates). I accordingly translate the text as emended by Meineke or Halbertsma (there is little to choose between their conjectures); but I suspect there may be slightly deeper corruption, since the normal way of saying "you're black" would be *melaina g(e) ei*, not just *melaina g(e)*. Possibly (see apparatus) a word or two may have been lost from the text and a stopgap later inserted in the wrong place, in which case the original text may have meant e.g. "By Zeus, you're black! It wasn't you, was it, that boiled the dye that ...?"

737 **maid-in-waiting:** Greek *kommōtria*, lit. "adorning-woman", normally applied to a maidservant responsible for a lady's dressing, skin-care, make-up and hair-styling (cf. Pl. *Rep.* 373c, *Gorg.* 465b). A *kanēphoros* would be carefully prepared in these respects *before* taking part in a procession, but it would disrupt the ritual if she received cosmetic attention *during* it, and Vetta is probably right to take *kommōtria* here as the designation of the attendant who we know accompanied her to carry a parasol for her comfort (*Birds* 1550-1; cf. last note but one). He ingeniously proposes that the utensil representing this attendant was a ladle, whose shape would suggest that of a parasol.

738 jar-bearer: the daughters of metics (free non-citizens) carried water-jars (*hydriai*) in festival processions (Demetrius of Phalerum, *FGrH* 228 F 5; Pollux 3.55). On the Parthenon frieze the jar-bearers are men; they may have been so represented for artistic reasons (there are no women or girls at all on the north or south frieze), but it is possibly significant that in our passage the jar-bearer is distinguished from the jar itself and presumably therefore is, for once, to be identified not with the (grammatically feminine) utensil but with the (male) slave who brings it out, even though it is of course the jar, not the slave, that is set down as part of the mock procession. It is not clear whether the format of the Panathenaic procession changed in this respect between Ar.'s time and Demetrius' (late fourth century), or whether the law referred to by Demetrius had never applied to the Panathenaea.

739 there: the point is that in the Panathenaic procession (as the Parthenon frieze shows) the "jar-bearers" did not walk directly behind the *kanēphoros* and her attendants, but were separated from them not only by the sacrificial animals (which the Neighbour does not include in his mock procession at all) but also by the "tray-bearers" (cf. 742); hence the Neighbour takes care to leave a gap between the ladle and the jar, into which he will later put the tray.

739 musician: lit. "lyre-player" (feminine). The musicians in the Panathenaic procession (who comprised both pipers and lyre-players, in that order) were male, so the use of the feminine gender here can only be explained if the object representing a musician is grammatically feminine. This rules out the otherwise attractive supposition (Brunck, Rogers, Ussher) that the "musician" who had so often woken the Neighbour early was a cock (cf. next note); we should follow the scholia ("a grinder") and identify the object as a hand-mill. A whole village might resound with the noise of grinding mills in the early morning (Pherecrates fr. 10; cf. *Odyssey* 20.105-119), which one writer (Nicostratus the Sophist) compared to the sound of a lyre (Stobaeus 4.22.102).

741 your song of dawning: Greek *orthrios nomos* "first-light melody", with a pun on the famous lyre melody by Terpander called the *orthios nomos* (*Ach.* 16, *Knights* 1279); the same pun appears, with reference to the cock's crow, at *Birds* 489.

742 the man with the tray ... the honeycombs: in the Panathenaic and other processions, metic *skaphēphoroi* carried cakes and honeycombs on trays (*skaphai*) (Pollux 3.55, Photius s.v. *skaphās*); on the Parthenon frieze, four men carrying trays walk just behind the sacrificial animals and in front of the men carrying water-jars.

743 the olive-branches: the Panathenaic procession included a group of old men (*thallophoroi*), chosen for their handsomeness, who carried olive-branches (cf. *Wasps* 544 with scholia, Xen. *Symp.* 4.17, Philochorus *FGrH* 328 F 9). In the procession on the Parthenon frieze, the musicians are followed by sixteen old men, who may well represent *thallophoroi* even though they are not shown as carrying olive-branches.

744 the two tripods: Greek *tripous* could denote anything from a bronze tripod-cauldron for ritual use to a three-legged table (cf. Xen. *Anab.* 7.3.21, Men. fr. 194, Pollux 10.80); here two of the latter (small and portable) serve to represent the former.

744 the oil-flask probably represents an amphora (a vessel holding some 39 litres of oil, and requiring two men to carry it when full); an amphora is shown being carried in a sacrificial procession, possibly that of the Great Panathenaea, on a black-figure vase by the Theseus Painter in the Joseph Beach Noble collection at Tampa (86.52; see J. Neils [et al.], *Goddess and Polis* [Hanover/Princeton, 1992] 181 no.53).

745 the crowd of little pots: lit. "the little pots and the crowd"; the smaller kitchen paraphernalia represent the general public who line the route of the procession and, when it has passed, follow it towards the Acropolis.

746 **DISSIDENT:** this man has not appeared before, for he can neither be Chremes (who at no point showed anything like this man's total and shameless contempt for anyone's good but his own) nor Blepyrus (who in the end expressed approval of the new dispensation, 710, and is extremely proud of being "the General's husband", 725-7). In theory he could be Blepyrus' other neighbour (the husband of First Woman, see on 327-356); but nothing in the text indicates that he has a house on stage or that he has any previous acquaintance with the Neighbour, and it is best to assume that he is a casual passer-by.

746 **an absolute loser:** Greek *kakodaimōn* "wretched", lit. "with an evil (hostile) divinity", the point being that to surrender one's goods would, to the speaker's mind, be so foolish an act that it could be explained only by supposing that some god must have put one out of one's right senses; so again 760.

755 **are you taking it to pawn?:** see on 567.

757 **preparing a display:** lit. "organizing a procession". Since the Dissident is trying to make sense of what he sees by associating it with something that commonly happens (or happened, before the revolution) in ordinary life, we should probably deduce that when goods were displayed for sale by public auction (see next note) they were often put out in a long row on a table or board, and that such a display was called a "procession" (*pompē*).

757 **Hieron** (*PA* 7522; *LGPN* 8) is not otherwise known; his occupation, though it seems to have made him a familiar figure in the Agora, was a lowly one (cf. Dem. 44.4, Thphr. *Char.* 6.5).

761 **that's easy to see—:** Greek *rhāidiōs* "easily", which normally, in contexts like this, introduces an explanation (cf. *Birds* 201, *Frogs* 642); Vetta therefore supposes, probably rightly, that the Neighbour (his "Man I") indignantly interrupts before the Dissident can say more.

767 **sound-headed:** Greek *sōphrōn* which can mean (1) "intelligent" (e.g. Thuc. 4.28.5; in *Peace* 1297 it is ironically applied to a coward, taken as knowing what is in his own best interests) and (2) "dutiful" (of those who "refrain from breaking moral or social rules for the gratification of their own ambitions or desires", Dover on *Clouds* 529); here the Dissident uses the word in sense 1 and the Neighbour understands it in sense 2 (Dover *AC* 192 n.1).

767 **ought to do what he's told:** the Athenian civic oath, taken by every citizen soon after attaining his majority, bound him to obey "those who for the time being exercise authority reasonably, and the established laws, and such laws as they establish reasonably in future" (Tod 204.11-14); the word "reasonably" (*emphronōs*) might seem to offer a loophole, but Athenian public speakers regularly assume that the obligation to obey the laws, and lawful authority, must *always* take priority over one's personal interests. The Dissident is thus virtually repudiating his duty as a citizen. (The obligation did not apply to laws that purported, or holders of authority who attempted, to overthrow the democracy, cf. Andoc. 1.96-98; but the Dissident does not try to justify his disobedience on that basis.)

772 **I'll believe that when I see it:** lit. "having seen, I believed", probably a catch-phrase used by those telling tall tales, and thus a means of saying in effect "that's just not credible"; similarly Xanthias' comment on Dionysus' account of his alleged achievements in naval warfare, "and then I woke up" (*Frogs* 51), is equivalent to "you were dreaming that, weren't you?"

773-6 Four times the Dissident echoes the verb just used by the Neighbour. The first and second times his meaning is clear: people are *saying* they will conform with the new law, and they will go on saying it – but they will not do it. Then the Neighbour loses patience, and says so – but the Dissident goes on playing the same verbal game, purely, it seems, to mock and annoy him (and, from Ar.'s point of view, to raise a laugh). Attempts to extract a literal meaning from his third and fourth responses are not persuasive; it is not even possible to determine what would be the object of "blast" (*epitrībein*, lit. "crush") in the last ("me"? "you"? "themselves"? "the women"?).

778-9 **You mean we should only take and not give?:** the last three words are added by the translator for clarity. These words were restored to the law-abiding citizen by J.C.B. Lowe, *Hermes* 95 (1967) 66-71 (cf. H.J. Newiger, *Hermes* 96 [1968] 122-3); all modern editors (including, since then, Ussher and Vetta) have treated 777-783 as a continuous speech by the Dissident, of which this section runs approximately thus:

> That's not our tradition; we ought only to take, by Zeus – that's what the gods do ...

Against this, note (i) that on the traditional view the late position in the sentence of *nē Dia* "(yes,) by Zeus" has "no real parallel in Aristophanes" (Lowe), (ii) that the mss. mark change of speaker before *nē Dia*, and (iii) that the Neighbour's naïve, incredulous question is thoroughly in character (cf. 762, 766, 769, 794-5, 830-1). It is more doubtful whether, as Newiger further suggested, the last four words of 777 should be given to the loyal citizen, yielding this exchange:

> DISSIDENT: Do you think anyone will hand it in?
> NEIGHBOUR: Any of them that's got any sense.
> DISSIDENT: No, that's not our tradition.

For in this scene it is invariably the Dissident (747, 751, 760, 764-8, 787, 793, 811), rather than the Neighbour, who treats those who disagree with him as stupid.

779 **that's what the gods do:** both in comedy and in tragedy it is a familiar line of argument by sophistic subverters of traditional morality to excuse human wrongdoings by pointing to (mythical) examples of similar wrongdoings on the part of the gods: cf. *Clouds* 902-6, 1079-82, Eur. *Hipp.* 451-8, *Tro.* 948-950. For the complaint that the gods take men's offerings but do not fulfil their prayers cf. *Birds* 584, *Wealth* 1116-25; for a theological argument based, like this one, on the appearance of cultic and other images of the gods, cf. *Birds* 514-9.

782 **holding out their hands palm upwards:** like a magistrate hoping for a bribe (cf. *Peace* 908, *Thesm.* 936-7, [Lys.] 6.29). The gods (that is, their cult-images) often did in fact "get something" in their outstretched hands in the form of a share of the internal organs (*splankhna*) of sacrificial animals (cf. *Birds* 518-9; at Chios *splankhna es kheiras* "offals for the hands" was a technical term of ritual law, cf. *LSCG* 119.4, *LSS* 76.4, 77.6, 129.4-6).

786 **or rather:** Greek *men oun* "on the contrary"; the Neighbour corrects his first answer – he is not merely *going* to take his property to the Agora, he is actually *now* in the process of doing so.

791 **if by any chance there was an earthquake:** this would be regarded as an evil omen for any enterprise in progress, and might lead to its being discontinued; cf. Thuc. 3.89.1, 5.45.4, 6.95.1, Xen. *Hell.* 3.2.24.

792 **a bolt of lightning:** lit. "fire from which one turns away"; for lightning and/or thunder treated as cause for the discontinuance of a political or military action cf. *Clouds* 579-580, Eupolis fr. 99.30-32, Xen. *Hell.* 4.7.7.

792 **or if a ferret** (lit. polecat) **ran across the street:** the Dissident evidently thinks most people will be ready to grasp at any straw of an excuse to hold on to their property: it is only a particularly superstitious man who "if a polecat runs across the road, will not

walk on until someone passes between them, or until he throws three stones over the road" (Thphr. *Char.* 16.3).

793 **you moonstruck idiot:** lit. "you struck-by-lightning (i.e. stupefied) one".

794 **nice thing it would be for me:** meaning the opposite, as in 190.

794 **if I came and found no space left:** sc. after waiting to see what others were doing.

795 **afraid you won't find space for it, is that it?:** the Greek is very elliptical, but this is the interpretation that best suits the context; lit. "<you fear> lest you may not get <a place> into which <to deposit it>?", the Dissident echoing the Neighbour's words before proceeding to answer them.

797-8 **they vote in haste, and then ... renege on what they've decided:** cf. 193-201, *Ach.* 630-2, Isoc. 8.52, and, for some notorious historical instances, Thuc. 3.35-50, 8.1.1, Xen. *Hell.* 1.7.34-35. The Dissident does not at present exemplify his assertion, but he will do so in 812-829.

799-803 Again (cf. 773-6) the Dissident repeats the same turn of phrase over and over again in successive answers, and again (803) the series ends in nonsense. Later the two will have a very similar exchange with the roles reversed (861-6).

801 **I'll go away and leave them be:** the Neighbour is not prepared to risk life and limb in the cause of communism; given that he is among its most enthusiastic supporters, it thus appears that the new order will survive only if the bulk of the population are willing to make it work. But then the bulk of the population are poor (cf. 408-426) and therefore should be better off under the new system.

802 **if they sell your stuff:** i.e. if the dissident faction, having *ex hypothesi* defeated their opponents and gained control of the Agora, treat the goods deposited there as ownerless property or booty and dispose of them for their own benefit. Those who have obeyed the new law will then be entirely destitute, with neither private property nor the promised public maintenance. Both the Neighbour and the audience will be reminded of the large-scale confiscations and sales by the Thirty, in 404-403, of the property of their exiled opponents: cf. Lysias, *Against Hippotherses* (*POxy* 1606.29-47, 118-124); Isoc. 18.23; Xen. *Hell.* 2.4.1.

805-6 **I see that my neighbours are taking theirs:** possibly, as the Neighbour says this, he gestures into the wings, beyond his own house.

806 **Antisthenes:** see on 366.

808 **to shit for a month or more:** the point is presumably that for Antisthenes, defaecation equals pain (cf. 366-8) – but parting with his wealth would give him even greater pain.

808 **Callimachus, the chorus-trainer** (*LGPN* 13) is not otherwise identifiable; it is not clear whether he was a minor lyric poet (who would be officially described as *didaskalos* "trainer" of the choruses who performed his compositions at festivals, cf. *Ach.* 628, *Knights* 507, 516, *Birds* 912, 1403, *Wealth* 797) or merely a *répétiteur* (as perhaps was the *didaskalos* of Demosthenes' chorus whom Meidias allegedly corrupted, cf. Dem. 21.17). The scholia say he was poor (like the poet of *Birds* 904-957), but this is probably only a deduction from the text, and a mistaken one: the Dissident's argument requires Callimachus to be, not poor, but mean – though the Neighbour (deliberately misunderstanding?) answers as if he had spoken of him as poor.

810 **Callias** (*PA* 7826; *LGPN* 84), son of Hipponicus of the deme Alopece, was born about 450 and died in 367/6 or later (*SEG* xii 100.64). He inherited a large fortune from his father, but was an extravagant debauchee, who by the late 390s had squandered almost his whole patrimony (cf. Lys. 19.48) – hence the expectation here that he will have hardly any property to surrender. He had been a magnet for spongers and parasites (as was graphically described as early as 421 in the lost *Flatterers* of Eupolis, and later in Xenophon's *Symposium*), was said to have spent more money on sophistic education

than all other men combined (Pl. *Apol.* 20a; cf. Pl. *Prot.* 314c-316a), kept a series of rapacious mistresses (*Birds* 286, Cratinus fr. 12) and was believed to have once escaped prosecution for adultery only by paying three talents to the woman's husband (Cratinus fr. 81; for his sexual reputation cf. further *Frogs* 428-430, Andoc. 1.124-9). All this was despite his being hereditary second chief priest (*dāidoukhos*) of the Eleusinian Mysteries (cf. Arist. *Rhet.* 1405a19-20, Andoc. 1.112, 124). Nevertheless, probably not long before the production of *Eccl.* (cf. Introduction, p. 7 and note 33), Callias was elected a general for 391/0, when he commanded the Athenian hoplite force based at Corinth and took part in the operation in which Iphicrates' light troops routed a battalion (*mora*) of Spartan hoplites at Lechaeum (Xen. *Hell.* 4.5.13-18). For a full discussion of the genealogy and property of his family, see Davies 254-270.

814 the one about salt: we know nothing about this decree, except that it was either soon repealed (cf. 815-822) or ineffective (cf. 823-9). The scholia say that it was aimed at reducing the price of salt, but this may be a mere guess.

815 that copper coinage: the reference is probably to the silver-plated bronze coins known to have been struck near the end of the fifth century (see J.H. Kroll, *GRBS* 17 [1976] 329-341) and mentioned in *Frogs* (725-6) as "these wretched coppers, struck only yesterday or the day before"; they were introduced as an emergency coinage in 406 (later than "the new gold" [*Frogs* 720, cf. Hellanicus *FGrH* 4 F 172, Philochorus *FGrH* 328 F 141] made during the year 407/6 from the gold plating of the Victory statues in the Parthenon) and, as 817-822 shows, demonetized (or drastically reduced in value, cf. on 821-2) some time between 403 and 392 – though perhaps more likely early than late in that period, since the taxation decree of 823-9 is described as "recent" in apparent contrast to the coinage changes.

818 cargo does not directly represent anything in the Greek text, but both *apairein* "start out, set sail" and *mestos* "full" are often used of ships, and Vetta is probably right to suggest that the Neighbour is picturing himself as a merchant-ship: as traders sailed to the Black Sea to buy corn, so he is "voyaging" to the Agora to buy meal.

818 in my mouth: classical Athenians, having "neither pockets nor a sense of oral hygiene" (MacDowell on *Wasps* 791), habitually carried low-value coins in their mouths (cf. *Wasps* 791-5, *Birds* 502-3, *Wealth* 379, Ar. fr. 3); tradesmen even used their mouths as tills (Alexis fr. 133.7, Thphr. *Char.* 6.9).

820 for it to be poured in: lit. "under" (sc. the dealer's sack).

821-2 no one to accept copper any longer: in fact bronze coins continued in use (Eubulus fr. 81; Alexis fr. 15.2; Philemon fr. 66, 76), but they were of very small value; a character in Ar.'s later play *Aeolosicon* (fr. 3) speaks of having had two obols left in his mouth and finding they had turned into two *kolluboi* (i.e., probably, one-eighth of an obol; see M.N. Tod, *Numismatic Chronicle* [6th ser.] 5 [1945] 108-116).

825 the two-and-a-half-per-cent tax: lit. "the fortieth <part>". The proposed tax was probably an *eisphorā*, i.e. a one-off direct tax levied on individuals' wealth (imposed, by an *ad hoc* Assembly decree, when money was required for special needs, usually in wartime). For a tax of 2.5% to have an expected yield of 500 talents implies that the tax base was believed to be 20,000 talents; most if not all fourth-century *eisphorai* were levied at 1% (cf. G.E.M. de Ste Croix, *C&M* 14 [1953] 34, 47-53), and it is probably no coincidence that the *eisphorā* of 428 had yielded 200 talents (Thuc. 3.19.1). It was, however, wildly optimistic to expect a proportionate yield in the 390s, and when a census was taken in 378/7 the total taxable wealth of Attica proved to be only 5,750 talents (Polybius 2.62.6-7, cf. Dem. 22.44); in 354 the generally accepted estimate was 6,000 talents (Dem. 14.19, cf. Philochorus *FGrH* 328 F 46). The object of levying an *eisphorā* will certainly have been to fund the creation of an effective Athenian fleet (cf.

on 197-8), and the measure is thus unlikely to have been proposed while Athenians thought they could rely on the Persian navy; probably therefore Heurippides made his suggestion after the arrest of Conon in the summer of 392. An earlier *eisphorā*, mentioned in Isoc. 17.41 (394/3), seems to have been imposed on aliens only.

825 **Heurippides:** this man is called Euripides in the mss. (as in those of Arist. *Rhet.* 1384b15) but he is certainly to be identified with Heurippides (*PA* 5949 = 5955 = 5956, *LGPN* Euripides 11), son of Adeimantus of the deme Myrrhinûs; the spelling of his name with *-pp-* is invariable in inscriptions, and is confirmed by the mention of another (or it may be the same) Heurippides of Myrrhinûs (*LGPN* Euripides 10) in an inscription of unknown date (*AD* 19 [1964] B 72). Between 403 and 400 (cf. Andoc. 1.112) Heurippides proposed a decree appointing one Eucles as "herald of the Council and People" in recognition of his services to the democratic cause in the civil war (*IG* ii^2 145); in 393 he served on an embassy to Syracuse sent, on Conon's proposal, in the hope of making an alliance with Dionysius I (Arist. *loc.cit.* with *CAG* xxi.2 p.106.32, cf. Lys. 19.19-20); some time later he won a victory as *chorēgos* with a boys' chorus at the City Dionysia (*IG* ii^2 1138.25-27 = 2812.1; cf. D.M. Lewis, *ABSA* 50 [1955] 17-19), but he cannot be traced on the political scene after 392/1, and his public career may have been finished by the fiasco of his tax scheme and the death of his patron Conon. Thereafter Heurippides' name seems to have been remembered only in the slang of dice players, where it denoted a score of 40 (obviously in memory of his tax of "one-fortieth", though Pollux 9.101 gives another, far-fetched explanation). See Wilamowitz *KS* iv 88-89, 430 = *Hermes* 34 (1899) 617-8, 61 (1926) 303; Davies 202-4.

826 **covering Heurippides with gold:** i.e. praising him extravagantly (cf. *Clouds* 912 "you're spangling me with gold"); the metaphor may be based on the gilding of statues (cf. J.E.G. Whitehorne, *G&R* 22 [1975] 111).

828 **the same old story:** lit. "Corinthus, son of Zeus", a catch-phrase meaning "something we've heard many times before" (cf. *Frogs* 439 with scholia, Pind. *Nem.* 7.105 with scholia, Pl. *Euthyd.* 292e, Ephorus *FGrH* 70 F 19, Demon *FGrH* 327 F 19), said to have originated at the time of a dispute between Corinth and Megara, when Corinthian ambassadors harped *ad nauseam* on the disrespect being shown by the Megarians to Corinthus son of Zeus, the eponymous hero of Corinth.

829 **covering Heurippides with pitch:** a preliminary to having him (here metaphorically) burnt alive, cf. Aesch. *Cho.* 267-8, *trag. adesp.* 226a, Pl. *Gorg.* 473c, Cratinus fr. 201, 397.

832 **piss over me:** i.e. treat me (sc. and all men) with arrogant contempt, in revenge for the way men have so long treated them; cf. on 640. The speaker's fears are strikingly belied, before he has said another word, by the Heraldess's announcement inviting all male citizens to feast.

833 **the pole:** hanging from this pole, which the slave will be carrying over his shoulder (like the slave on the "Berlin Heracles" vase, formerly Berlin Staatl.Mus. F3046, which seems to depict the opening scene of *Frogs*; see O.P. Taplin, *Comic Angels* [Oxford, 1993] 45-47 and pl. 13.7), will be a sack or sacks containing all the goods brought out of the Neighbour's house except for the two three-legged tables (744, 784-7) which will be carried separately by the other slave.

834-852 HERALDESS: cf. 713.

834 **because that's the way it is now:** whereas formerly meals had been provided at public expense (in the Prytaneum) only as a special honour (e.g. to Olympic victors, descendants of the "tyrannicides" Harmodius and Aristogeiton, distinguished foreign visitors, and occasionally to successful generals; cf. *Ach.* 124-5, *Knights* 280-3, 1404-5, *Peace* 1084, *Frogs* 764, Pl. *Apol.* 36d-37a, *IG* i^3 131).

835 the Lady General: hitherto Praxagora's title has been *stratēgos*; here and in 870 she is given the feminine designation *stratēgis*, which is said to have been used by Pherecrates (fr. 269) – possibly in *Tyrannis* (see Introduction, p. 9 and note 42) – but which in ordinary usage meant "ship in which a fleet commander was sailing" (Thuc. 2.84.3, Andoc. 1.11).

836 so that you can be entered ... to dine: cf. 681ff.

840 the couches: on which the diners would recline (cf. on 675); there will be ample provision for their warmth and comfort (cf. *Wasps* 675-7 where "rugs" [*dapides*, as here] and also "pillows" figure among the mainly symposium-oriented bribes in kind said to be offered to Athenian politicians by the subject states of the Athenian empire).

841-2 the women perfume-sellers are standing in a row: not of course to *sell* perfume (since no one now has money to buy perfume or anything else), but to supply it free to the incoming diners (cf. Pherecrates fr. 105); on the use of perfume at symposia, see Athenaeus 15.685c-692f.

842 fanned on the fire: i.e. cooked over a fire which is being fanned to keep it strong (cf. *Ach.* 668-671, Eubulus fr. 75.7, both also on cooking fish).

843 hare: frequently mentioned as a delicacy (*Ach.* 1006, 1110-2; *Knights* 1192ff; *Wasps* 709; *Peace* 1150, 1196).

843 cakelets: Greek *popana*, small, flat, round cakes, which elsewhere in Ar. appear only as religious offerings (*Thesm.* 285, *Wealth* 660, 680) but which were also made for human consumption (cf. Pl. *Rep.* 455c).

845 juniors: Greek *neōtatai* (feminine), whose masculine equivalent (*neōtatoi*) was a military term denoting under-age soldiers (cf. *Knights* 604-5, Thuc. 1.105.4; also called *peripoloi*, cf. *Birds* 1177, Eupolis fr. 340, Thuc. 4.67.2-5, 8.92.2) who normally performed patrol and garrison duties, but sometimes went on campaign as light troops (Thuc. 4.67) or for non-combatant duties such as digging and foraging (*Knights* loc.cit.) or, as this passage implies, cooking.

845 pea-soup: Greek *etnos*, a soup normally based on vegetables (especially pulses), to be distinguished from meat soup (*zōmos*). After 846-7, however, an allusion will be discerned, in retrospect, to vaginal secretion (cf. *Lys.* 1061, and *zōmos* in *Peace* 716, 885). Henderson 144 detects sexual *double-entendres* also in the food items listed in 842-4, but there is nothing in the words used that would indicate this to a listener, any more than in numerous other comic descriptions of banquets and preparations for them. Pl. com. fr. 188 (from *Phaon*, also produced in 391), cited by Vetta as a parallel, differs fundamentally in that (i) the speaker is almost certainly Aphrodite (see R.M. Rosen in G.W. Dobrov ed. *Beyond Aristophanes: Transition and Diversity in Greek Comedy* [Atlanta, 1995] 132-3), who is giving a list of "offerings" to be made to herself and her subordinate divinities (cf. *Ach.* 792-4, *Birds* 565, *Lys.* 898) and (ii) the first item in her list, *plakous enorkhēs* (lit. "a flat-cake with testicles"), gives a further clear hint that what follows is to be given a sexual interpretation whenever possible.

846 Smoeus is otherwise unknown (the "information" offered in the scholia is transparently guesswork based on the text), but evidently had the reputation of being addicted to cunnilingus (cf. Ariphrades in *Knights* 1280-9, *Wasps* 1275-83, *Peace* 883-5). His name does not recur at Athens.

846 wearing a cavalry outfit: he has chosen this, or been assigned it, from among the stock of surrendered property. Cavalrymen were typically young and rich (like the chorus of *Knights*, or the speaker of Lysias 16), so it is likely that Smoeus was middle-aged to elderly and/or poor. There may be an allusion to the "equestrian" sexual position (woman astride man; cf. *Wasps* 501-2, *Peace* 899-900, *Lys.* 60, 676-8, *Thesm.* 153); this is not, however, mentioned elsewhere in connection with cunnilingus.

847 licking the women's bowls clean: cf. *Knights* 1285 ("licking 'the abominable dew' in brothels"), *Peace* 885 ("he'll fall upon her and lap up her broth"); "bowl" (Greek *trublion*) = vulva + labia as a container for "soup" (cf. on 845). See Henderson 143-4, 185-6.

848 Geron (*LGPN* 1) is again unknown, and the name (which means "old man") may be corrupt; it is not otherwise found at Athens before Roman imperial times. Might the man described here be the Hieron of 757, the humble and despised auctioneer now acting and dressing like a young aristocrat? It would be very easy for ΙΕΡΩΝ to become ΓΕΡΩΝ, especially since the person spoken of clearly *is* an old man.

848 light sandals: Greek *konīpodes* "dusty-feet", skimpy sandals that covered only a small part of the foot and exposed most of it to the dust of the streets, suitable for social evening wear when one was only going to walk a short distance (see Stone 233). The mss. actually have the singular form *konīpoda* (accusative case), which could be right (cf. the singular *embas* "rough shoe" in 850); but the Suda (κ2035), whose entry seems to be based on a fuller version of the scholia, refers to *konīpoda* as an *alternative* reading, implying that the *text* known to the compiler read something different.

848 fine cloak: Greek *khlanis*, a fine outer garment worn on special occasions such as weddings (cf. *Birds* 1693) and festivals; see Stone 163-4.

849 with another young man: the point is that Geron, though not himself a young man, is behaving like one; as often, the triumph of the comic project results in the rejuvenation of the old (cf. *Knights* 1316-end, *Wasps* 1299-end, *Peace* 335-6, 349-353, 860-2, *Wealth* 757-761; see Introduction, pp. 22, 32).

850 old coat: Greek *tribōn*, a coarse outer garment worn mainly by poor men (Stone 162-3); cf. *Wasps* 1131-2, *Lys.* 278, *Wealth* 714-5, 842-6, 882.

851 barley-cake: a cereal-based food (*sītos*) was the staple of every meal, to which all the other items served as relish (*opson*); see Davidson 20-26. *Sītos* and *opson* were brought in together at the start of a dinner (cf. Athenaeus 3.109b with 116a).

852-862 The Dissident suddenly becomes very willing to obey the decrees of the City (contrast 758-768) when, and to the extent that, he sees a chance of getting something for nothing out of them!

858 then what will it be?: Greek *ti dai?*, "in a question motivated by what precedes" (Denniston 263); *dai* is very liable to corruption (e.g. of its seven or eight occurrences in *Frogs* there is not one in which it appears in all mss.), and it has become *dē* (the mss.' reading here) in R at *Clouds* 656 and in most mss. at *Peace* 929.

862-6 echoes 799-804 with the roles reversed.

863 I'll lower my head and charge them: like a bull or a boar, cf. *Frogs* 804 and see Taillardat 206-7.

863 if they flog you: the Scythian archers (see on 143) carried whips in addition to their bows and quivers (cf. *Thesm.* 933, 1125, 1135) and were entitled to use them, on the instructions of a state official, against persons openly defying state authority (e.g., in *Thesm.*, attempting to release a condemned criminal). The Neighbour assumes that the new women rulers would use similar methods to deal with violence against themselves such as the Dissident envisages.

864 if they laugh at that: as they surely would: the Dissident would have no cause of action against them, for the flogging would have been perfectly legal (see previous note); what is more, he would be facing a female magistrate at the preliminary hearing and a female jury (cf. 460) if the case ever came to trial, and, being subject, as a man, to all the disabilities formerly imposed on women (cf. 1024-5), he would not even be able to plead his own case in court. The Dissident, recognizing that his first idea of forcing his way into the dining-hall is likely to fail, now adopts an alternative plan (865-6).

866 **snatch the food from the people bringing it in:** implying that the food for the first communal meal will have come from the stores of individuals who have surrendered it to the community with the rest of their property.

867 **then you can come *after* me:** sc. so that I will have had my dinner before you start snatching food brought in by others.

867-8 **Sicon ... Parmenon:** Parmenon ("he who sticks by one", "loyal, trusty") is a regular name for a slave in later comedy (e.g. in Menander's *Samia*; cf. Men. fr. 300, 373, 798, 901, Philemon fr. 45, *com.adesp.* 1035.22, 1089.12, Terence's *Eunuchus*, *Adelphoe* and *Hecyra*, and the Mytilene mosaic of Menander's *Theophoroumene* [*CGFP* 143]). Sicon ("Sicilian"?) is also a slave-name in Middle Comedy (Eubulus fr. 123, Alexis fr. 25.4; cf. the calyx-krater from Paestum published by A.D. Trendall, *JHS* 55 [1935] 48-50 and pl. 6b = *com.adesp.* 63), but in Menander's *Dyskolos* it is borne by a cook (cf. Sosipater fr. 1.14); the status of the title-character of Ar.'s *Aeolosicon* is not clear.

868 **worldly goods:** Greek *pampēsiā* "whole possessions", a tragic word (Aesch. *Seven* 817, Eur. *Ion* 1305).

871 **you may claim ... that my goods are yours:** and therefore that, having surrendered them, you (and not I) are entitled to dine.

872 **I certainly need some scheme:** he has already thought of, and had to abandon, three plans (to force his way in to the meal, 860-4; to snatch food at the door, 865-6; to use the Neighbour's property, instead of his own, to secure admission, 869-871).

873 **these people:** not the Neighbour and his slaves (for the slaves are not members of the new commonwealth – cf. 651-2, 721-4 – and will not be sharing in the communal feasts), but, more generally, those who are obeying the new law.

874 **the communal meal that's being prepared:** lit. "the things that are being communally kneaded", with reference primarily to the (kneaded, uncooked) barley cake (*māza*) mentioned in 851.

875 **that's got it right:** many modern spectators and readers find it objectionable that the Dissident is thus made to depart with a thought-out plan for gaining entry to the communal dinner without giving up his property, a plan, however, of whose nature, and whose outcome, we are never informed. However, it is not uncommon in Ar. for characters who have been worsted to depart threatening to avenge their discomfiture or frustration, after which neither they nor their threats are heard of again; cf. 1044, *Clouds* 1254-5, *Wasps* 1332-4, 1441, *Birds* 1052, *Wealth* 608-9, 944-950. The unique feature of this scene is not that the Dissident believes he will be able to turn the tables on the supporters of the new order, but that he is allowed to have the last word in the scene; it should, however, be remembered that the scene was followed by a choral song (cf. on 876/7) which may have commented on his selfishness and predicted his deserved failure.

875-6 **get into the thick of things on the dinner front:** lit. "come to grips for the purpose of dining"; the Greek adjective *homose* "to the same place, to grips" often refers to closing with an enemy in battle (cf. 863, *Lys.* 451, Thuc. 2.81.5, Xen. *Anab.* 3.4.4). The phrase gives no clue to the scheme the Dissident has in mind, telling us only that he is going to go immediately to where the action is.

876/7 The arguments for positing a choral song between 729 and 730, as indicated by R, apply even more strongly here, since a substantial time interval has to be posited between the two scenes 730-876 and 877-1111. At the end of the former scene the Neighbour (and, we are to understand, many others) were on their way to the Agora for dinner, while at the beginning of the latter one the dinner, and the drinking that would follow it (cf. 948), are over and the diners are believed to be already on their way home. Moreover, the houses seen on stage have changed identity, representing now the residences of women apparently unconnected with any characters who have appeared previously (see next note).

877-1111 As the previous scene illustrated the institution of communism in property, so this one will illustrate the institution of communism in sex. The women who figure in this scene, though they speak and act like *hetairai* (compare the old woman of *Wealth* 959-1096, whom her reluctant toy-boy estimates [1082-3] to have had thirteen thousand lovers), are not in fact *hetairai* (for all commercial sex has been outlawed, cf. 718ff) but women of citizen status. None appears to be living, or to have recently been living, in a household headed by a man: like the garland-seller of *Thesm.* 443-458, and possibly the spinning-woman of *Frogs* 1331-63, they represent a substantial submerged class of citizen women, of whom speeches and inscriptions tell us little, who were "devoid of a guardian or relatives" (Antiphanes fr. 210) and had to make their own living as best they could. The three old women are presumably to be taken as widows living alone; the young girl is living with her mother (912-3). At least three, and probably all, of the four have residences represented by parts of the *skēnē*. The Girl appears at an upper level (cf. 962 "run down"), i.e. at a window, no doubt the same one at which the Neighbour appeared in 327-356; this leaves the three ground-floor flats, as it were, to be distributed among the three old women, and it will be most convenient if the First Old Woman is assigned the central door, leaving the two flanking doors to form a symmetrical background for the tug-of-war between the Second and Third. The Girl's apartment is reached via a door at stage level (962-3, cf. 989) which must be identical with the door of one of the old women if they all have onstage residences, but this does not compel us to suppose that one of them must live offstage: the Girl's door can become that of the Third Old Woman, who makes her (completely unexpected and unforeshadowed) appearance at 1065, well after the Girl has vanished beyond recall. I have placed the Girl, and therefore the window, on the *right* side (the side further from the Agora) because the Old Woman identifies Epigenes at 934 but the Girl does not do so till 951, suggesting that she has a more distant view of him.

878 **white-lead:** Greek *psimūthion* "lead carbonate" (on its preparation see Thphr. *On Stones* 56), used both to whiten the complexion (cf. on 732) and to conceal wrinkles (cf. *Wealth* 1064-5, *AP* 11.408).

879 **a saffron dress:** see on 332.

883 **in the Ionian style:** in connection with music and poetry, "Ionian" implied "luxurious, voluptuous, effeminate" (cf. *Thesm.* 163, Athenaeus 12.524f-526d) and/or "sexually suggestive" (cf. Pl. com. fr. 71.14; Athenaeus 13.573b-c, 14.620e-621b).

884 **you rotting hulk:** lit. "O decaying one"; so again 926.

885-6 **strip an unwatched vineyard:** i.e. achieve success unopposed; cf. *Wasps* 634.

888 **even if the audience find that tiresome:** this should not be taken (as by Vetta) as evidence that song in drama was becoming unpopular in the 390s: if that was Ar.'s reading of spectator opinion, why did he go out of his way to include *two* lyric duets (893-923 and 952-975) in the present scene, following quite closely after a choral song (see on 876/7)? Rather, as Rogers saw, Ar. is confident that the audience's reaction to the suggestion that they may find the songs tiresome will be to shout out that they won't; cf. *Lys.* 1218-21 where a character at first refuses to perform a piece of slapstick because it is "vulgar" but then relents ("if it's absolutely necessary ... to do you a favour") in the face, evidently, of protests from the audience which the script had been deliberately designed to elicit.

890 talk to *that*: as often (e.g. *Clouds* 1146, *Lys.* 863), the text uses a demonstrative pronoun to refer to an object which the audience could see, with the result that we as readers cannot identify the object with certainty: here we know only that the object is masculine or neuter in grammatical gender, that the invitation to talk to it is an insult, and that, in view of the whole tenor of the scene, the insult is likely to have some sexual content or connotation. The most plausible identifications of "that" are (i) the speaker's anus (for farting in a person's face as a gesture of contempt, cf. *Wasps* 618, *Peace* 547, *Frogs* 1074, *Wealth* 617-8), (ii) her middle finger, suggesting that self-administered sexual stimulation is the only kind the girl is likely to get (in this case *dialegesthai* "talk, converse" would bear a sexual sense as in Hypereides fr. 171, Plut. *Sol.* 20.3 and perhaps *Wealth* 1082; see V. Coulon, *RhM* 105 [1962] 20), or (iii) a dildo, which she would throw up to the girl (but 915-7 suggests that dildos have not been mentioned previously in the scene).

891 piper sweetie: this is the first known occasion on which a character in a comedy explicitly addresses the theatrical piper (cf. Men. *Dysk.* 880-1), but this may well be an accident of preservation (characters in flying scenes often address the theatrical crane-operator, cf. *Peace* 174-6, Ar. fr. 160, Strattis fr. 4). O.P. Taplin, *Comic Angels* (Oxford, 1993) 105-110 discusses other cases where the theatrical piper *may* have been addressed or referred to by characters or choruses in Old or Middle Comedy; in most cases the evidence is poor or even adverse (see e.g. my note on *Thesm.* 1160-75, and Olson's [in his forthcoming commentary] on *Peace* 950-5), but Nicophon fr. 8 may well be a (near-contemporary) parallel to the present passage. The word translated "sweetie" is *philottarion*, a coined portmanteau formed from *philotēs* "love" (used in addressing cherished friends in Pl. *Phdr.* 228d and frequently in Lucian; see Dickey 138) and *nēttarion* "duckie", an endearment used in addressing a beloved or a child (cf. *Wealth* 1011, Men. fr. 652).

892 a tune to show your quality – and mine: lit. "a tune worthy of me and you".

893-910 Metre: while there is no strophic correspondence (Parker 538-9 posits correspondence between 900-5 and 906-910, but this requires at least two otherwise unmotivated emendations) the rhythm is consistently trochaic, except that several times in the second and third stanzas (902, 905, 908, 910) and possibly in the first (898; on the metrical difficulties of the transmitted text here, see Parker 536-7) a trochaic run is ended by an aristophanean (–∪∪–∪– –).

898 my boyfriend: lit. "the (male) friend whom I was with", the relative clause being indefinite (verb in optative mood) and thus indicating that the reference is not to a particular person but to any man with whom the speaker might have a relationship.

899/900 The last line of the Old Woman's song is a complete trochaic dimeter, a verse-form which is not normally final; a similar verse does appear at the end of a song in *Wasps* 1014, but here it is at least as likely that the Girl interrupts the song (cf. *Clouds* 706/7; see Zimmermann ii 64).

903 firm breasts: Greek *mēla*, lit. "apples" or "quinces"; cf. *Ach.* 1199, *Lys.* 155, *Thesm.* 1185 ("like a turnip"), Crates fr. 43, Cantharus fr. 6, Theocr. 27.50.

904 plucked: the reference here (contrast 724) must be to something the Girl can see, i.e. to the removal of *facial* hair; this is confirmed by the ancient lexicographers (e.g. Hesychius π566 Schmidt), who associate the Greek verb used here specifically with the plucking of *eyebrows*.

904 plastered: the Greek verb is the same as that translated "well-powdered" in 732 (see note there).

905 the darling of Death: the first appearance of a theme that will pervade this scene throughout; for the particular variant of it found here (Death as the *lover* of the aged and ugly) cf. 994-7.

906 may your hole fall out: she is wishing upon the Girl an affliction that was all too common among older women, a prolapse of the uterus or bladder, which can result in internal tissues hanging out of the vulva and making intercourse difficult and unpleasant or even impossible; cf. Hippocr. *Gyn.* 144, 145. Archilochus fr. 66 ("a growth between the thighs") may have a similar reference.

907 may you lose your lie-upon: Greek *epiklintron* normally denotes the headrest of a bed or couch (cf. Ar. fr. 41, *IG* i^3 422.286, Pollux 6.9; see W.K. Pritchett, *Hesperia* 25 [1956] 232-3); but it is hard to see how losing a headrest would prevent the Girl from satisfying her desires, or (if *apoballein* here means "throw away" rather than "lose") how, if she was suffering from the affliction described in the previous note, throwing away her headrest would serve to remedy it. More likely *epiklintron* is here being used in its literal sense "something to recline on", with reference to a body-part; i.e. "may you lose your bum". Cf. Semonides fr. 7.71-76 on the ugly "monkey-woman" who is "short in the neck ... fixed legs, no bum" (tr. M.L. West, *Greek Lyric Poetry* [Oxford, 1993] 18); on the erogenousness of buttocks cf. 965, *Peace* 876, *Thesm.* 1187, Alexis fr. 103.10-12, Athenaeus 12.554c-e.

909 draw a snake to your arms: the mss. read "find a snake and draw it to you", which is highly dubious in metre and bad in sense: no sane person, finding a snake in her bed, would draw it to her arms and attempt to kiss it! If we accept Wilamowitz's deletion, which restores a trochaic trimeter (as in 897 and 903), the curse is that the Girl, in bed with her lover, will draw him towards her *and find that he has turned into a snake*; it is probably relevant that *ophis* "snake" can refer metaphorically to a treacherous lover (cf. Theognis 602 and Philostratus, *Life of Apollonius* 4.25; the word could also, at least later, mean "penis", cf. *AP* 11.22.2, but the Greek texts cited by Henderson 127 give no support to his claim that it denotes specifically a *limp* penis, and its phallic sense, if it had one in Ar.'s time, is therefore probably irrelevant here).

911-923 This portion of the duet falls into two halves (911-7 and 918-923) which seem in part to correspond metrically and in part not to; both metre and text are often very uncertain. Each half can be divided into three portions:

(i) 911-3 and 918-9: basically iambic, with extensive syncopation (i.e. omission of short syllables), so that the basic iambic *metron* ⏑–⏑– can be reduced to –⏑–, ⏑– –, or even – –. The "strophe" is much longer than the "antistrophe" (ten *metra* against four, on the text here adopted); nothing in 918-9 suggests that the text there is incomplete, and nothing in 911-3 (except its last word, here deleted; see on 913) shows any real sign of being interpolated. It seems impossible to suppose that these sections were designed to correspond; the mismatch between them may be connected with the probability that 911-3 is a quotation from a popular song.

(ii) 914 = 920: an iambic trimeter, probably spoken rather than sung.

(iii) 915-7 = 921-3: these two sections, as transmitted, match exactly, except at one point (in 917) where emendation is necessary anyway on grammatical grounds. The rhythm is aeolic (thus the first verse, – – –⏑⏑–⏑–, is a glyconic, one of the commonest aeolic verse-types), but the sequence of verse-types is susceptible of more than one analysis and is in any case very unusual (see Parker 540-3; I follow the analysis she hesitantly prefers, which is that of U. von Wilamowitz-Moellendorff, *Griechische Verskunst* [Berlin, 1921] 478).

911-3 "Ah me ... somewhere else": these lines bear no relation to the argument between the Girl and the Old Woman, and are probably part of a popular song (for the theme cf. Sappho fr. 168b).

912 boyfriend: Greek *hetairos* "(male) companion"; cf. on 609-610.

913 my mother's somewhere else: the mss. add an extra word at the end, giving the sense "my mother's gone somewhere else", which spoils the structure of the verse (six long syllables, or three maximally syncopated iambic *metra*, identical with 912; see on 911-923). Either (i) as assumed here, the extra word is a gloss wrongly incorporated in the text (cf. J. Jackson, *Marginalia Scaenica* [Oxford, 1955] 109) or (ii) it is the beginning of a new verse which the Girl leaves incomplete (cf. next note).

914 and I've no need to add what comes after that: either because the song is familiar to all (so Vetta), or because her meaning (viz. that a golden opportunity for a tryst is being squandered) is clear from what she has already said.

915 "Oh, nurse, I implore you": probably a further quotation from the same or another song; the girl in the song is using her nurse as a go-between, like Phaedra or Juliet (cf. *Thesm.* 340-2). To the extent that the line is sung to (or at) the Old Woman it may convey an insult, since to call a woman *maia* "nurse" would imply that she was, or had been, a slave: it is true that *maia* had once been a respectful way of addressing older women (cf. *h.Hom.Dem.* 147), but there is no evidence that it was still so used in classical Attic except by young children (cf. Eur. *Alc.* 393, of a dead mother).

916 invite the Hard Man round: the first word, *kalei* "call, invite", may possibly continue the song-quotation (the girl asking her nurse to go to her lover's house and ask him to come, cf. Lys. 1.20, Theocr. 2.94-103), but from that point on, as the next line shows, the words are being improvised on the spot. The phrase "the Hard Man" renders the Greek name Orthagoras; this was a genuine Athenian name, but is used here (with a play on its first element *orth-* "straight, upright, erect") as a nickname for a device wherewith a woman can "give [her]self some pleasure", i.e. a dildo (cf. *Lys.* 108-9, Ar. fr. 592.16-28, Herodas 6 passim): for the name cf. Orthannes, an erotic divinity in Pl. com. fr. 188.12 and the eponym of a play by Eubulus.

917 "I beg of you": here we are probably back in the song-quotation (cf. 915 "I implore you"), since if the Girl were speaking in her own person she would *advise* rather than *beg* the Old Woman to order a dildo.

918-927 For the assignment of lines in this passage, see M. Vetta, *QUCC* 9 (1981) 95-100. I differ from Vetta, however, when he gives the spoken line 920 to the Girl: a rejoinder by her would probably have begun *su de* ... "and *you* ..." (cf. 930, *Knights* 443, *Clouds* 915, 920, 1277), and continuing the line to the Old Woman is just as effective comically. She first accuses the Girl, in mockingly pitying tones, of being desperate for sex (including oral sex, she adds with climactic contempt, cf. on 470); after which the Girl replies, with a defiant reprise of her melody of 915-7 (see on 911-923), returning to the theme of her first stanza (900-4) – that she has youth and beauty on her side, and that no jealous rival can deprive her of them.

918-9 in the Ionian fashion: cf. on 883.

920 you've got the big L as in Lesbos: lit. "you also *labda* in the manner of the Lesbians" – *labda*, the classical name of the letter L (*lambda* is not securely attested till much later), probably standing for the infinitive of a verb beginning with this letter (so the scholia; cf. H.D. Jocelyn, *PCPS* 26 [1980] 21-22). Reference to Lesbos and Lesbians, in an ancient Greek sexual context, invariably suggests, *not* female homosexuality (the first person known to have used "Lesbian" in this sense is Arethas in AD 914; see A.C. Cassio, *CQ* 33 [1983] 296), but fellatio (cf. *Wasps* 1346, *Frogs* 1308, Pherecrates fr. 136, Strattis fr. 42, Theopompus fr. 36; see Jocelyn *op.cit.* 31-34); hence the verb lying behind the abbreviation is probably the highly obscene *laikazein* "fellate" (cf. *Knights* 167, *Thesm.* 57; it might then be desirable, with Blaydes, to change *kai* to *kān* = *kai an*, to give the sense "you want to suck", parallel to *knēsiāis* "you want to scratch, you itch" in 919, rather than "you suck") or perhaps **laikaseiein* (not attested) a desiderative formation which would mean "want to fellate". The use of a euphemism here may be connected with the fact that women *never* in surviving comic texts actually utter the verb *laikazein* or any of its derivatives, whereas they can use most other primary obscenities freely if no man is present (see my discussion in F. De Martino and A.H. Sommerstein ed. *Lo spettacolo delle voci* [Bari, 1995] ii 78-80; among the sixteen words or word-families there considered, only *kusthos* "cunt", *prōktos* "arsehole", and *pūgizein* "bugger", apart from *laikazein*, are entirely absent from women's speech in comedy). The insult to the Girl is climactic, submission to oral penetration (let alone actual *desire* for it) being the worst imaginable form of sexual degradation (see on 470).

922 **playmates:** Greek *paignia*, lit. "playthings", used of sexual partners in Anaxandrides fr. 9.3 (a woman), Plut. *Ant.* 59.8 (a catamite). In neither of these passages (pace LSJ) is the plural used of one person, and it is best to take it as a genuine plural here also: the Girl quite rightly assumes (cf. 925) that the Old Woman wants to rob her not just of one particular lover but of *all* access to men except, in the phraseology of 634, as "second pressings".

923 **grab a share of:** in classical Greek *apolambanein* does not mean "take away", but it can mean "take a part of" (LSJ s.v. §I 3; cf. Thuc. 6.87.3); if the object ("youth") had been repeated with the second verb, it would have been in the (partitive) genitive case. The Girl is telling the Old Woman that she cannot deprive her of the advantage that youth and beauty give either (i) by destroying that youth and beauty or (ii) by taking some of it for herself: as yet neither side has mentioned the one way in which the Old Woman can and will deprive her rival of this advantage, viz. by invoking the law (first mentioned in this scene at 944).

924 **peep out** shows (cf. 930) that the Old Woman has never gone far from her door, though it cannot be literally true that she is only poking her head out (otherwise she could hardly converse with the Girl at the window above).

924 **like a ferret** (cf. on 792): the point of comparison may, as Ussher suggests, be that the polecat (tolerated around the house for its efficiency in catching mice; cf. *Wasps* 1182 and the papyrus mock-epic *War of the Polecats and Mice* published by H.S. Schibli, *ZPE* 53 [1983] 1-25) "kept stealthy watch ... for a chance to snatch away a tasty morsel" of meat (cf. *Wasps* 363-4, *Peace* 794-6, 1151-2, *Thesm.* 559).

929 **rouge:** Greek *enkhousa* "alkanet", the red dye obtained from the root of *Alkanna tinctoria*. For its cosmetic use cf. *Lys.* 48, Ar. fr. 332.3, Ameipsias fr. 3, Xen. *Oec.* 10.2; in most of these passages, as here, it is mentioned together with white-lead, the two being used in conjunction to create a white complexion with rosy cheeks.

931 **I'm singing to myself a song to ... Epigenes:** lit. "I'm singing to myself to ... Epigenes", i.e. singing to myself a love-song in which he is the addressee. The name Epigenes can be etymologized as "born after", i.e. "young" (cf. V. Tammaro, *Eikasmos* 5 [1994] 133-4); there is no reason to believe that the name is meant to make the audience think of a real individual, since although its bearer is on stage for a long time he is given no characteristics at all that serve to distinguish him from any other young male Athenian. Rather the name should be regarded (like e.g. Blepyrus and Chremes) as a fictitious one, though it does not recur as such in comedy.

932 **Geres** might be thought to be another fictitious name (suggesting *gerōn* "old man", cf. on 848), but the scholia explicitly deny this and state that Geres was a "bald and poor"

man. It is true that the Geres of *Ach.* 605 (*LGPN* 1; a youngish man who had served in the 420s on an embassy in north-western Greece) is also described as bald (and, incidentally, as descended from slaves and as a passive homosexual – perfectly compatible, in ancient Greek eyes, with being a dedicated woman-chaser, cf. Lys. 14.25-28, Aeschines 1.75) by the scholia there, so ancient commentators seem to have identified the two men; but they may have been right to do so (no other Athenian named Geres is known, and if our man was about forty – not unduly young, even for an ambassador – in 426/5 he would be in his middle seventies by 391; compare the painter Pauson, who is satirized in *Ach.* 854 and thirty-seven years later in *Wealth* 602). The Girl's assumption that Geres is the *only* possible boyfriend the Old Woman could have tells against the view that he merely represents the typical old man; rather we may infer that he was (or could be thought of as) so exceptionally ugly and/or poor that no woman, unless totally desperate, would be prepared to look at him.

933 **he'll show you:** or, with the mss., "you'll <soon> think so yourself too", which is, however, a curiously weak way for the speaker to anticipate her coming triumph (why "think" rather than "know", which Ar. could easily have written?).

934 **you old ruin:** Greek *ō (o)lethre*, lit. "O destruction", which can mean "person deserving destruction" (cf. Eupolis fr. 406, Men. *Dysk.* 366, *Sam.* 348) but may here, like *ō tumbe* "O tomb" (*Lys.* 372), mean "person close to death"; it is striking that when *olethros* denotes a person in Ar. it always refers to an *old* person (cf. *Lys.* 325, *Thesm.* 860).

935 **Miss Anorexia:** Greek *phthinulla*, lit. "little consumptive" (cf. *phthisis* "consumption"). The Old Woman (padded to look ludicrously fat, like most old men and women in terracottas and vase-paintings illustrating comedy; see e.g. Stone 127-143 and figs. 1-5, 8-14, though Stone wrongly follows Ussher in supposing, on the basis of a far-fetched interpretation of 1002, that this particular character is *not* fat) is jealous of the Girl's slim and well-proportioned figure, and affects to regard it as due to chronic disease (cf. on 330).

937 **more confident:** *mega* (comparative *meizon*) *phronein*, lit. "think big(ger)", usually means "be proud(er)", but in appropriate contexts it need mean no more than "be (more) self-confident", e.g. in Xen. *Hell.* 3.5.21 where an army that has been put to flight, but learns next morning that most of the enemy have gone home and recovers its morale, is said *meizon phronein* (so again *ib.* 22, after the arrival of new allies).

938-945 Metre: each character sings an aeolic stanza in the metre of, and doubtless to the melody of, a whole series of Athenian symposiac songs (*skolia*), most famously the *Harmodius* skolion in honour of the "tyrannicides" Harmodius and Aristogeiton (quoted in several different forms, *PMG* 893-6 and *Wasps* 1226; alluded to in *Ach.* 1093, *Lys.* 632, Ar. fr. 444); the stanza comprises (i/ii) two lines of the form – – –⏑⏑–⏑–⏑– – (phalaecian hendecasyllable), (iii) ⏑⏑–⏑– –⏑⏑–, (iv) –⏑⏑–⏑– –⏑⏑–⏑– ("dodrans A" twice). "The two singers [thus] trumpet out their conflicting assertions of civil rights to the tune of the anthem of Athenian democracy" (Parker 544-5), one emphasizing freedom (941), the other legality and popular sovereignty (944-5); the exchange is reminiscent of the symposiac game of song-capping, exemplified in *Wasps* 1222-49.

938 **the young one:** the Girl, listening to this from inside, cannot be sure that *she* is the young one meant (similarly when Epigenes speaks of "the pretty one" at 947); he has not yet seen her (nor has he seen the Old Woman – who is nearer to him, cf. on 877-1111 – otherwise he would not refer indefinitely to "*an* old woman or one with a turned-up nose"), and for all she yet knows he might be making for another house further on.

940 one with a turned-up nose: cf. on 617.

942-5 Whether it is to be understood that the Old Woman is singing this for Epigenes to hear is of little importance to the action, since he takes no notice of her, and if he had he would have learned nothing that he does not know already. Probably she does mean him to hear, since the desire to remind him of his legal duty provides a motive, otherwise lacking, for her reappearance. She should certainly sing at least as loudly as he did: she is legally more powerful than he, and physically she will prove strong enough to drag him off (1037), so she ought to be heard to defeat him vocally.

942 you'll howl: i.e. you will be severely punished.

942 if you do screw her: sc. first. The last five syllables of this line (*Dia spodēseis*, lit. "[by] Zeus you will screw"), are almost identical to the last five syllables of 939 (*diaspodēsai* "to screw [through]").

943 the days of Charixene clearly means "the olden days", but who was Charixene? She is mentioned by Cratinus fr. 153 (an unidentified woman "doesn't know that these things are no longer as they were in Charixene's time") and Theopompus com. fr. 51 (a girl piper plays old-fashioned tunes "like those of Charixene's time"). Ancient lexicographers (e.g. *Et.Mag.* 367.21, Hesychius ϵ5413) tell us nothing that could not be guesswork based on the known comic texts. All the three passages are compatible with, and two of them (the present one and Theopompus *loc.cit.*) give some positive support to, the hypothesis that Charixene was a *hetairā*, and her name ("she who gratifies strangers/visitors") would be appropriate for one; I therefore agree with *LGPN*'s view that she was a famous *hetairā*; she may have lived in the late sixth century (at any rate early enough to have been associated with long-past times by the early 430s when Cratinus' *Odyssês* was produced), and with the passage of time become a semi-legendary and proverbial figure like her near-contemporary, the aristocratic matriarch Coesyra of Eretria (*Ach.* 614; *Clouds* 48, 800). The contrast made here between "the days of Charixene" and "democracy" might suggest that Charixene was associated with a pre-democratic Athenian regime; had she perhaps been the mistress of Hipparchus, the "tyrant" (or rather tyrant's brother) whom Harmodius and Aristogeiton had assassinated in 514? Myrrhine, the wife of Hipparchus' brother Hippias, was still well enough remembered in Athens in 424 to be the subject of a joke based on a distorted form of her name (*Knights* 447-9).

946 what he finally does (*ho ti ... drāsei*): or, with RΛ, "what you finally do" (*ho ti ... drāseis*). Either reading makes sense, but *drāsei* has the advantage of being, as it were, equidistant between the reading of RΛ and that of Γ (*drāsoi*, ungrammatical and meaningless in this context): it is more likely that there has been one scribal error in each branch of the tradition than that there have been two in one branch and none in the other.

948 with a few inside: lit. "having drunk"; we may be meant to infer that he needed some drink to give him the self-confidence to bring his long-standing desire to the point of an actual attempt at seduction; cf. Ion fr. 27.9-10 West. Nothing in the text indicates that the two young people had arranged an assignation beforehand (note that the Girl speaks of "the very man *we were talking about*" rather than "the very man *I was expecting*"); rather, each has seen and desired the other, and in the coming duet each will discover with (short-lived) delight that their desire is mutual.

950 thinking I was going to stay inside: both women had initially withdrawn inside till they heard which of them (if either) it was that Epigenes wanted. His song made it very clear that it was not the Old Woman (nor any other old woman), and she then came out to remind him of his legal duty (cf. on 942-5); the Girl lay low, hoping her rival would take her to be admitting defeat, and now, the Old Woman having gone inside again, the

Girl thinks the coast is clear. In fact, however, the Girl will prove to have been herself deceived by precisely the same kind of ruse that she supposes she has successfully practised on her rival.

952-975 This "love-duet" (C.M. Bowra, *AJP* 79 [1958] 376-391) appears to be modelled largely on the genre of love-song later known as the *paraklausithyron*, the song of the "shut-out lover" (*exclusus amator*) outside his beloved's door, a genre which can possibly be traced back as far as Alcaeus (fr. 374; cf. also Eur. *Cycl.* 502) and of which Ovid, *Amores* 1.6 provides a sophisticated later example. Here, however, there are some remarkable reversals, quite apart from the fact that the beloved is a citizen maiden and not, as would be normal, a *hetairā*. Most notably, in accordance with the new social order, the woman takes the initiative and sings first; and though the man does ask for the door to be opened (962-3), and threatens, in true *paraklausithyron* style, to lie down outside it all night if denied admission (see on 963), he already knows that he will not be denied. The mutuality of their desire is strongly emphasized by the verbal repetitions from the song of one to that of the other, which are sometimes extended to the point of illogicality (e.g. at 967-8, "make *her* come to *my* bed"); and the language of the Girl's solo would have been thought by contemporaries far more appropriate on the lips of a man (it could in fact, without the alteration of a single word, have been sung by a man to a boy with whom he was in love – or, with a change of gender in one pronoun, to a girl). See S.D. Olson, *CQ* 38 (1988) 328-330. The repetitions make it appropriate to speak in terms of strophes and antistrophes, even though the responsion outside the repeated sections is far from exact. The rhythm is mainly iambic and trochaic, with syncopation (cf. on 911-923) facilitating passage from one to the other; but in one or two (textually uncertain) sections it seems to be anapaestic (954, 963-4), and 966 is aeolic (an anaclastic hipponactean, o o–x–∪∪– –). The second strophic pair (969-972 = 973-5) is in iambo-choriambic rhythm (based on the units x–∪– and –∪∪–), ending with an aeolic verse, apparently a form of telesillean (∪∪–∪∪–∪–).

952 **come hither:** the Greek phrase (*deuro dē*) was an amatory cliché which passed into Latin slang as a noun meaning "sex-object" (cf. Petronius *Sat.* 58.7).

953 **my love:** the Greek phrase is in the neuter gender (as are similar vocative phrases used by Epigenes in 960, 970 and 1046); this use of the neuter adjective as an endearing form of address may originally have been associated with the affectionate use of neuter diminutives in addressing cherished (or professedly cherished) persons (cf. *Ach.* 475, *Clouds* 746, *Lys.* 872, 889).

954 **fierce** (Greek *deinos*) is a conjectural supplement: in the text as transmitted the adverb *panu* "very" has nothing to modify.

955 **those locks of yours** suggests that Epigenes has the long hair affected by rich young men (cf. *Knights* 580*, *Clouds* 14, *Wasps* 463-470*, *Birds* 1282*, Lys. 16.18*, Pl. *Phd.* 89b) and thought to be very attractive to women (cf. Eur. *Ba.* 235-6, 453-6) – and also, by some, to be a badge of anti-democratic leanings (as in the passages asterisked above; cf. 944-5).

957 **release me:** sc. from torment.

962 **I'll fall to the ground and lie there:** for this *topos* cf. Theocr. 3.52-53; Hor. *Carm.* 3.10.3; Tibullus 2.4.22; and the allusions in Pl. *Symp.* 183a, 203d to "sleeping at doors". The rejected/excluded lover either threatens to lie down and die (Theocr. *loc.cit.*) or spends the night outside the beloved's door, demonstrating a passion too strong for cold, wind or rain to deter.

963-4 **I want ... with your bum:** lit. "I want, in your *kolpos* [see below], to exchange blows (*plēktizesthai*) with your bottom"; the physical explicitness of this sentence (reminiscent e.g. of Archilochus fr. 119) is designedly incongruous with the emotional lyricism that dominates most of the rest of the song. When the word *kolpos* is first heard, it will probably be taken in its most common sense of "lap, bosom"; but in the light of what follows it may well be retrospectively reinterpreted as "vagina" (cf. *Lys.* 1169-70, Pollux 2.222, LSJ s.v. *kolpos* I 2; see J.J. Henderson, *AJP* 95 [1974] 344-7).

965 Cypris: a very common poetic designation for Aphrodite (cf. on 722).

969 my state of distress (Greek *anankē* "necessity, compulsion, pressing need") is one of several touches which cumulatively make it likely, though not certain, that the costume of the actor playing Epigenes included an erect phallus (cf. 978-9, 1020, 1048). In Ar. the erect phallus indicates that sexual release is either eagerly anticipated (*Ach.* 1216-21, *Thesm.* 1187-8, possibly *Peace* 1351) or frustratingly denied (*Lys.* 831-1187); in our scene both these ideas are present together with a third, as the phallus is threatened with being forced into action against the will of its owner. That Epigenes is ithyphallic was first, so far as I know, suggested by D. Sewart in a note to his translation (Open University, Milton Keynes, 1979).

971 open and welcome me: we may be meant to catch a double meaning in these words, an invitation to the Girl to open the "door" of her body (cf. 990, Eur. *Cycl.* 502, Archilochus fr. 196a.21) as well as the door of her house.

973-4 you golden work of art ... the very image of Delight: many of these expressions echo archaic love lyric; cf. Sappho fr. 163, Alcman *PMG* 3.68, and especially Ibycus *PMG* 288.

974 honeybee of the Muses (strictly "of the Muse"): presumably "a compliment to her song" (Ussher); cf. *Birds* 748-751, *Frogs* 1299-1301, Pl. *Ion* 534a-b.

974 Delight: Greek *Truphē* "voluptuousness, self-indulgent pleasure". Delight, like any other abstraction, might at any time be personified *ad hoc* and spoken of as a divinity, and our passage shows that this personification was well established in poetry by Ar.'s time, though there is no other archaic or classical attestation of it; for later appearances of this goddess in literature and art, see Lucian, *The Double Accusation* 23 (where she appears alongside such implausible personages as Stoicism and Moneychanging), Stobaeus 4.31.34, and *LIMC* s.v. Tryphe.

977 strike me dead if I did: lit. "then may I die".

978 torch: since there would be nothing surprising in a man carrying a torch when walking through the streets at night, Vetta is probably right to suppose that the Old Woman is coyly alluding to Epigenes' phallus (cf. on 969); certainly Epigenes' answer suggests that that is how he understands her.

979 a man from Wanksbury: lit. "a man from Anaphlystus", a deme on the Attic coast north-west of Sunium whose name invited puns on the verb *anaphlān* ("get up an erection", whence also "masturbate"; cf. *Frogs* 427 where the name appears together with *Sebīnos* for which see next note). Epigenes knows that if he admits the real reason for his being here, the Old Woman will assert her legal rights over him; accordingly, in the first of a long and varied series of evasions, he tries to pretend that he is not visiting a woman but means to give himself solitary satisfaction.

980 Shagathon: Greek *Sebīnos*. This is, or would be, a personal name of a common pattern (cf. Cratinus, Philinus, Archinus) derived from the root of *eu-seb-ēs* "pious"; but it does not appear to have been in actual use, very likely because it was so liable to be interpreted, as here, to mean "Fuck-you" (from the verb *bīnein* and the second-person pronoun *se*). Here the meaning the speaker intends to convey is clearly "someone willing to sleep with you, never mind who".

981 yes, it is, by Aphrodite: i.e. "yes, I *am* expecting a lover, <and it's you>" – the last clause being expressed by action rather than by words.

982-4 we're not entering cases over sixty ... those under twenty first: Epigenes speaks in the language of decrees relating to the scheduling of court cases. Sometimes in the fourth century a moratorium was placed on certain types of cases, usually because of a shortage of money for jury pay in wartime (thus in the 360s there was for some time a moratorium on all private actions, and in 348 even prosecutions for deserting the army were being stayed: cf. Dem. 39.17, 45.4), and our passage is evidence that there had been such a moratorium not long before the production of *Ecclesiazusae*. The moratorium is not mentioned in surviving court speeches of the period, but the language used here probably explains why not: cases were being prioritized or delayed according to the *value in dispute*. The phrase "under twenty" (lit. "within twenty") corresponds to expressions used in lawcourt contexts to denote the value (in drachmas) in dispute in a case (e.g. "within a thousand", Arist. *Ath.Pol.* 53.3; "within fifty drachmas", Pl. *Laws* 953b); it is likely therefore that the recent moratorium had applied only to cases involving small sums, hence not to those which would have been of concern to leading speechwriters or their clients. The moratorium dreamed up by Epigenes is, of course, based on *age*, and this is signalled in the Greek by the first key word, *huper(h)exēkonteteis*, lit. "over sixty *years*"; and unlike any real lawcourt moratorium, it adversely affects, not those below a specified limit, but those above it.

982-6 entering ... enter: the *double entendre* in the translation is probably also present in the Greek; *eisagein* in a legal context means (of the presiding magistrate) "bring (a case) into court", but just as *hupagein* could in colloquial Greek mean "move" (e.g. *Wasps* 290) and *anagein* "move back" (e.g. *Birds* 383, 400), so *eisagein* could mean "go in, enter" (cf. schol. bT to *Iliad* 6.252).

984 finishing dealing with: lit. "finishing judging, completing the trial of".

987 "at the player's option": lit. "for him who wishes".

987 backgammon: I have used this as the nearest (but a very rough) equivalent of Greek *pettoi*, a generic name for several board games in which pieces were moved according to the throw of (usually three) dice: see –. Lamer, *RE* 13 (1927) 1900-2029, esp. 1967-76. It is likely (so rightly Ussher) that *eisagein* was a technical term of the game (perhaps = "reintroduce a captured piece to the board"?), and that the rules of the game allowed a player to *eisagein* a piece if he wished but did not compel him to do so. The manuscripts (except Γ) offer, and the scholia explain, a different reading which refers to a law of the *Paitoi*, an obscure East Thracian tribe (cf. Hdt. 7.110). It is just possible that this tribe may, in writings that have not survived, acquired notoriety for its sexual customs (like the promiscuous Massagetae and Agathyrsi in Hdt. 1.216, 4.104) and that "for him who wishes" (cf. previous note) had become a catch-phrase in this connection (though against this, note that Hdt. 5.6 claims that unmarried women in Thrace were allowed to sleep with any man *they* wished to); but more likely B's conjecture is correct.

988 you didn't follow ... a question of having dinner: lit. "you didn't dine according to the rules of backgammon, either", i.e. "<the rules of backgammon cannot be invoked to bar my claim on you, because> no more would you have accepted it if they had been invoked to bar your claim to a free dinner" – if, that is, the women had asserted that it was for them to choose whether to feed him or not.

990 when you've *knocked* my door first: for the sexual sense of *krouein* "knock" cf. on 256; for the use of *thurā* "door" (and synonyms) in the sense of "vulva" cf. on 971, and see Henderson 137-8 (although here as elsewhere the warning of Henderson[2] 246 about "the glossarial method" should be borne in mind).

991 we're not wanting to borrow a flour-sieve just now: Epigenes ignores the *double entendre* and takes 990 literally, relating it to the common practice of knocking on a neighbour's door to borrow some household utensil (cf. on 446-9); this explains his use of the first person plural ("we" = the household from which the borrower comes, cf. Men. *Dysk.* 922-3). The choice of a flour-sieve (*krēserā*) as the article to be borrowed is probably suggested by the Old Woman's whitened face (a mirror-image of the sieve/*kanēphoros* joke in 730-3).

992 **that I'm loved:** van Leeuwen's conjecture, "that you love me" (Greek *phileis me* in place of *philoumai*), is very tempting, because the Old Woman's opening words as transmitted would be wide open to the riposte "Maybe, but not by me!"

993 **you found me out of doors:** if a *hetairā* who had committed herself to a monogamous relationship was found roaming abroad at night, her lover would be very likely to suspect that she was seeking other men ...

994-7 ... but Epigenes, contrariwise, affects to fear that *he* is the "other man" whom the Old Woman is pursuing in disregard of an existing relationship, and that at any moment her partner may appear and attack him or her. Cf. Men. *Perik.* 153ff: Glycera, who was living with Polemon, happened to be at her door, sending her maidservant on an errand, when Moschion (whom she knew, but Polemon did not, to be her brother) ran up and embraced her; Polemon arrived at that moment, saw the two part, heard (and misinterpreted) what they said to each other, and in a rage cut off Glycera's hair.

996 **the one who paints jars for funerals** (lit. "for corpses"): see on 538. The phrase is probably not to be taken literally: there were not one, but very many, artists who painted *lēkuthoi* for funerary use, and such an artist would have no more reason than anyone else to become the lover of a decrepit old woman – if anything he would have *less* reason, since on her death he would probably find himself responsible for the funeral and would have to make a batch of jars for which he would not be paid! It has been suggested (N.W. Slater, *Lexis* 3 [1989] 43-47; cf. Taaffe 190 n.48) that the point of the joke is the fancied resemblance between the Old Woman's face (i.e. mask) and a white-ground *lēkuthos* of the kind often deposited in tombs, on which the figures and their features were outlined in black on the white background with some added red: her supposed boyfriend must be a *lēkuthos* painter, because only such a painter could have created the colour-scheme that has been imposed on her face! This is an attractive idea, but it does not meet the objection made above to any literal interpretation of the passage; moreover white-ground *lēkuthoi* were virtually obsolete by 391 (see e.g. R.M. Cook, *Greek Painted Pottery*[3] [London, 1997] 221). Ussher is therefore probably right to identify the painter with Death himself (cf. 905); he "paints" the *lēkuthoi* in the sense of causing them to be painted (cf. *Frogs* 14-15 where certain comic dramatists are said to "carry luggage", i.e. to write scenes featuring slaves carrying luggage), and he is the "best" of painters because "his" products are the only ones that *everyone* sooner or later has to buy.

998 **and I know what *you're* after:** so the mss. (except that they make the second-person pronoun unemphatic – this reflects the judgement of an ancient editor, since written accents did not exist in Ar.'s time); the scholia, however, comment on a different reading which gives the sense "yes, and *I* know what I'm after too" (viz., presumably, to escape from her grip and get to the Girl – though the scholiast's own explanation is "I want you to go away to death"). Both readings make good sense, and either could reasonably provoke the reply that follows.

999 **to whose allotted realm I belong:** i.e. Aphrodite is "my patron goddess" (Barrett); cf. *Peace* 347-8 (campaigning and its hardships are "allotted" to Phormio, i.e. he is their patron hero), Pl. *Tim.* 23d (both Athens and the Egyptian city of Saïs have been "allotted" to, and nurtured and educated by, the same goddess Athena/Neith).

1002 hooks: Greek *kreagrā* (lit. "meat-catcher", i.e. a hook for extracting meat from boiling pots; cf. *Wasps* 1155-6) is here applied to hooks that could be lowered on the end of a rope to extract a water-bucket from a well (also called *harpagai* "grabs", cf. Men. fr. 421, Pollux 6.88). They were shaped like a hand with bent fingers (schol. *Knights* 772); the comparison is with the bent, bony hand and arm that are now gripping the speaker with a force that would be sufficient, he feels, to haul up a very heavy weight.

1006-7 unless you've paid the City 0.2 per cent of what I'm worth (lit. "of what is mine"): this must refer to a tax, probably recently introduced and probably short-lived (no Athenian tax at this rate of "one five-hundredth" is mentioned in any other source). The allusion does not make clear the nature of the tax, but Epigenes implies that if the old woman had paid it he *would* be obliged to follow her, which suggests that he is equating his situation with that of a slave (cf. 1023-4, 1037). Van Leeuwen was therefore probably right to suggest that the tax was one on sales: at so low a rate it would not be worth collecting except on large transactions, and most people would probably pay it only when they bought a new slave (on whom the average tax due would be about two obols; cf. on 593). Epigenes, of course, is not actually a slave and has no purchase price on which the tax can be calculated; so for the value of his person he substitutes the value of his property. This attempt by Epigenes to evade the old woman's clutches, like others later (1023-4, 1027), is based on the laws as they were before the revolution; it is meaningless in the new society where private property and money purchase no longer exist. All such ploys are either rebutted by the old woman with a brief reference to the new order of things (as in 1024-5) or simply brushed aside.

1013 a decree: we are not expected to wonder when this was passed, only to be amused by the very idea of a legal regulation such as this, and by its language which mixes standard Athenian legal phraseology (*edoxe* "resolved by ...", *anātei* "without penalty") with vulgar obscenity. The decree corresponds almost precisely to Praxagora's exposition of her plan (617-8); indeed its first sentence is a paraphrase of 618.

1015 a young man: Praxagora had not specified this; indeed in 619-622 Blepyrus had assumed that the law would apply to him too, and Praxagora did not then say otherwise. Her next proposal, however (626-9), did give sexual privileges to old men over young ones (cf. too 846-7, 1138), and in this scene it is fitting that the law should be phrased so as to apply as closely as possible to the actual case before us.

1017-8 has first screwed ... such pre-screwing: the Greek verb is not *krouein* "knock" as in 990, or *hupokrouein* as in 618, but *prokrouein*, lit. "knock beforehand"; this verb is not found elsewhere in a sexual sense, and is used here purely in order to prepare for the pun in 1021.

1017 her elderly neighbour: lit. "the old woman". The definite article is illogical, since no old woman has been mentioned previously in the decree; probably Ar. has mistakenly copied the phraseology of 618, where "the ugly one" meant "the ugly woman sitting next to the good-looking one" as described in 617.

1020 the peg: on the double meaning of Greek *pattalos* ("peg" and "penis") cf. on 284. To have a woman hale one off in this particular way (cf. *Lys.*1119), using the very emblem of masculine power to exercise control over a man, would be seen by Greek males as an insult of measureless depth.

1021 I'm going to get screwered alive: lit. "I will become a Procrustes", with a pun on *prokrouein* (see on 1017-8). Procrustes (also called Procoptes, Damastes or Polypemon; our passage is the earliest to give him his best-known name) was the brigand who invited travellers to stay with him and stretched or cut their limbs to match the size of his bed; Theseus killed him by his own method (Plut. *Thes.* 11.1; cf. Bacch. 18.27-30, D.S. 4.59.5, Apoll. *Ep.* 1.4).

1022 ***our* laws:** sc. and not your (men's) laws as hitherto.

1023-4 someone from my deme: members of the same deme were expected to be ready to do each other favours; cf. *Clouds* 1214-9, 1322-3, *Lys.* 685, Arist. *Eth.Nic.* 1160a18, and see D. Whitehead, *The Demes of Attica* (Princeton, 1986) 223-234. For the pairing of "friends" and "fellow-demesmen" cf. *Knights* 320, *Clouds* 1209-10, *Wealth* 254; in *Lys.* 333 *dēmotides*, lit. "fellow-demeswomen", seems to *mean* "friends".

1023-4 to go bail for my freedom: lit. "to take me away" (*aphaireisthai*), an abbreviation of the technical term "to take (someone) away to freedom" (*aphaireisthai eis eleutheriān*). When one person seized another and claimed him/her for a slave, any third party could intervene, assert that the person seized was really free, and take him/her under his protection; the intervener would, however, be required to lodge a security deposit to guarantee that he would produce the alleged slave in court when the dispute came to trial. Cf. Lys. 23.9-12; Isoc. 17.14; [Dem.] 58.19, 21; 59.40, 45; Aeschines 1.62; see Harrison i 178-9, 221.

1024-5 no *man* ... over the value of a bushel: a reversal of the actual Athenian law which "expressly forbids a child to make a contract, or a woman beyond the value of a *medimnos* [about 50 litres or 1½ bushels] of barley" (Isaeus 10.10), i.e., at this time, rather less than three drachmas (cf. on 547; barley was cheaper than wheat). The point is that no male would be in a position to lodge a security deposit (cf. previous note; for the purpose of this exchange it is forgotten that no man, or indeed woman, now has any money or property in any case).

1026 an oath of excusal: Greek *exōmosiā*, an oath declaring that one had a proper reason for failing to perform what would otherwise be one's legal duty; normally applied (1) to a witness swearing that he knew nothing of the facts about which he had been called to testify (cf. Isaeus 9.18-19, Dem. 29.20) or (2) to a man elected to public office claiming that illness, pressure of work, etc., made it impossible for him to take the position (cf. Dem. 19.124, Thphr. *Char.* 24.5). The allusion here is probably to (2); the passages cited show that to decline office in this way on any but medical grounds, though legally permissible, was offensive to public sentiment, and the old woman's retort is in line with this attitude.

1027 I'll claim to be a merchant: merchants trading by sea had the right to be tried before a special court (the court of the *nautodikai*) and probably at a time of year convenient to them (cf. Lys. 17.5, where defendants stop a lawsuit by claiming to be merchants and the plaintiff has to bring a new case before the *nautodikai* in the month of Gamelion, during the winter, when sea travel was normally avoided). Thus to claim merchant status gave one a chance of delaying an opponent's lawsuit by anything up to six or nine months; no wonder the informer in *Wealth* (904), when asked if he is a merchant, replies "Yes, I claim to be one, when occasion arises." See E.E. Cohen, *Ancient Athenian Maritime Courts* (Princeton, 1973), esp. 42-59, 162-184.

1029 I absolutely must? – By Diomedes' compulsion!: lit. "And this is a necessity for me? – Yes, a Diomedean one." The proverbial phrase "Diomedean necessity/compulsion", which also appears in Pl. *Rep.* 493d, is said by Hesychius δ1881 to have been first used in the *Little Iliad* (fr. 9) in connection with the theft of the Palladion from Troy by Diomedes and Odysseus. Other sources (e.g. schol. Pl. *Rep.* 493d and Conon, *FGrH* 26 F 1.34) give the details: as the two men were returning to the Greek camp, Odysseus drew his sword to kill Diomedes, but Diomedes saw what he was doing, drew his own sword, tied Odysseus' hands, and forced Odysseus to walk in front of him the rest of the way, driving him on from behind with blows from the flat of his sword: thus a "Diomedean necessity" is a situation in which one has to obey orders or die. I suspect that the old woman may well have reinforced her words with action – though, having no sword, she would have to use the flat of her hand. Hesychius *loc.cit.* also gives an alternative explanation (the only one offered by the scholia to our passage) which takes the reference to be to another Diomedes, the Thracian son of Ares whose mares Heracles captured in the eighth of his labours, and cites from Clearchus of Soli (fr. 68 Wehrli) a story that would be very apposite to Epigenes' situation: this Diomedes, we are told, had daughters who were prostitutes, and forced passing travellers to have intercourse with them until they (the men) were exhausted and helpless, whereupon he killed them. The scholia add, however, that these daughters "are those whom the myth spoke of as man-eating mares", and this stamps the tale as a rationalization of the myth, of a kind that was popular among intellectuals at least from the early fourth century (cf. Pl. *Phdr.* 229c-e) but that cannot possibly have become generally accepted and acquired proverbial status at so early a date. No other source, literary or artistic, early or late, makes Diomedes' horses anything other than horses.

1030-4 Epigenes, professing to believe the old woman is so decrepit that sex will kill her (cf. 1036), advises her to prepare a funeral bier for her *prothesis* (cf. on 537; for details see following notes; contrast 1105-11 where Epigenes gives instructions for *his own* funeral). One or two of the items he mentions, however, would also be appropriate in the context of a wedding, and the old woman chooses to interpret the whole speech accordingly.

1030 marjoram: strictly "oregano" (Dalby 85); Timotheus *PMG* 799 may well likewise refer to the strewing of funeral biers with this herb.

1031 vine branches have been found laid under buried corpses in Athenian graves; cf. A. Brückner and E. Pernice, *MDAI(A)* 18 (1893) 165, 179, 184-5.

1032 put on ribbons: ribbons or fillets (*tainiai*) were often draped over a corpse at its *prothesis*, or attached to funerary monuments; cf. Ar. fr. 205.1 and probably *Lys.* 603, and see R. Garland, *The Greek Way of Death* (London, 1985) 170. But *tainiai* were also associated with weddings: in vase-paintings they sometimes figure in scenes of the bride's preparations, and Eros is often shown flying towards the bride or groom bringing a *tainiā* to deck his/her head. See Oakley & Sinos 12 and figs. 2, 23, 60.

1032 flasks: Greek *lēkuthoi* (cf. 538, 996). The old woman apparently chooses to take the word as referring to flasks of perfume (cf. Ar. fr. 210): perfume had strong erotic connotations (cf. on 524) and bride and groom would both perfume themselves for their wedding (cf. *Wealth* 529; see Oakley & Sinos 16).

1033 the pot of water: for those leaving a house of death to purify themselves with; cf. Eur. *Alc.* 98-100, and see R. Parker, *Miasma* (Oxford, 1983) 35.

1034 you'll buy me a tiara (Greek *stephanē* "diadem"): either the old woman is thinking of the *stephanē* regularly worn by a bride on her wedding day (cf. Eur. *IA* 905; see Oakley & Sinos 16 and figs. 28, 30, 39, etc.), or she is hoping, as a *hetairā* might, to receive one as an expensive present from a grateful lover (cf. Davidson 120-7). The verbal context (see on 1032) suggests the former interpretation; the situational context suggests the latter (for the bridal crown was worn only *before* the consummation of the marriage, whereas here Epigenes is being dragged straight off to bed); and since the idea underlying the whole scene is that citizen women are now behaving like *hetairai*, it is very likely that spectators would be unsure which of the two interpretations to adopt.

1035 one of the wax ones: cf. on 538.

1037-1097 In this scene Epigenes is fought over by three pairs of women (the winner of each contest meeting a new challenger within a few moments of her victory), inverting the common real-life scenario of a *hetairā* (cf. Lys. 4.9, Dem. 54.14) or an attractive youth (cf. Lys. 3 passim, Xen. *Anab.* 5.8.4) being fought over by male rivals (see Davidson 82; K.J. Dover, *Greek Homosexuality* [London, 1978] 56-57).

1037 I'm taking him in here; he's *mine*!: or, with Meineke, "I'm taking him into my house".

1042 you'll fill the whole country with Oedipuses: this assertion is designed to shock the old woman by raising the appalling spectre of mother-son incest, which in Sophocles' *Oedipus Tyrannus* (362-7, 457-460, 791-3, 1207-15, 1256-7, 1288-9, 1403-8) is repeatedly spoken of with more horror even than parricide. This scare-tactic is completely illogical, for Praxagora, unlike Plato (*Rep.* 460b-d), has not been concerned with preventing mothers from knowing who their own children are, nor would any of the rules of her society have that effect; but it works for the second or two necessary for Epigenes to escape from his captor ...

1043-4 ... and when the old woman realizes she has been tricked, it is too late for anything but impotent rage.

1044 I'll get my own back on you yet: the audience will not be surprised when nothing comes of this threat; see on 875.

1048 a long thick reward: *megalēn* "great, big, long", said of a returned favour (*kharis*), might by itself mean no more than "generous", but *pakheian* "thick" ensures that the precise nature of the reward is not left either to the Girl's or to the audience's imagination; for this pair of phallic epithets cf. *Ach.* 787, *Peace* 1351, *Lys.* 23-24.

1050 when it says in black and white: lit. "when the writing has said".

1051-70 In reconstructing the staging of this passage, the key facts to be accounted for are that Epigenes cannot see that the Girl is no longer there (1054-5) and that similarly, when the Third Old Woman appears on the scene, he hears her voice at 1065-6 but does not see her face until 1068. Since one normally looks at a person when one is either appealing for his/her assistance or expressing gratitude for having received it, it follows that at these two moments Epigenes is unable to turn his head, which is most easily explained if the Second Old Woman is holding him in a headlock. On the orientation that I have been assuming, she comes from her door (left) to confront the young couple who are moving towards the Girl's door (right); at that moment, therefore, Epigenes is facing up right, and if he is not to see the Girl running away, she must flee in the direction that is behind him, i.e. left. He knows, of course, that she is no longer at his side, but he does not know that she has disappeared altogether. After this the Second Old Woman begins to march him towards her door (i.e. up left), and accordingly the Third Old Woman, emerging from *her* door (right, cf. on 877-1111), is behind him and he cannot see her.

1056-7 It's not *me* dragging you off, it's the *law*: almost the same words that Euphiletus claimed to have used, a few years earlier, before killing his wife's lover (Lys. 1.26); the old woman, like Euphiletus, is taking advantage of a law that mandates her to do something she very much wants to do. Less disingenuously Iphigeneia, constrained to perform human sacrifices in the land of the Taurians, says that one of her victims "did not think that it was my hand that would be slaying him, but that he was being killed by the [Taurian] law" (Eur. *IT* 585-7).

1056 a sort of Empusa: Empusa was a female monster or bogy who could take many shapes; in *Frogs* 285-306 Xanthias sees her (or maybe pretends to see her) and recognizes her as Empusa because "her whole face is blazing with fire" (293-4). Here, it seems, the Second Old Woman has so much rouge on that her face looks even *more* fiery than Empusa's: Empusa would only look as red as that if she was "covered in bleeding blisters"! For later evidence regarding Empusa, see O. Waser, *RE* 5 (1905) 2540-3.

1058 softie: Greek *malakiōn* is taken by the scholia as a term of endearment, but elsewhere *malakos* "soft" is normally pejorative when applied to males, and probably the old woman is taunting Epigenes for being so unmanly as to be frightened of an ugly face.

1059-60 let me ... go to the bog and give myself some courage: Epigenes professes to want a little time on his own in order (i) to pluck up courage for the ordeal ahead and (ii) to defaecate in decent privacy (for he is on the point of losing control of his bowels from terror, cf. *Knights* 1057, *Wasps* 627, *Peace* 241, 1176, *Birds* 65-68, *Frogs* 308, 479-491). His subsequent offer of sureties (1064-5) shows that he thinks the old woman may suspect that his request is a ruse to enable him to escape from her altogether.

1061 doing something yellow: see on 329.

1064-5 I'll appoint two competent sureties: sc. to guarantee that I will duly return from the privy – as a defendant might in certain cases, to avoid imprisonment pending trial, be required to name sureties (usually two or three) who would guarantee his appearance for trial and be subject to punishment if he failed to appear (cf. Antiphon 5.17 [three]; Andoc. 1.2, 44; Dem. 24.144 [three], 32.29, 59.65-66 [two]). "Competent" renders *axiokhreōs*, lit. "worth the debt", i.e. with means to pay the fine to which they might become liable (cf. Pl. *Apol.* 38b where Socrates names four sureties who he says are *axiokhreōi* to guarantee payment of the half-talent fine he suggests as his penalty). Epigenes once again (cf. on 1024-5) ignores the fact that in the new society there is no such thing as a competent (male) surety.

1064-5 if you want: lit. "for you".

1065 I'm not having any sureties: lit. "don't appoint (sc. sureties) for me".

1068-9 O Heracles! ... O Sons of Zeus!: Epigenes, like many characters in Ar. at moments of alarm or astonishment, appeals to Heracles as "the Averter of Evils" (*Alexikakos*); cf. *Ach.* 94, *Peace* 180, *Birds* 277, *Lys.* 296, *Frogs* 298. The three following invocations are of less frequent occurrence. The Pans (Pan is usually a single god, but cf. Aesch. fr. 25b, Soph. fr. 136, Pl. *Laws* 815c, Theocr. 4.63, D.S. 1.88.3) and the Corybantes (Phrygian divinities attendant on the mother-goddess Cybele) were both thought capable of causing madness (cf. *Wasps* 8, Eur. *Med.* 1172, *Hipp.* 141-4; the reference to the Pans might also suggest "panic" fear, first definitely associated with Pan in [Eur.] *Rhes.* 36-37), while the "Sons of Zeus" (*Dioskoroi*), Castor and Polydeuces (Pollux), were saviours of those in peril (*h.Hom.* 33; Terpander fr. 5 Campbell; Alcaeus fr. 34; Eur. *El.* 1241-2, 1347-53; Callim. fr. 64.11-14; Theocr. 22.5-23). Hence these four appeals indicate that Epigenes is afraid he is going mad (i.e. he momentarily takes the Third Old Woman for a hallucination) and is desperate for divine aid.

1070 another evil creature ... than this one: almost an exact repetition of 1053.

1071-3 For this type of question asked on seeing a bizarre sight ("what is this, an X or a Y?") cf. *Wasps* 1509, *Birds* 102, *Lys.* 982.

1071 I beg you: "you" is not in the Greek, and the question should not be taken to be addressed to anyone in particular.

1072 a monkey: proverbially ugly, cf. Pl. *Hipp.Maj.* 289a, Arist. *Top.* 117b17-19, *AP* 11.196.1; see P. Demont in P. Thiercy & M. Menu ed. *Aristophane: la langue, la scène, la cité* (Bari, 1997) 462-3.

1073 the ... majority: i.e. the dead; cf. Polyb. 8.28.7; Plautus, *Trinummus* 291 *ad pluris penetravi*; *AP* 7.731.6, 11.42.5-6; Paus. 1.43.3. Not only does Epigenes find it impossible to believe that someone looking so ancient is still among the living (cf. *Wealth* 1033-5), but in addition her face is so white that she resembles a (bloodless) ghost (so the pallid Chaerephon is called "half a corpse" in *Clouds* 504, and pictured coming up from the underworld in *Birds* 1564).

1074-97 The assignment of lines in this passage, as between the two old women, is sometimes uncertain, though it is clear e.g. that 1077 must be spoken by the Second and 1078 by the "even uglier" Third. The principles I have followed are: (i) that the winner of the tug-of-war should be the Third Old Woman, to maintain a pattern whereby in this scene the winner of each duel is defeated in the next; (ii) that unprompted references to the law (1077, 1081) should come from the Second Old Woman (cf. 1049-51, 1055-6); (iii) that so far as possible the two women should speak in strict alternation, so that Epigenes, held between them, is constantly turning to look first at one, then at the other. The application of these principles leaves a residual doubt only in 1075, where there is some case for continuing "I tell you, I'm never going to let you go" to the Second Old Woman and giving the retort "Neither am I" to the Third; this would create a strict alternation of speakers in the passage as a whole, but at the expense of the symmetry of thrust and parry in 1074-5.

1076 **curse and blast you both:** lit. "O you (pl.) who will perish miserably".

1077 **you've got to:** the mss.' division of words would give the sense "you ought to" or "you would have to", rather mild and tentative expressions, out of character for a speaker who has always demanded immediate, unconditional obedience to the law, and whose interest it is to convince Epigenes that he has no alternative whatever.

1079 **if I've first been massacred by you two:** lit. "if I first perish miserably by your (pl.) agency".

1080 **how will I ... get to that lovely girl?:** with both his arms held, Epigenes has no way to indicate the direction in which the Girl is now to be found. This is very convenient for the author, since any indication Epigenes might have given would have raised unwanted questions: if the Girl is imagined as being in her upstairs flat, how did she get back there? and if she is somewhere offstage in the direction in which she fled at 1051 or thereabouts (see on 877-1111 and 1051-70), how will Epigenes find her?

1087 **you'd ... bruise them to death:** the scholia explain that "ferrymen compel passers-by to embark on their own boats [sc. rather than on those of their competitors]", and such a scenario, with two ferrymen (say on the Peiraeus-Salamis run, cf. Aeschines 3.158) fighting over a passenger whom each claims as his own, provides the only imaginable situation in which ferrymen might "drag ... passengers about". It is, however, hardly to be credited that, as Vetta implies, such fights, with passengers being injured as a result, were a regular occurrence; more likely Ar. is alluding to a specific recent case which had come to public notice (probably in the courts).

1089 **Cannonus,** son of Sibyrtius, of the deme Lamptrae (*PA* 8249, *LGPN* 2) was a minor politician of the Persian War period; some ostracism ballots cast against him survive (see F. Willemsen, *MDAI(A)* 106 [1991] 152). He was the mover of a decree making regulations for the trial of those charged with "injuring the Athenian people"; they were not only to be imprisoned until trial, but to be tried before the whole people, in bonds and held on each side by a guard, and executed by precipitation into the *barathron* if found guilty (Xen. *Hell.* 1.7.20 and the scholia here). In 406 an unsuccessful attempt was made to have the commanders of the fleet at the battle of Arginusae, who had allegedly failed to pick up shipwrecked men, tried individually under this decree rather than *en bloc* (Xen. *Hell.* 1.7.20-21 and 34); we know of no case in which the decree was actually put into effect – unless indeed it had been activated, and perhaps even expressly designed, for the prosecution of Miltiades in 489 (cf. Bonner & Smith i 205-9).

1090 **held by two warders:** Greek *dialelēmmenon*, lit. "having been seized between [two or more persons]"; cf. Hdt. 1.114.3, 4.94.2, Pl. *Rep.* 615e.

1091 to ply the oar in both holes at once: lit. "to row-with-two-oars both <women>"; for rowing as a sexual metaphor cf. on 39.

1092 bulbs: strictly, the bulbs of the purse-tassel or grape-hyacinth (*Muscari comosum*). These, and also the bulbs of other plants, were considered to be aphrodisiac, partly no doubt because of their testicle-like shape; cf. Pl. com. fr. 188.12, 189.9-10, Alexis fr. 175.3, 281.2, Xenarchus fr. 1.4-6, Athenaeus 2.63e-64b. See E. Degani in A. López Eire ed. *Sociedad, política y literatura: comedia griega antigua* (Salamanca, 1997) 16-19.

1098-1111 The action is in effect suspended to enable Epigenes to deliver this "dying" soliloquy: this is a tragic device comparable, though on a much smaller scale, with Eur. *Or.* 1369-1502 where a Phrygian slave escapes from the palace where Helen has supposedly been murdered and Hermione has been made a hostage, and has "time" to sing an aria of prodigious length before Orestes comes out in pursuit of him. Here the artificiality of the device is more patent than it is ever allowed to be in tragedy, for the three characters must visibly loiter for a considerable time on the Third Old Woman's threshold (Epigenes was already "almost ... [at] the door" at 1093) before they can be allowed to disappear inside.

1098-1101 I see no way to tell from the script alone which of the two women is spoken of first and which second. On stage the identifications could be made obvious by movements of the speaker's head.

1101 a toad: Greek *phrūnē*. The scholia treat this as a proper name (Phryne – which was the name of a famous *hetairā* of fifty or sixty years later), but this is clearly a guess (all they can say about this Phryne is that she was an "ancient woman"), and "toad" (i.e. "hideous creature") gives wholly appropriate sense.

1101 a carbuncle: the Greek word is *lēkuthos*, on which the scholia have the gloss "swollen"; and since *lēkuthos* can denote a swelling in the neck (cf. Clearchus fr. 72 Müller), there is no reason why it should not also have denoted a swelling or boil in the cheek or chin, probably hemispherical and so reminiscent of the small globular vessel used to carry oil for use at the gymnasium, wrestling-school or baths, which Athenians called a *lēkuthos* (cf. *Frogs* 1200-47, Dem. 24.114) though modern scholars call it an "aryballos" (see C. Rolley, *AC* 43 [1974] 168-171). There may be a pun on the two senses of *lēkuthos*, "oil-flask" and "swelling", in *Frogs* 1246-7. Most recent interpreters (Ussher, Vetta; N.W. Slater, *Lexis* 3 [1989] 47-48) have sought to associate the *lēkuthos* of this line with the funerary *lēkuthoi* of 538, 996, 1032 and 1111, but none has convincingly explained how any feature of even an ugly face could plausibly be metaphorically described as a *lēkuthos* of funerary shape. Nevertheless the use of this particular word, even in a different sense, still serves to evoke yet again the aura of death that has pervaded this scene.

1101 on her cheek: lit. "near the jaws", which might also mean on the chin (the audience, of course, could see from the character's mask which was meant).

1102 wretched ... accursed: Greek *kakodaimōn* ... *barudaimōn*, lit. "with an evil attendant spirit ... with a grievous attendant spirit".

1104 to be shut up with wild beasts like these: the Greek verb *sun(kath)eirgein* can be used both (i) of being shut up (e.g. in a cave) with a beast or monster (cf. Philoxenus *PMG* 824, Aeschines 1.182) or (ii) of a bride and groom being shut into the bridal chamber (cf. Pl. *Rep.* 461b, Plut. *Alex.* 2.3). This double sense makes *suneirxomai* "be shut up with" a better emendation than the imaginative sixteenth-century conjecture *sunnēxomai* "swim with" (a sexual metaphor based on the similarity of the body movements involved, cf. Henderson 164).

1105 if ... something does happen to me meant in Greek, as in English, "if I die"; cf. *Wasps* 385, *Peace* 169-170, Lys. 19.51, Dem. 4.11.

1106 these whores: the old women are not in fact prostitutes (see on 877-1111), and if they were they would hardly be likely to attract any clients, but their dress (cf. 879), make-up and demeanour corresponds precisely to that of cheap whores (the Greek word is not the regular *pornai* but the even more contemptuous *kasalbades*) before the revolution.

1106 when I sail into this port: lit. "sailing in hither"; the harbour into which he is sailing is the Third Old Woman's house (not, even secondarily, her vagina, as tentatively suggested by P. Murgatroyd, *CQ* 45 [1995] 11 – though he could have cited Soph. *OT* 422-3, 1208-10 in support; such a *double entendre* could hardly be understood without hand gestures, which Epigenes is still unable to make, and what the audience can *see* is that he is about to be taken through the door and swallowed up in the darkness within).

1107 bury me right at the mouth of the strait: Willems may be right to suspect an allusion to the tomb (or cenotaph) of Themistocles at the entrance to the main harbour of Peiraeus, which may have been begun in 394/3 on the initiative of Conon (Plato com. fr. 199; Plut. *Them.* 32.5-6; Paus. 1.1.2; see P.W. Wallace, *Hesperia* 41 [1972] 451-462, and P. Funke, *ZPE* 53 [1983] 182-3).

1109 cover her alive with pitch: cf. on 829.

1110 pour molten lead over her feet: both (i) as a further torture, and (ii) to ensure that she stands upright (like a statue; cf. Eur. *Andr.* 266-7, and see S. Adam, *The Technique of Greek Sculpture* [London, 1966] 81).

1111 a monumental urn: Greek *lēkuthos* (see on 538), referring this time to the large marble *lēkuthoi* which were sometimes placed over graves (see B. Schmaltz, *Untersuchungen zu den attischen Marmorlekythen* [Berlin, 1970]; C. Rolley, *AC* 43 [1974] 167).

1111/2 In *BICS* 31 (1984) 145 I argued that there was a choral performance at this point (cf. on 729/730 and 876/7; here, however, R does *not* have the note *khorou*), on the not very strong grounds that this would enable the play to be performed by three actors and that the Girl's quick exit at or about 1051 suggested that only three actors were being used – and also because if (as I then believed) there was no choral interlude at 729/730, such an interlude was required here to bring the total number of choral performances (including 289-310 and 478-503) up to four, the number that became canonical in later comedy and apparently in later tragedy also (cf. Horace *AP* 189-190). Once, however, it is accepted that there are no good grounds for rejecting R's evidence at 729/730 (see note there), there are also no good grounds for rejecting the evidence of R's silence here: we do not need to posit a choral performance every time the stage is left empty of actors (cf. *Clouds* 1212/3, *Wasps* 1325/6, Men. *Dysk.* 49/50, 392/3, 455/6, 486/7, 521/2, 665/6, 873/4), and, as Vetta argues, there are actual dramatic advantages in having the Maid's entrance follow the exit of Epigenes and his captors without a break (see next note). Cf. R. Hamilton, *CQ* 41 (1991) 352 (though I disagree with him on *Wealth*, which cannot be performed even by four actors unless there is a choral interlude at 1096/7; see now D.M. MacDowell, *CQ* 44 [1994] 334).

1112-26 There is a sharp, and obviously designed, contrast between this soliloquy ("Oh, happy people! ...") and that of Epigenes ("Oh, wretched, wretched me ..."), the one redolent of misery and death, the other of wine and perfumes. The contrast extends to the scenes as a whole: in the first we saw the young man Epigenes compelled by the new female authorities to become the sexual prisoner of two hideous old women, in the second we see the old man Blepyrus invited by those same authorities, indeed by his own wife, to feast in the company of (at least) two beautiful young women. Thus the conclusion of this play vividly presents the common Old Comic motif of the triumph of age over arrogant youth; see *CQ* 34 (1984) 320-1 = Segal 261-3, and Introduction, pp. 13, 22, 32.

1112 Oh, blest country!: the mss.' reading is "Oh, blest me!", which would not only make the Maid list herself twice in the enumeration (cf. 1116) but would also make her first exclude herself from the group labelled "happiest of all" (1113) and then, a moment later, not only include herself within this group but spend nine lines (1116-24) dilating on her own felicity in the most gushing terms. Dobree's emendation creates a logical progression: all Athens is happy (1112), but my mistress is happiest of all (1113) and next to her all those who have any connection with her (1114-5) including myself (1116ff). It is more likely that a scribe miscopied one letter (which may have been e.g. obscured by a damp spot) than that Ar. spoiled the rhetorical effect of the speech's opening merely in order to indicate that the speaker was drunk (so Ussher) when this was going to be made abundantly clear very shortly in any case (cf. 1118-24).

1113 my mistress: one would have thought it obvious that this can only be Praxagora, the "Lady General" (246, 491, 500, 727, 835, 870) who has been the leader of the women's revolution from the start and the sole elected magistrate (that we have heard of) since they took over power; no other woman has achieved anything in the play except on her orders or in pursuance of her plans, and it is asking far too much of the audience to expect them to imagine that any of these other women, ciphers hitherto, has attained a state of glory and felicity so great that all her "neighbours and fellow-demesmen", and even the "ladies ... standing near [her] door", have a share in it. It follows that the mistress's husband, who is first mentioned at 1125 and comes on stage shortly afterwards, must be Blepyrus. This, however, raises some logical difficulties. Blepyrus went off at 727, following his wife, to the Agora, which is where the communal dinner was to be held; he now returns, obviously not from the Agora (otherwise there would have been no need to send the Maid in search of him), and not having had dinner (1133). Attempts to evade this inconsistency – such as the suggestion by R.G. Ussher, *Hermes* 97 (1969) 36, that Blepyrus changed his mind before reaching the Agora and went off in search of other pleasures, or that by P. Sewart in a note to his Open University translation (Milton Keynes, 1979) that Blepyrus actually *has* had a dinner and is being invited, by a mistake very agreeable to him, to have another – fail because they require the audience to make complex assumptions about characters' offstage activities to which the text itself offers no direct clue. Accordingly U. von Wilamowitz-Moellendorff, *SAWB* (1903) 451-2, E. Fraenkel in *Greek Poetry and Life: Essays Presented to Gilbert Murray* (Oxford, 1936) 270-4, and S.D. Olson, *GRBS* 28 (1987) 161-6 and *CQ* 41 (1991) 36-40, have all held that the Maid's master cannot be Blepyrus: Wilamowitz, and Olson (1987), took him to be an entirely new character, Fraenkel identified him with the loyal citizen of 730-876 (but if Blepyrus is disqualified because he has already gone to the Agora, the loyal citizen should be too), and Olson (1991) with Chremes (who in his view, as in mine, last appeared at 477). None of these scholars succeeds in explaining how this character's wife has come to be spoken of in such exalted terms; only Olson (1987) 161-2 even tries, and he supports his claim that the Maid "does not mark [her mistress] out as in any way unusual" only by citing 1114-6 which actually proves the reverse (see the first sentence of this note). The only satisfactory solution is to accept the inconsistency, which it is unlikely that any spectator in the theatre would even notice (cf. Dover *AC* 193 n.3).

1114 all of you ladies: i.e. the chorus.

1114 near our door: lit. "near the doors", but the speaker must mean the door of her mistress's house, not only because the following two lines likewise define a sphere of special happiness centred on Praxagora (her neighbours, the members of her deme, her servant) but also because the only other interpretation grammatically possible, viz. "near *your* doors", would be inconsistent with the rest of the play (none of the doors of the *skēnē* has at any time been identified as that of the house of any member of the chorus) and arithmetically impossible (there are twenty-four women in the chorus and only three doors in the *skēnē*).

1115 **fellow-demesmen:** cf. on 1023-4. Here, as at 1125, the Maid's linguistic usage is not fully in tune with the principles of the new society. In pre-revolutionary Athens, only men had been registered as members of demes: thus, for example, the father of the speaker of Demosthenes 57 was "Thucritus of Halimûs" (*Thoukritos Halimousios*), but his wife was not "Nicarete of Halimûs" (**Nikaretē Halimousiā*) but either "Nicarete, daughter of Damostratus of Melite" (Dem. 57.68) or "Nicarete, wife of Thucritus of Halimûs"; accordingly Isaeus 8.20 speaks of the men of his father's deme as "the demesmen" and their womenfolk as "the wives of the demesmen". Since registration in a deme was an essential prerequisite for full citizenship with its political rights, this gender distinction would necessarily be reversed when political power was transferred to women; but the Maid still speaks in the old fashion.

1117 **my head's all scented with scents:** cf. on 841-2; this would be an unheard-of luxury for a slave (unless she was employed as a prostitute).

1119 **those darling jars of Thasian:** the wine of Thasos was a much-praised variety (Athenaeus 1.28e-29e) noted for its dark colour (*Lys.* 205, Ar. fr. 364) and its sweet aroma (*Lys.* 206, *Wealth* 1021; Hermippus fr. 77.3). See F. Salviat, *BCH* Suppl. 13 (1986) 145-196; Davidson 42-43.

1120-1 **they stay in your head:** it is not clear whether it is the aroma that is being said to linger, or the intoxication, or (most probably) both.

1123 **mix it neat and it'll give you pleasure ... :** i.e. if you mix it neat, it'll give you pleasure; for this "paratactic" way of expressing a conditional statement cf. e.g. *Wealth* 1027 "speak, and it shall be done". The self-contradictory expression "mix it neat" (lit. "mix it unmixed") is symptomatic both of the speaker's drunkenness and of her ("typically feminine") liking for wine drunk very strong (cf. 227, *Lys.* 197; in Ar. fr. 364 a group of old women are drinking neat Thasian). It was considered improper to drink wine undiluted except, in small quantities, when the initial libation to "the Good Spirit" (*Agathos Daimōn*) was poured at the beginning of a symposium (*Knights* 85, *Wasps* 525, Xenarchus fr. 2); but the rules were sometimes broken (cf. *Ach.* 1229, *Knights* 354-5, Men. fr. 401, *com. adesp.* 101.13; see Davidson 48). The subject of "mix" is singular (i.e. the individual preparing the wine for consumption), but "you" is (feminine) plural (i.e. the women drinking it).

1125-6 **my master – I mean, ... my mistress's husband:** cf. on 727 and 1115: women are now the heads of households and the owners of the household slaves (one might have expected that in a society which has communal property and communal sex, marriage, households and privately owned slaves would have disappeared, but cf. 727, 867-8).

1127-8 **I think you'll be most likely ... on his way to dinner:** Vetta is the first modern editor to have followed RΛ and given both these lines to the chorus(-leader). Previous editors divided them between the chorus-leader ("I think you'll find him if you stay right here") and the Maid ("That's right; here he comes, on his way to dinner"); but this is unsatisfactory. The chorus-leader cannot know in advance that Blepyrus will shortly return to, or come past, his own home (cf. 668-9!): her confident prediction indicates that she has seen him coming, and in that case she, not the Maid, should be the one to identify him.

1128 on his way to dinner: this probably indicates that Blepyrus is wearing a garland (cf. *Wealth* 1041, and see on 691-2); the speaker knows that he is going *to* dinner, rather than coming *from* it, because he is walking towards, not away from, the Agora.

1132-3 numbering more than thirty thousand: a conventional figure for the adult male citizen population of Athens (cf. Hdt. 5.97.2, Men. *Epitr.* 1088-9), but possibly not far from the truth in the fourth century (see M.H. Hansen, *Demography and Democracy* [Herning, 1985]; E. Ruschenbusch, *ZPE* 54 [1984] 253-267, had argued for a considerably lower figure).

1133 the only one who hasn't had his dinner: sc. and therefore still has it to look forward to.

1138 and these girls with you: the scholia, followed by Wilamowitz (*SAWB* [1903] 452) and more recently by J.E. Stephanis, *O doulos stis komodies tou Aristophani* (Thessaloniki, 1980) 64-70, and Thiercy 1310, identify the "girls" (*meirakes* "nubile young women") with the chorus; but (i) as Thiercy sees, this would require the Maid not only to speak 1151-3 and 1166-78 but also (since there is no hint of a change of speaker at 1154) to make the parabasis-like appeal to the contest judges in 1154-62, and more importantly (ii) *meirax* never elsewhere denotes a woman who is or has been married: see E. Fraenkel in *Greek Poetry and Life: Essays Presented to Gilbert Murray* (Oxford, 1936) 266-270. It follows that these "girls" (brought on stage partly for the sake of the dance which they are instructed in 1166-7 to perform) are mute extras, corresponding to the young females who come into the possession of a leading (normally elderly) male character near the end of *Acharnians*, *Knights*, *Wasps*, *Peace*, *Birds* and *Thesmophoriazusae*; the performers probably, but not certainly, wear costumes simulating nudity (cf. B. Zweig in A. Richlin ed. *Pornography and Representation in Greece and Rome* [Oxford, 1992] 73-89). We cannot be certain how many of them there are, but two, as in *Acharnians*, is most likely (cf. also on 1165-6 and 1166-7). Has Blepyrus arrived with them, or has the Maid brought them to him? The former is more logical, since Praxagora could perfectly well have informed her husband that there were girls awaiting his pleasure in the Agora without sending them along with her messenger. In any case, the world has indeed turned topsy-turvy if a wife, instead of bitterly resenting it when her husband brings a mistress into the marital home (this is called *hybris* in [Andoc.] 4.14, and in tragedy it is invariably fatal to the husband: see E.M. Hall in P.E. Easterling ed. *The Cambridge Companion to Greek Tragedy* [Cambridge, 1997] 122), actually invites his casual pick-ups to a dinner presided over by herself, or maybe even acts as his procuress! As promised in 623-634 (cf. 702-9), elderly men are certainly getting the best of things sexually (see *CQ* 34 [1984] 320-1).

1139 Chian wine, which came in several varieties, is sometimes rated even more highly than Thasian (1119): cf. Hermippus fr. 77.5, Athenaeus 1.32f, and see Dalby 100.

1140 don't you dilly-dally: the Greek verb is plural, and must denote the chorus: their words later (1163-5) show that they have been included in the dinner invitation, and this is the only part of it that could refer to them.

1142 who isn't turning his eyes away: sc. because he is already committed (through friendship or through corruption) to vote for another play.

1146 old men, youths and little boys alike: i.e. the whole audience (or at least all spectators who are male and of citizen status). For somewhat more elaborate classifications of (this portion of) the audience cf. *Peace* 50-53 and Pl. com. fr. 222; Menander's plays seem regularly to have ended with an appeal for applause directed to "youths, (pretty) boys, men" (the order varies: cf. *Dysk.* 967, *Mis.* 463-4 [= 993-4 Arnott], *Sik.* 420; *Sam.* 733-4, in trochaic tetrameters, adds "old men").

1148 if they go off home should not be taken (as e.g. by W. Süss, *RhM* 97 [1954] 292-4) as indicating that the feast has no real existence: it is merely an instance of a comic *topos* whereby a character offers free gifts or invitations to the audience and then immediately cancels the offer (cf. *Lys.* 1043-71, 1189-1215; Plautus, *Rudens* 1418-22, *Pseudolus* 1331-4).

1150 this torch: cf. on 691-2. The fact that Blepyrus specially draws attention to the torch, and does so only now (not e.g. at 1135 when he was also just about to go off to dinner), suggests that he has only recently (and fortuitously, as *kalōs* "conveniently" indicates) come into possession of it. Most probably (Rogers, Vetta) the torch is that of Epigenes (cf. 978), dropped while he was struggling with the old women. Another possibility is that the "torch" is actually one of the girls (whom Blepyrus might squeeze or kiss as he speaks this line): a naked girl is compared to a torch in *Wasps* 1372-7, Lampas "Torch" was the name of a noted *hetairā* (Athenaeus 13.583e), and in later comedy there was a young female mask-type called *lampadion* "little torch" (Pollux 4.151, cf. L. Bernabò Brea, *Menandro e il teatro greco nelle terracotte liparesi* [Genoa, 1981] 233-4) because of its high tapering quiff of hair rising like a torch-flame above the forehead, which we may be sure was a *hetairā* mask (neither a maiden nor a domestic slave could have been portrayed with so eye-catching a hair-style).

1152 making your way down there: lit. "going down", sc. from his home to the (relatively low-lying) Agora; not from the stage-platform to the orchestra, since Blepyrus is already in the orchestra, dancing, by 1166 when the "pre-dining celebration song" has hardly begun.

1153 pre-dining celebration song: Greek *melos mellodeipnikon* "song for one about to dine", possibly punning on some such phrase as **melos mellonumphikon* "song for one about to be married, song for a pre-wedding celebration": cf. perhaps Soph. *Trach.* 205ff "Let the house about to receive a bride(groom) (*domos ... ho mellonumphos*) shout for joy!"

1154 advice to the judges: cf. *Clouds* 1115-30, *Birds* 1102-17, each from the second parabasis of its play.

1155-62 This short speech in trochaic tetrameters seems like an abbreviated version of the epirrhema of a traditional Old Comic parabasis, in which the chorus often praised or defended itself either in its dramatic character (*Ach.* 676-691, 703-718; *Clouds* 575-594; *Wasps* 1071-90, 1102-21) or *qua* competitor for the festival prize (as in the *Clouds* and *Birds* passages cited above). It must have been the last part of the script to be written (after the draw for the order of performance, cf. 1158-9), and it holds up the action uncomfortably (Blepyrus has just been urged to get moving at once, yet the song promised to speed him on his way does not begin till 1163): Ar. was apparently unusually nervous about how the judges would react to some features of his play (possibly the "intellectual bits", cf. next note).

1155 the intellectual bits: such as Praxagora's "philosophic" (571) exposition of the structure of her new society.

1155-7 vote for me ... vote for me ... vote for me: cf. on 221-8.

1156 the laughs they've had: notably perhaps from the scatology of 311-373 and the song, slapstick and sexual innuendo of 877-1111.

1158-9 the lottery ... the fact that we were drawn first: the draw to determine the order in which the competing plays would be performed will have been conducted by the magistrate responsible for the festival, probably at this date by means of an allotment machine (see on 681); the fact that it was possible for Ar. to insert this passage into his script shows that the draw was held at least some days before the start of the contest. The perception that, in any contest where the competitors perform in succession, the last to perform has an advantage over the other(s), is reflected in the convention of Old Comedy whereby the first speaker in a debate (*agōn*) is invariably defeated.

1159 all these things: i.e. "the intellectual bits" and "the laughs" (1155-6).

1160 break your oath: cf. Pherecrates fr. 102 "don't perjure yourselves or judge unfairly", Dem. 21.17, Plut. *Cim.* 8.8.

1161 supertarts: Greek *hetairā* (cf. on 22-23) can refer to any woman who makes her living by mercenary sex; here it probably denotes not "fourpenny prostitutes" (Del Corno) but courtesans of a higher grade (see Davidson 90-136), who were ready, if sufficiently well paid and maintained, to live with one man for an indefinite period – but equally ready to abandon him if they received a better offer. That a woman has no memory of, or thought for, any man but her current partner was evidently a cliché (among men) even before Homer made Athene use it to arouse Telemachus' suspicions about his mother (*Odyssey* 15.20-23).

1163-7 Metre: 1163, as transmitted, consists of five long syllables (a "pentamakron", cf. Dale 60); Zimmermann's deletion of the first syllable would create an anapaestic *metron* such as introduces an iambic choral passage at 478 above and a trochaic one at *Thesm.* 953. 1164-7 are trochaic tetrameters.

1164 to do the thing: to achieve what we want to achieve, viz. to have dinner.

1165-6 in Cretan fashion: from the time of Homer (*Iliad* 16.617, 18.590-606) Cretans had been famous as dancers, and there may be a special reference to "leaping solo dancers" (Edwards on *Iliad* 18.605-6); Pindar fr. 107b speaks of a "light dancing of the feet [which] they call the Cretan style". Probably Blepyrus performs a clumsy, comic version of a spectacular *pas seul* while the two girls and the Maid dance more expertly – a pattern similar to the dance of Philocleon and the three sons of Carcinus at the end of *Wasps* (1516-37; cf. also 1482-95). Philocleon's dances too may have been "Cretan" in style, though they are not explicitly so called: when he "cowers like a cock" (*Wasps* 1490), his attitude will have been rather similar to that of the Cretan Meriones when he bent low to avoid Aeneas' spear (*Iliad* 16.611), which was the occasion of Aeneas' taunting him as a "dancer" (*ib.* 617).

1166-7 these girls as well ... to the rhythm: about ten syllables appear to have dropped out of the text; my tentative restoration is based largely on *Thesm.* 953-6. Whatever the exact words that were used here, they must have constituted a direct instruction by the speaker to those whom she desires to dance (on the identification of the addressees, see next note). The restorations of van Leeuwen and Coulon both make one person (the Maid, in their view; see on 1138) tell another person to tell "these girls" to dance; this is unsatisfactory because the supposed addressee (the chorus-leader, if the Maid is the speaker here; Blepyrus, if the chorus-leader is speaking) does not in fact carry out the supposed instruction.

1166-7 these girls: if it is the chorus-leader who utters these words, they cannot refer to the chorus, since "you get your feet moving *too*" (1165-6), addressed to Blepyrus, implies that the chorus are dancing already. The other females present are the two girls accompanying Blepyrus, and the Maid. The two girls are *hetairai* – or at any rate are fulfilling the role assigned to *hetairai* in pre-revolutionary Athens – and a lively, perhaps sexually-suggestive dance would be appropriate to them; the Maid is drunk, a condition often associated with dancing in comedy (e.g. at the end of *Wasps*; cf. last note but one), and since the script provides no clear cue for a separate exit by her, the only plausible way to get her off stage is to have her dance off with the rest of the company. For dancing by drunken women servants as a symbol of joyful celebration cf. Men. *Dysk.* 950-3.

1168-78 Metre: the short introductory colon (⏑⏑⏑⏑–⏑) is metrically obscure, possibly a resolved iambic "penthemimer" (M.L. West, *Greek Metre* [Oxford, 1982] 131). The long word of 1169-75 (see next note) can be analysed as dactylic throughout, with some feet resolved into proceleusmatics (⏑⏑⏑⏑), provided that in 1171 (where see note) we read something like Blaydes' *-tūro-* "cheesy" rather than my suggestion *-paralo-* "bit-salty"; alternatively 1169 can be taken as trochaic (West *loc.cit.*, Zimmermann iii 100) or iambic (Parker 550-1) and the rest as dactylic, or (possibly best) the whole can be treated, with Rogers, as a sequence of dactyls (–⏑⏑) and tribrachs (⏑⏑⏑) in free alternation (cf. *Lys.* 1279-90 which likewise begins with pure tribrachs and ends with pure dactyls; see Dale 90-91 and, for comparable phenomena in Ar. and Euripides, Dale 56, 62-66, West *op.cit.* 107-8, 132 n.136). By 1174-6, at any rate, the rhythm is firmly dactylic. The metre of 1177 is uncertain; R's word-order, here adopted, gives a colon –⏑⏑– –⏑– which likewise follows a long dactylic sequence in Soph. *OC* 249 (see Parker 552). 1178 ends this part of the song with a resolved ithyphallic (⏑⏑⏑⏑⏑⏑– –).

1169-75 presents us with the longest word ever known to have been created in the Greek language, comprising (subject to textual uncertainties) 170 letters and 79 syllables, and describing a gargantuan dish consisting mainly of fish (1169-70) and birds (1172-4), plus hare (1174), well sauced and seasoned (1170-1, 1174). It is tempting to associate this *tour de force* with the recent fashion for gastronomic poetry evidenced, in the same year, by two references in Plato's *Phaon* to poems of this kind by Philoxenus, a hexameter poem on cookery (Plato com. fr. 189) and the lyric poem *The Dinner* of which large portions survive in quotations by Athenaeus (*PMG* 836; Plato is cited as having mentioned the poem by Athenaeus 1.5b and 4.146f) and which is, precisely, a description of a superb feast. (There were two lyric poets named Philoxenus active at this time, natives respectively of Cythera and Leucas; Athenaeus was not sure which of them Plato was referring to, and neither can we be, but the Leucadian is more likely if only because we have no record of any *other* work of his, and it is hence more likely that poems by the Leucadian were wrongly ascribed to the more famous Cytherian than vice versa.)

1169 -slicy-: Greek *temakhos* denotes specifically a slice of *fish.*

1170 -heady-: after three words referring to fish, Greek *krānio(n)* "skull, head" will probably be taken to mean the head of a bass (*krānion labrākos*), which appears in lists of delicacies in Ar. fr. 380, Eubulus fr. 109.4 and Eriphus fr. 3.

1171 -silphiumy-: *silphion* was a wild umbelliferous plant (now long extinct) growing in Cyrenaica, whose stalk was both eaten as a vegetable (*Knights* 894-8, Eubulus fr. 6.3) and used as a condiment (*Birds* 534, 1582).

1171 -bit-salty-: Greek *-paralo-* "lightly salted", cf. *Ach.* 1158; the mss. read *-parao-*, which is meaningless. See *CQ* 34 (1984) 322 n.54

1172 -thrush-upon-blackbirdy-ringdovey-: these three birds, particularly thrush, are frequently mentioned as desirable foods: cf. *Ach.* 970, 1007-11, 1104, 1116, *Clouds* 539, *Peace* 531, 1149, 1195-7, Ar. fr. 402.7, 581.3, Ephippus fr. 3.8, and (on shopkeepers' displays) *Birds* 1080-1.

1173 -roast-cooty-: the mss.' reading, *-optenkephallio-*, is meaningless, and *-optenkephalio-* "-roast-brainy-" would violate the rhythmic pattern on which this mega-word is built (see on 1168-78). Coulon's *-optokephalio-* "-roast-mullety-" is open to the objection that no fish has been mentioned since the beginning of 1170 and we are now in the middle of a run of at least seven birds. It is, however, difficult to find a bird-name that could plausibly have given rise to the transmitted reading: Ussher's conjecture is based on *piphallis* (a name found only in Hesychius and said to mean *korudallos* "crested lark"), my tentative suggestion on *phalēris* "coot" (cf. *Ach.* 875).

1174 -haremeaty-: cf. on 843.

1174 -boiled-winy-: Greek *siraio(n)*, new wine boiled down to a third of its volume and sweetened with honey (Plin. *NH* 14.80; cf. *Wasps* 878); it was sometimes used to colour food (Alexis fr. 193.4).

1174-5 -deliciousy-: Greek *tragalo-*, connected with *trōgein* "eat", and seemingly meaning "fit to regale oneself on" (cf. its derivative verb *tragalizein* in *Wasps* 674). The mss. read *tragano-* "gristle", hardly an appetizing ingredient.

1176 get yourself a plate, quick and fast: or, with Blaydes, "run and get yourself a plate"; in either case, as the next line shows, Blepyrus is to equip himself with a plate *before* going to the Agora. For him to go into his house for this purpose, however, would disrupt the dance, so he is made to ignore the suggestion (and that of 1177-8) in his impatience to be off (1179).

1177 raise the dust: i.e. hurry as fast as you can; cf. on 291.

1177-8 take some porridge to dine on: a notable anticlimax: just as the prospect of a mouth-watering feast was snatched away from the audience (1148), so now it is snatched away from Blepyrus. Once again it does not follow that the communal dinner is a mirage: the point may rather be that Blepyrus, as the last comer (1133: note the references to the food and drink "left (over)" at 1139 and 1170), is likely to find that not much of the feast now remains uneaten (see *CQ* 34 [1984] 322-3 – but I should not have cited 1181 as evidence, cf. below).

1179-83 Metre: basically iambic (the interjections *euoi* and *euai*, if susceptible of metrical analysis at all, are probably to be scanned ⏑–). 1182 as transmitted is a pherecratean (x– –⏑⏑– –), which does not normally occur on its own in an iambic context; hence H.J. Newiger (see Zimmermann ii 88) emended 1181 (cf. below) to make it a glyconic (x– –⏑⏑–⏑–), which very often precedes a pherecratean. Alternatively one might move *euai* from the beginning to the end of 1182, making it metrically identical with the penultimate verse of the parallel passage *Lys.* 1291-4.

1179 but they must be shovelling it down: sc. so I had better go without a moment's delay. Greek *laimattein* (from *laimos* "throat, gullet") may have had the basic meaning "have a voracious appetite", whence either "be very hungry" (cf. Herodas 6.97) or, as here, "eat greedily".

1180-3 is virtually identical with *Lys.* 1292-4 (sung by a chorus half of old men, half of old women) except for the addition of a reference to feasting (the *Lysistrata* passage, however, does *not* conclude the play and can neither accompany nor be followed by the exit of the chorus).

1180 raise it high probably indicates that the dance includes high kicks; cf. *Wasps* 1524-7, 1530-1, *Lys.* 1292.

1181 we're going to feast refers not so much to the communal dinner in the Agora (for this confident prediction is hardly consistent with 1177-8) as to the feast which the *khorēgos* will give his chorus if (or rather, they here imply, *when*) they are victorious in the comic competition (cf. *Ach.* 1154-5, Pl. *Symp.* 173a). Newiger's emendation (see on 1179-83) gives the sense "let's feast/dine"; but that would imply that the feast is to be held immediately, and one does not have "a feast of victory" when the result has yet to be declared.

1182 a feast of victory: lit. "as on the occasion of a victory". *Acharnians*, *Birds*, *Lysistrata*, *Thesmophoriazusae*, and all comedies of Menander whose final lines survive, likewise end with an anticipation of, or a prayer for, victory in the festival competition; prayers for victory (perhaps added by fourth-century producers in accordance with a practice of their day) are also found in the mss. at the end of Euripides' *Iphigeneia in Tauris*, *Phoenician Maidens*, *Orestes*, and (in two mss. only) *Hippolytus*.

ARIS & PHILLIPS CLASSICAL TEXTS

Published and forthcoming books

AESCHYLUS: EUMENIDES ed. A.J. Podlecki, PERSIANS ed. E. Hall

ARISTOPHANES ed. Alan H. Sommerstein :ACHARNIANS, BIRDS, CLOUDS, FROGS, KNIGHTS, LYSISTRATA, PEACE, THESMOPHORIAZUSAE, WASPS, ECCLESIAZUSAE

ARISTOTLE: ON THE HEAVENS I & II ed. S. Leggatt, ON SLEEP AND DREAMS ed. D. Gallop

AUGUSTINE: SOLILOQUIES *and* IMMORTALITY OF THE SOUL ed. G. Watson

CAESAR: CIVIL WAR I & II ed. J.M. Carter, CIVIL WAR III ed. J.M. Carter

CASSIUS DIO: ROMAN HISTORY Books 53.1-55.9, ed. J.W. Rich,

CATULLUS: POEMS 61–8 ed. J. Godwin,

CICERO: TUSCULAN DISPUTATIONS I, ed. A.E. Douglas, TUSCULAN DISPUTATIONS II & V ed. A.E. Douglas. ON FATE with **BOETHIUS** CONSOLATION V ed. R.W. Sharples, PHILIPPICS II, ed. W.K. Lacey, VERRINES II, ed. T.N. Mitchell, ON STOIC GOOD AND EVIL ed. M.R. Wright, LAELIUS ON FRIENDSHIP and THE DREAM OF SCIPIO ed. J.G.F. Powell, LETTERS (Jan– Apr. 43 B.C.) ed. M. Willcock

EURIPIDES: ALCESTIS ed. D. Conacher, ANDROMACHE ed. M. Lloyd, BACCHAE ed. R. Seaford, ELECTRA ed. M.J. Cropp, HECUBA ed. C. Collard, HERACLES ed. S. Barlow, HIPPOLYTUS ed. M.R. Halleran, ION ed. K.H. Lee, ORESTES ed. M.L. West, PHOENICIAN WOMEN ed. E. Craik, TROJAN WOMEN ed. S. Barlow, FRAGMENTARY PLAYS VOLUME I eds C. Collard, M.J. Cropp & K.H. Lee

GREEK ORATORS: I ANTIPHON, LYSIAS ed. M. Edwards & S. Usher, III ISOCRATES PANEGYRICUS and TO NICOCLES ed. S. Usher, IV ANDOCIDES ed. M. Edwards, V DEMOSTHENES On the Crown ed. S. Usher, VI APOLLODORUS Against Neaira ed. C. Carey

HELLENICA OXYRHYNCHIA ed. P.R. McKechnie & S.J. Kern

HOMER: ODYSSEY I & II ed. P.V. Jones, ILIAD VIII & IX ed. C.H. Wilson,

HORACE: SATIRES I, ed. P. Michael Brown, SATIRES II ed. Frances Muecke

JOSEPH OF EXETER: THE TROJAN WAR I-III ed. A.K. Bate

LIVY ed. P.G. Walsh: Book XXXVI, Book XXXVII, Book XXXVIII, Book XXXIX, Book XL

LUCAN: CIVIL WAR VIII ed. R. Mayer

LUCIAN: A SELECTION ed. M.D. McLeod

LUCRETIUS: DE RERUM NATURA III ed. P.M. Brown, DE RERUM NATURA IV ed. J. Godwin, DE RERUM NATURA VI ed. J. Godwin,

MARTIAL: EPIGRAMS V ed. P. Howell

MENANDER: SAMIA ed. D.M. Bain, THE BAD-TEMPERED MAN ed. S. Ireland

OVID: AMORES II ed. J. Booth, METAMORPHOSES I-IV ed. D.E. Hill, METAMORPHOSES V-VIII ed. D.E. Hill, METAMORPHOSES IX–XII ed. D.E. Hill *(for 1999)*

PERSIUS: THE SATIRES ed. J.R. Jenkinson

PINDAR: SELECTED ODES ed. S. Instone

PLATO: APOLOGY ed. M. Stokes, MENO ed. R.W. Sharples, PHAEDRUS ed. C.J. Rowe, REPUBLIC V ed. S. Halliwell, REPUBLIC X, ed. S. Halliwell, STATESMAN ed. C.J. Rowe, SYMPOSIUM ed. C.J.Rowe

PLAUTUS: BACCHIDES ed. J.A. Barsby

PLINY: CORRESPONDENCE WITH TRAJAN FROM BITHYNIA ed. W. Williams

PLUTARCH: LIVES OF ARISTEIDES AND CATO ed. D. Sansone, LIFE OF CICERO ed. J.L. Moles, MALICE OF HERODOTUS ed. A.J. Bowen, THEMISTOCLES ed. J, Marr

THE RUODLIEB ed. C.W. Grocock

SENECA: LETTERS: A SELECTION ed. C.D.N. Costa, FOUR DIALOGUES, ed. C.D.N. Costa

SOPHOCLES: AJAX ed. A. Garvie, ANTIGONE ed. A.L. Brown, PHILOCTETES ed. R.G. Ussher

SUETONIUS: LIVES OF GALBA, OTHO & VITELLIUS ed. D.C.A. Shotter

TACITUS: ANNALS IV ed. D.C.A. Shotter

TERENCE: THE BROTHERS ed. A.S. Gratwick, THE SELF-TORMENTOR ed. A.J. Brothers, THE MOTHER-IN-LAW ed. S. Ireland

THUCYDIDES: HISTORY Book II ed. P.J. Rhodes, HISTORY Book III ed. P.J. Rhodes, HISTORY Book IV–V. ed. P.J. Rhodes, PYLOS BC: Book IV, 2-41, ed. J. Wilson

WILLIAM OF NEWBURGH: THE HISTORY OF ENGLISH AFFAIRS I ed. P.G. Walsh & M. Kennedy

XENOPHON: HELLENIKA I-II.. ed. Peter Krentz, HELLENIKA II.–IV. ed. Peter Krentz, SYMPOSIUM ed. A.J. Bowen, ON HUNTING with **ARRIAN** eds A.A. Phillips & M.M. Wilcock *(for 1999)*